Samantha Tross

A PROFILE

Verna Wilkins
illustrated by Gillian Hunt

Tamarind Ltd

Other books in the

Black Profiles Series

Lord John Taylor of Warwick
Benjamin Zephaniah
Malorie Blackman
Baroness Scotland of Asthal
Jim Brathwaite

Samantha Tross is currently working towards being
a Consultant Orthopaedic Surgeon.

Published by Tamarind Ltd 2000
PO Box 52, Northwood
Middlesex HA6 1UN, UK

Text © Verna Wilkins
Illustrations © Gillian Hunt
Series editor: Simona Sideri

ISBN 1-870516-48-6

Printed in Singapore

Contents

CHAPTER ONE

The Early Years

SAMANTHA TROSS WAS BORN IN JUNE 1968 into an extended family in Guyana in South America. Along with her mother, father, sisters and brother, there were two grandparents living in the family house. There was never any need for babysitters. When Samantha was five, her family grew even larger when old Great Aunt Rosa came to stay. Aunt Rosa was a fabulous cook and a brilliant storyteller.

In Guyana, stories are passed down through the generations by word of mouth, and Aunt Rosa continued this tradition.

Every evening, in the spectacular tropical twilight, Samantha sat and listened to Aunt Rosa's stories. Some stories were ghostly and grim and made her frightened to go to bed in the dark. Others, especially the Annancy stories about a cunning spider, were funny and made her laugh. Samantha loved listening to them all.

CHAPTER TWO

Sweet Child

GUYANA LIES JUST ABOVE THE EQUATOR. The Caribbean Sea forms its northern border and to the south is dense rainforest and the enormous Amazon River.

Samantha's family lived near Georgetown, the capital city of Guyana. The family home was large and comfortable, with huge square windows that let in the bright sunshine. For many months of the year, the garden was awash with colour. There were orangey-red blossoms on the towering flamboyant tree, pink and white oleander and hibiscus, and wide borders of rambling purple bougainvillaea. It was a butterfly heaven.

Samantha's father worked as a Government Accountant, her mother as a <u>Lecturer</u> in Health Science. Samantha was the second born of four children, three girls and a boy. Each child was given two names, one of which was African.

Samantha's African middle name, Zoisa, means Sweet Child.

"Where did you get that name when you're so horrible!" her brother would shout when she ran off with one of his <u>precious</u> toys.

Samantha loved her brother's ˙<u>trucks</u> and go-carts, and he did not want to share.

CHAPTER THREE
Death in the Family

WHEN SHE WAS SIX YEARS OLD, Samantha's happy family life was thrown into deep sorrow when Great Aunt Rosa died suddenly.

Soon afterwards, Grandfather also fell ill. The doctor visited every day, but the old man never left his bed.

"Why doesn't Dr Ambrose make Grandad better?" Samantha asked her mother.

"He's doing his best, my dear, but Grandad is very old and very sick."

The doctor came every day to visit Grandad, but soon the old man died. Samantha was extremely upset and cried for a very long time.

There was worse to come. Samantha's grandmother missed her two best companions and she soon took to her bed. The doctor's visits started again.

"Promise you won't let Grandma die, too," Samantha pleaded with the doctor.

"I'll try, my dear," he said.

But Grandma grew weaker and weaker until she too passed away, leaving the once bustling household half empty.

Samantha missed the old people terribly. No one else seemed to have the time to sit for hours and tell such wonderful stories. Three deaths under the same roof, in such a short space of time, had a tremendous effect on Samantha's young mind.

"I'm going to be a doctor when I grow up," vowed Samantha to her parents, "and I'll never let anybody die."

CHAPTER FOUR

A White Christmas?

IN GUYANA, there are only two seasons – the wet and the dry – and both seasons are warm.

Christmas falls in the dry season, and every year Samantha's father cut a large branch from the huge casuarina tree in the garden. The whole family would decorate the branch with brightly coloured ribbons and balloons.

Although the weather was hot and sunny, all the Christmas cards on sale in the shops showed snow and snowmen, and many of the Christmas carols the children learned mentioned snow.

Sitting in her garden, Samantha thought about snow and sleet, fog and hail. She wondered what they looked and felt like.

Everyone in the family always received two Christmas presents. But Samantha's presents did not always please her. She was easily bored with many of her birthday presents, too. She longed for the kind of presents her brothers were given. The boys had trucks and cars, adventure stories and planes. Samantha was given pink dolls in frilly dresses and books about helpless princesses with bright yellow hair.

None of the dolls looked like Samantha or her family, and neither did any of the characters in her books.

There was one character in a book who puzzled Samantha a great deal. She was called Little Red Riding Hood. "This girl is silly, Mum," said Samantha. "She can't tell the difference between her grandma and a wolf!"

Samantha soon abandoned her books of fairy tales and started sneaking into her brother's room to borrow his adventure books and comics. This was easy to do because her father and brother spent a great deal of time outdoors, building treehouses and going on exciting trips. One weekend, Samantha spent hours crying when the men and boys in the family went for a long hike, deep in the rainforest.

"Why can't I go, too?" Samantha complained to her mother.

"Your father thought you mightn't like it. They get very wet and very dirty in the rainforest."

"I don't mind getting wet and dirty, and I'm old enough. I'm seven now. Can I go next time, Mum?"

"We'll see," said her mother, but she was shaking her head from side to side. Samantha knew that meant 'no'.

CHAPTER FIVE

"I Want to Be..."

WHEN SAMANTHA WAS NEARLY EIGHT years old, she asked her father, "Why do boys get to do all the great things?"

"Well," replied her father, "girls get to do great things, too."

"Like what, Dad?"

"Like playing with beautiful dolls and sewing and cooking..."

"But I don't want to play with dolls!" replied Samantha.

"Well then, my girl, what *do* you want to do?" asked her father.

"I want to be a doctor," said Samantha. "I want to fix people when they are broken. I want to be like Dr Ambrose who looked after Grandma, Grandad and Aunt Rosa, but I'd never let anyone die."

"*That* decision might not be yours," said her father, smiling, "but I'm glad that you want to be a doctor. You'll be a very good one. I'm sure of that."

Samantha raced indoors to tell the rest of the family her news.

"That's wonderful!" said her mother.

"Girls are nurses, aren't they?" said her brother.

"They can be doctors and boys can be nurses too," said their mother. "Now, off you go, you two, and don't start quarrelling."

CHAPTER SIX

Playing at Doctors

FOR HER EIGHTH BIRTHDAY, Samantha's aunt gave her a nurse's uniform. Her parents gave her a stethoscope. Samantha hid the nurse's uniform and wore the stethoscope around her neck. She collected all the toys she had abandoned and borrowed her sister's toys as  well. Eventually, every doll and every teddy bear became a patient.

Most weekends and sometimes after school, Samantha put on her stethoscope and opened a doctor's surgery in her bedroom. She lined up

her patients outside her door. Then, one by one, she took them in and examined them thoroughly. She would then set aside at least two of them to perform surgery.

All her operations were successful, but some were very messy. Her stitches were not wonderful, and sometimes bits of stomach and intestine had to be put in the bin.

One day, when her mother stopped to look at Samantha's packed surgery, she spotted a familiar piece of red cloth sticking out of the bandages around a teddy bear's stomach.

"Operating again?" asked her mother, as she tried to get past the pile of bandaged patients outside her daughter's door.

"Yes, Teddy is doing well. I've made his tummy better and he's leaving hospital today," replied Samantha.

"Isn't that your father's best tie?" asked her mother, pointing to the red cloth.

"I need it for the operation. It's Teddy's blood, you see."

"I think I'll just have it back, Samantha," said her mother. "Try and find some other type of blood. And please don't operate on your baby sister, okay?"

Eventually, everyone learned to hide their valuables.

CHAPTER SEVEN

Bad News

THEN SUDDENLY, Samantha's whole world changed.

One night, soon after her eleventh birthday, her mother and father sat the oldest children around them and said that they had to leave their home, their

family and friends, their school and their country. They were to go to school five and a half thousand kilometres away.

There was more to come. They were to live at the school. And even worse, their parents were not going to be there. They were going to live in a different country.

"But why?" asked Samantha, really scared.

"I've been given a very important government job, my dear," explained her father. "It means I'll be travelling from country to country, all of the time."

"Why can't we come with you, Daddy?" asked Samantha.

"Because I'll be staying only a short time in some countries..." he replied.

"That sounds like fun, then," said Samantha.

"But what about school!" said her father. "Your mother and I think that your education is very important. We can't drag you around from country to country with us all the time. By the time you've settled in one school, we'll be on the move again. You won't have time to make friends and you won't learn anything. Believe me, we are doing what we think is best for us all."

Samantha's mother looked sad through all this. "We'll make sure that you're well looked after," she

said, "and we'll visit you as often as we can. And of course we'll spend the holidays as a family."

"Where are we going to live?" Samantha's brother asked.

"England," replied their dad. "And I've bought lots of storybooks about schools there for you to read."

Samantha already knew a lot about England. Nearly all the textbooks at her school in Guyana – in history, geography, maths and science – were written in English. All her storybooks were written in English and often set in England, too. But Samantha still read the books her father had bought.

Some of the stories were about boarding schools. The girls lived there and slept in huge bedrooms called dormitories. They seemed to have fun. They had midnight feasts and pillow fights and played strange ball games with funny names, like hockey and lacrosse.

In some stories though, the girls were miserable.

They missed their parents and went hungry because the food at school was horrid.

Much too soon it was time to start packing to leave Guyana. The children had to buy new clothes that would be more suited to the cold English weather.

When Samantha saw how sad her younger sister was about going to England, she tried to cheer her up. Even though she was miserable, too.

"We'll get to see snow at last... have snowball fights and build enormous snowmen," chirped Samantha.

Her sister managed a weak smile.

"Oh yeah," said her brother. "And we'll freeze to death in the snow and ice and disappear in the fog. Still... at least I won't have to share my comics with you any more."

Soon it was time to leave. Their friends and family came to the airport to say goodbye. Samantha was sad, but as she ran towards the plane, perched on the tarmac in the sizzling heat, she was determined not to look back.

CHAPTER EIGHT

England

THE PLANE RIDE SEEMED NEVER-ENDING, but after ten hours and one stop in Trinidad to pick up some passengers, they landed in England. It was a bright sunny day. The sunshine made Samantha less homesick and she skipped out of the plane.

Immediately, she froze in her tracks.

"It's really cold! Even though the sun is shining!" exclaimed Samantha to her father. "This country is going to be really… different…" she continued. But her voice came out all funny as she shivered in the chilly September air.

Samantha and her brother gazed out of the window of the taxi as they raced along wide smooth roads past neat green fields.

"Why are all those houses stuck together?" asked her brother.

"They're called terraced houses," replied their mother.

"But they all look the same. How can anyone tell them apart?"

"Numbers, dear. All the houses are numbered."

At last they arrived in Hertfordshire. They turned off the motorway and drove down winding lanes and through woods. Finally they passed through a gate and along a drive until they came to a stop in front of a large building.

"Is this it?" chimed the three older children.

The school was not stuck to anything. It sat alone in the middle of a huge plot of land. It was very big and seemed very grand. Samantha's knees were shaking uncontrollably as she stood looking up at it.

The senior girl who showed them to Samantha's dormitory was very polite. There wasn't much room for Samantha's things, and it was freezing.

Saying goodbye to her parents and her youngest sister made Samantha completely miserable.

"I mustn't cry," she kept muttering to herself, "I mustn't cry. I mustn't cry."

But she did because she had to say goodbye to her brother too. He was taken to a different boarding school a long way away. Her other sister stayed at the same school as Samantha, but not in the same building.

CHAPTER NINE
School Life

SAMANTHA SHARED A DORMITORY with three other girls. She was unhappy and, at first, the girls were horrid. She was teased because of the way she spoke and she was always shivering from the cold.

"You talk funny," said Penny, the girl in the next bed. "Do you live in trees in your country?"

They asked loads of really stupid questions. Samantha wondered why they hadn't read about her country, the way she had read all about theirs. Then they wouldn't have asked such ridiculous things.

As the weeks went by, however, Samantha made a couple of friends. She made more when the girls found out that she was a whiz at homework. She could read better than anyone in her class. She was brilliant at remembering things, and she found sums easy. Samantha and her new friends started a system. She helped them with maths and science. They helped her with needlework and pottery.

The school was very keen that their girls were good at sewing and cooking and everything to do with the

home. Samantha was not, so she did very little work.

Then, one wonderful day, her parents came to visit. They couldn't stop hugging her and they brought bags full of gifts.

"Are you happy here?" asked her parents over and over again.

"Yes," replied Samantha. "I'm fine, and I have some great friends, but I miss you."

They all went out for the day and, when they left, Samantha's tuck box was stuffed with biscuits, sweets and cakes. She had some new clothes, too.

Saying goodbye to her mother and father again was heartbreaking, but easier than before. This time, her parents and her little sister were going to Africa.

That night, however, Samantha and her room-mates had a fantastic midnight feast. There was enough food left for a whole week of midnight feasts. Samantha fell in love with chocolate.

CHAPTER TEN
Africa

WHEN THE HOLIDAYS CAME, Samantha, her brother and her sister were escorted to the airport. There, they waited in the airport lounge for their flight to their parents in Zambia, in Africa.

"Look," said Samantha, "over there!" She pointed to an enormous sweet shop filled with hundreds of different kinds of chocolate and sweets.

"Let's go!" they shouted.

Six gigantic chocolate Easter bunnies guarded the entrance and millions of tiny jelly babies lay in huge trays. The shop was called Sweet Paradise. The children bought bagfuls of everything. Samantha chose one of every chocolate she could reach and ate them all. She then spent the entire flight being horribly sick.

Samantha fell out of love with chocolate.

Samantha was thrilled to be with her family again. To begin with they just talked and talked. Then, once they had told all their news, the children spent hours exploring the house and garden. Zambia reminded Samantha of Guyana in many ways. She loved it.

Living in England, she was surrounded by white people. Nearly all her school books and storybooks had only white images. Science, her favourite subject, showed only white men in white coats doing all the interesting experiments. And in England, she hadn't seen any black doctors. Samantha was beginning to think that she couldn't be a doctor after all.

Then one day, during the holiday, Samantha went with her mother to visit a neighbour.

Suddenly the phone rang and a young woman came running down to answer it. As soon as she put the phone down, she dashed out. They heard the door slam and then a car drove off.

"That's Chanda, my youngest daughter," her mother's friend explained to Samantha. "She's a doctor and she's on call today. She told me earlier that she would probably have to leave suddenly."

Samantha turned to her mother with great excitement. "Mum, I really *can* be a doctor, can't I?" she said.

"Of course you can. You can be anything you want to be," replied her mother. "Why? Has anyone said anything to you at school?"

"No, but it's the first time I've seen a doctor who looks like me. In England, I was beginning to think that doctors had to be white."

"And Mum," she continued, "Dr Martin Luther King was a doctor, wasn't he?"

"Yes, but he wasn't a medical doctor," answered her mother. "He was an academic doctor."

That night, both her parents had a talk with her.

"You've been at school for two years now. Are you happy there?" asked her father.

He was holding her school report. Although she was clever, Samantha had done very little work, and her grades were not very good.

"Sometimes," replied Samantha.

"What makes you unhappy?" he asked.

"We do lots of games and needlework and pottery, and I'm no good at them."

"So I see," said her father. "Your mother and I have decided to move you to another school."

"Here, in Zambia?" Samantha asked hopefully.

"I'm sorry, I'm going to be moving again soon, Samantha," explained her dad. "Your new school is in Nottinghamshire, in England."

CHAPTER ELEVEN
A Change for the Better

THE NEW SCHOOL WAS MUCH BETTER. There were other black girls there and the Head Prefect was a kind girl from Jamaica. Nearly everyone was friendly.

Samantha enjoyed being. there and worked well. She took her maths 'O' level at fourteen. She passed. She was still determined to be a doctor, and was delighted when she passed her biology and chemistry exams.

By the time Samantha was ready for her 'A' levels, her mother couldn't bear to be away from her children any longer. She moved to England so that Samantha and her brother could go to a Sixth Form College and all the children could live with her.

They were delighted. Their father visited as often as he could. They settled down to family life. Her mother's presence – and the fact that she cooked delicious Caribbean food – was wonderful.

Samantha never lost her love for calypso music. Living with her family meant that she had her own bedroom. She could now play her favourite tunes for

as long – and as loudly – as she liked. Reggae and soul echoed around her room constantly.

During her final year at school, she went to the Careers teacher. "You're a bright girl. What do you plan to do with your life?" she asked Samantha. "I want to be a doctor. Ever since I was a little girl that's all I have ever wanted to do."

"Well, I don't really think that's a good idea, Samantha. My daughter is a doctor and it's no life for a woman. She's dreadfully overworked and not very happy. Why not be a lawyer? I'm sure you can cope with that."

Samantha didn't listen. She knew her own mind. She applied to medical school and she was accepted.

CHAPTER TWELVE

Becoming a Doctor

SAMANTHA'S YEARS AS A MEDICAL STUDENT were wonderful. Much better by far than her earlier education. She spent a great deal of time socialising. She went to one nightclub so often, they made her an honorary member.

Samantha worked hard too, and after six successful years, she graduated from medical school.

When she was just newly-qualified she was always nervous the first time she had to meet a patient.

One day, she walked into an examination room where a middle-aged man was waiting to be examined.

"How old are you?" he asked.

Samantha said she was nearly twenty-four.

The patient looked at the stethoscope around her neck and asked, "Are you going to examine me?"

He seemed rather suspicious.

"Yes, of course," she answered.

"Are you a nurse?" he asked.

"No," explained Samantha. "I'm the doctor in charge of your case."

"Are you qualified?" he asked a bit crossly. "You look like a teenager."

"I should be asking the questions here," said Samantha, smiling.

"Okay, Doc," the patient replied. "I'm all yours."

"Fine," said Samantha, "I'll take good care of you."

And she did.

Samantha's first AIDS patient filled her with fear, and it was some time before she was comfortable operating on patients who were HIV-positive or who had full-blown AIDS. She knew quite well that the chances of becoming infected were small, but she still held that irrational fear.

At the back of her mind, too, was the sad fact that soon after qualifying from medical school, one of her classmates had died from AIDS. Samantha made a huge, positive effort and, after a while, she found working with people suffering from AIDS to be hugely rewarding.

Soon after her twenty-sixth birthday, Samantha was put in charge of her first cancer patient. The patient was also twenty-six years old, and she was dying. Samantha was desperately unhappy that she could not save her life. All she could do was lessen the pain.

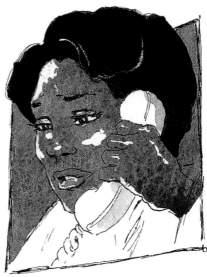

When the patient finally died, Samantha phoned her mother in tears.

"Mum, it's too much," she cried. "I can't bear it."

"It's good that you have such sympathy for your patients, my dear," said her mother, "but try to remember that there are also millions of healthy young and old people in the world. You're doing a great job, and you're doing the best you can!"

"But she was only my age," Samantha said.

Her mother reminded her, "Do you remember when you were six how angry you were with Dr Ambrose, in Guyana? You didn't want Great Aunt Rosa, or Granny or Grandad to die, either."

"I remember, Mum. Thanks for listening."

Samantha dried her tears and went back to work. However, giving bad news to patients and their families has never got any easier.

Samantha's love of children led her to work in paediatrics for some time.

Many of the children looked forward to her visits. She spent time explaining to the older children what

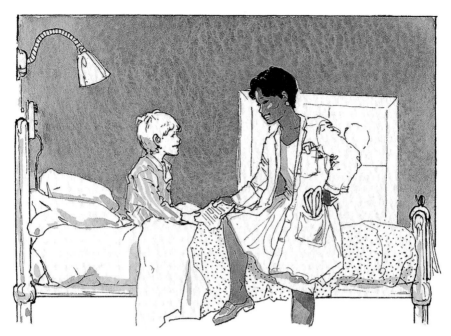

was happening around them in the hospital. She loved tiny babies, but if a baby died Samantha was devastated and couldn't bear having to tell the baby's parents the terrible news. Samantha decided to change to another branch of medicine.

CHAPTER THIRTEEN

An Orthopaedic Surgeon

THE SIGHT OF BLOOD had never bothered Samantha. She loved operating, so she decided to concentrate on surgery – orthopaedic surgery.

This side of the medical profession is usually where the men work. The tools of the orthopaedic surgeon include a knife, saw, drill, chisel, bolts, nails and many other tools traditionally used in carpentry or metalwork. They need these tools to saw into bones and to repair them.

"So what's so special about orthopaedics?" asked a friend one day.

"It's a sophisticated form of carpentry," replied Samantha.

"Is that why women mostly don't choose to work in this field?" asked her friend.

"Well spotted," replied Samantha. "It can be heavy work, but I loved woodwork at school. By the time I was seven, I'd sawed the legs off at least five dolls and given them new hips. The teddies too!"

"Did the new hips work?" asked her friend.

"Not always. But sticky tape and a bit of sewing helped a bit," giggled Samantha.

"How do you cope with real amputations, on real people?" asked her friend, fascinated.

"Difficult one. The decision to cut off a limb is sometimes the only way to save a patient's life and that's my job. And I have to do it."

Her friend shuddered. "Think I'll stick to architecture!"

"But, for me," Samantha continued, "there's nothing better than freeing someone from pain and sickness and, even better, saving a life."

Samantha is now a Fellow of the Royal College of Surgeons and works in a large hospital.

CHAPTER FOURTEEN
A Snowy Day is a Busy Day

WHEN SAMANTHA WAS A LITTLE GIRL sitting in her tropical garden in Guyana, reading and wondering about snow, she had no idea it could be so dangerous. Moving to England taught her that the cold, white fluffy stuff can leave roads dangerous for drivers and pedestrians alike. As a doctor, she has learned that snow can change an ordinary working day into a whirlwind of activity, and keep her busy far into the night.

One January morning turned into such a day. Samantha was getting ready to go to work, when she heard the weather forecast.

"Oh no," Samantha muttered to herself. "That's going to play havoc with my schedule."

Her first operation was on an old woman. Samantha had to replace her worn-out hip joint. When one doctor had put the old woman to sleep, Samantha cut through her hip and sawed off the top of the diseased bone. She replaced it with smooth metal just the right shape and size.

"You'll be fine now," she murmured to the sleeping patient.

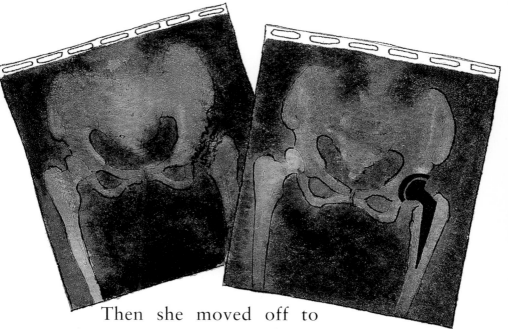

Then she moved off to another operating theatre where she operated on a boy who had been born with one hip joint out of

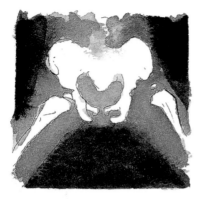

place. Samantha moved the bones into the right position, and a plaster was fitted on, to hold them until they settled in the right place.

Then it was time to check on some of the patients she had already operated on. That's when Samantha noticed the thick carpet of snow outside.

As she was eating her lunch, Samantha was bleeped

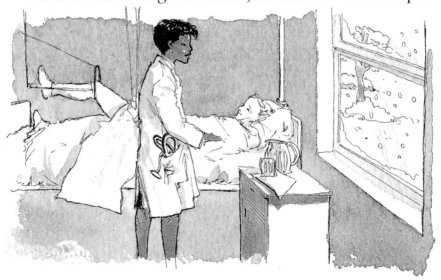

from the Accident and Emergency department.

"Dr Tross," she was told when she rang through, "three people have just come into A&E and need attention: an old lady who slipped in the snow and

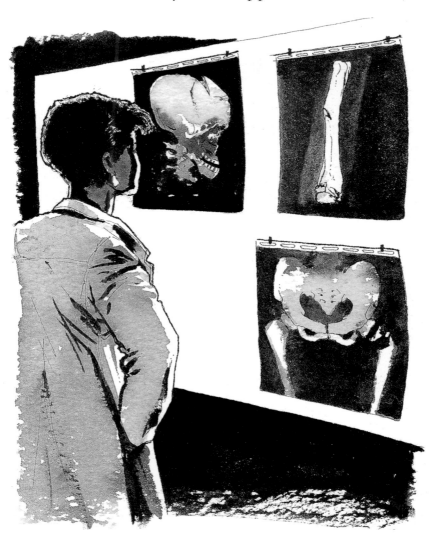

has broken a hip, and two people who have been in a car accident. One has a head injury while the other one has an arm injury."

Operating on all these people was going to keep Samantha busy for quite a few hours.

Samantha Zoisa Tross loves her work. She is successful and happy in her chosen career. If there is a road or rail accident, many people can be injured at once. Samantha has to lead her team and allocate duties to all her colleagues to make their work successful and to save lives. It is hard and very demanding work, but Samantha would not change it for the world.

KRAFTWERK
PUBLIKATION

A BIOGRAPHY BY

DAVID BUCKLEY
in collabortion with **NIGEL FORREST**

FOREWORD BY

KARL BARTOS

OMNIBUS PRESS
London / New York / Paris / Sydney / Copenhagen / Berlin / Madrid / Tokyo

© 2012 Omnibus Press
A Division of Music Sales Limited

Book designed by Malcolm Garrett RDI
Picture research by Jacqui Black & David Buckley

ISBN: 9781847729316
Order No: OP52943

Exclusive Distributors
Music Sales Limited,
14/15 Berners Street,
London, W1T 3LJ.

Music Sales Corporation,
257 Park Avenue South,
New York, NY 10010, USA.

Macmillan Distribution Services,
56 Parkwest Drive
Derrimut, Vic 3030,
Australia.

Every effort has been made to trace the copyright holders of the photographs in this book but one or two were unreachable. We would be grateful if the photographers concerned would contact us.

Typeset by Phoenix Photosetting, Chatham, Kent
Printed in the EU

A catalogue record for this book is available from the British Library.

Visit Omnibus Press on the web at www.omnibuspress.com

LOG IN

YOUR NAME

YOUR EMAIL

PLEASE VERIFY YOU ARE NOT A ROBOT

A 64-BIT HISTORY OF KRAFTWERK

ACKNOWLEDGMENTS

WHEN I began researching this book back in 2009, I could not have imagined having the co-operation and input from four ex-members of Kraftwerk. Karl Bartos not only offered his help, but remained in regular contact through Skype during this period. Much of what he told me remains private and confidential, but I cannot thank him enough for his contribution to the book, for his friendship and for his terrific and wicked sense of humour.

In November 2010 I spent two days with Wolfgang Flür in Düsseldorf. Wolfgang was charming and warm and remarked after the interview that it was the longest he had ever given! Indeed, the transcription of our marathon chat came to a whopping 40,000 words.

Eberhard Kranemann, a member of the pre-fame Kraftwerk, also supplied excellent information and many rare photographs. It was a privilege to speak to Michael Rother who was also briefly a member of Kraftwerk before forming Neu! in 1971.

In alphabetical order, my other interviewees were: Rebecca Allen, Joe Black, Henning Dedekind, Ralf Dörper, Rusty Egan, John Foxx, Malcolm Garrett, Manfred Gillig-Degrave, Ian Harrison, Andy McCluskey, Moby, Steve Redhead, Hans-Joachim Roedelius, Jon Savage, Peter Saville, John Taylor, Kristoff Tilkin, Martyn Ware and Simon Winder.

The quotes from Paul Buckmaster and John Peel come from interviews I conducted with them about David Bowie. The quotes from Chris Cross and Billy Curie of Ultravox, Gary Numan and Philip Oakey come from interviews conducted for *Mojo* magazine.

My editor, Chris Charlesworth, was simply everything you want an editor to be. Not only is he an excellent editor but his knowledge of popular music history means that he acts as a much-needed 'back stop' when one gets things wrong, or forgets important matters. My wife, Ann Henrickson, as she has done for all my books, read the manuscript and made some important changes. Nigel Forrest acted as a sort of 'project manager' and brought the book to fruition by organising, collating and annotating the transcriptions, commenting on the text and adding important slabs of information. Ros Edwards, my agent at Edwards/Fugelwicz, was also a wonderful support. My thanks too to Helenka Fuglewicz, Julia Forrest and Ann Waterhouse at E/F.

The book's designer, Malcolm Garrett, not only came up with, for my money, a classic book cover (Kraftwerk fans have already been contacting me to ask if they can buy the design as a poster!) but also suggested that I make the book as 'Kraftwerk-like' as possible. It was his idea to call the book 'Publikation' and to make the chapter headings read like Kling Klang Produkt. Without this suggestion I would not have had the idea of writing the book in eight chapters and in 64-bits in homage to Kraftwerk's obsession with numerology and computerised history.

I would also like to thank Jacqui Black, who helped source the photographs for the book and designed the photo sections and the book's PR and right's manager, Helen Donlon, who waited so patiently for the text.

The transcriptions for my interviews were completed with great skill by Maria Stone, Helen Williams and Jackie Roper. John

Ellis, was a huge support during the writing of the book, and also designed the 'captcha' page. Essential Kraftwerk material was provided by my friend Michael Wiegers.

I would also like to thank my friends in the UK for their support: Bob and Eirwen Adkins, Mike Baker, David and Oonagh Blackshaw, John Ellis, Richard Freeman, Pete Gibbons, Richard and Ann Goosey, Robin Hartwell, Phill and Anne Humphries, Ian Craig Marsh, Jo and Rick Ord, Steve Jopson, Graham Lidster, Ron Moy and Paul Du Noyer, as well as my friends in Germany and elsewhere: Timo, Colin and Shona Andrews, Grant and Liz Coles, Matthew Hawkes, Klaus and Veronika Federa, Graham and Carol Johnstone, Simon Johnstone, Jim Lucas, Christel Keters, Birgit and Jakob Mayr, Lisa Meinecke, Brigitte Niehues, Steve Jones, Stella Kingsbury, Renate Krakowczyk, Jim Ready, Karl Siebengartner, Steve Thornewill and Karen Weilbrenner. I would also like to mention a close family friend, Angi Andrews, who passed away in 2010 and who is much missed.

Finally, much love to my wife, Ann, daughters, Louise and Elsa, my mum and dad, Harold and Mabel, John and Beth Buckley, Harry and Gill Buckley, Ruth, James, Hannah and Peter, Ziggy, and Hoggle (RIP).

FOREWORD

KARL BARTOS

ONE DAY in April 2009 I opened my inbox to find the following e-mail:

> *Dear Karl, I'm writing a book about Kraftwerk. Would you be available for an interview? It would be wonderful to speak to you, and any help you could give would be very much appreciated. Best wishes from Munich, David.*

Here's what I replied:

> *Hello David, thank you for your inquiry. Please understand that I can't make a contribution to a book on Kraftwerk. I have stopped giving interviews on that topic. I wish you all the best, however. Kind regards, Karl.*

When you think about it, that should have been the end of the story. But here I am, writing a foreword to the book. So what happened?

Somehow, over the three years since that first contact, David and I have found ourselves emailing and Skyping about all sorts: writing, musicians we know or admire, art, success, failure, personal stuff and, it goes without saying, a load of old nonsense as well, something which both the Brits and the Germans do very well, as it happens.

I soon came to realise just how much this man from Liverpool knows about pop and music. I also realised just how skilled he has been at squeezing a few Kraftwerk quotes out of me after all, although I always had what I like to call my 'emergency exit'. Any time it got too much for me, I simply posted the words 'I have just closed my quotation department'.

Now, in the spring of 2012, I have just read the draft manuscript. For me, this is the first serious book written by an outsider about the band I was a member of for 15 years, both as a musician and then later as a co-writer. David Buckley paints a vivid picture of the social and cultural background to Kraftwerk, putting the band and its music into detailed context with the aid of numerous interviews with insiders and observers alike. In doing so, he provides an in-depth insight into how this strange band from Düsseldorf managed to produce pop music that was – and still is – understood around the world.

That's the feeling I get at my concerts as well. The fans from the seventies – when the sound of the synthesizer was still regarded as something out of the ordinary – stand side by side with a younger generation for whom electronic music is as familiar as social networking. What connects them all is the mysterious power of music to speak to us, to reach deep into our hearts.

That means a lot to me. And it's what makes me do what I do.

Karl Bartos, Hamburg, 31 May, 2012

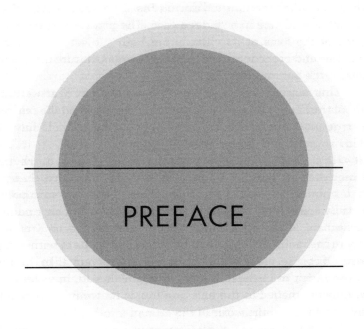

PREFACE

GERMANY HAS played a big part in my life. It's been my home for 20 years. It fascinates me, it frustrates me. It's true, trains do run on time, and orderly and appropriate behaviour is expected at all times (when a German friend is invited to dinner for 20.00, expect them to come bang on time, even a few minutes early, not tactfully late, as a Brit would).

Living in southern Germany I have encountered rules encouraging proper and decent behaviour, such as not cooking on a barbecue more than six times during the summer if you live in a flat with a terrace area, and never using a lawnmower on a Sunday. During *Fasching* (the Carnival time, immediately before Lent), it is, however, expected of you to don a wig, engage in face painting and to embark on an orderly revelry which would ideally include the humorously-entitled *Krapfen* (doughnuts), all washed down by endless mugs of strong coffee or cloudy wheat beer. *Fasching* can literally be explosive. It has been claimed, although it is possibly an urban myth, that adultery committed during *Fasching* was not regarded as permissible evidence in a divorce case. The private and the public spheres of the lives of its citizens are both subject to the sort of formalities and procedures which make German culture unique and, of course, the butt of jokes worldwide.

This sense of *Ordnung* is at the very heart of Kraftwerk. Not for them the Dionysian excesses of rock music; instead the reasoned and structured Apollonian constraints of a music which only very seldom sounds as if it was created organically at all. At its best, Kraftwerk's music sounds so perfectly pre-arranged, its rhythms and melodies so completely perfect in their simplicity, that they offer a chimera of ideals, Platonic forms, made not so much by man as by something altogether less fallible, less human, and more superhuman. Kraftwerk's music, in an odd way, seems to exist purely in the realm of the artificial, the mechanic, the cybernetic, the cyborg. Of course, many of the songs you will encounter in this book were the result of chance, of luck, of mistakes and, in at least one case, musical theft. But the end product, what we hear, very often seems to bear no imprimatur of the human mind at all.

My first encounter with a German came when I was 18 months old. Although when I mention this many people respond with a disbelieving look, my memory starts when I was still a baby. My brother, Harry, had invited a German exchange student to stay at our home. I think we even shared the same bed, so I can claim that I have actually slept with a German. He gave my mum a bottle of Eau de Cologne. It was the time of the World Cup, 1966. I'd be lying if I said I could remember the final.

A few years later, school age at least, I noticed that my parents' bed had broken (I shudder to think how), and one corner was being propped up by an old, yellowing, battered book. It was an English-language copy of *Mein Kampf*, a mighty tome indeed. Its front cover, as I remember, had fallen off, although it did look as if it had been read. According to family folkore, two of my uncles were briefly followers of Oswald Mosley in the thirties, and yet one later went on to befriend the enemy, visiting Germany on several occasions after striking up a friendship with a wartime adversary.

As a child, like anyone born in the fifties and sixties, I was subjected to a tawdry diet of anti-German light entertainment. Of course, I knew the basics of what had occurred during the Second World War. My dad had served in the air force and my mum was in the Women's Land Army in 1946. It wasn't, however, much of a topic of conversation. Hitler, if he was mentioned at all, was reduced to a figure of grotesque hilarity as personified by Basil Fawlty's squirm-inducing caricature of a Nazi in a 1975 episode of *Fawlty Towers*. German autobahns, however, were widely praised, though annoyance was expressed at West Germany's post-war economy – how they lost the war, but won the peace. Nevertheless, the close proximity of the war was evidenced in concrete terms, literally, when on an excursion to the bottom of the local playing field, I saw a huge triangular concrete bollard which dwarfed me. "It's a tank trap," my brother informed me. As a child, I collected plastic toy soldiers and re-enacted World War Two scenarios. It was taken as a given that Hitler himself was one testicle light, and that his wartime high command were similarly short of manhood, as we sang a popular anti-German song to the tune of 'Colonel Bogey' which ended in 'and poor old Goebbels, he has no balls at all'. When we went for day trips in the summer, we would drive past areas a mile or so from our house which then looked like huge ponds, but which 25 years or so before had been bomb craters. My English teacher in my first year at secondary school, who was yet to celebrate his 40th birthday, told tales of being evacuated as a child during the hostilities. My friends, many of them Jewish, had family and friends who had suffered directly at the hands of the Nazi regime. I grew up not in the shadow of the War itself, but certainly at a time when the events of 1939–45 were within the living memory of a majority of the population, and when Winston Churchill, the wartime Prime Minster who led us to victory, was regarded by young and old, rich and poor, as 'the greatest living Englishman'.

In truth, it was hard to find anyone whose views didn't conform to a very British stereotype of what a German was. Pete Townshend of the Who spoke for many of the baby-boomer generation about what was tantamount to cultural brainwashing: 'As a young man, every bone in my body wanted to pick up a machine gun and kill Germans. And yet I had absolutely no reason to do so. Certainly nobody invited me to do the job. But that's what I felt that I was trained to do. Now no part of my upbringing was militaristic.' Force-fed on a weekly diet of war films, the average British teenager of the seventies would have received very little by way of unbiased commentary. Almost without exception, wartime Germans were sinister, ruthless henchmen (the squaddies) or scheming, cold, cruel and clinical (the officer class). The British, when killed, died heroically, or stoically, and with honour. German soldiers however were much more likely to be blown up, or to die in as gruesome, undignified a manner as possible. As a child, I remember one war film where a German soldier was shot and a whole magazine of bullets unloaded into his body as he twitched and convulsed. One had to make sure such evil was truly dead. There was one notable exception, the 1957 movie *The One That Got Away*, starring Hardy Krüger as a bold and handsome Luftwaffe pilot who escaped British clutches while being transferred to a POW camp in Canada. In the early seventies, the BBC TV drama *Colditz*, although a popular hit and largely well-acted, sent out mixed signals about the propriety of German high command, whilst *Dad's Army*, the popular sitcom featuring the buffoonish goings on of the Warmington-on-Sea Home Guard, famously poked fun at German punctiliousness, most notably in an episode in which the Home Guard were briefly entrusted with the task of guarding some German captives. The German officer (played by Philip Madoc) threatens future retribution to anyone who crosses him by including them on his 'list', whilst he warns his captors when they send out for fish and chips that his chips must be crisp, not soggy. Many children's favourite programme, *Dr Who*, also included distinct Third Reich-style references (as we would go on to discover later). The Daleks' cry of 'Exterminate', and their indefatigably evil creator, Davros, both had obvious Nazi connotations. Hitler was fair game to be lampooned on primetime national television by the likes of Spike Milligan, and, a little later, by Freddie Starr. We had won the war, and so had the moral right to be as offensive, as insensitive, and as uncritical as we liked.

Elsewhere, German presence on British TV was minimal. Andrew Sachs (born Andreas Siegfried Sachs), who played Manuel in *Fawlty Towers*, was in fact German, although one would never have known given how convincing his portrayal of the inept Spanish waiter was to the Brits. Smiley Heinz Wolf, with his dicky-bow, flyaway hair, and distracted eccentric mad-professor-like *mien*, spoke a heavily German-accented English on children's TV's *The Great Egg Race* and *Young Scientist Of The Year*. He was one of the very few positive images of German identity on television, and even that, one suspected, was rather rehearsed, as if Professor Wolf was performing the stereotype of the friendly, bumbling and absent-minded German scientist for his pre-teen audience.

It was hardly surprising therefore, that it wasn't through television, but through radio that I met my first, very different, imaginary German friend, someone who wasn't evil, or buffoonish, but something altogether more human. I was lucky enough to grow up in a house full of music. Not only were my elder brothers pop fans, but my dad, then in his mid-fifties, was a lover of progressive rock. His Focus and Pink Floyd albums would compete with my brother's Genesis and Roxy Music. I would watch *Top Of The Pops* for sightings of Slade and Wizzard, Bowie and Sparks. Even my mum listened to Terry Wogan playing the unthreatening songs of Elton John and Simon & Garfunkel on the kitchen radio each morning. One sunny early summer's day in 1975, upstairs in our tiny bathroom, I switched on the Top 30 countdown in my school lunch break. While sitting on the loo, I heard, well, the future. I had no musical compass for this song – naive, simple, childlike almost, and the words – the first time I had heard German being spoken or sung, added to the strangeness. It certainly wasn't rock music, but it wasn't really pop either. What was it? Thirty-five years later, I'm determined to find out.

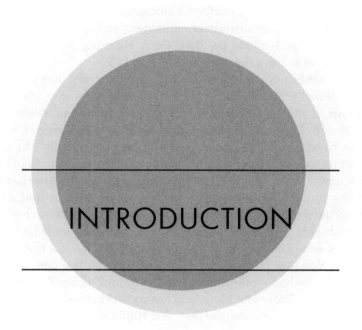

INTRODUCTION

**'Meine Damen und Herren, Ladies and Gentlemen,
Heute abend (aus Deutschland)
Die Mensch Maschine Kraftwerk'**

DÜSSELDORF, NOVEMBER 2010

I'M NERVOUS. More nervous than usual when I meet pop people.

I'm being driven to Kling Klang Studio by ex-Kraftwerk member Wolfgang Flür. Wolfgang, now in his early sixties, is wearing loose-fitting brown cords and a short, casual jacket, his slightly thinning hair is dyed brown, and his complexion looks tanned. I'm more nervous than usual because, unlike the majority of pop people I have met, Wolfgang, if he only but knew it, is close to being one of my favourite music icons, ever. For 13 years he was part of Kraftwerk's classic line-up. In fact, it's the only line-up which, to this day, really means Kraftwerk to most of their fans – Wolfgang, Karl, Ralf and Florian. However competent and reassuring for fans the current band might be, Ralf, Fritz, Henning and Stefan just doesn't seem to have the same iconic ring to it.

Tracking down Kraftwerk has proved tricky. For a start, it wasn't actually clear what or who Kraftwerk were any more. The first port of call, as a matter of courtesy, was the band as currently constituted. Only one of the original members, Ralf Hütter, is still in the band but he has been and still is, undoubtedly, the most important one. It was always his vision of the band that held sway and it is true to say that to all intents and purposes, Kraftwerk is Ralf Hütter's project. My publishers had written a letter to Ralf which was passed on to him by a third party. A few weeks later, we received a formal reply from Patrick Strauch at Sony, which let it be known that they would contact us if they liked the idea, but not to hold our breath. I also sent polite requests to Ralf through two people in the business who had worked with Kraftwerk and whom Ralf trusted, Paul Baines at EMI, then Mute, and Stuart Kirkham who had worked with the band on the release of their last studio album, *Tour de France Soundtracks*. I had also tried to contact current member Henning Schmitz through a circuitous route via a member of his side project band. None of these stratagems brought forth the desired result, an audience with Ralf.

However, Kraftwerk certainly have the 'EX-Factor' since, to date, if we include every musician who has played with the band both live and in the studio, there are no fewer than 19 ex-members. Of these, Eberhard Kranemann, who was in the band even before it was called Kraftwerk, back in the late sixties and early seventies, and Michael Rother, most famously 50% of Neu!, who again spent a brief period in the early band, both spoke to me. Wolfgang Flür gave me the longest interview he had ever done, spread over two days in Düsseldorf and punctuated by some delicious food and much laughter. The strangest moment certainly was when, emboldened by a couple of beers, I decided it was a good idea to sing 'The Model' to him in 'pub-singer-style' late one evening. A mildly bemused Wolfgang took it with good humour.

2

The charming and wickedly funny Karl Bartos, who left the band in 1990, had spoken to me on many occasions via Skype and we became internet buddies on email and Facebook. Karl had told me that his reservoir of Kraftwerk anecdotes had run dry. He was bored with answering the same old questions and, besides, because he was obliged to speak English he was often dissatisfied with his answers in print and on television, feeling that they lack the nuances he could give them if he had answered in German. Reluctant to commit fully to co-operating on the book, mindful of his own memoirs in the pipeline, he was nevertheless open and friendly to me off the record, and agreed to answer several questions in writing, in German, especially for this book. 'Write about the radiation coming from Kraftwerk,' he advised me. 'You weren't there at the time.' There was a private history of the band which I was able to piece together by off-the-record comments and through information that research work gleans as part of a natural process. Karl suggested it was better to concentrate on this 'radiation', the fallout, the significance, rather than the internal logic of his 'autistic friends'. In fact, Karl had met up with Florian Schneider-Esleben just after the founding member had left the band in December 2008. He seemed 'happy and relaxed', considerably more relaxed than he had been during his final years in the band. But Karl claimed to have no contact number or even email address for him. Wolfgang simply expressed a certain surprise that the last time he saw Florian on TV he was wearing a cap.

Of all the past members, it is Wolfgang who is most comfortable speaking to journalists; and 'part of the service' is a trip down to his old hunting ground, his place of work for almost 15 years, the Kling Klang Studio in Düsseldorf. He picks me up from my hotel, and, as he drives, he talks about Kraftwerk more openly than he did when the voice recorder was switched on (and that was candid enough). It's well over 20 years since he left the band. He told of how he was merely an employee; how Kraftwerk stalled as a project and became a poor second, in Ralf's eyes, to his 'addiction' to cycling; how he felt he had to leave because he felt Kraftwerk had reached a standstill, and how, in the late nineties, a meeting with Ralf, which led to him being asked to rejoin the band, ended in disaster; and how he felt it strange, and not a little embarrassing, that Kraftwerk continued when it had almost nothing new to say. Ralf, he told me, was driven to take the project on and on, when he and Karl had known it was over decades before.

He flashes a smile as we get out of the car, and it's then that I can see clearly how he could have become 'the Tom Jones of electro-pop', as Andy McCluskey from Orchestral Manoeuvres In The Dark put it. Charming, funny and beaming, he switches back into the present. He parks his car right outside what looks to me like a porn shop – tacky, seedy. Indeed, Kling Klang is in a rather unprepossessing street, Mintropstrasse 16, a few minutes' walk from the Hauptbahnhof. We walk down the road 50 yards and then cross over to Kling Klang, or rather, what *was* Kling Klang. Several years earlier, Ralf had upped sticks and moved to a new Kling Klang several miles outside Düsseldorf. The sign 'Electro-Müller GmbH' is still there, in red livery, with the proprietor 'Joachim Dehmann, Tontech' the name on the doorbell. Joachim, who had for many years worked with Kraftwerk, now works with Florian who has retained the old premises. Florian, Ralf's original comrade-in-arms, had left the group 18 months earlier, without explanation, although some journalists theorised that only in Kraftwerk, where the pace of artistic endeavour had run so slowly, could it take almost four decades for the two to discover that they finally had irreconcilable musical differences. I had sent Joachim an email to say I was coming and would it be OK if I spoke to him, and had asked, casually, but with very little real hope, if Florian was around. Good-naturedly, Wolfgang poses with the covers of some vinyl Kraftwerk albums and 12" singles, and we pretend that we're tradesmen trying to sell dodgy contraband to passing fans.

'Oh look, Florian is here!' says Wolfgang, 'There's his car in the courtyard. Perhaps he likes you?' As the last sentence is spoken, the drawbridge, or, rather, the shutters of Kling Klang are closed. I peer up, and notice that I am obviously being watched, through two small surveillance cameras. I burst out laughing, all of my nervousness now replaced with a sneaking admiration for such a clinical piece of territorialism. I had been refused entrance to Kling Klang and I had most certainly been refused an audience. Never had rejection come with such classic comic timing. Like so many others before me, it was a case of so far... and no further.

4

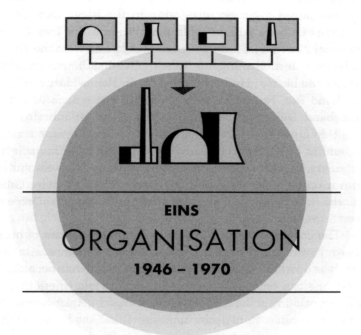

EINS

ORGANISATION
1946 – 1970

1.1 Mediaphobia

THEY ALMOST always refuse to grant interviews, publicise their work, or to have photographs taken, except when they have new product to promote, which, at the current rate, is about once a decade. They certainly refuse to talk about their private lives, to appear on chat shows, game shows or entertainment programmes. Throughout their career they have refused big-name collaborations with the likes of David Bowie (the band's first major media supporter) and even the biggest star on the planet, Michael Jackson. They have yet even to release a 'best of' record. They are not celebrities, they are not rock stars. Even in their home country, only music fans know who they are. If they are remembered by the wider population at all, it is for two songs, 'Autobahn', largely dismissed as a novelty hit, and 'The Model'. 'Are they even still going?' is probably the most commonly posed question in relation to the band. One German friend even asked me, 'Are they German?' When, in 2003, the German TV channel ZDF ran its public vote to decide who were the Top 200 most famous Germans, *Unsere Besten* ('Our Best'), there would be places for the likes of Herbert Grönemeyer, Nena, Hartmut Engler of the band Pur, Heino, Marlene Dietrich, Peter Kraus, Campino (of the band Die Toten Hosen), Nicole, Farin Urlaub (from Die Ärzte), Udo Lindenberg, Peter Maffay and Nina Hagen, but not for any member of Kraftwerk. A motley collection of Eurovison light entertainers, earnest singer songwriters, and hard rockers virtually unknown outside German-speaking territories were prized above those who have been by far and away their most important export of the last 50 years.

The core members of this most intensely private of groups have always retained the right to keep their private selves away from the public; and when odd facts about their off-stage lives occasionally emerge, one can only imagine the discomfort felt. Bristling at the revelatory, bridling at the task of having to explain, Kraftwerk are less a pop act and much more performance artists. They have a lot more in common with Gilbert & George and Andy Warhol. They have had nothing whatsoever to do with the celebrity aspects of the record industry. 'They are really defined by what they don't subscribe to – and much of the list is a merciful release,' says electronic musician John Foxx. 'No loose sex vids or confessional addiction recovery blogs.' The focus would always be on their work, their music as part of a wider cultural package, a *Gesamtkunstwerk* – a universal work of art. 'That means we're not just musicians. We're rounded artists,' confirmed Hütter. Although very much a band interested in and informed by technology, their own website has almost no content at all, no band history, no news section, and certainly no blog or link to a Twitter account. Its most developed feature is the online merchandising store, which dispatches Kraftwerk-endorsed product with typical efficiency. Kraftwerk are possibly the most mediaphobic band in music history.

'Mediaphobic is not a bad way to describe us,' says Karl Bartos, a member of Kraftwerk between 1975 and 1990, the period in which Kraftwerk changed the musical world. 'Looking back, I would say what actually happened was that we controlled the way we were reported in the media. Ralf Hütter and Florian Schneider had a pretty good idea of how they wanted Kraftwerk to be perceived in and by the media: one campaign per album – in other words, only when we had a relevant message (*Botschaft*). And we preferred to use our own photos and films wherever possible. The media landscape was completely different then, of course, and the internet was a long way off.'

Florian's interview with a female Brazilian journalist in 1998 sums up this non-cooperation policy with brutal perfection. Speaking in a foreign language she interviews Florian, also speaking in a foreign language, and whilst we could blame the confused semantic nexus of a native Portuguese speaker and a native German speaker conducting an interview in English as the reason why the interview has absolutely no content, it's also hard not to see the art of non-co-operation as a tactic, with hilarious consequences. The hapless journalist asks a succession of admittedly not-terribly-inspiring questions to Florian. Asked about Brazil, he's at his most animated: 'A wonderful country; we stay here forever.' Later in the three-minute interview, Florian simply smiles and answers every question with an increasingly unrevealing range of conversational gambits:

Q: 'What are the songs you are going to play tonight?'
A: 'All.'
Q: 'I've heard you're preparing a new album?'
A: 'Yeah.'
Q: 'Do you like the new generation of Techno music?'
A: '*Ja.*'
Q: 'Do you think you are the father of this new generation?'
A: 'What shall I say? [laughs] I don't know,'

before the interview ends with a classic piece of pate-wiping from Florian. Throughout, Florian cannot help but grin wildly after almost every question to his off-camera table-mate.

This is the crux of their success, of course, too. By giving nothing away, Ralf Hütter and Florian Schneider have created a mythic corona around the band. The central tenet of myth-making is never to explain. Create a cult by remaining silent. The act of explanation should be unnecessary. It's all in the work for those with the correct critical faculties. Kraftwerk have clearly defined their audience, and they want an audience of inquiring and literate minds, not an audience of passive and boorish thrill-seekers.

Where does this elitism come from? Such high-minded aesthetics are uncommon in popular music, certainly in a group who, for a time, were actual pop stars, if only by default. The answer to this can partly be explained by the personal backgrounds of Kraftwerk's undoubted leaders, Ralf Hütter and Florian Schneider, their affluent family backgrounds, their emotional geography, and their analyses of what post-war German music had become, and what future it had to have.

1.2 'Bombed Cities ...Rotten Corpses...'

Simon Winder, author of the best-selling book on German culture, *Germania*,[*] a book which, incidentally ends, to all intents and purposes, in 1933, speaks of the terrible emotional legacy of the Nazi period: 'There is a great comment in Thomas Bernhard's memoirs about the way that whenever someone was killed by bombing in Salzburg everyone simply pretended that they had either gone away or had never existed. I feel a bit sorry for Germans (but not Austrians) on this issue as perhaps the best response to 1933–45 is to be democratic, inclusive, collaborative with other countries, be internationalized, eunuchized and chuck money into aid projects – all of which the Germans have done. There is perhaps little value in saying sorry – particularly as such colossal numbers of Germans wound up dying themselves. Just after the war a group of senior Protestant clerics got together and said that the bombing of German cities had been legitimate because Christianity had failed to stand up to Nazism and this was God's punishment. I thought that pretty much summed it up – hundreds of thousands of convinced Nazis were killed, many others committed suicide, others were executed or gaoled (although not enough) – there must be a point when moving ahead again is not a bad response.'

The overriding feeling for the German baby-boom generation was one of shame. To this day, German people seldom, if at all, mention the name of Adolf Hitler. His Austrian birthplace, Braunau

---

* Germania: a Personal History of Germans Ancient and Modern, 2009.

am Inn, has the memorial stone against war and fascism, on which is written:

FÜR FRIEDEN FREIHEIT
UND DEMOKRATIE
NIE WIEDER FASCHISMUS
MILLIONEN TOTE MAHNEN*

Impersonating Hitler, even for comedic effect, is fraught with danger. His image is seldom, if ever, seen in paintings, photographs or posters. His bunker in Berlin has never been opened to the public. Madame Tussauds' decision to include a wax effigy of the Führer in their Berlin exhibition was widely condemned. 'Distasteful beyond comparison,' said the centre-right Christian Democrat Union (CDU). 'Tasteless, disgusting and in bad style,' said the Greens. The second visitor to the exhibition broke through security and tore off Hitler's head. Likewise, unless for strictly satirical use or in serious documentaries and films, it is strictly forbidden by law to display the swastika. One coin collector even pointed out recently that coins from the period of the Third Reich (1933–45) had the swastika symbol stickered or pixellated out in photographic representations.

And yet, despite all this, many Germans born in the post-war period and into the sixties were horrified that despite the public display of guilt, many high-ranking members of the Nazi Party somehow avoided trial and returned to public life. They voiced the concern that the Allies hadn't gone far enough, or quickly enough, to make sure that the guilty were seen to pay. The fact that some high-ranking officials subsequently became captains of industry and important politicians would lead, in the seventies, to a violent youth-inspired backlash. Modernity and economic power were all well and good – but at what price? 'Many people from that period who kept their sympathy for the Nazi ideology survived and got employed in the government, in the education and economical system,' says Berlin-born Hans-Joachim Roedelius, a young musician in the sixties who would later go on to form the hugely influential bands Cluster and Harmonia. 'It was hard for the young

---

* English translation: 'For peace, freedom and democracy. No more fascism. Millions of dead will not let us forget.'

to find their own way to express in art what was necessary at the time. The youngsters in the sixties had had nothing to do with the war, and the older generation that had survived the war and the mess afterwards didn't care much about it.'

'The key events for German youth must have been the unease over the War,' agrees Simon Winder. 'I always thought that if I was a teen in the early fifties in East Germany I would definitely have been an enthusiastic Red Pioneer, eager to erase the shame of the past to create a bright new socialist future. West German youth did not really have that opportunity and the consumerist conservatism of official politics must have been an utter dead hand.'

Henning Dedekind, Krautrock expert and translator, recalled speaking to Irmin Schmidt of Can. Schmidt was born in the Nazi era, in 1937, and the devastation left by Allied bombing left an indelible and brutal picture in his child's imagination: 'Irmin told me what it was like to see all those bombed cities and rotten corpses lying around as a child, and after that, not being a victim, but being brought up as a sinner in the eyes of the world, and all the time suspecting that their parents' generation was responsible for these terrible crimes and this terrible outcome of the war. They saw the guilty generation, their parents, fall silent at the end of the war. It was an unwritten law not to talk about Hitler and the Second World War. Irmin, and his generation, had the feeling that this was unjust, and they wanted to talk to their parents and to their teachers... So they rebelled, because they thought it was like a whole country was living a lie, like the Second World War suddenly had never happened; and they wanted to, in their sometimes destructive sounds or very open sounds or experimental sounds, question this atmosphere of a cultural standstill.'

If Germany was the site of a complicated generational battle for the soul of a country, it was also forced into two decades of rebuilding a nation whose structure was almost completely destroyed. This forced modernity on the country, beginning with its architecture. Britain, meanwhile, was financially exhausted, and though its Labour government may have embarked on a wildly audacious piece of welfare reform in the form of the National Health Service, its solution to the effects of years of Luftwaffe bombing was largely of the make-do-and-mend patch-up rather than wholesale physical rebuilding of a society. 'The Second World War changed everything' says Andy McCluskey, co-founder of Orchestral Manoeuvres In The Dark, and a Kraftwerk fanatic, born just 14 years after the end of the war into a Northern Industrial landscape that had changed very little since the days of midnight Luftwaffe bombing raids. 'Britain came out of the Second World War with its railways and industry and its housing much more intact than Germany, so what we had was a very worn, tired mess. Germany was obliterated and was rebuilt after the war. With this attitude of positive brave new future, the brave new world, the confidence that science and technology, and medicine and electronics were going to make a wonderful new future and it was also paid for by the Marshall Plan. Do you know that Britain was still repaying its debt to America until 1976? We were in this dystopian dirty mess; and actually Kraftwerk were growing up in, of all places, Düsseldorf. You find me an original building in Düsseldorf of pre 1945! There aren't many of them. I think that is where their music reflected that wonderful utopian vision of the future which is now of course a vision of modernity.'

Germany may have had modernity forced upon it in the decades after 1945. The British might have looked on at Germany's newness with a certain envy; but the route towards embracing and achieving modernity in terms of popular culture would, as we will see, take much, much longer to achieve.

1.3 The Colonising of the Subconscious

In the post-war period of economic and cultural reconstruction, German youth largely turned to the West, to British and American popular music for their musical language and for escapism. German film-maker Wim Wenders called it 'the colonising of our subconscious'. An examination of the West-German best-selling singles of the late fifties and early sixties discloses an assortment of safe, sentimental folk songs, copies of American originals, and the occasional home-grown hit. In the late sixties, when the constituent members of what would become known as Kraftwerk were coming together, the overriding idea behind music-making was to produce something that was culturally of its time and place. 'We were obliged to rediscover the sound of everyday life because it didn't exist any more,' opined Kraftwerk's supremo Ralf Hütter in the seventies, reminding us that, when his group began, there was no real German popular culture to speak of. 'We had to redefine our musical culture. Not only our musical culture, however: at the end of the sixties all German artists had the same problems. Writers, directors, painters ... all of them had to invent a new language.'

The bands grouped together by the British press as Krautrockers in the late sixties and early seventies shared one common vision: to release the pause button on German culture. For almost three decades, German music had stood still. There was the on-going affection for serious art music and the avant-garde at which the Germans had always excelled, but in terms of popular music, as American youth rocked to Little Richard and Chuck Berry, and, a little later, as Britain was shaken to its foundations by the Beatles and Rolling Stones, Germany had almost no home-grown popular culture whatsoever. In the East, Western popular music was censored, radio output strictly regulated. Such music that existed, whether it was jazz or pop, existed only because the Communist government permitted it.

The dominant form of indigenous popular music in West Germany was the *Schlager*. Literally translated as 'hits', *Schlager* came to refer to a whole genre of lightweight popular music, and its scions; as Magnus Palm writes in *Bright Lights, Dark Shadows*, his definitive biography of Abba, in which he explores the Swedish group's musical roots: 'Typical schlager music has its roots in genres as diverse as German military marches, Austrian operettas, Italian and Eastern European folk music, and the French chanson.' Britain had its own *Schlager*: the wholesome, clean-cut Cliff Richard's 'Bachelor Boy', its banal Eurovision Song Contest entries 'Puppet On A String' (Sandie Shaw), 'Congratulations' (Richard) and 'Boom Bang-A-Bang' (Lulu), and, in the late sixties and early seventies, the bubblegum music of the 'Chirpy Chirpy Cheep Cheep' (Middle Of The Road) and 'Co-Co' (Sweet) variety. Americans too had their own *Schlager* – the endlessly bland country & western Nashville spewed out, the tortuous 'Death Discs' typified by Bobby Goldsboro's 'Honey', or the post-Army Elvis, evidently influenced by his posting to Bad Nauheim in early 1959. But nowhere in the West was pop as banal, as conformist, as cringe-making or as platitudinous as in Germany.

Literally shell-shocked by the Second World War, and, in part, in denial about the true extent of the Hitler-led Holocaust,

West Germany retreated into sentimentality of the stickiest sort. The songs of the fifties deified courtship, marriage, homeland, and cosiness. Take, for example (if we must), the success of Berlin-born René Carol, doyen of all things *gemütlich* ('cosy', 'warm' or 'congenial'), with hits such as ' Rote Rosen, rote Lippen, roter Wein' ('Red Roses, Red Lips, Red Wine'). Then there was Freddy (Quinn), real name Franz Eugen Helmut Manfred Nidl, an Austrian-born musician whose repertoire included 'Heimweh' ('Homesickness'), 'Dort wo die Blumen blüh'n' ('Where The Flowers Bloom'), 'Schön war die Zeit', a German-language version of Dean Martin's 'Memories Are Made Of This', 'Ich bin bald wieder hier' ('I'll Be Back Soon'), 'Heimatlos' ('Homeless'), and 'Die Gitarre und das Meer'. ('The Guitar And The Sea'). To listen to and watch the *Schlager* singer Dorthe, for example, with her horrendous number from 1968, 'Wärst Du doch in Düsseldorf geblieben?' ('If You Had Only Stayed In Düsseldorf'), is to realise how the rationale for a new genus of home-grown German music in the post-war culture became all too compelling. It is as if the boom-bang-a-bang style had got caught in a hideous, let's-give-up-the-will-to-live time warp. Meanwhile, from outside the German-speaking world, came equally bathetic songs from the likes of Edith Piaf, the Kingston Trio, Petula Clarke and Pat Boone. In a country so riven with guilt and shame, core mythic German values took precedence, as if to remind its shell-shocked masses of a less brutal and more civilised time.

Compared to the United States and Britain, West Germany had next to no youth culture to speak of. It took until the late seventies and early eighties for any kind of youth-based ethos to emerge as a strong component of its social life. Peter Saville, born in Manchester in 1955, and, like his future working partner, Andy McCluskey, a Northerner in awe of Kraftwerk, explains the cultural differences in the following terms: 'In my opinion Germany is only just becoming a holistically pop society, so that the young German people that I know in the significant conurbations like Cologne, Munich possibly, and Hamburg certainly, the 40 year olds and younger are only now becoming a society of shared pop values. Whereas Britain has been disseminating and sharing a kind of pop socio-culture for 40 years, and pop culture is what has become the universal connector between [parts of the] British previously class-orientated structure, in the post-war period during which Britain's class structure has been entirely dismantled. The shared value system between these formerly disparate classes, the one shared thing has been pop culture, the common language of formative society so the people [have been] growing up. The common language of people in society in Britain is pop – pop in its broader sense of music, fashion, image, identity, design and increasingly art. We have got that kind of joined up sensibility in Britain; and we kind of see it through a pair of pop spectacles.'

Saville continues: 'Germany has not been like that. Germany has got a more structured set of political, cultural and academic ideas. They have high cultural values which we tend to underplay because of class. You know, working class people basically didn't want to know about high culture because of its associations with an upper class. Middle class people were either leaning one way or another or were on some kind of aspirational course towards higher culture, but depending on their background it was pretty much beyond them. Pop has stepped in to, in a way, appease all. Now Germany, after the war, Germany had to set itself on an entirely different pathway to Britain. All notions of tradition were temporarily "off message". Germany went forward with its cultural programme the same way that it went forward with its socio-economic and industrial programme. They took high culture seriously and were progressive with it.'

High Art dominated; West German pop music, such as it was, imitated established Anglo-American themes, forms and codes. What Germany had in abundance was culture with a capital 'C'. Germany excelled in literature, poetry, opera, classical music and theatre. Whilst the *Schlager* was king until at least the early sixties, in the field of abstract experimental music, advances were being made which would, a decade or more later, have a crucial influence on groups such as Kraftwerk. A landmark recording from the mid-fifties is *Gesang der Jünglinge* ('Song Of The Youths') recorded in Cologne by Karlheinz Stockhausen. Noted for his ground-breaking, aleatory works, here Stockhausen fashioned what many critics regard as the first modern classic electronic piece. Stockhausen created a unique soundscape by fading in and out the sound of a young boy reciting a poem whose voice was pitched to match exactly the sound of a manipulated sine wave. The result was artificially created phonemes, a language of sound. Such experiments in voice and electronic manipulation would have a direct impact on the most innovative of the new West-German bands that formed in the late sixties. What many of these new bands would have in common was a classical training aligned to a love of all sorts of Anglo-American music, from soul and funk to rock and pop; high art would be set on a collision path with street music, and thus would change the currency of popular music for ever.

1.4 '... My name is called Disturbance...'*

The sixties was the decade in which the baby-boomers, whilst not taking control, started to make their opinions, prejudices and desires heard. Today, there is much debate about this generation, born roughly between the end of the Second World War and the years between 1955 or 1960, depending on which social parameters one accepts. It has been argued, not without merit, that this generation has been the least responsible, and most spoilt, of any generation in the history of humankind. Even those born into relative poverty in the UK benefitted from many freedoms – free healthcare and prescriptions, almost full employment, free education, a relatively well-funded welfare state. Those born in more affluent circumstances also benefitted from these self-same privileges and yet seemed to accept them as natural and deserved, unaware, or perhaps even simply uninterested, in the struggle and the sacrifice that had gone into making their lives the safest, most comfortable and with the greatest potential for freedom of expression in the twentieth century. Under their auspices, as the baby-boomer generation came into power in the eighties and nineties, they bequeathed tuition fees, a crumbling welfare state and a huge carbon footprint, a legacy which, on first glance, confirms the baby boomers as selfish at best, or at worst self-interested hedonists. The fact that this was a generation that could express their sexuality in the pre-AIDS era as well merely confirms that they were a historical quirk, the most fortunate of the fortunate.

Of course, this is an oversimplification, and deliberately polemical. Not everyone born in the era of the baby boom was unaware of the relatively privileged nature of their lot, nor was

---

* From the Rolling Stones' 'Street Fighting Man' (1969).

everyone greedy, self-interested or uncaring. What was unique about the baby-boomers however was the sense of generational angst felt by so many. Unlike today, in which the gap between father and son, mother and daughter is often quite marginal in terms of interests and views, the gulf between the post-war generation and the pre-war generation was massive. Theirs was a hip, alternative, optimistic credo set against their parents' buttoned-up, parochial, repressed and deferential world view.

The Kraftwerk band members – those of the seventies and eighties line-ups, at least – belonged to the baby-boomer generation. By the time they were reaching adulthood, in the late sixties, the crossing of cultural frontiers was commonplace throughout the western world. Television, radio and cinema reflected the momentous developments in transport, communications and continent-hopping trends in thinking and behaviour. Only Germany and Japan shared the common experience of having passed through years of occupation following the end of hostilities in 1945 and the recovery that followed – especially dynamic in West Germany in the fifties and in Japan during the following decade – the trauma of the post-war experience. In both countries the dominant feature of political and cultural life, as we have seen, was conservatism. However, this was mingled with an appetite for tasting the cultural offerings of the occupying nations. Put simply, by the late sixties, the cultural life of the German baby-boomer generation and their parents was characterised by what was safe, conservative, non-controversial (in the case of locally generated material) and by what was internationally available (in the case of non-German material).

By 'Germany' we mean West Germany of course, as the East was to remain largely closed to influences from outside and, until the eighties, certainly closed to the free expression of ideas and of innovative cultural trends. State control of the radio and live performance stifled creativity. Western cultural forms were seen as imperialistic, corrupting and decadent. Such indigenous popular music that existed was made to divert and to educate East Germans. That said, Western music did, of course, make its way into the Eastern Bloc countries. Here, even the Beatles at their most simple – a song such as 'I Wanna Hold Your Hand', for example – became, in the hands of an East German, a highly politicised symbol of freedom and liberty.

16

In West Germany, the supply of cultural output, in all its forms, was aided by the presence of Allied Forces personnel and their families, first as occupying powers up to the foundation of the Federal Republic in 1949, and later as a substantial NATO presence, which still exists today, albeit with reduced numbers. One speciality generated largely within West Germany was free jazz, and this was to influence the early musical exploits of most of those who were later to be both at the core and around the fringes of Kraftwerk. West Berlin was one of the centres of the counterculture movement; the concert there by Frank Zappa's Mothers of Invention in 1968, which ended in a riot, is now perceived as a landmark event. It was also in Berlin that Benno Ohnesorg, a 27-year-old university student from Hanover, was shot and killed by a policeman in June 1967, during a protest against the State visit by the Shah of Iran. That event was to lead to the foundation of a political movement and to aftershocks for many years.

The year 1968 was pivotal in West Germany. Indeed, it has been argued on many occasions, most recently and most forcefully by the American writer Mark Kurlansky, that 1968 was *the* most important year not only in his lifetime, but of the century. 'What was unique about 1968 was that people were rebelling over disparate issues and had in common only that desire to rebel, ideas about how to do it, a sense of alienation from the established order and a profound distaste for authoritarianism.' In the States, and across Europe, revolution was in the air, protest on the wing... barricades in the streets. 'The generational split was dramatic, affecting households as well as whole communities,' continues Simon Winder. 'I'm always struck though by the way that the great German moment (1968) has become first stuck and then ossified so that for amazing numbers of people long hair and faded jeans remain de rigueur even though their original proponents now draw pensions. It was an authentic German appropriation of Vietnam War-era Americana, but in the US and the UK everyone moved on long ago, whereas I don't feel that is quite the case in Germany.'

1.5 Krautrock Deconstruction

THE YEAR 1968 was also ground zero for popular music in Germany. Karl Bartos, in 1968 a 16-year-old gifted classical musician, puts it like this: 'We don't have the blues in our genes and we weren't born in the Mississippi Delta. There were no black people in Germany. So instead we thought we'd had this development in the twenties which was very, very strong and was audio-visual. We had the Bauhaus school before the war; and then after the war we had tremendous people like Karlheinz Stockhausen and the development of the classical and the electronic classical. This was very strong and it all happened very close to Düsseldorf, in Cologne, and all the great composers at that time came there. During the late forties up until the seventies they all came to Germany; people like John Cage, Pierre Boulez and Pierre Schaeffer, and they all had this fantastic approach to modern music, and we felt it would make more sense to see Kraftwerk as part of that tradition more than anything else.'

In the late sixties, Germany had no national pop culture beyond the *Schlager*. Rather, local scenes developed on often divergent paths, unaware or uncaring about music made in other parts of the country. Munich formed cultural waves of its own, notably with the creation of Amon Düül*, a radical arts commune which became best known as a musical group of the same name. They travelled the country, with spouses and children in tow, varying their line-up and fomenting activity off- as well as on-stage. On Kraftwerk's home turf, the Ruhrgebiet and surrounding areas, a musical revolution had been underway since the fifties. The pivotal figure was Karlheinz Stockhausen, who, in turn, was strongly influenced by Pierre Schaeffer. Schaeffer, born in Lorraine in 1910, trained initially as an engineer but had turned to creating music, experimenting with naturally generated or industrially produced sounds (water and railway trains, for example), a style which became known as *musique concrète*; and this movement was espoused by Stockhausen, who had worked with Schaeffer in the early fifties. He was based for many years in the fifties and sixties at the Nordwestdeutscher Rundfunk studios at Cologne. It has been reported that Ralf and Florian were students at the Robert Schumann Conservatory in Düsseldorf in the late sixties. 'In fact,'

---

* One should make a distinction between Amon Düül and Amon Düül II. The former was the arts collective and for a short time a band who made a couple of fairly free-form albums. The latter was a breakaway second band. They made a complete split from the collective and went on to become the archetypal 'Krautrock' band.

says Karl Bartos, 'Ralf was studying architecture in Aachen. He had a few piano lessons in Krefeld. Florian had some private lessons from Rosemarie Popp (she was a teacher at the Robert Schumann Conservatorium, which was very close to where Florian lived on Leo-Statz-Strasse in the north of Dusseldorf).'

Elsewhere, 'noise' was the watchword of young musicians such as Conrad Schnitzler, who was a founder member of one of the most famous and influential groups of the late sixties, Kluster. (They became Cluster in 1971, after Hans-Joachim Roedelius had been invited to join the band.) Their music was to become dubbed 'industrial'. There is a perceptible link to the earliest manifestation of Kraftwerk – the one-and-only LP of Organisation (forerunner of Kraftwerk), which was called *Tone Float*. Here percussion was to the fore; and it was clearly distinguishable from the style of, for example, Amon Düül, perhaps the best-known of the German groups of the day. The producer Conny Plank, of whom we will hear much more later in this story, was involved in *Tone Float* and managed to sell it to RCA in London. Interestingly, the LP was not distributed in Germany.

By this stage (1968/1969) many bands had come on to the scene in West Germany. One of the most interesting was Popul Vuh, a reclusive trio based in Bavaria. Not only is their reclusiveness an echo of how Kraftwerk were to evolve, but also their fascination with new electronic instruments only then coming on to the market. Florian Fricke of Popul Vuh was an early and enthusiastic purchaser of a new Moog synthesizer in the late sixties.

Overall, three characteristics were to become key features of music groups in West Germany in this period: firstly, very few had the financial resources to buy quality and/or cutting-edge musical instruments; secondly, most were touring the country, using their own cars or vans as transport, for most of the time; and lastly, most had a high level of turnover among their members. These three traits are, of course, linked; and they led to most of the groups being short-lived or at best having a peripheral existence.

This music on the scene at the time was called *Kosmische Musik* ('cosmic music'). It was music that broke away almost completely from the orderliness of the Anglo-American verse/chorus/middle eight song structure. It was music which was improvised, free, anarchic and unbound by constraints of length or of what instruments could and should be used. John Taylor, who in the eighties became the bass player of Duran Duran, has a strong interest in the culture of West Germany in the fifties and sixties. 'You have this kind of anarchy, really. German art doesn't really come into focus until the mid to late sixties – it's almost like it's stunned,' he says. 'Through the fifties it's just stunned, nothing is really happening, everybody's just trapped. Nobody knows what has happened, right? But, as you get into the sixties, and the late sixties, in fine art and in music, things start to happen, and people start to think, and people start to express this vacuum, this blackness.'

However, for most music fans, even some German music fans, the style of music was and still is known as Krautrock. Some find the term offensive; some inaccurate. Others see in the name a relatively harmless form of ethnic stereotyping. Henning Dedekind, author of the book *Krautrock*, and translator of books on musicians including Roxy Music, is unequalled in his qualifications to speak about the origins of the term. 'There are different legends around. One is that the term was forged by John Peel; and there is another story that Amon Düül put a single out, or a song out, entitled 'Amon Düül und ihre Sauerkraut Band'. Possibly it's an English invention for silly Germans and Teutons making music which doesn't fit. I have tried not to take any of those sides because there's too many legends around; and after all this time everybody claims to have invented the term Krautrock. For example, the band Faust had a title called "Krautrock" on their fourth album, because everybody was talking about Krautrock. But I think that was more of a reaction than an invention: so they reacted to this common term which was not so well-meaning, I believe, by making a step forward and saying, "OK then, we are Krautrockers – so what?" it was used among German musicians, so they'd say, "Oh, that's Krautrock, that's what it sounds like, Krautrock, means something that doesn't fit together or that doesn't sound good, doesn't sound American." I remember a friend in the nineties, a German guy, who played what he called Krautrock, and he liked it. And it meant experimental, dissonant, a lack of virtuosity, sense of irony.' As for the characteristics of Krautrock, Henning comments: 'The aesthetic... I would say... it's the will to experiment and the will to throw over everything that ever was before that's a little bit too fake. The will to question each and everything, to be a little cheeky, so to speak, and to just try out anything new.'

1.6 The New *Volksmusik*

The sound of so much cosmic music was indeed the sound of a new musical identity being born, albeit somewhat painfully. The music of many of the artists mentioned above is challenging, an off-shoot of the musical avant-garde and determinedly not made for mass consumption or, indeed, escapism. Kraftwerk were born out of this free-spirited chaos but chose to impose order upon it. For Ralf Hütter and Florian Schneider, musical boundaries were there to be redefined, but never at the cost of sacrificing melody on the altar of dissonance. 'Germany is very open to new music,' Ralf Hütter opined in 1976. 'It is not like America, where there is a strong entertainment thing. Everything in America is measured by its entertainment value... In Germany, it's not measured this way.'

As a young musician, Hütter had a clear idea of the task that lay ahead. 'Music was maybe the most reactionary form. Music was maybe the last art form to adopt the 20th century, and I think it had to do with electronic instruments from the forties, the tape recorder.' Germany's thriving arts scene in the twenties had to all intents been destroyed with the exodus of prominent filmmakers, playwrights and musicians, particularly to France and America, after 1933. 'After the war everything was replaced and turned into American culture, Coca-Cola and whatever, whisky. So we were in a way lucky since we lived in the British sector because their system was not that overpowering,' is how Ralf put it in a 1981 interview. 'These two streams of culture we have, the modernistic and the more, let's say, pathetic, historical, Teutonic. Both streams were wiped out: one before the Nazis and one with the war. So when we knew there was more to life than a house and a Mercedes Benz for the husband and a Volkswagen for the housewife... We have no father figures, so we might as well get ourselves something going. It's very open. It's that old fascination with science in Germany that we share because we are a mix between music and science. Germany is not really big on the entertaining side of the world. They're not very entertaining.'

From the start, they were interested in creating an indigenous music, a new folk music which was essentially middle-European and which reflected contemporary German life. The rise of Kraftwerk mirrored the rise of West Germany's self-confidence after the destruction and terror of the war. Culturally, Kraftwerk

21

would become enormously important for their homeland. At a time when 75% of all music on German radio was in English*, Kraftwerk sang in their mother tongue. Hütter: 'Our music is electronic, but we like to think of it as ethnic music from the German industrial area – industrial folk music.' As we have seen, they would also brand their peculiar repertoire *Kosmische Musik*. 'It was never called Krautrock,' Hütter is keen to point out. 'The word was invented by the English press, and it was never used in Germany.' Against the backdrop of technology advancement, US-Soviet space-race rivalry, and the liberation of popular culture by countercultural progressives, Kraftwerk began making music during a time when the future of mankind seemed to be being radically re-directed.

To many, the idea that Kraftwerk was a folk group might sound contradictory. Folk music has always implied music made by and for the people, easy to play and usually on simple acoustic instruments, and certainly not music made by electronics. Yet, as we know, so many artists singing traditional songs have had very few shared experiences with the problems and deprivations so often portrayed in their lyrics. John Peel, the noted broadcaster and promoter of left-field music, had this to say about folk music back in 1996: 'Marketing people put labels on things. I mean, how can you tell if it's Britpop or folk? The sort of stuff Bowie was doing when he was at his best, and the stuff Oasis and Blur are doing now, particularly Blur, is folk music, because it's music by the folk, whereas the stuff that's described as folk music is done by sociology lecturers at Leicester Polytechnic.'

'I think we predicted that electronic music was going to be the next phase in popular music – Volksmusik,' said Hütter in 1992. 'People said it was crazy, very elitist, intellectual, and we had to say no, this was everyday music – cars, noises, microphones picking up music for everybody...'

With no unified music business in Germany in the late sixties and early seventies, the scenes that sprang up across the country were largely independent of one another, but all with the same questing vision. Promotion and record business infrastructure in the Düsseldorf areas were, according to Ralf, 'non-existent'. 'It was a

---

* This figure comes from Simon Witter's 1991 article in the *NME*, 'Kraftwerk: Robopop'.

completely anarchic situation... In Cologne it was Can, other bands in Munich, Tangerine Dream in Berlin; it was all happening with different aspects coming from the different cities. We would meet at festivals, there was some knowledge of each other, but we came clearly from the Düsseldorf scene.'

Kraftwerk, in order to get heard at all, played multi-media events, seeing their work as a fusion of multiple art forms. 'You can imagine, in the late sixties, we wouldn't even get a spot to perform. So we sneaked into the art world. Within the music world, there were all these rock bands, so we went into some of these happenings situations in the art world, and we would use light shows or projections,' said Hütter. 'We were doing little drawings and comics and album covers; we were preparing projections; we worked on the lights; we worked on the tunes; we built speaker cabinets. Everything around Kraftwerk was part of our creative ideas.'

Rather than play the rock circuit as one would have done in America or Britain, Kraftwerk were born out of the tail end of the sixties 'happenings' scene. Like the Velvet Underground in mid-sixties New York, they were conceived as a mixed-media event, but on a much smaller scale, and without the patronage of a famous and wealthy art guru. Pink Floyd's psychedelic work in the mid-to-late sixties would be another attempt to fuse sound, noise, and the visual. In their case, the use of film, slide projections, lighting and sheer volume would create an all-embracing experience to mirror the addled minds of their acid-taking audience. Another group on a parallel course in the UK would be Roxy Music. Although they convened a few years after Ralf and Florian started working together, there were similarities, particularly an initial disdain for the tried-and-tested routine of gigging in a transit van and 'paying one's dues' on the live circuit. Roxy Music's first live appearances were at private parties at *vernissages*. The important thing is that Kraftwerk were never just about the music. Like their contemporaries, David Bowie, Roxy Music, even the more populist shock-rock of Alice Cooper, the visual presentation was central. The task was always to make something new: 'We started working with the waste products of the media – rather intuitively,' says Karl Bartos of his pre-fame self when he was studying classical music but also fascinated by film and television. 'I remember one performance where a ballet ensemble and we musicians were standing around a television tower dancing.

Such a happening was euphoric and completely naive.' This was an era before the forced contrivance of MTV obliged patently un-photogenic acts with no acting talent, and no interest in the visual arts at all, to dress in designer suits, suffer death-by-stylist and pretend to be deep and meaningful; an era in which the connections between various art forms were still being made and explored with a sense of genuine intellectual curiosity.

However, the very act of making music, getting it heard and building up a fanbase in early seventies Germany was a difficult proposition because the country lacked the music industry superstructure of Britain and the US. Naturally mistrustful of gatekeepers and potential benefactors who might claim influence over the creative process as a quid pro quo for financial backing, Kraftwerk, from the very start, set themselves up not so much as a pop and rock band, but as a business located on one fixed site. Ralf Hütter: 'We wanted a place where we could actually work, because in Germany there's no music industry, or no fabrication that you can rely on, or that is existing or picking people up; an exploitation system that takes people from the streets, fabricates them into other situations and marketing channels; productivity. And we had this idea of... ah... since we didn't have that anyway, and we're not... politically we don't like it anyway, so we would be our own factory, our own industrial productivity. And then we started renting some space in some workshops. And we are still actually in the same place, although now we have taken over other parts of the building, so it's quite magnetic. And we started producing there, and started making our own sounds, tapes, with cassette recorders or a simplistic two-track Revox machine. And then we made all the sounds. And since we didn't have enough money to mix it down in a studio we met Conny Plank and he helped us out. We actually worked together, but he had no part in producing the music.'

1.7 'Loners...Mavericks'

But just who were Kraftwerk? According to the accepted band history, Kraftwerk were formed in 1970 by Ralf Hütter and Florian Schneider. But the real history behind the formation of the band is less neat. Like so many of their contemporaries, Kraftwerk were originally a loose aggregation of musicians. True, Ralf and Florian were almost always at the core, hiring, directing, firing, but the origin of the band dates not from 1970 but from 1967.

In that year, the year of the so-called 'Summer Of Love', but in reality the prelude to the convulsive violence of the year to follow, Florian Schneider-Esleben (his full name) began playing music with Eberhard Kranemann. Florian's main instrument was the flute. Eberhard, two years his senior, had been playing for several months with his (Eberhard's) band, PISSOFF. They often practised at the home of Florian's father, Paul, then in his early fifties. He was a successful architect with several high-profile commissions already to his name, including the Mannesmann-Hochhaus and Commerzbank Tower in Düsseldorf. At the time of the birth of Kraftwerk, Paul was working on a huge project – the design of Cologne-Bonn Airport.

Eberhard had fostered a real link with the avant-garde at this time. 'Joseph Beuys was a professor at the Kunstakademie in Düsseldorf and most of the students in my band PISSOFF were students in this class,' he recalls, giving a real flavour of the free-form experimentalism which was the order of the day. 'I was a student in the class of Rupprecht Geiger. Normally a professor would have 20 students at the art university. Rupprecht Geiger was very strict; he had only seven. He only took the best. Joseph Beuys wanted to take everyone. He said, everyone is an artist so I will take everyone who wants to join. He was in trouble with the university – he had 300 students! Joseph Beuys was the most interesting professor at this time because he was interested in "happenings". He asked PISSOFF to take part. He set up the Cream Cheese club in Düsseldorf, in 1968. At the time, it was the most important club in Düsseldorf, an alternative club mixing art and music. It was an old building in the *Altstadt*. In the building there was one very long room. It was 20 metres wide and 30 metres long, with a bar near the entrance, and a stage and dance floor at the back. Joseph Beuys would stand doing his *Handaktion* ['hand movements']. For three hours standing in the corner of the room, raised up, and he was very concentrated. All he did was move his hands a little bit in front of his face. It was something like theatre, but theatre has too many rules; something like theatre without language, just showing the body doing something. So Joseph Beuys stood there moving his hands. The five of us in PISSOFF, we stood there making a noise. It

25

was so loud, it was so incredibly loud, it was very dissonant. It was a disaster, it was the Third World War or something like it. We made everything *kaputt*. It was so very hot and very full of people: and the television was there, WDR-3, who filmed us.'

Florian was born on April 7, 1947 in the village of Kattenhorn near Lake Constance in Baden-Württemberg. At the age of three he moved to Düsseldorf. A future member of Kraftwerk and founder of Neu!, one of the most important bands of the seventies, Michael Rother, attended the same *Gymnasium** as Florian as a boy. 'Florian was an outsider,' says Rother. 'People made jokes about Florian, the way he walked and his sharp nose and so he was a figure that stuck out. I just knew him by sight. I got to know him better of course, in 1971. He was older than me. He was spiky, edgy.'

'I met his father in 1971,' continues Rother. 'I think his mother was mentally troubled, very troubled. I think I felt pity for her. His father was just a nasty, famous and rich guy. That's the way I experienced him, a very, very nasty man. Yes, very unpleasant, bullying. At dinner in their house we discussed politics, and of course being a young guy, 20 or so, with much less experience than this great architect, it's quite likely that I was talking nonsense. But the way he treated people, and treated me, and treated everyone, was so disgusting. That's the only way I can describe it. I think this background can make people turn out a *Menschmaschine*,' says Rother.

In the very early days of the band, Florian's opulent house would have been the site of some of their first music-making. 'Florian Schneider-Esleben is a boy with very rich parents,' says Eberhard Kranemann. 'They had everything in the house, champagne, plenty to eat and drink. I am from middle-class parents. For me it was interesting to see how other people lived, in this world of money. So, Florian grew up with a lot of money and this was important for the development of Kraftwerk because other musicians had no money and he had a lot of money. His home was a detached, in the best area of Düsseldorf. He had two younger sisters, one was studying architecture and the other one was studying design. Most of the time the parents were not at home; they had a woman working in the house, a kind of maid. I don't think rich people are interested in

---

* A school comparable to a grammar school in the UK.

being at home; they like to be in Ibiza or Mallorca or New York or something like this. The father had a lot of money, so the wife had the job of spending it.'

Having more disposable income put Florian in a position to immerse himself in his major teenage passion: music: 'He bought very expensive, very good flutes with the newest electronics. Nobody else had it, only he had it in Germany,' recalls Kranemann. 'He also had very good LPs from America I didn't know at the time. The parents had music from India, Ravi Shankar.'

According to Kranemann, Florian's father encouraged his son's musical ambitions, and was, indeed, happy that he had friends and could enjoy himself: 'One time Florian and I made music in his father's office or studio. He was an architect and a lot of people worked for him, for the design of all the houses. He had very huge rooms and studios to work in. Florian's father came and took photos. He was very glad that Florian had me as a friend. Now, 40 years later, I know why. I think that Florian was a difficult son. He was very shy. I think he was a difficult young man because he had no family. He had a family, but the family was not there. Florian, I think, was very intelligent but his protest was not working for school and only playing music for himself. So his father took him out from school and put him into a special boarding school in the Bad-Godesberg district of Bonn, where all the rich people sent their sons. It was a special school to get pupils through the *Abitur*.* So, when I met him he was still in Bonn, and was only at home at the weekend.

'There is another thing, I don't know whether you know about it; the first five years of Kraftwerk when I was together with the guys was very good,' continues Kranemann. 'We were all friends. Florian's father had a swimming pool in the house. One night we were in the pool naked together with girls and smoking joints, wonderful parties. This was a good time. We were in the outdoor swimming pool 20/30 young people all naked smoking joints, consuming LSD, drinking champagne and all this and one night the father and mother came home earlier from a holiday, and did not know that there was a party. They liked it and joined the party! There was no problem; they were glad that young people made a party in their house [laughs].'

---

* The final exam and qualification at the end of the period of study in a *Gymnasium*.

Florian's upbringing made for an eccentric personality, a mixture of shyness and wonderful dry humour. 'For me Florian in the beginning was the founder of Kraftwerk,' claims Kranemann. 'He was the most important person in Kraftwerk. Later on it changed, and I have the feeling that Ralf Hütter was the boss of the band, but in the beginning the whole idea was Florian's.'

Meanwhile, in Aachen, near the border with Belgium and Luxembourg, Ralf Hütter, then a student, was a talented musician looking for like-minded adventurers. Florian and Ralf met for the first time at a summer 'jazz-academy' in 1968 at Remscheid-Küppelstein. Florian had gone there on the recommendation of Eberhard Kranemann who had attended the previous year.

Ralf was born on August 20, 1946 in the city of Krefeld, northwest of Düsseldorf. To suggest that Ralf Hütter has been secretive about his upbringing is no understatement. Whereas most musicians are often keen to reveal their childhood obsessions, embellish acts of abuse by tyrannical and unloving parents, or detail their adolescent dysfunctions, Hütter, perhaps demonstrating nothing more than a stereotypical German reserve, has said almost nothing about his formative years. According to Kraftwerk biographer Pascal Bussy, he spent a number of years studying the piano. 'Ralf's father was a textile merchant in Krefeld and was quite rich I think. I have heard that Ralf still lives in his father's house in Krefeld,' says Eberhard Kranemann. 'Ralf was cool but he did not speak much. He is a very nice guy, and a very good musician, wonderful. At that time I talked a lot with Florian but Ralf kept himself to himself. We went on stage, we put instruments together in the car, which was OK, but he didn't like to speak about it.'

'We talked the same language,' said Ralf of meeting Florian. 'We were *Einzelgänger* – loners, mavericks. Mr Kling and Mr Klang. Two *Einzelgänger* produce a doppelgänger.' In interviews in the mid-seventies, Hütter and Schneider were already keen to portray the origins of Kraftwerk as a collaboration. That Ralf actually left the band for a short period to finish his degree is glossed over; likewise the contributions of their earlier collaborators, although mentioned, are not personalised. 'We started to perform live concerts of amplified music in 1968 and that led directly to getting into what we call repeat music,' Ralf told *Synapse* magazine in 1976, 'and from then on we started to continually work.'

1.8 Two Kraftwerks?

The album *Tone Float*, recorded by the proto-Kraftwerk group, Organisation, demonstrates almost none of the musical leitmotifs and obsessions which would later form the Kraftwerk imprimatur. It is improvisatory, almost jazzy, and totally unremarkable. It was music which sounded of its time, perfectly proficient, but lacking either originality or spark.

Apart from (unintentionally) causing Florian to meet Ralf, Eberhard Kranemann brought another crucial player in the story into their lives: 'The first thing is that before Kraftwerk I made this kind of experimental music. Florian learned it from me, and then later Ralf Hütter. Then, because I was two years older, I was a studio musician earning money. I had contact with the sound engineer and producer Conny Plank. I sometimes worked in Conny Plank's studio in order to make money. I became his friend because we made music together and I noticed that he had other ideas, not just to make studio jobs, he had his own ideas about making new kinds of music. Sometimes I went into his studio to speak to him and try something, some sounds. Then I got a job in Rhenus Studio, Godorf, with some people who made music for the *Schauspielhaus*, a new theatre in Düsseldorf which was due to be opened with our music. It wasn't a band; it was our music that was going to be played at the opening of the theatre. We realised that we needed someone to play the flute. No-one knew a flute player. I said, I know a flute player. It was Florian. So Florian came into the studio and played the flute with me and some other guys. And the theatre opened with our music. This was the first time Florian and Conny Plank met. After that, there was more contact. So when Florian and Ralf did their first recordings they went to Conny Plank; again I initiated this contact. I think without this contact Kraftwerk would not have existed. Before *Autobahn* Kraftwerk were a normal experimental band – the same thing as I do today. I am still doing experimental things, and I love it, being free to express myself.'

Asked about *Tone Float*, the album by Organisation, Eberhard Kranemann replies: 'Yes, this was very interesting. This was Conny Plank, too. It was the Kraftwerk production made by Conny Plank. I investigated 10 or 20 years later what happened at this time with me in Kraftwerk. There were two Kraftwerk bands at the same time.

The reason is that Florian lived in Düsseldorf, whereas Ralf lived in Aachen, a town near the border with the Netherlands. Ralf studied architecture in Aachen. So Ralf lived in Aachen to study, and he had some musicians that he played with. Florian lived in Düsseldorf, and he had some musicians in Düsseldorf that he played with. So I made music with Florian in Düsseldorf; and Ralf played with some other musicians in Aachen. But Florian sometimes played with Organisation, Ralf's band in Aachen, and Ralf sometimes played in the band in Düsseldorf with me with the Hammond organ and flute. At the time I did not know that there were two bands. I only knew that there was a band I played in, with Ralf and a drummer, Paul Lovens. Paul now is one of the most famous free jazz drummers in Europe, touring with the extraordinary Schlippenbach Trio, for example.'

Eberhard describes those early days when he and Florian played music together: 'It was very simple. We came together. I had a guitar, a cello, and a bass. Florian played electric violin and flute. His main instrument was the flute. He was a very good musician. I think it is a pity that, in the last 30 years, he hasn't played the flute – only electronic, and electronic was the style of Ralf Hütter. He had an enormous C-flute with special electronics to modify the sound, a bass flute, and a tenor flute. He also had a special style of violin-playing. He put the violin on his knees, in his lap, and played from the side. He always played on an Arabian scale, very abnormal scales. For me it was the beginning of Kraftwerk, because in the beginning Kraftwerk was an experimental group, looking for what is "over the horizon", for new things. In 1967, Florian and I started to do something like this with experiments, and then, in 1968, Ralf Hütter joined us, and he brought the drummer, from Aachen. So we were two guys from Düsseldorf, Florian and me, two from Aachen – Ralf and the drummer, Paul Lovens. Then we met up and performed together, in Düsseldorf and in North-Rhine Westphalia. It was something like jazz music. We played in jazz clubs, including one famous jazz club called Dum Dum. Sometimes we played in Dum Dum, sometimes we played in Down-Town (both jazz clubs in Düsseldorf). The most famous Hammond organ player in the world was Jimmy Smith, a black musician. He gave a big concert in Düsseldorf, in the Tonhalle, in 1968. Normally, when musicians give a concert, afterwards they go to the most famous jazz club in the town. At this time it was Dum Dum; and we played there. Ralf Hütter, Florian, me and Paul Lovens. The interesting thing is that at the time Ralf Hütter tried to play like Jimmy Smith. So, that evening, Jimmy Smith came to Dum Dum when we were playing there. He came with his whole band to look at what we were doing there. It was very crowded, very hot and very full, and with very hot music. We played very good Jimmy Smith music! Jimmy Smith came in, and the normal thing would have been for him to have sat down and played the Ha..mmond organ with us. He did not. He looked for the Hammond organ. It was a Hammond M-100. He said "Oh, this is a Mickey Mouse organ. I won't play on this" – because the M-100 is a small organ, costs maybe 10,000 Euros, the big one was the Hammond B3, which costs about 100,000. So he went away. But he had a very famous guitar player, Kenny Burrell. He stayed, and we played with him the whole night.'

But were they called Kraftwerk? 'I don't know, I don't remember any name. My feeling is that it was a "no name" band. I don't have any posters or announcements of that time and we did not even record this music. But I just met the drummer Paul Lovens at a concert and we spoke about the old times. And he remembered everything. Maybe it was already Kraftwerk, maybe it was not. I don't know when the name came up. But for me the name was not so important. The people who develop the music together are important. For me Kraftwerk begins in 1967, with the work of Florian and me: and one year later, in 1968, Ralf joined the band. But when you look on the homepage of Kraftwerk on the internet, you will see as *Gründungsmitglieder* [founder members] only two people, Ralf Hütter and Florian Schneider-Esleben, in 1970. For me, this is not right. For me Kraftwerk began with Florian and me in 1967. One year ago, I found tape recordings in a forgotten cardboard banana box in the attic of my house that I made with Florian at his father's house in 1967. It already sounds like Kraftwerk. On the other side Ralf Hütter says it begins in 1970. But the interesting thing is that in 1970 Ralf was not even a member of Kraftwerk, because he went away to study architecture in Aachen, and in 1970 and beginning of 1971 Florian and me made up the band.'

Where did the name 'Kraftwerk' even come from? Eberhard Kranemann replies: 'I think from Florian, because in the early days of Kraftwerk, Florian was the most important person. It was his idea, his plan. He was, as we say in German, *die treibende Kraft* [the driving force], the man behind the idea of the music. And the design, this Kraftwerk design, was made by Florian, this I know to be 100 per cent true. So I think the name "Kraftwerk" comes from Florian, too.'

Quizzed by a journalist in the mid-seventies Ralf Hütter was vague and impersonal about the band's origins. 'We have always worked with different people according to the music we have been writing. Sometimes we have six, four, five, three members. We even played a series of concerts with just the two of us.' For him, Kraftwerk began when Kling Klang began, not before. 'In 1970 we opened our studios, Kling Klang Studio, Düsseldorf, just with some tape recorders and that was the beginning of our recording activities.' Again, this version of events in strongly contested by Eberhard Kranemann: 'In 1970 Ralf was not even a member of Kraftwerk because he finished his architecture studies at the Aaachen University. The Kraftwerk studio between the main station and the red light district of Düsseldorf was rented by Florian.'

ZWEI

REISEN

1970 – 1974

2.1 Traffic Management

SO FAR; no further.

The first Kraftwerk album proper arrived in November 1970 on the Philips label. Long unavailable, it has never been given an official release on CD, although at various times illegal copies have appeared for sale. Today it remains largely unheard, apart from by a minority of Krautrock fans; furthermore, it is unloved, one suspects, by its creators. Florian has reportedly called this period of the band, 'archaeology'. When Kraftwerk's back catalogue was remastered and reissued in 2008, it began not with their first album but with their fourth.

The album itself is as significant for its cover as for its

musical contents. A painting of a red and white traffic cone set against a pure white background has the word 'KRAFTWERK' ('POWER PLANT') stamped over it on the diagonal. In taking ready-made everyday objects, Kraftwerk were in the tradition of Dada and, more significantly, Andy Warhol, who had turned such banal icons of modern capitalism as the Brillo box and the soup can into art. The lettering of the band's name was functional and industrial, it was no more or less impersonal than a franked stamp on a letter, a piece of cargo or a large consignment for a warehouse on which a label of its contents is stamped solely for reasons of recognition. This art does not seek to do anything other than to signify that this product is functional, factory-made and one of several thousand identical copies. Kraftwerk were a product of the industrial age and an industrial environment.

But what is more interesting is the use of the image of the traffic cone itself. It warns us of danger; it diverts us on to a different route. It blocks us; it maybe even puts a barrier between audience and musician. There is an echo here of the leading German twentieth century playwright Bertolt Brecht, whose signature style was the *Verfremdungseffekt* – the alienation effect. We might ponder the significance of the cover, but the inescapable conclusion is that it is an instant signifier for the band. Throughout their career, they have been masters in economic minimalism of graphic art.

What linked the cover artwork to the music was motion. In this, Hütter and Schneider's second album together, the propulsive beat which would later be dubbed 'the Apache Beat', or, more famously, the *Motorik* beat, is clearly being developed. It is plainly evident on the album's most fully realised piece, 'Ruckzuck'. Staccato flute, an insistent electronic pulse, and a fast-tempo drum beat all create the feeling of a music in-motion. The word, *Ruckzuck*, means something like 'Avanti' – it carries with it the idea that something has to be done immediately, straightaway, *schnell*. It's the sort of thing a parent might say to a child in order to get him out of the house on time. This is music that still has one foot in the old – fans at the time of Jethro Tull and Focus would clearly hear it as part of progressive rock – and now that we know what would come later, the seeds of musical modernity are clearly there.

What Kraftwerk were doing was no different from what all the great musical innovators did, whether it be the Beatles, David

Bowie, or whoever – they copied. The Beatles began their career as a teenage band enthralled by the rhythms of black America. Bowie began as a style copyist – first jazz, then rhythm and blues, then mod pop, then as a singer songwriter. Some artists become hugely successful, and write fantastic songs, simply by copying styles – one could make this claim, however controversial it might sound, for the Rolling Stones. But the true innovators, the genuine pop artists, build on the appropriation of teenage enthusiasms and create something new. In 1970, Kraftwerk were not a wholly original project; by 1975, that had changed, and changed dramatically.

The album itself was recorded with two drummers, Andreas Hohmann and Klaus Dinger, soon to be 50% of Neu! with Michael Rother, and, like *Tone Float*, was produced by Conny Plank. Central to the band's new sound, Konrad (known to most as 'Conny') Plank was a much admired producer and a well-liked colleague whose studio, in Neunkirchen-Seelscheid, within 25Km of both Bonn and Cologne, was the locus for many of the seminal West German electronic recordings of the day. Supremely musical, he wanted to foster a democratically creative environment for the musicians with whom he worked. 'I'm just the co-producer,' he told *Record Mirror* in 1975. 'I firmly believe in getting the group equally involved in the production of their record.'

'I'm not a musician,' Plank posited. 'I'm a medium between musicians, sounds, and tape. I'm like a conductor or traffic policeman.' In many respects, Plank was West Germany's answer to Brian Eno, a 'roving clarifier', part producer, part collaborator, part ideas man. People who met him spoke of his 'Papa Bear cuddliness'. 'Standing at a lumbering 6′4″, looking like a centre for the New York Giants, Conny rules over his studio with Buddha-like serenity,' wrote John Diliberto in one of the last interviews with Plank in 1987. 'His enthusiasm and joy [were] contained behind a bemused grin.'

Plank was born in Hütschenhausen near Kaiserslautern in May 1940. Like many musicians of his generation, he was fascinated by psychedelia in the sixties, but, as a record producer, moved well beyond the genre to develop a recording technique which was based on free improvisation and was also indebted to some of the dub and scratch techniques being developed in Jamaica by the likes of Lee 'Scratch' Perry. Conny called his style 'live dub mixing'. He worked with the highly influential Karlheinz Stockhausen. 'At that time we all were influenced by English and American music,' said Plank in 1987. 'We also listened to Koenig, Stockhausen, Varese. I used to work with these people in '67, '68, and '69. Mauricio Kagel gave me a lot of ideas about sounds. In those recordings I worked with very academic musicians being very precise doing these sounds, and to me it seemed lifeless, and dry. I then tried to find people that looked in a different way to these materials, that tried to improvise with these dirty sounds, these electronic sounds – to have a feeling like a jazz musician has to his instrument.' Plank continues: 'We were also influenced by the Velvet Underground. When I got this "banana" record produced by Warhol, we were immediately influenced by that. We said this is a fresh approach. They didn't care about the beauty of sound, they just went for a basic feeling of a true situation.'

According to Eberhard Kranemann, the live version of Kraftwerk at the time included himself and a drummer, Charly Weiss. These musicians were, however, not asked to play on the first Kraftwerk record. 'We practised hard, and made music 10 hours a day, even at weekends. Then, one day, Florian and Ralf told me, "We cannot make music with you at the weekend. We won't be there."…. I said, "OK, then we can meet again on Monday." OK, OK, so on Monday we worked, no-one spoke about what happened at the weekend, and later this record came out… So they made the record without me and without Charly Weiss or whoever was the drummer. This is typical of Kraftwerk… No, only the two boys made it, and this is one reason why, later, I left the band. Florian and Ralf they are both businessmen.'

'Ruckzuck', the album's opener, became the first Kraftwerk song to make an impact and was played as the theme music for a popular German TV arts programme called *Die Zeichen*. A black-and-white WDR (*Westdeutscher Rundfunk*) recording of the band performing the instrumental, dating from 1970, shows Kraftwerk as a three-piece of Hütter, Schneider – the dominant musician – and Klaus Dinger on drums. The studio is packed, a cross-section of West-German youth, approximately 50–50 male and female, half sitting cross-legged, and half standing. There is no dancing; the audience look on quietly appreciative. A large screen projects images of the band in performance.

'"Ruckzuck" was played heavily by the presenter Winfried Trenkler at the radio station WDR,' according to Ralf Dörper, then a teenage Düsseldorfer, later to find fame as part of the groups Die Krupps and Propaganda, who were signed by ZTT and, for a while, became one of Germany's biggest musical exports. 'Westdeutscher Rundfunk was very progressive at that time. And Trenkler played all kinds of electronic music in his "Radiothek". I think the programme went on for 20 years or so. Later it became purely electronic and was called "Schwingungen", which translates as "Oscillations". I used to tape "Radiothek" – and recall a recording where he played Pink Floyd, followed by a German band – I think it was Amon Düül – and then "Ruckzuck". I thought "Wow!" [for the music] and "wow" a second time when Trenkler gave away the name of the band and the track. I thought both "Kraftwerk" and "Ruckzuck" were fantastic names – a perfect fit. And since then I had that more or less in the back of my mind. That was the first electronic music that left an impression. After then I noticed that parts of "Ruckzuck" were used on German TV in the background for some cultural and even political programmes.' I even dared to record a cover version of "Ruckzuck" in 1991.'

Ralf and Florian's moneyed background put them in a position of strength in that they could afford the new technology. The biggest technological advance, according to Ralf, was the availability of the first monophonic synthesizers: 'Before that it used to be these big machines from Bell Laboratories or government radio stations. Being able, as an individual musician – an independent musician – to get your hands on some of this electronic gear, I think that was the most significant change, around the late sixties.'

Along with 'Ruckzuck', there are just three other tracks. 'Stratovarius' combines Hütter's Hammond organ with more conventional rock structures, whilst 'Megaherz' is dissonant and jarring. 'Vom Himmel Hoch' contains the electronically generated sound of aircraft and explosions, almost a decade before Pink Floyd's excursion into the same sonic territory on their double album *The Wall*. Rather than coming from the winning side, however, this is a piece of music from the defeated.

Later, in 1981, Ralf spoke about Kraftwerk's neophyte work: 'Not only were we interested in *musique concrète* but also in playing organ tone clusters and flute feedback sounds that added variety to the repeated note sequences that we recorded and mixed on tape. Then we used several acoustic drummers as we turned our attention to more rhythmic music, and soon found that amplifying drums with contact microphones was desirable for us but not readily accepted by the players. We started off Kling Klang studio in 1970, which really marked the beginning of Kraftwerk. The studio was, in fact, just an empty room in workshop premises that was a part of an industrial area in Düsseldorf. We fitted sound isolation material into the 60 square metre room, and we now use other adjoining rooms where we make instruments. When we first moved in, we started recording with stereo tape machines and cassette recorders in preparation for our first record. The master tapes were then taken to the recording studio for final mix-down. This allowed us to be 'self-producing' at the time as far as we could with our own limited resources, so we did another three LPs in this way. Don't forget in those days successful musicians used important producers to promote and launch their records, but we took on every aspect of the production ourselves.'

Ralf's testimony gives a good idea of his artistic intent, but, like so many of his interviews, imposes a neat rationale on what must have been uncertain times. Was the studio really called Kling Klang as early as 1970? Could the 'self-producing' unit really have made such sonically faithful records without the massive input of Conny Plank?

That said, it is clear that Kraftwerk were developing along singular and headstrong lines. In some important aspects, the early Kraftwerk, through a determination to retain control, prefigured by half a dozen years the do-it-yourself credo which would become one of punk's clarion calls (until 99% of them, of course, allowed themselves to be bought out by major records labels). 'It's been quite a common thing for groups to have their own "home studios" in Germany, with the emphasis very much on "do-it-yourself" activities,' affirmed Ralf in the same interview. 'We made our own record covers by taking Polaroid pictures and designing the artwork, and did our own management.'

Live appearances were sporadic – the opportunity to do a formal tour was not yet available. It is known that the band played gigs in Karlsruhe and Essen in April 1970, and then in July at the Tivoli Pop Festival at the Reitstadion in Aachen. On Boxing Day, the band played the Cream Cheese club in their home town. At the time, Düsseldorf had a thriving arts scene centred on the Kunstmuseum [art museum] and the Altstadt [the old town].

Eberhard Kranemann was the poster-designer for the group: 'I took the photos and I made the designs for the posters. They were just like the Andy Warhol silk screens of that time (Marilyn, Elvis) but in black and white with strong contrasts. It was something like "anti-design", something against the mainstream with an underground feeling, dirty like the Kraftwerk music of this early time. We didn't earn much money. When we performed a concert, we got maybe 50 marks, or 100 marks, each. That wasn't very much.' Incidentally, after Eberhard left the band, the posters took a racier turn. For example, a colour poster for an appearance in July 1971 in Karlsruhe shows a naked blonde with her back turned to the camera sitting astride a red and white traffic cone.

2.2 Ralf Departs, Then Returns

Kraftwerk were evolving, ever-changing, and, at one point, even existed without the man who, in time, would come to dominate the group above all others. In late 1970 or early '71, Ralf returned to Aachen to finish his architecture studies and, given his later pre-eminence, the fact that during this period he had effectively left the band is often overlooked. According to Eberhard Kranemann: 'First there was, in 1970, Florian, Charly Weiss and me. Only three people, for a long time – nearly one year – 1970/1971.' Then came Peter Schmidt and Houschäng Néjadepour. 'Houschäng Néjadepour lived in Düsseldorf. His father had a carpet business. He was from India. He played guitar with an Indian touch, and he liked to smoke joints. He was nice, but not the right musician for Kraftwerk, because he played too much solo guitar, and he played too much blues guitar with blue notes in it. We didn't like this, so he wasn't in the band too long.' Michael Rother: 'Houschäng was the best Jimi Hendrix impersonator in Düsseldorf. He could play Jimi's guitar so much better than me and in 1968 I envied him that ability.'

According to Eberhard, Kraftwerk published a promotional booklet. 'It was called *Media News Of Kraftwerk*, produced by Florian. It was maybe 10 pages or so and was produced in January of 1971. There are four names – Florian Schneider-Esleben, Eberhard Kranemann, Houschäng Néjadepour (the guitar player) and Karl Weiss (drums) I still have some of the original pamphlets.'

39

Eberhard confirms that around this time, the future Neu! duo, guitarist Michael Rother and drummer Klaus Dinger were also members of the group. 'One of the band's biggest concerts was at the Forum, Leverkusen in January 1971. We played to about 1,200 people, a concert of two or three hours. This was with Michael Rother and Klaus Dinger, who were the rhythm section. They made powerful music with a heavy, driving rhythm. And the solo players were Florian Schneider-Esleben and I. Florian played the electric flute and violin, and I played the Hawaiian guitar and cello with sound manipulations. I liked Klaus's drumming. He played like an animal! At this time I played like an animal, too, with full power.'

'In January 1971, I jammed with Ralf in the Kraftwerk studio,' explains Rother. 'A friend of mine, Georg, introduced me. 'We were all demonstrating for some improvement in the *Ersatzdienst*, some issue. And he had an invitation to go to a studio in Düsseldorf to record some music and he asked me, because he was also a guitar player, whether I'd like to join in. I didn't know the name of the band; Kraftwerk sounded silly! The next thing I remember was being in the studio, taking a bass and jamming with Ralf Hütter. My memory is so fresh because what happened in the studio was amazing. There was Ralf Hütter playing with a drummer, Charly Weiss. I picked up a bass, and jammed with Ralf. It was at that moment that I realised, for the first time, that there was another musician, on a similar road with a music that was free of the blues influence that I grew up with. Ralf was playing all those notes in the octave that I liked and which were definitely non-blues. Florian and Klaus [Dinger] were just sitting on a sofa and listening. A few weeks later Florian called me and asked me to join the band. Florian played amazing things on his flute, very rough, very rhythmic, and quite crazy... Later on, especially when we played live and had a good night, the three of us played very, very exciting music together.'

Today Michael Rother is one of the most respected German artists still working. He inspires affection and respect from his fellow musicians. 'One of the finest guys, still today,' says Wolfgang Flür. A 2010 concert at the Institute for Contemporary Arts in London was spoken about in the sort of hushed tones of reverence reserved only for the truly important and original. Back in the late sixties, Rother, several years younger than Kranemann, Schneider-Esleben and Hütter, was a young musical colt, who had attended the same

Rethel-Gymnasium in Düsseldorf as Florian Schneider. Michael's band, the Spirits Of Sound, used to play at dance evenings at the school. From 1969 to early 1971, Rother served in the *Ersatzdienst*, the civilian alternative to military service and later to be known as *Zivildienst*. 'Spirits Of Sound started out in 1965 as a band imitating bands like the Kinks and Beatles,' he says, 'and a bit later, moving on to Cream, Jimi Hendrix and the likes. At the end of the sixties we were already playing more freely using ideas from famous rock bands only as starting points for our own improvisations.'

Rother, like Ralf and Florian, was looking for a new musical path, something that was neither bluesy, nor jazzy. Being a conscientious objector also shaped his personality. 'Out of my great interest in psychology, I chose a psychiatric hospital* to do service in and saw all the troubled minds of the patients, young and old. This, and the discussions with the other objectors shaped my views on life. I began to think about my own identity.'

Michael Rother's family background and upbringing were unusual for the time and, for the other Kraftwerk members, quite exotic: 'I lived in Pakistan from 1960 to 1963 with my parents, in Karachi. I think that was another very important musical experience for me. The hypnotic music I heard there, I have some very vivid memories of bands... walking in the streets, playing in front of the house. I listened to them and this kind of music that has no beginning and no end.'

Before Karachi, Michael had lived with his parents in the Cheshire town of Wilmslow, at a time when his father was working for British European Airways (BEA), which merged with the British Overseas Airways Corporation (BOAC) in 1974 to become British Airways. The move to Karachi, in 1960, was caused by Rother senior moving job to Lufthansa.

Kranemann would finally leave the group in the spring of 1971 to resume his studies at art school. His style of playing and his musical obsessions were perhaps never fully shared by Florian and his new band mates by this time. There is still, after more than 40 years, a sense of injustice that the true origins of the band have been

---

* In Germany at the time conscientious objectors who declined to join the military were required to work in hospitals or in other forms of community service.

obfuscated. 'For Florian and Ralf, Kraftwerk begins with *Autobahn* in 1974. So, the period before this, 1967–1973, doesn't count. They don't speak about it, and they don't want other people to speak about it. I don't understand it. Because we early musicians, we are the roots of Florian and Ralf; and they learned a lot of things from me.'

For a short period, maybe six months, Kraftwerk were down to a trio of Schneider-Esleben, Rother and Dinger. Several clips of this Kraftwerk trio exist on *YouTube*, and the sound is closer to what would become Neu! than it is to Kraftwerk. At times, for example on the instrumental, 'Heavy Metal Kids', the sonics were astonishingly raw and almost Black Sabbath-like with their dark, pounding rhythms and hard-rock riffing. Michael Rother: 'The first Kraftwerk album was released in 1970, and when I joined them this album was starting to become quite a big success. People were crazy about 'Ruckzuck'. I remember Conny Plank saying that on the heavy drug scene in Munich they listened to Kraftwerk all the time. Everyone was on drugs apart from us guys!' A fan of this often overlooked era of Kraftwerk would be someone who would go on to play a crucial role, if only indirectly, in bringing the band to a wider audience: David Bowie. In 1978, speaking about Kraftwerk's early albums, he said: 'I've found a lot of their earlier work more invigorating than their later stuff, actually. I liked a lot of the stuff that seemed to be free-form... That was when Neu! were with them, of course, and you had two very frictional elements working against each other – Neu! who were into complete volume against Florian's very methodical planning.'

Michael Rother: 'We played festivals and toured in Germany, appeared in two TV shows *Okidoki* (WDR) and *Beat Club* (Radio Bremen), did a radio live recording (Radio Bremen) and recordings for the second Kraftwerk album in a Hamburg studio with Conny Plank. Our last Kraftwerk concert happened in a place called Langelsheim not so far from my current home in the Weserbergland on July 31, 1971. Sometimes we created music that was so powerful and exciting the crowds went completely wild. During these great concerts I was swept away and totally happy but when the atmosphere wasn't right, the sound wasn't right. I think on the bad nights it was quite terrible and apart from those good times on stage there were a lot of arguments, especially between Florian and Klaus. They were arguing a lot. So we tried to do the sessions for the second

Kraftwerk album in summer of 1971; and that failed because it was quite clear that we were dependent on some rough live atmosphere to make us create that excitement. So it was just natural for us to separate. Klaus and I, we had the idea that our aims were closer so we should carry on together. So we got in touch with Conny again, and so in December we recorded the first Neu! album.'

It should not come as a great surprise, perhaps, that the line-up of early Kraftwerk was so fluid. In fact, no single member of the band has had an unbroken tenure. In the years before Ralf and Florian hit upon a workable, stable band in the mid-seventies, they simply jammed and tried out people, all the while seeking out musical minds that clicked. For example, Cluster's Hans-Joachim Roedelius remembers playing live with the band. 'I knew Ralf and Florian, because in the beginning we jammed with each other in live shows and I was a friend of Florian Schneider's sister.' In August or September 1971, Ralf re-joined Florian for the second Kraftwerk album; no outside musicians were used, apart, of course, from the band's co-producer, the experienced innovator of the Krautock sound, Conny Plank.

'In 1971 Kraftwerk was still without a drummer, so I bought a cheap drum machine giving some pre-set dance rhythms,' said Hütter in 1981. 'By changing the basic sounds with tape echo and filtering we made the rhythm tracks for our second album. Our instrumental sounds came from home-made oscillators and an old Hammond organ that gave us varied tonal harmonies with its drawbars. We manipulated the tapes at different speeds for further effects.' In a later interview, Ralf gives a flavour of what an early Kraftwerk gig must have been like, the moment when the machines took over. 'I had this little drum machine. At a certain moment we had it going with some loops and some feedback and we just left the stage and joined the dancers.' The pair would stay in the crowd dancing to the proto-house beat until the primitive equipment stopped working or burst into flames. Superstar DJ? Here we go!

The band's second album, with typical Industrial functionality entitled *Kraftwerk 2*, arrived in January 1972, again on the Philips label, and is also out of print. The cover sees the red and white traffic cone now painted a luminous green and white, with the number 2 stamped beneath the band's name.

43

The album is an electro-acoustic exploration into the manipulation of conventional instrumentation, and it positions the musicians very firmly within the tradition of the avant-garde pioneers of the fifties and sixties, although the band would later be at pains to distance themselves in interviews from the sterile nature of much experimental music. There are loops, repeats, tape manipulation to slow and quicken the pulse of the instruments, and, in the track 'Atem', which features the eerie, heavily-treated sound of breathing, a prefiguring of Florian's later, and more fully realised, interest in speech modulation. The 17-minute opening track, 'Klingklang', which sees the debut of Florian's rhythm or beatbox, would later provide the name of the band's studio.

Although never less than interesting, this is the sound of appropriation; listening to both *Kraftwerk* and *Kraftwerk 2*, one senses that this was music that could have been made by many young German musicians with the right technology at the time. It was music which seemed frustrated with itself, locked into a mode of expression it sought to overturn. 'We started with amplified instruments and then we found that the traditional instruments were too limited for our imaginations,' Florian would later say.

All this was to change with the release of the band's third album. Suddenly, this was a music that was *sui generis*, music which no one else was making. And the reason for this paradigm musical shift? The arrival of the synthesizer.

2.3 Mr Kling and Mr Klang

The first classic Kraftwerk album is not *Autobahn*, as received wisdom would have it, but its predecessor. Recorded in 1973, and entitled *Ralf And Florian*, it is, like the band's first two albums, currently unavailable on an official release. Yet many of the musical leitmotifs that would bring the band to global recognition are already here present. And while acoustic instruments are still used – Ralf's organ and piano, Florian's flute, some pedal-steel guitar, and, on one track, some *Motorik*-style percussion, which may or may not be electronically generated, along with handclaps and heavily treated wordless vocalisations on another, and a rudimentary vocodor sound on a third – Moog and EMS synthesizers are also used, and one instrumental is totally

44

electronic. *Ralf And Florian* offers the earliest taste of classic Kraftwerk sound. But what is it?

By 1973, Florian had built a rudimentary drum machine from an organ rhythm unit. This is the first element of the Kraftwerk sound – the beginnings of the demotion of the drum kit to antiquity. Although Kraftwerk's music is heavily percussive and, later, outrageously danceable, the beat is electronically generated. So, on *Ralf And Florian*, the beautifully quaint melody of 'Tanzmusik' ('Dance Music')*, a tune which seems as if it might be an undiscovered piece of classical music from the previous century, is framed by Florian's synthetic percussion.

This leads us to the second characteristic of the Kraftwerk sound: the melodies. The first two Kraftwerk albums, 'Ruckzuck' aside, were not graced with many distinctive tunes. However, by 1973, Kraftwerk had developed, by an internal alchemy, into pop writers. In interviews, a love of the Beach Boys would later become apparent. Ralf was a huge fan of the Doors. Just as there is with Brian Wilson's best work for the group he founded with his two brothers, there is a purity to Kraftwerk's melodies and an almost childlike simplicity. The melodies are often quite beautiful, and sound as if they could be played by a Grade 2 piano student, or a precocious child on a toy xylophone. And yet, they sound totally fresh, and new, and, mostly, but not entirely, non-referential.

The third and most obvious characteristic of the Kraftwerk sound is that, despite the admiration for Anglo-American pop, their music is conceived outside, totally, the Anglo-American rock, blues, folk and country tradition. It has been remarked that for any artists, post-1970, to innovate, then their music, even to this day, must sound as little like the Beatles as possible. Although the members of Kraftwerk would turn out to be huge Beatles fans, indeed huge fans of many of Britain's best, their music would always seek to distance itself from the lineage of rock 'n' roll.

Finally, leading on from this rejection of the Anglo-American tradition of popular music comes a rejection of music being conceived of as being *purely* about music. 'The ideas reflected in our work are both internationalism and the mixing of different

---

* The English translations of these tracks are taken from the 1975 US release of the album by Vertigo.

art forms,' said Ralf in 2006. '[It's] the idea that you don't separate dance over here and architecture over there, painting over there. We do everything, and the marriage of art and technology was Kraftwerk right from the beginning, even though we didn't have the tools we have today – we used old tape recorders, small echo units and distortion. We broke down the barrier between craftsmen and artists, we were music workers.'

Ralf And Florian begins with the deep synth booms of 'Elektrisches Roulette' ('Electric Roulette'), a bright sprinkling of electronic fairy dust, Florian's flute motif, before firing up into a fast percussive beat. It doesn't sound like anything the band had hitherto recorded. Track two, 'Tongebirge' ('Mountain Of Sound'), and track four, 'Heimatklang' ('The Bells Of Home'), are pastoral, almost ambient instrumentals which prefigure the later ambient music composed by Brain Eno. They evoke a sense of place, an immersion in a sonic environment which appears a long way from industrial Düsseldorf, and far more Alpine in its sense of stillness and solitude. 'Ananas Symphonie' ('Pineapple Symphony'), with its Hawaiian guitar and washes of white surf white noise, moves further into the meditative. If it had been made 10 years later, it would have been called New Age. But the real musical interloper from the future comes in the form of 'Kristallo' ('Crystals'): odd, strangely unformed. Hütter's melody appears to be played in and out of time to a much darker synth pulse which, had it appeared on a 1995 dance track by Orbital, wouldn't have caused anyone to bat an eyelid.

So, there we have it – Ambient, New Age, Classical, Synth, Dance Music. Listening to Ralf and Florian's Nostradamus-like manifesto makes for thrilling listening.

The album artwork, as ever, is crucial to the music's meaning. In the original German release, the inside gatefold sleeve shows a photograph of the duo inside their Düsseldorf studios (yet to be named Kling Klang, although, interestingly, Kraftwerk's publishing wing was, by this time, already known by that name). Even though the album was, in fact, recorded with Conny Plank in studios in Munich, Cologne and Düsseldorf, Ralf and Florian were evidently keen to create the impression that the album was recorded at one venue, the better to reinforce their DIY ethos. Ralf and Florian sit smiling facing one another, their names in neon, surrounded by a clutter of instrumentation.

The original German front cover was a black and white photograph of the two with their names in heavy Gothic script underneath. Ralf, wearing glasses, his hair parted and still long at the back, is in stark contrast to the taller Florian, who is dressed in a formal suit, his hair cut short, and with a treble-clef badge on his lapel. Their gaze is now at us; but to our side, as if they demur. Ex-member Eberhard Kranemann was struck by the image: 'On the cover photo you see Ralf and Florian looking like... *wie ein altes Ehepaar* – an old married couple. You see Florian with the short hair. He is the man, the boss; and Ralf, he looks sweet like a woman, with long hair.' Kranemann's analysis of the album cover notwithstanding, there is undoubtedly something of Gilbert and George about the 1973 Kraftwerk – a twosome as divorced from the clichés of accepted rock presentation as one could imagine.

In Britain, the album was released with a very different cover, one which would prove to be an inspiration for Malcolm Garrett, who in the eighties would design some of the most iconic record sleeves of the era for Simple Minds, Duran Duran and Peter Gabriel. 'I bought the *Ralf And Florian* album, a brilliant album, with the embossed circuit board on the cover.'

His fellow graphic design student at Manchester Polytechnic, Peter Saville, was equally impressed. Kraftwerk were a portal to another world: 'I have only recently appreciated that the cover of *Ralf and Florian* is massively significant in relation to the intuitive approach that I took to creating the Factory covers. The cover of *Ralf And Florian* that I have has a circuit diagram on the front, printed in bronze ink and embossed, with a 'Kraftwerk' in day-glo colour. The colour palette alone, the day-glow and the metallic, is very like my own work, but there is one other quintessential influence that it made on me. I was familiar with the imagery of pop that gave you an insight. It gave you a window into other possibilities. So, the Roxy Music covers are the ones that I always use as examples of that. But, particularly, the easiest example of it is the cover of Bryan's second solo album, *Another Time, Another Place*. It is like a picture window into other societies that I found alluring and which I wanted to know more about. Before I was buying Italian and French *Vogue* etc., etc., a picture of other worlds was brought to me by Roxy Music, other worlds that I was interested in, but in the same way with Velvet Underground covers and the same with

Bob Dylan covers and the same with Leonard Cohen covers, and covers that I grew up with as a kid, courtesy of my older brothers. They showed me pictures of other worlds but I felt the *Ralf And Florian* cover *gave* me a piece of another world. The cover was a simulation, like owning a piece of Kraftwerk. The fact that it was embossed, the tactile quality of a circuit diagram of all things, was like an object given to me by Kraftwerk. So, it was not a picture of their world, although there was a picture of them on the back, but I can forgive that. Only recently I realised that so many of my Factory covers were just like *Ralf And Florian*. They were things given to our audience. Factory was an opportunity for me to make cultural propositions, to ask "Why can't pop culture be more broadly informed?" – which is a motivation and inspiration from Kraftwerk. For me in my late teens in the North West of England in the mid-seventies, Kraftwerk were an entry-point to a canon of European and technological culture.'

Kraftwerk did not invent electronic music. Outside the more academic schools, this is most popularly credited to the American Walter Carlos, whose 1968 album *Switched-On Bach* relied on the modular Moog synthesizer, as did his highly influential soundtrack to 1971's *A Clockwork Orange* (the march sections of which were later used by both David Bowie and Kraftwerk as intro music). The work of the BBC Radiophonic Workshop for a variety of television programmes dating back to the early sixties, most famously the theme tune to *Dr Who*, had also raised the profile of electronic music. The Beatles used synths on their later albums, whilst in 1972, the UK's first-ever synth number one, 'Son Of My Father' by Chicory Tip (including the future electronic artist and producer Giorgio Moroder), had been released. Bowie had used the Moog on his *The Man Who Sold The World* album in 1970. In 1971, the Who married synth loops with hard rock on their album *Who's Next*, most notably on the tracks 'Baba O'Riley' and 'Won't Get Fooled Again', though winding synthesizer lines could be detected down in the mix on other songs too. And there were, of course, any number of progressive rock acts – Pink Floyd, Genesis and Mike Oldfield at the forefront – who made music with synths, and in the US Stevie Wonder on his remarkable trio of early seventies albums, *Music Of My Mind, Talking Book* and *Innervisions*. Kraftwerk were also not the first people to use a drum machine. That honour probably goes to progressive legend Arthur Brown and his band Kingdom Come.

But Kraftwerk *were* the first *pop* group to move away from traditional instrumentation towards a completely synthetic sound template. They were not interested in re-interpreting the classics, and they were not a rock band with electronic *longueurs*. Kraftwerk were on the road to re-invent modern pop music itself.

2.4 The World's First Synthetic Drummer?

Playing live, as a twosome, would prove unworkable, given the highly percussive style of their music. Live, they needed a drummer, but not one who was still in love with the idea of becoming the next Keith Moon. They wanted someone who didn't want to play a drum kit at all. Enter: Wolfgang Flür.

Wolfgang Flür had started his musical career with a Beatles tribute band, the Beathovens. 'We were the best Beatles cover band in the whole North Rhine Westphalia region,' he says. 'We had gigs on Friday, Saturday and Sunday nights, every weekend. We were earning 400, 500, 600 or even 700 marks a night – yes, a night! This was in the sixties. And we didn't even need the money, because we were all young men, living at home, with our parents. We were just schoolboys. Do you know what we did with that money? It all went into buying new equipment. We had a Rickenbacker bass, an Epiphone guitar. We had, not really the whole set of Ludwig drums, but most of it, the big Selmer amplification, the Vox Goliath bass-box. We had Vox guitar amps, Vox stand-by speakers, Shure microphones. We had everything. We bought it from a Düsseldorf dealer; and he laughed at us, because every week we came with money to buy more.'

After the demise of the Beathovens, Wolfgang played in two subsequent groups, the Fruit and the Anyway. 'It had to be "the" this, or "the" that! Then I played in the Spirits of Sound, who recruited me. I loved their music. That's how I came to meet Michael Rother. Michael was our best guitarist, but we lost him to a semi-professional group called "Kraftwerk" – whatever that was! It was usual, in those days, for German bands to have names in English. We followed the example of names like "the Beatles", "the Pretty Things", "the Hollies", "the Who".... the "So-and-So's!" So we copied them. We had to be like them, the groups from England or America. So a group with its name in German was very unusual. To have an English name was modern, futuristic. That was how it was for young men, and for girls. We copied English and American music. We had only *Schlager* in Germany in those days. It was horrifying: good for our parents' generation, but not for us.'

After school, Wolfgang opted to join the *Zivildienst*, the civilian alternative to military service. 'It was in Düsseldorf, in a hospital for diabetics. It was a nice, beautiful old building in the middle of a forest. I used to take the train, about 20 kilometres to and from Düsseldorf. I had to be back to rehearse with my band in the evenings. It was a wonderful time! In the hospital they wanted to educate me. I was working in the laboratory, doing research into blood samples all day. The head of the laboratory wanted me to stay. He said "We'll give you a good future here." So, I could have stayed there, and become a medical assistant. Or I could have become an architect. Or a musician. And music was the most unsafe choice of the three!'

In 1973, Kraftwerk came calling. 'They came to the office of my architects' bureau. They knocked on the door, and said, "Hello, my name is Ralf Hütter, and this is Florian Schneider. We are from the group Kraftwerk. We have seen you playing with Michael Rother in Monchengladbach (a small town close to Düsseldorf) in the Boudike club. We found your drumming quite nice and it was steady drumming and 'minimal' drumming. We like that, and we wanted to ask you if you would join us for a session." I was sitting at my drawing board, drawing, and drawing ... "I have no time," I said, "I don't have any time". They said, "You don't need much time, maybe tonight?" I said, "Why should I? My group has broken up because you took our guitarist, you know, so why should I be friendly to you?" On the other hand, I knew that this was really an up-and-coming avant-garde band. They had a hit on the radio every day and that made me a little bit jealous, of course. You can understand that, as a young man who had just thrown away his musical career with his last band. So I said no, I am going to be an architect, you know. I was jealous and I said maybe, maybe, not tonight. We exchanged telephone numbers. I already had a telephone in 1973 in my little student flat. It was a luxury to have your own telephone line, you know.'

Soon Wolfgang had his introduction to the Kling Klang studio: 'The courtyard was just as ugly as the rest of the building,' he recalled in his memoirs, *I Was A Robot*. 'Everything was painted dark brown. I hated dark brown.'

Wolfgang's Kraftwerk debut came on the TV show *Aspekte*, a prestigious arts programme which aired on the ZDF channel. 'I looked like one of the four musketeers, like d'Artagnan, with long black hair. I had a lot of hair at the time, and a big moustache, I was still a hippy, you know. In those first appearances in the shows I told myself, "OK, they are paying me". I was young; I was a student; I needed money. I was offered 300 marks. That was a lot of money, you know, for just one hour playing. But I didn't like it all that much. I thought, oh, this is not like being a real drummer.'

Despite some initial misgivings, Wolfgang accepted his role as an electronic drummer comparatively quickly. Instead of sitting behind a huge kit of snares, tom-toms, hi-hats and cymbals, he would stand before a lectern and beat out the electronic rhythms with what looked like a wand or a knitting needle. 'By that time, Wolfgang Flür had joined us to play a custom-built drum system and was our first percussion player to accept electronically produced drums,' said Ralf in 1981. 'Electronic music was quite new as a musical medium in the early seventies, of course, and many people were just starting, like the Can group in Cologne. I think we were one of the first groups to have an electric drummer, with Wolfgang Flür. As well as the custom drum console, we now have two sets of drums that consist of six metal pads triggered by metal sticks on contact. These are not touch sensitive, so accents and dynamics come from separate volume foot pedals. Sometimes we link one or more pedals to change other parameters, such as tone or pitch.'

Wolfgang was born on July 17, 1947 in Frankfurt. 'I'm a twin. But we are not, as we say in German, "one-egg twins", but "two-egg twins". So we look different and have different personalities.' Wolfgang spent his childhood in and around the city of Koblenz, at the confluence of the Rhine and Moselle rivers. His father had been in the army during the Second World War, later becoming an optician. He had affection and respect for his mother, but little of either for his father. With age, however, contempt for his father seems to have mellowed into more of a feeling of pity. One of his most vivid recollections is of seeing the families of Moroccan troops (part of the occupying French army at that time) bivouacked in the woods outside Koblenz. As a boy of nine or 10 he hatched a plan to marry a dusky girl like the Moroccan children he saw on those family walks in the woods. "Their children were more beautiful than the white-skinned German children in our street. We saw colourful clothes, long black hair." His father, however, admonished his son: 'Don't run off to the Moroccans', which meant, in his family, 'Don't bother with what's foreign.' 'My father said that Moroccans eat their children,' says an incredulous Wolfgang today. 'Crazy! He was not very well educated, I think. I didn't like my father at all. He was a weak man. My mother was different, she had something special about her.'

Although it was apparent that Ralf and Florian were from moneyed backgrounds, Wolfgang disputes the idea that they were of a different social class. 'We all came from the middle class. They – the others – had a better education. Karl and I didn't have the *Abitur*: we just had the *Mittlere Reife*.* Florian's father was a very successful architect. I would imagine that in the early seventies, he was a millionaire. Florian, however, didn't receive much money from his father. His father was a very hard guy. He wanted all his children, including Florian's sisters, Claudia and Tina to earn their own money. So he was very disappointed that Florian did not want to take over the whole architecture empire that he had. But Florian's sister Claudia did become an architect. The problem was that Florian's father had problems with women, with his wife as well as with his daughters, Claudia and Tina.'

Shortly after Wolfgang joined the band, the lease ran out on the flat he was renting. As an interim measure, Florian invited him to stay chez Schneider-Esleben. The Schneider-Esleben parents' marriage was, according to Wolfgang, a troubled one: 'I think her biggest problem was that her husband wanted to leave her, and she was concerned that she might have had to lose her famous name. She just wanted to be Frau. Dr. Professor Professor Schneider-Esleben. That was her problem and also the fear that she might lose the big money. He was always travelling; she was always alone. From the day I got to know them – I don't know what happened before – but it

---

* The first public exam in secondary school – the equivalent of GCSEs in the U.K.

seemed to be not a nice family. The children grew up with gardeners and cooks and a nanny.'

Wolfgang's initial impression of Ralf was of a talented musician, but not a young man who was comfortable in his own skin: 'When I met Ralf for the first time, he was self-conscious about his physicality. He was a bit flabby; he was not a *geiler Junge* [fanciable young man]. Maybe this was also one of the reasons why he got to be a musician, because musicians are viewed in a special way by the girls. Otherwise he is really talented, really outstanding and this is beyond dispute. He is more than talented, he has a kind of genius, that's for sure. It must be clear that he is the star, the big one, the talented and shining hero. And Ralf always needed that position. Even with us, he wanted to be the leader.'

2.5 Wanderlust

To this day Germans quizzed about their miraculous post-war boom and solid economy respond simply: 'We make things.' Today, brands such as Siemens, Sennheiser, Hugo Boss, BMW, Bosch, Bayer and ThyssenKrupp are guarantors of quality. This pride in performance and quality of construction was nowhere more evident than in the car industry: *Vorsprung durch Technik**, as they said.

Germans love their cars and are rightly proud of producing some of the world's top brands. In addition to BMW, there is Audi, Volkswagen, Mercedes-Benz and Porsche. With effectively no speed limit, and with hundreds of kilometres of autobahns to discover, Germany has an infrastructure to match any in Europe. Today, one can get around at a pace that would impress even the most un-reconstituted UK petrolhead.

Linked with this passion for elegant, efficient and speedy travel is the very German fondness of the outdoors. A facet of the German psyche for centuries, many of its countrymen and women love nothing better than a thorough and often highly time-consuming commune with Nature. *Der Wanderer über dem Nebelmeer* (*The Wanderer Over A Sea Of Fog*), an oil painting from 1818 by Caspar David Friedrich, depicts a man dressed in long frock

---

* Roughly translated as 'advancement through technology', the strapline was part of Audi's TV commercials from the seventies to the nineties.

coat, boots and walking stick, gazing out from his vantage point over a mountain range enveloped dramatically in swirls of mist and cloud. It is one of the most emblematic images of the Romantic period, a walk in the mountains elevated to a contemplation of the nature of existence itself.

Unlike the UK, where a weekend trip to Snowdonia or the Lake District might lead to an accurate impersonation of a drowned rat, Germany, particularly the south, has the weather for it. Sunny weather brings out walkers and climbers everywhere, the boom in Nordic walking inspiring people of any ages equipped with cross-country gear *and* poles similar to ski poles to walk determinedly along mountain pathways almost all year round. Indeed *Wandern* (to take a walk, hike or ramble), whether it be in the countryside or in the mountains, is almost a pre-requisite for residence in southern Germany in particular. Many of the accessible Alpine regions have mountains with safe tracks; the prize at the top, a hut or even a restaurant with the ubiquitous *Kaffee und Kuchen* (coffee and cake), or a bowl of homemade soup. Germans like their rewards for being on the move so much.

For many Germans, their cars, the performance and maintenance thereof, and the possibilities afforded in terms of sating their passion for touring and travelling, are major signifiers of status. 'I remember that my first synthesizer cost as much as my Volkswagen,' said Ralf in 2003. 'Studying and being in Kraftwerk was almost impossible. But still I did. I had to have that synthesizer, and I wanted that Volkswagen – both meant freedom to me.' Ralf's grey Volkswagen would be the star of the cover artwork of the band's next album.

Motion emerges as a central ordering mechanism in the lives of Ralf and Florian. The heartbeat of everyday industrial life is encoded directly in their aesthetic. Florian: 'Several years ago we were on tour and it happened that we just came off the autobahn after a long ride, and when we came in to play we had this speed in our music. Our hearts were still beating fast so the whole rhythm became very fast.' Ralf adds: 'The idea is to capture non-static phenomenon because music itself is a non-static phenomenon. It deals with time and movement in time. It can never be the same.'

This sense of motion, of time and space and travel, would be absorbed into the music that dominated the group's next album, effectively their fourth but in the minds of many the first record to reflect truly the sound of Kraftwerk as it is nowadays recognised worldwide. 'The construction of the entire *Autobahn* album took place between 1973 and 1974, in Konrad Plank's studio and in the Kling Klang studio,' says Wolfgang Flür. 'Konrad Plank had mobile equipment in a lorry he had bought: and he put a little recording board inside his lorry, a recording machine and so on. He sometimes came to Düsseldorf and put that lorry in the yard where we were. He put some cables in; and we would record from there. Sometimes they recorded in the little village where he lived.' By now, Kraftwerk had purchased some of the most cutting-edge synths on the market. Along with the Minimoog, there was an ARP Odyssey, and the EMS Synthi AKS. Another distinctive part of the Kraftwerk sound was the use of vocoded voices on the album's title track.

The track 'Autobahn' was written by Ralf and Florian, with lyrics co-written by friend and artwork co-ordinator Emil Schult. Ralf's vocal on 'Autobahn', instantly recognisable, likeable, but slightly self-conscious, would become his trademark vocal delivery. 'It's called *Sprechsingen*,' he says. 'I don't know the English word. Sprechsingen means 'talk-sing'. It's like a form of rap. This started with 'Autobahn' (*'Wir fahr'n, fahr'n, fahr'n auf der Autobahn'*)*.

It is no coincidence that the rhythm of the words is virtually identical to the cadence of the Beach Boys' 1966 single 'Barbara Ann'.† Kraftwerk were creating the West German equivalent of a Californian road song: *'Vor uns liegt ein weites Tal/Die Sonne scheint mit Glitzerstrahl'* ('Before us is a wide valley/the sun is shining with glittering rays'). According to Ralf, the Beach Boys 'managed to concentrate a maximum of fundamental ideas. In a hundred years from now when people want to know what California was like in the sixties, they only have to listen to a single by the Beach Boys.'

There were no real equivalents in the UK of a road song up to this point, possibly because the motorways were famous for being congested, with three-mile tailbacks, overturned heavy

---

* In English: 'We're driving, driving, driving on the autobahn.'
† Although generally associated with the Beach Boys, their recording of 'Barbara Ann' was actually a cover of a 1961 number 13 US hit by Bronx band the Regents, written by their leader Fred Fassett.

goods lorries, and hard shoulders full of cars with smoke pouring out of an open bonnet. In America, of course, with many miles of open highway, all was different; from beat literature that included Kerouac's ground-breaking 1957 novel *On The Road*, together with a host of rock 'n' roll songs whose raison d'être was the pleasure of nothing more than, in the words of Chuck Berry's 1964 hit 'No Particular Place To Go', 'riding along in my automobile'. But to have a road song made by Germans, that was something else altogether, for ultimately a song about the joys of car travel would, at some point, reflect back to the architect of most of the *Autobahnen* himself. This was a landmark German song, a song which reinstated a sense of pride in being German, without, in any way, denying or forgetting the nation's past. The autobahn now meant freedom, modernity, fun.

Again, the album's cover artwork was an integral part of the overall product. The original album cover in Germany was a painting by Emil Schult from the perspective of the driver, a literal, some might say too literal, depiction of a journey down the autobahn looking out along the endless road towards a rising sun, mountains and a large fir tree. However, it was the cover designed for the UK and US markets that would become iconic.

Peter Saville, in the spring of 1975, was in his foundation year at art school 'It was Malcolm (Garrett) who told me that there was a 20-minute long version on their album. I was just astonished and fascinated by that, so I immediately went and bought the album. the UK cover was the blue motorway sign. There was a significant thing that happened because of that. The other cover, the rather quaint Heimat-style illustration, I really don't like. It's not as important as the music. But, at 20 years of age, the "Autobahn" sign had a markedly profound and enlightening influence upon me. In a way, I would say it was my first basic lesson in semiotics – not a term I would apply to it at the time, but I now know. I saw the vast landscape of past, present and future Europe unfold in my mind. Listening to "Autobahn" was entirely summarised in a monochromatic symbol. So, it advanced my notions of visual communication enormously.'

Later, when Saville was given the job of creating a brand visual signifier for Manchester's Factory Records, the influence of the *Autobahn* cover was crucial. 'In '78 for Factory I used a hearing protection symbol. It is the direct consequence of the "Autobahn" sign. It was the first work of significance that I got the opportunity to make. I "appropriated" a sign that I had been admiring on a workshop door at the art school, it was an industrial warning sign and I loved it; and I loved it for the landscape of possibilities and ideas that it opened up – in the same way that "Autobahn" had. The rapid transition through notions of Europe – that was what the Autobahn sign evoked. The hearing protection sign evoked the world of industry, the relationship between man and machine, the past, present and future of the industrial experience. So the "Use Hearing Protection" sign for me was a sort of symbol of industrial culture and in a way the "Autobahn" sign was a symbol of European culture, you know, geography and history – of kind of time and place – *times* and place. My first romantic Kraftwerk notion, even before I ever went to Germany, was of motorways and a cathedral. And then when I started to visit Germany I found a place in Cologne where an elevated roadway passes by the cathedral and it is quintessentially Kraftwerk. You pass at speed through a millennium. That is my relationship to Kraftwerk and it started with that motorway sign.'

Autobahn was musically ordered so that the title track took over the whole of side one, and a sequence of shorter songs was found on side two. Such a split was not uncommon in progressive rock. One side of Genesis' 1972 album *Foxtrot* was almost completely taken up with the 20-minute-plus progressive rock epic 'Supper's Ready', Yes were stretching things out on *Fragile* and *Close To The Edge* and Mike Oldfield was making his name with the long conceptual pieces that straddled both sides of his early albums for Virgin. And, of course, contemporary German music did this too – Can's 1972 LP *Tago Mago* ran to 73 minutes over four sides of music with two tracks, 'Halleluhwah' and 'Aumgn', taking up a side each. In an email from 2009, Ralf alludes directly to the fact that the technology available at the time focused and formed the music: 'Autobahn ... the endless journey ... the timing of the composition resulting from the technical possibilities of the vinyl long-playing record ...'

This was an era of longhair stoner parties, rooms of teenagers seeking cosmic significance, and the longer the song, the deeper the meaning, obviously. But unlike some of the inflated creations inspired by too much Old Nick's Navy Cut, 'Autobahn' is no noodling piece of music. It is utterly modern, sleek and liberating. Today, it still sounds astonishing, its ambient beats and cadences echoing down through the years and informing so much of today's contemporary music. It is also a piece of music which would confound and perplex a new community of music fans used to downloading off-the-peg songs from popular music's seven-decade-long canon from Bing Crosby to Adele. This was music which took time to listen to. Twenty-three minutes devoted not simply to one artist, but one track, now seems like both an extravagance and a monumental effort.

The shorter pieces were no less impressive. 'Kometenmelodie 1' ('Comet Melody 1') was inspired by Comet Kohoutek, a much hyped visitation by a heavenly body which turned out to be a milky blur at best. The soaring melody of 'Kometenmelodie 2' ('Comet Melody 2') has an almost French way with a melody, and sounds reminiscent of some of the later work of synthesizer composer Jean-Michel Jarre. With the third short instrumental, 'Mitternacht' ('Midnight'), with its eerie melody, creepy synthesizer footsteps and overall air of Gothic 'he's-behind-you' creepiness, the mood darkens. Bowie's 1977 instrumental 'Sense Of Doubt' is its psychic, sonic partner. Klaus Röder, featured in the inside cover artwork, and briefly a member of the band, plays electric violin on this track.* But then the heart lifts, the mood lightens. 'Morgenspaziergang' ('Morning Walk') has a lovely, simple descant recorder tune, and the busy chatter of synthesized birdsong appears in a piece which could easily have fitted thematically and musically with the pastoral excursions on *Ralf And Florian*. It was the last time acoustic instrumentation would be used by Kraftwerk.

Finally, what *Autobahn* did was to drive a wedge between Kraftwerk and the other German bands. Although some electro-acoustic instruments were used on the album, the playing and purpose was now all about the synthesizer. This was music which had very little to do with the experimental music of Can, not that there were ever major similarities, but now Kraftwerk were also distanced from all their peers on the German scene too. One senses that for some

---

* Indeed the inside artwork of 'Autobahn' originally had a painting of Ralf, Florian, Klaus Röder and Emil Schult as band members positioned on the back seat of a car. Wolfgang's position within the line-up was only later confirmed, and so his head then replaced Emil's body in the finished artwork.

German musicians, Kraftwerk had now lost their sense of adventure. This was now music which had none of the jazzy or progressive feel of their early work. Kraftwerk had ditched artistic integrity in search of a hit tune, or a gimmick.

'There were other musicians, possibly more important in terms of authenticity/originality,' says Hans-Joachim Roedelius. 'Florian Fricke (Popol Vuh), Paul and Limpe Fuchs (Popol Vuh), Konrad Schnitzler, Asmus Tietchens and of course my own work with Kluster/Cluster, which had nothing to do with Kraftwerk. It's another world philosophically and spiritually.' Sell out? 'Not at all,' says John Foxx, then the twenty-something Dennis Leigh, and about to embark on a long musical journey, first with the original Ultravox, then as a solo artist and in collaboration, which, at the time of writing, shows no sign of running out of gas. 'This is akin to the accusations levelled at Bob Dylan for going electric long, long ago. It's actually more honest than continuing with a set of outgrown ideals that you are now able to see as naïve, yet dare not abandon for fear of peer disapproval. That always leads to a cosy consensual asphyxiation. The distillation into Kraftwerk proper entailed a swift purging of all conflicting elements, leaving them with that clear identity, one that effectively differentiated them from their peers. I think it takes an unusual amount of intellectual courage and vision to carry this through.'

In reality with *Autobahn* Kraftwerk made a significant portion of German music sound old-fashioned; the days of long hair, flares and the hippy happenings were now most definitely over.

2.6 Tomorrow's World, Today

When did truly modern pop music begin? Did it begin in 1966, when circular time replaced linear time with the release of the Beatles' 'Tomorrow Never Knows', and the Velvet Underground's 'Venus In Furs' with music which jettisoned the intro/verse/chorus/middle eight bedrock of traditional pop, and replaced it with repeats, beats, a modern mantra? Or did we reach pop modernity later, in the summer of 1972, with Bowie's *The Rise And Fall Of Ziggy Stardust And The Spiders From Mars*, an album about a fictitious rock messiah which examined the whole concept of what rock idolatry was, and, by extension, broke with the past by saying that rock was simply a construct, and a rock star might simply be a poseur, a player, an actor? Also that summer, Roxy Music's debut album did musically what Bowie's album had done conceptually: it laid bare the tangled weave of music that made up rock 'n' roll by parodying the past whilst playing, simultaneously, courtesy of Brian Eno, the synth soundtrack of the future. In 1972, popular music was becoming parodic, and self-referential, something it has been ever since.

But for many, modern music would truly begin in the spring of 1975 with the release of the 'Autobahn' single.* For Andy McCluskey, it began in the bathroom. 'I can remember distinctly that we had a little transistor radio in the bathroom on the window shelf; and I wasn't in the bath but I was in the bathroom. I might have been brushing my teeth or something. I heard "Autobahn". It was a bit like "Where were you when Kennedy was shot?" I remember because I heard "Autobahn", and it stopped me in my tracks. I thought, "What the heck is that?" – because it was so different, yet so melodic and had a good rhythm. It was everything that a teenage English boy who was looking for something different could possibly want to find.'

John Foxx's reaction to the single, like many at the time, was not to dismiss it but to categorise it as a novelty record: 'When "Autobahn" was released. I was intrigued because it was electronic, and thought it was very funny – a rewrite of "Barbara Ann" by the Beach Boys. I didn't then think of them as something really new – because "Autobahn" seemed like some sort of one-off novelty record, chiming more with the Shadows and various strands of Europop I'd already come across when hitch-hiking across Northern Europe in 1965/1966. I didn't really connect them with Neu! or other German bands until the mid-seventies, because their music sounded so different. It was only when I realised that Conny Plank had recorded both that I was aware of any connection. Conny is really "Mr Connective" – all the lines of European music run through that station. If it has a centre, he is it. Then I remember talking to Caroline Coon backstage at the Rainbow in London in 1976. We were

---

* In the introduction to the article 'From Neu! To Kraftwerk: Football, Motorik And The Pulse Of Modernity,' January 6, 2010, in the online music magazine *The Quietus*, John Doran writes: 'When we started The Quietus we made the fairly arbitrary decision that modern popular music started with Kraftwerk's *'Autobahn'* in 1974.'

all talking about sound – I said I was interested in the Futurists and wanted the band to sound like a jet plane or some sort of massive industrial engine. Caroline said I should check Kraftwerk out again, so I did. It wasn't until I learned from Conny that the Beach Boys were among Kraftwerk's more serious influences. Then "Autobahn" made more sense as a Germanic transposition of American beach/ surf music into Euro/motorway music. Apparently they had even attempted songs with Beach Boys harmonies – using vocoders. I would love to hear that.'

Joe Black, a massive fan of Krautrock, and for many years Senior Marketing Manager at Universal Music, heard 'Autobahn' as a boy in Scotland and remembers that 'it probably sounded very, very, romantic and very exotic. I think I got the Beach Boys reference straightaway as well. Seeing it on *Tomorrow's World* just confirmed it. Here were these Germans just playing things that looked like electric cookers rather than drum machines, with knitting needles... If there's one word that I always associate with Kraftwerk it's romance. It's the romance of travel, and the romance of technology.' Joe Black echoes many listeners' experience that 'it was made for the car, really'.

The band's appearance on the popular science programme *Tomorrow's World* in 1975 was the first time people in the UK had seen them in action. By now, all four members had short hair and were dressed stylishly though conservatively in shirts, ties and jackets. 'Kraftwerk have a name for this; they call it *Machine Music*,' intoned presenter Raymond Baxter. The short report concentrated on the synthetic drums: 'Each disc gives a different sound – rolls, bongos, snares – just by completing the contact with the spring-steeled batons. Next year, Kraftwerk aim to eliminate the keyboards altogether, and build jackets with electronic lapels which can be played by touch.' Then, at the very end of the piece, comes one of the band's most iconic images – Florian's wide, mad-professor smile to the camera.

By now, Kraftwerk had become a foursome with the addition of 23-year-old Karl Bartos. For Andy McCluskey the arrival of Wolfgang and Karl Bartos was a masterstroke: 'I think they were wonderful, and I think that [it was] a very clever and wonderful addition that Ralf and Florian made actually by getting in the two drummers.' The fact that Wolfgang, with his dark, good looks, and

Karl, youthful looking even today, aged 60, were telegenic, even sexy, was also a key advantage.

Wolfgang Flür recalls that the three Kraftwerk members were performing at some 'stupid' clubs and, in particular, at a French club when 'we thought, all three of us, that we were a little bit too light in number as a band on the stage. We should have one more.' Florian knew a professor at the Robert Schumann Conservatory in Düsseldorf and consulted him. "It can only be Karl Bartos," responded the professor. "It can only be him. Why? Because he is the best percussionist."'

'I went to the studio and we got along very well from the first day,' says Bartos. 'They didn't really know that I was growing up in the sixties as well and I had a good concept of pop music in general. I started off playing songs by the Beatles and Chuck Berry – rock 'n' roll really. When I was 18 or 20 I went to the conservatory to study music and I was already able to understand the concept of pop music then.' He continues: 'At that time Düsseldorf was on British-occupied soil and my brother-in-law was actually a British soldier. And this guy, Peter, he brought into our house the first rock 'n' roll records, the Beatles and the Rolling Stones.'

What was unusual in the recruiting of Bartos was that Kraftwerk would now have two percussionists, and that, together, they made up half the band. Moreover, Karl Bartos was, by Wolfgang's open admission, a far superior musician to him. Even more offputting, perhaps, was the fact that Wolfgang had already been a member for two years but that he and Karl were destined to have equal status. Karl went on the following year to take his final exams at the Robert Schumann Conservatory and graduated with an advanced performer's degree in percussion.

However, Karl and Wolfgang seem to have hit it off from the start, partly from a joint desire to improve the music in the band. 'Like me, Karl didn't think the sound was very good.' Strengthening the bond between Wolfgang and Karl was their shared similarity in character and temperament, as well as a kindred spirit that contrasted starkly with the Florian/Ralf combination. Although Ralf and Florian are characters fundamentally different from one another, they (collectively and as individuals) were quite unlike Wolfgang and Karl. Somehow, this unlikely cocktail worked.

For Karl Bartos, perhaps with just the merest hint of false

modesty, *Autobahn* is the most important Kraftwerk album: 'The legendary Conny Plank was involved. I joined in 1975 and was initially booked for the upcoming live stuff in the USA. I had no idea at that time that I would be part of the *Mensch Maschine* for the next 15 years.'

2.7 Midnight Special

Bartos joined at a turning point in the band's career, the moment when something quite improbable happened. The *Autobahn* album had broken into the US *Billboard* charts. Kraftwerk's peaceful invasion of the USA began in early April 1975. The catalyst was Ira Blacker, the CEO of Mr I. Mouse Ltd., a company that looked after the professional interests of rock stars, and 21 concerts were planned. Wolfgang Flür is among many with vivid memories of this larger-than-life manager. He was told: 'The big manager, Ira Blacker, flew over to Hamburg with a huge bag full of dollars, to sign them up to a contract, and he gave Ralf and Florian the money in cash. It must have been a big amount. I don't know how much. They had an appointment in a cheap backstage hotel. He came in, he was sweating. He was hot, so he took off his jacket, and he had a belt with a gun. An American, he flew with that outfit. In the seventies, nobody asked about guns. He flew back the same day. So the deal was done, and they made some millions of marks or dollars in America with the album, then the single cut.'

According to ex-member Eberhard Kranemann, producer Conny Plank lost out badly: 'Conny Plank got a phone call from an American music businessman [Ira Blacker]. He said to him "Hey, Conny Plank, I like this Kraftwerk *Autobahn*: but it is too long. I want to cut it to three minutes to make a single out of it. Conny said, OK, we can do it. Then this businessman wanted to meet Conny. Today I would have to say that Conny Plank made a very big mistake. He said "I don't have time to meet you. Please meet Florian and Ralf." Conny gave his personal contact to Florian and Ralf. So they met this big businessman and they made a contract with him, without Conny. They kicked the discoverer, promoter and producer out of the business. And this is a shame. After that I often spoke about this in details with Conny – and he was very angry about it. They changed their behaviour after *Autobahn*. They were very,

very strong. They did not want to speak to other people, they had lawyers to look after their rights. If someone said something about Kraftwerk that they didn't like, then a letter from the lawyer came, and you were not allowed to say this or that.'

Up until 1975, the band had had solid, but modest success. *Kraftwerk* and *Kraftwerk 2* charted inside the Top 40 in Germany although *Ralf And Florian* had sold poorly. By 1975, Kraftwerk had sold around 150,000 albums in West Germany, yet their media presence in their homeland was still minimal. 'They don't do interviews, one is told, and they hardly do any concerts either, because apparently they don't really need the money,' is how *Record Mirror* put it in May 1975 when their single 'Autobahn' was breaking into the British and West German charts. It was, however, America that took the band fully to its heart. This was an American music scene dominated by multi-platinum albums by Elton John, Led Zeppelin, Chicago, the Eagles and Jefferson Starship. Pre-punk and pre-new-wave America, circa 1975, was the land where FM radio was king and AOR (album-oriented rock) had it in a stranglehold. The success of an album of radical synthetic sounds such as *Autobahn* was, therefore, all the more startling. In some ways, the record's success, particularly its adoption by the college set as the latest cool music from Europe, put the band in the same broad category as Bowie and Roxy Music, music for outsiders, at a time when there was very little in American music, especially on FM radio, that was catering for that community.

Suddenly, everything had changed. The single 'Autobahn' reached number 11 in the UK charts, and number nine in Germany. It also charted inside the US Top 30, while the album would reach the giddy heights of number five on the *Billboard* charts. 'I didn't even know that "Autobahn" was released as a single,' Conny Plank told *Record Mirror*. 'It was the Chicago boss of Phonogram who cut the track down to three minutes. It was purely meant for radio promotion in the States, but we were rather pleased when we heard it, that's exactly how we would have done it.'

The US tour got off to a bad start with Wolfgang slamming a car door shut on his left thumb before they had even left the ground in Düsseldorf. The schedule took them to snow-bound upstate New York, muggy Florida (where Wolfgang suffered from stomach trouble in the heat), to southern California and New York. The tour also included TV appearances: 'I can remember one,' Wolfgang Flür recalls: '*Midnight Special* in LA. It was fantastic. The compere was crazy about us. What I really remember was the Jackson 5 before us on stage.' Kraftwerk played an eight-minute version of 'Autobahn' on prime-time American TV. Four young Germans who looked like lawyers next to one of America's funkiest, most colourful and biggest acts on a high-rating NBC production? It was one of pop's strangest but most significant moments.

In a neat piece of self-fulfilling prophecy, the band would hear their song on the radio driving on the freeways. 'On ["Autobahn"] we have this story of our music being played over the car radio while we are sitting in the car and driving,' says Ralf. 'This is what actually happened while we were in America. We were driving from the airport to the hotel and turned on the radio and our music was coming out. The composition was about this and it is reality for us.'

But unlike many of their British musical contemporaries for whom America represented a mythic land of almost unlimited potential (and, of course, a huge commercial market to be tapped into), Ralf and Florian seemed positively turned off by the superficiality of American culture, particularly its network TV. 'Oh sure, I can watch *Bonanza* if I have nothing else to do,' said Ralf in 1976, 'but there is a very large portion of people that are lazy and they take whatever is on television for given. Once you realise how it's done and what it really means, you come even to the point that you cannot watch it because you get physically sick. It makes me sick.' 'I can't stand American TV,' is Florian's terse assessment.

Kraftwerk's aesthetic was a studied rejection of almost everything Anglo-American culture stood for, and an often witty take on Germanness: 'I think they long ago became conscious of the rest of the world's stereotypical view of the efficient, intellectual German, and decided to play up to this,' is John Foxx's analysis. 'The suits and haircuts that Florian introduced seem to bear this out, and so does their general demeanour – unexcitable yet engaged, dignified, precise, detached, analytical, dryly humorous or comically over-earnest – or both. Part of a wider culture, of which they allow us just a glimpse, through music titles, or references, or self-made myths – the Franz Schubert title, the story of watching Stockhausen after taking LSD etc., of independent means – financially capable of maintaining a career outside music business norms. Intellectually independent too – not reliant on the usual strained constructs resulting from an over-eagerness to establish credibility through spurious artistic connections. Then there is the music – again, it deliberately excludes all British and American pop elements. Instead, it refers to repurposed German music, much simplified, from Schubert to Stockhausen, incorporating elements from *Schlager*, disco and folk melodies. I think the specifically German element in their stage image lies mainly in an apparent inability to dance. But we're again talking about stereotypes that they have great fun exploiting. Their use of techno-mythology also seems to reinforce this. Some of the themes that Fritz Lang manifested through *Metropolis* seem to have been incorporated into the heraldry of German life from then on – the possibility of improvement through work, good behaviour, good citizenship, into a kind of technologically enabled progress. This is manifested clearly in Kraftwerk's use of German public information films, usually promoting a sort of 'Autobahn Optimism' – families picnicking on the grass verge of motorways, etc. These are much like the American films of the same era and equally charming and naïve, but they always refer to that specifically German environment – family-friendly industrial sites and especially the road system. It's a sort of knowing, affectionate acknowledgement of naivety. Magical kitsch.'

2.8 Papa Bear Departs

The success came at a personal price. Conny Plank, so crucial in developing and refining the Kraftwerk sound, would be dropped. Plank had had a crucial role to play sonically. Plank was basically bought out by the band. Offered DM 5,000 by Ralf and Florian for his stake in *Autobahn,* he took it, and thus did not benefit from the album's enduring popularity in the years up to his death in 1987.

Before we rush to judgement, DM 5,000, in 1975, was a lot of money, and probably the largest pay cheque Conny had ever seen. We must also have some sympathy with Ralf and Florian, two young musicians, young businessmen seeking to run their band as just that, a business. The model was a pop group as a small business, with Ralf and Florian the managing directors, hiring and firing. Maybe, by 1975, they felt they had learnt enough from Plank? Perhaps they found his approach limiting and needed a clean break, artistically? With both Ralf and Florian unavailable for comment, we don't know their side of the story. However, what is certain is that two ex-members of Kraftwerk were dismayed, even outraged, by the way Plank was treated.

'Conny Plank was very open and very friendly. He did not care about money,' says Eberhard Kranemann. 'He was interested in sound experiments. Musicians would come to try out his studio and he wouldn't charge them. For the previous Kraftwerk albums he had a 50/50 deal with Ralf and Florian. *Autobahn* had been produced by Conny Plank, but Florian and Ralf – and this is not right – they kicked him out and put him out of business. They gave him DM 5,000 for producing the album. How much did Ralf and Florian earn from the album? That's not OK. Conny Plank wanted to have the money back. He went to a lawyer and said. "Here, I am the producer, I must have 30/40/50 per cent of the whole thing." Kraftwerk said, "No, it was our idea, we did it all ourselves", or something like that. But it was Conny Plank's mistake, too, because he was very friendly and naive. He did everything on a handshake, nothing was written down. Normally in business you have written documents, and you write, Florian 50% production, 50% production for Conny Plank, etc. But they had nothing written down on paper. It was just the way Conny did things. So Ralf and Florian thought, "Oh, we can kick him out." This is not OK, because at first they were his friends. You can't do something like that to a friend. I know the music, the early music, of Kraftwerk without Conny Plank: and I know exactly the work that Conny Plank did for the band. The sound of the band in the early stages was 70–80% Conny Plank; and not Florian and Ralf. It was so important what he was doing at the mixer with the sound and what kind of music he selected and how he supported Ralf and Florian. The sound is very important for Kraftwerk; and the sound has been made by Conny Plank, the great master.'

'He only lived for music. All his life was music,' continues Eberhard. 'He was not interested in normal life. Day and night he was in his studio working on sounds. A lot of the sounds of Kraftwerk and Neu! were made by Conny Plank, not by Kraftwerk and not by Neu! This is so important. Without Conny Plank, these bands would not have been possible. And I made the first contact.'

'He was a fantastic man, very talented, and he was the one, by the way, who brought the synthesizer into Florian and Ralf's lives,' Wolfgang Flür points out. 'They played the organ, Florian played the flute, and Mr Plank had a big relationship with American companies. He was over there a lot, and he knew some very famous people from the music scene, from record companies and so on. He was also involved with American soldiers that were stationed in Germany – in Wiesbaden and Hessen – the guys who brought rock music to Germany. He knew that Americans could do rock the best. He told Ralf and Florian, "Forget your rock attitudes. The US musicians can do that best. Forget it, do something special and invent some special German music, a kind of pop music which is reliable and which is close to your education and artistic visions." He was familiar with the new synthesizer from the Moog company, from Bob Moog. It was a device which was like a little organ or a toy, it was really lightweight. He brought it with him and said, "Boys, come on, forget your organ. Put it away. It's too big. It's not modern. They made the sound of the cars with it on 'Autobahn'. So he was the visionary man, not Ralf and Florian.

'He understood them; he knew how visionary they were with their themes,' continues Wolfgang. 'I was at his studio two times with them there in Neuenkirchen, close to Hennef, in the Rhineland area. He had bought an old farm, turned the pigs out, and put his recording studio in the pig sty. The smell went away very soon because he was a big smoker of pot.' Wolfgang was told by Christa Fast, Conny's wife: 'Conny played the Moog and Ralf and Florian would react with words such as: "Go back, go back over what you played five minutes ago. Yes OK. This is good. We'll take that." That was their way of working with him. He was working; they were just sitting elegantly in the chairs and deciding what was to be taken, what was to be done.'

So, is Conny Plank an un-credited composer? 'Absolutely,' affirms Wolfgang. 'He is not credited as the co-producer and composer. He was not just the "engineer". And this is not OK. When I met Christa she started to cry about it, because her husband was so upset about it, how they handled him after *Autobahn*, which became so famous and which was only possible thanks to him, his ideas and his direction. All they wrote on this record was "Engineered by Konrad Plank".' For Wolfgang, Plank was crucial in developing many of the LP's sounds, 'Especially the cars, the buildings, and all these things. Sound is really important, as much as melody. Sound is really important, that you get something in the brain, it's the whole feeling, the sound, especially electronic music, because in normal, average pop music, you only have guitars, or maybe an organ, that was the standard set-up. The guitar can never sound like rubber or like grass or carpets, you know.

'That was the first time in Konrad Plank's life that he went to a lawyer and asked what he could do against it,' continues an emotional Wolfgang. 'He had nearly no chance, because he couldn't prove it without a written contract. He wrote some letters to Kraftwerk which they didn't answer properly; and so it broke his heart. Christa told me, it really broke his heart, that he was handled so badly. I just wanted to tell you that because this is the truth, and I have no reason not to believe what Christa told me. They have a son: he was old enough to realise all these things and he also confirmed what his mother told me.'

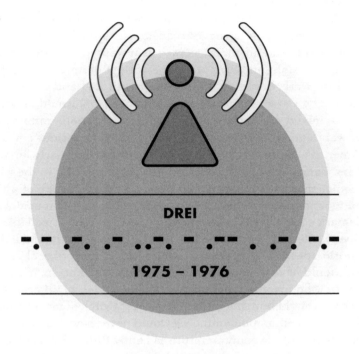

DREI

1975 – 1976

3.1 Lester Bangs Versus Kraftwerk

'**ALL GREAT** things must first wear terrifying and monstrous masks in order to inscribe themselves on the hearts of humanity.' So wrote German philosopher Friedrich Nietzsche. As individuals, the men in Kraftwerk were neither terrifying nor monstrous, but they were a sufficiently disruptive force in how they looked, what they played, and, in interviews, what they said, as to appear, to some, to be possessed of some sort of superhuman potency. The talk about *Machine Music* and their obvious admiration for technology sounded odd, even ominous to some who might equate Germanness with a more sinister, Nietzschean view of the future of mankind as the takeover of the 'Übermensch'. Today, Kraftwerk are respected and appreciated but back in the un-reconstituted seventies, all was different. In some areas, Kraftwerk were not simply misunderstood but actively disliked.

In 1975, Lester Bangs was the champion of a new breed of maverick, gonzo-style music journalism. His verbal sparring is the stuff of legend, and his prose, as racy as it was witty, burnt through with a rare insight and love of a huge variety of music. His article about Kraftwerk, based on an interview with Ralf and Florian and published by *Creem* magazine in September 1975, would, however, prove a mixed blessing. Entitled with appropriate minimalism 'Kraftwerkfeature', it provided the band with some serious coverage in America's second-best-selling music magazine early in their careers. Bangs liked Kraftwerk and was the first critic in the world to predict that their music would herald a techno future at a time when most observers viewed Kraftwerk as the end of music. With trademark contrariness he ascribed the birth of rock 'n' roll itself to Germany, offering as proof the fact that German scientists had given the world speed, a drug without which the history of rock 'n' roll music would have been very different: 'As is well known, it was the Germans who invented methamphetamine, which of all accessible tools has brought humans within the closest twitch of machinehood, and without methamphetamine we would never have had such high plasma marks of the counterculture as Lenny Bruce, Bob Dylan, Lou Reed and the Velvet Underground, Neal Cassady, Jack Kerouac, Allen Ginsberg's "Howl", Blue Cheer, Cream and Creem (the Reich never died, it just re-incarnated in American stereotypes ground out by hollow-eyed, jerky-fingered mannequins locked into their typewriters and guitars like rhinoceroses copulating)...'

'When was the last time you heard a German band go galloping off at 965 mph, hot on the heels of oblivion?' continued Bangs, nailing the orderly aesthetic of many of the German bands of the time. 'No, they realise that the ultimate power is exercised calmly, whether it's Can with their endless rotary connections, Tangerine Dream plumbing the Sargassian depths, or Kraftwerk sailing air-locked down the Autobahn.'

The preamble over, the interview starts. Throughout the piece, Bangs has an agenda – to portray Kraftwerk as soulless, and to reinforce as many of the damaging stereotypes of their national character as possible, but with a certain wit and irony too. Perhaps either knowingly complicit or naively blundering, depending on whether you gauge Bangs' feature as leg-pulling or bigoted, Ralf and Florian provide ample ammunition. They emerge as cold, calculating, machine-like, able to ponder (if also to reject) the effects of using sound, as posited by William Burroughs, as a means to destroy an audience. Taken out of context, the line 'It is also possible to damage your mind' makes music sound like torture.

In the UK, *NME* editor Nick Logan had cut a deal to reprint Bangs' work. On September 6, 1975, his paper ran the article under a new title: 'Kraftwerk: the final solution to the Musical Problem? Lester Bangs vivisects the German Scientific Approach', and in this incarnation any remaining level of irony had been well and truly stripped away. Florian is described as a man whose countenance gives the appearance that 'he could build a computer or push a button and blow up half the world with the same amount of emotion'. 'We want the whole world to know our background. We cannot deny we are from Germany,' Ralf is quoted as saying, 'because the German mentality, which is more advanced, will always be part of our behaviour. We create out of the German language, the mother language, which is very mechanical, we use as the basic structure of our music. Also the machines, from the industries of Germany.'

Kraftwerk wouldn't be the first to claim intellectual superiority over the Americans, of course. The same year, Jean Jacques Burnel of the Stranglers said of America, 'There was nothing there we could appreciate, nothing in the American culture that appealed to our superior Europeanism', before adding, with what was clearly a premeditated wind-up, 'Everyone knows that Americans have smaller brains. Fact of life, you know – they're just inferior specimens.'

Such criticism of the group was generally laughed off. 'We laughed about that craziness. They didn't understand our humour,' says Wolfgang. 'We knew it was satire – poor satire, of course.' Karl Bartos however, remembers differently: 'In the early years there was some negative reaction to our German background, that's true. The most famous example is the *NME* centrefold, which showed the black-and-white photograph of the band taken in New York by Maurice Seymour, and later used for the *Trans-Europe Express* artwork copied into a scene from the *Reichsparteitag* [The Reich's Party Convention]. As far as I recall, our concerts in England were not that well attended after that... In fact, it became clear to me on tour just how critically we Germans are viewed in general abroad.'

Political correctness was unheard of in 1975. Ralf, Florian, Karl and Wolfgang had been turned into Adolf, Hermann, Rudolf and Heinrich.

3.2 'This Ain't Rock 'n' Roll'*

The UK music press in the early-to-mid-seventies was almost to a man (there were still very few women involved) a dissolute bunch of drug addicts, alcoholics, failed academics and chancers.[†] While *Melody Maker* tended to employ qualified reporters from provincial dailies sidetracked by their love of rock music, its main rival *NME* relied on a rump of writers left over from the 1970 spirit of subversion fostered by *IT* and *Oz*. Both also employed an older generation of Tin Pan Alley-era jazz enthusiasts who, although gradually moving on and moving out, made for sometimes uneasy bedfellows with the newer breed. Kraftwerk, again, remained unintelligible to the rock literati by means of their patent lack of good rock breeding. Here was a group that not only didn't play rock music, but also didn't take drugs. And, unlike so many music journalists, Kraftwerk were actually university educated, like many a middle-class journo's mum and dad had always wanted them to be. This, of course, was not apparent to anyone at the time, but it does further explain Kraftwerk's singularity. So many music journalists were rock stars manqué, wearing trousers of the tight leather kind, obsessed with having their photos taken with their interviewees, shagging the PAs, and hanging out with superstars so as to bask in reflected glory. Kraftwerk were singularly unimpressed with all of this. They offered journalists scant encouragement and had absolutely no interest in celebrity and fame.

It was clear that what was being presented had absolutely nothing to do with rock music. 'When I joined up with Kraftwerk

---

* The opening line of David Bowie's 1974 song 'Diamond Dogs'. Bowie was about to abandon rock almost completely for the next half a dozen years.
† I oversimplify, admittedly, although the lifestyle choices of those on *NME* in the seventies, as described by Pat Long in *The History Of The NME: High Times And Low Lives At The World's Most Famous Music Magazine* (London, Portico, 2012), do little to disprove my main point.

in 1975 I found an already existing visual identity,' says Karl Bartos. 'Looking at the record covers, a proximity to the visual arts was evident. Also, the stage design resembled an audio-visual installation. Everything was dipped into neon light and looked extremely artificial. And then there were our names Ralf, Karl, Wolfgang and Florian being faded in as neon characters at dramaturgical points, every time causing frenetic applause. Even at my first concerts with the band we had slide projections, which were later replaced by video projections.'

The only time in their careers that Kraftwerk played without their stage gear would be in 1976 in France. Wolfgang puts this down to a 'logistical mishap' on the journey to a live concert in Lyon. 'Driving to Lyon in our black Mercedes, we drove straight into the rush-hour traffic jam. Time passed, and it got later and later. I can't remember where we'd played the previous day, but I know that it was a long way from Lyon, and that we had a very long car journey, during which we changed drivers constantly. At any rate one of the trucks had got stuck somewhere, and when we arrived at the large, unfriendly hall, in which cattle auctions took place on weekdays, we were very late. Fortunately, the audience had waited for us and no-one had left, even though we turned up a whole hour late, and didn't have any stage clothes because these were in the clothes case in the lost vehicle... During the show, a synthesizer gave up the ghost in an acrid-smelling cloud of thick black smoke... It was the only concert we gave in jeans and leather jackets after the release of *Autobahn*. We looked like an electronic punk band.'

Many critics were put off by Kraftwerk. This was a group that had none of the heat of rock'n'roll. There was no focal point, no lead singer with whom to identify. On stage, Kraftwerk were static, an electronic chamber orchestra with no real attempt to engage the audience. There was also a complete absence of the traditional drama of popular music, no songs of passion, envy, desire, love won and lost. Critics and audiences were, instead, treated to a de-sexualised form of contemporary music, detached, cool. Miles, perhaps the voice of the London underground scene of the late sixties, regarded Kraftwerk with a mixture of cold opprobrium and pity: 'They are a very neat band, all dressed in suits and ties and short hair like bank managers. They all stand stock still except Karl and Wolfgang, who have to move their arms a bit to play bass and drums – not ordinary bass and drums, but small flat suitcases on legs like electric pianos – that's right, electronic pads. Bryan Ferry might strive for this forties' decadent look but underneath everyone knows he's really a scruffy art student. But with these guys – they would actually look weird in a pair of jeans. Since it was dark on stage and we couldn't see what they looked like they showed slides of themselves wearing bow ties and looking blank. Their music was blank too. The electronic melodies flowed as slowly as a piece of garbage floating down the polluted Rhine.'

'In Germany we were not very successful,' says Wolfgang. 'We had incredibly bad reviews in the papers. They called us *verrückte Knöpfchendreher* [mad knob-twirlers], crazy, electronic dolls, emotionless, cold puppets. "This should be the future? Ha-ha" [sarcastically]. "Let us see where they are in two years!" ... and so on.'

It was clear that Kraftwerk were largely unintelligible to those reared on the politics of the counterculture, the longhairs now into their thirties, as well as the mid-twenties writers who expected their rock stars to look like Robert Plant or Roger Daltrey. However, for a new breed of teenager just waiting for an excuse to lop off their locks, bin the flares and throw away the plectrum and the drumstick, Kraftwerk were a message from and to another world. 'We're not trying to create some kind of safe, "Baby I love you" kind of atmosphere, but to put some realism into it,' said Ralf. Of their onstage presence, he would say, 'The attitude of the player is a non-physical one. Our drummers don't sweat. So they are like us. They are not subhumans doing the dirty work. They are like computer programmers.'

In a 1975 interview with *Triad* magazine, the interviewer then presciently turns their attention to the importance of dance in their music. Ralf answers first: 'Yes, in Germany some modern ballet companies have used our music to create their own versions of ballet for this music.' Then Florian adds, 'The choreography was like a computer dance, like robot dance. Very mechanical in its movement on stage.' Ralf expands, 'We also kind of dance when we perform. It's not that we actually move our bodies but it's this awareness of your whole body. You feel like a dancer.' Florian embellishes: 'Your brain is dancing. The electronics are dancing around in the speakers,' and Ralf concludes with an overall statement of the band's mission statement, the *Gesamtkunstwerk*: 'We've had this idea for a long time

rl Bartos, Ralf Hütter, Wolfgang Fleur and Florian Schneider: the classic line-up of Kraftwerk, urbane and elegant, photographed by ymour Stein, 1975. MICHAEL OCHS ARCHIVES/GETTY IMAGES

Kraftwerk as a trio: Michael Rother with Kraftwerk, Germany, 1971. ELLEN POPPINGA · K & K/REDFERNS

Florian Schneider from Kraftwerk, Germany, 1971. ELLEN POPPINGA · K & K/REDFERNS

Klaus Dinger, soon to depart with Rother to form Neu! on stage, Germany, 1971. ELLEN POPPINGA · K & K/REDFERNS

raftwerk promote *Radio-Activity* in the control room of a nuclear power plant, 1975.

ıe early 1971 line-up of Kraftwerk: Houschäng Néjadepour, Klaus Dinger, Florian Schneider and Eberahrd Kranemann.
ERHARD KRANEMANN

KRAFTWERK

Öffnungszeiten der Kasse:
werktags 11 - 13 Uhr, außerdem
montags und donnerstags 17 -
19 Uhr sowie 1 Stunde vor Ver-
anstaltungsbeginn

Montag, 15. Februar 1971 - 20.15 Uhr - Kleiner Saal

FLORIAN SCHNEIDER-ESLEBEN	- Flöte
PETER A. SCHMIDT	- Schlagzeug
EBERHARD KRANEMANN	- Bass
HOUSCHÄNG NEJADEPOUR	- Gitarre

Kölner Stadtanzeiger vom 12. 12. 1970: "Die gesamte überschau-
bare Rock-Szene von hier bis San Franzisco bietet zu der eigen-
artigen Musik dieses Düsseldorf-Krefelder Trios keinen Vergleich
an."

Kölnische Rundschau: "Bestes Beispiel für die Existenz der neuen
deutschen Pop-Avantgarde war die Düsseldorfer Gruppe Kraftwerk,
deren "musikalische Energien im Spannungsfeld von Rock und Elek-
tronik wirksam werden".

Kartenpreise an der FORUM-Kasse: DM 5,--
                                DM 3,50 Schüler u. Studenten

| Houschäng Nejadepour | Klaus Dinger | Florian Schneider – Esleben | Eberhard Kranema |
| electric guitar | drums | electric flute
electric violin | bass
electric cello
hawaiian guitar |

KRAFTWERK

in der

W E R K K U N S T S C H U L E

Krefeld   Petersstraße

Mittwoch 17. Februar 1971 20.00 Uhr   Eintritt : DM 3,-

Promotional posters from early 1971 – the band without Ralf Hütter. (Eberhard Kranemann)

alf and Florian, 1973 MICHAEL OCHS ARCHIVES/GETTY IMAGES

e pre-all-electronic Kraftwerk; Florian on the flute at the Forum, Leverkusen, February 1971. EBERHARD KRANEMANN

From the art work for *Trans-Europe Express*: the 'electronic quartet'. MICHAEL OCHS ARCHIVES/GETTY IMAGES

Rebecca Allen and Karl's head share an intimate moment. COURTESY REBECCA ALLEN

Rebecca Allen gives Wolfgang's robot head a quick cuddle. COURTESY REBECCA ALLEN

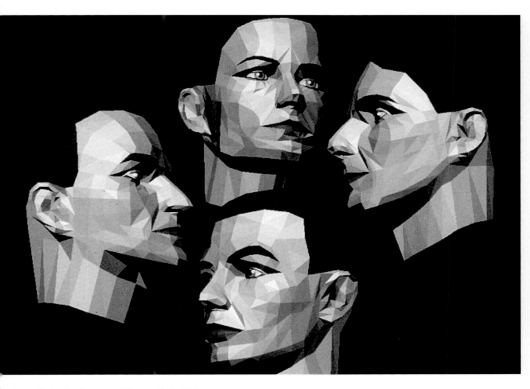

The iconic design for the cover of *Electric Café*, 1986. COURTESY REBECCA ALLEN

All smiles: mid-Seventies Kraftwerk in the King Klang Studio. MICHAEL OCHS ARCHIVES/GETTY IMAGES

but it has only been in the past year that we've been able to create what we feel is a loudspeaker orchestra. This is what we consider Kraftwerk to be, a non-acoustic electronic loudspeaker orchestra. The whole thing is one instrument. We play mixers, we play tapes, we play phasers, we play the whole apparatus of Kraftwerk. That's the instrument. Including the lights and the atmosphere.'

But the key to the hostility meted out was the assertion that Kraftwerk somehow made a form of un-music; that machine music was a confidence trick, almost on a par with the greater sin of 'not playing on your own records'. It was putting 'real' musicians out of work. Music made on the synthesizer was a debased form of music which anyone could do. No musical skill was required. Underlying the critique was possibly also a form of xenophobia. Synth music wasn't British and was, therefore, a harbinger of some sort of European takeover. 'All these impulses come from Germany. It is not British. We copied British pop and American pop for 20 years,' says Wolfgang Flür. 'We loved that because we said this is the future and we adapted it, and we came with the synthesizers in Germany. America had the instruments, but they didn't make interesting music with them.'

3.3 Radio-therapy

'Autobahn' had surprised its creators. At no stage during the making of the LP had Kraftwerk envisaged that their 22-minute long title track would or even could be edited to become a three-and-a-half-minute pop hit. 'Autobahn' was the first Kraftwerk song to have lyrics; now, on the next album, Kraftwerk became writers of text. The album itself would be the first of five to feature the iconic line-up of Schneider/Hütter/Bartos/Flür. The new work would be written and recorded in a matter of months during the summer of 1975, and released that October on EMI in Europe (through Kraftwerk's vanity label, Kling Klang) and Capitol in the USA. All songs would be composed by Ralf and Florian although, as on *Kraftwerk*, Emil Schult would make an important contribution as lyricist. Their new record would be thematically their most coherent yet, a set of short songs and instrumentals inspired by an unusual source.

On their recent tour, Ralf and Florian had been leafing through an American music trade magazine. One section detailed the movers and shakers in the *Billboard* charts, and included in this section were songs most played on the radio. The section was called 'Radio Activity'. Inspired by the name, they began writing a selection of songs which would be thematically linked around radio, radio wave, and communication. The album moves seamlessly through, songs dissolve into curious interludes, announcements, the sound of static, silence, and the transistor dial being moved from station to station. As a piece, it works completely.

The title track, re-recorded in 1991 with a very different lyric, was originally beguiling, nostalgic and indeterminate. It opens with the quickening pulse of the minute-long 'Geiger Counter'. The song, now detected, moves initially with the same time signature, Morse code punching out the band's name, and then a choir effect courtesy of one of their newly-bought toys, the Vako Orchestron, and an ominous Minimoog beat. Then Ralf's fragile though unique delivery: 'Radioactivity/ Is in the air for you and me/Radioactivity/ Discovered by Madame Curie[*]/Radioactivity/Tune in to the melody.' The song refers *both* to radioactivity, the potentially highly dangerous substance[†], and to radio-activity, the act of listening to recorded sound and the physical sending of radio waves. Both are in 'the air for you and me'.

The title track has gone on to be the highpoint of the Kraftwerk live show. But today it is performed in a very different version. According to John Foxx, the US critical reception of 'Radio-Activity' 'almost wrecked them in America. I understand they fell afoul of an intense, anti-nuclear climate of opinion at one point, with much fierce criticism for appearing to be pro-nuclear. I thought this was interesting, because the song is actually as neutral as a Warhol statement, as all their songs tend to be. Yet they seemed rattled by the reception, because they have since made it almost painfully clear

---

[*] Radioactivity was, in fact, discovered in 1896 by the French scientist Henri Becquerel. Marie Curie coined the term 'radioactivity', developed the theory of radioactivity, and discovered two elements, polonium and radium.

[†] 'Radioactivity is the process whereby unstable atomic nuclei release energetic subatomic particles. The word radioactivity is also used to refer to the subatomic particles themselves. This phenomenon is observed in the heavy elements, like uranium, and unstable isotopes, like carbon-14.' Source: http://www.wisegeek.com/what-is-radioactivity.htm

that their position is the opposite of pro-nuclear [1991's remake of the song contained a new intro, 'Sellafield 2']. That was the only time they appeared to bend a knee to popular opinion.'

'The original idea for the concept came from the *Billboard* charts where there is a column "Radioactivity" i.e. radio play... In 1975 I had no idea what an atomic power plant was all about,' says Karl Bartos. 'They (our record company) sent us into a real *Atomkraftwerk* (nuclear power plant) for silly promo pics! During the shooting I seem to remember that we suddenly had strange feelings and I think it was Florian who said, "We can't do this any more; we've gotta get out of here." The feelings became so strange during the session that we had to leave. The lyrics, ambivalent in 1975, were changed to 'Stop! Radio-Activity' on *The Mix* in 1991.' Indeed, the photographs of the band to promote the record tended to trivialise the music. Arguably, it is the last time that Kraftwerk would bow to record label pressure. The four are photographed in white protective gear, Bartos stern, Ralf and Florian bemused, Wolfgang, ludicrously, in shades, all four wearing protective anti-radiation bags over their shoes.

The British painter David Hockney once said, 'People who understand music, understand silence,' and the LP is full of moments when the music drifts to almost nothing, or is slowed so that the spaces between beats are exaggerated. *Radio-Activity* is sonically muted, at times fragile and beautiful, Ralf's vocal uncertain yet magical. The album delights in wordplay and allusion. One cannot help but chuckle at a German band that had the cleverness to entitle a track, 'Ohm Sweet Ohm'. 'Radioland' possesses one of the slowest time signatures in modern pop, overlaid by Moog synth in a way which would bring to mind Ultravox's huge single 'Vienna' five years later. Ralf and Florian sing alternate lines over a mournful melody: 'Turn the dials with your hand/Till you find the short wave band,' before a vocal so heavily vocodorised as to sound totally non-human: 'Electronic music sounds from Radioland.' *Pitchfork* effused: '*Radio-Activity*, a sometimes-overlooked record on par with any of the band's seventies masterpieces, is filled with deeply emotional vocals, both cleanly recorded and warped into dazzling shapes,' and went on, 'The breath-taking "Radioland" shows the full range. A shimmering synth drone and steady drum pulse create a drifting, ethereal quality, and then Ralf Hütter's flat, half-spoken lead vocal sets up a feeling of icy loneliness. When the static-riddled vocoder kicks in about two minutes in, it's like a dial cranked suddenly to the right, ratcheting up the feeling of both loneliness and wonder. The effect is shattering.'

When 'Radioland' links into the fast-tempoed 'Airwaves', the mood changes to one of wonder at the achievement of modern communication: '*Wenn Wellen schwingen/Ferne Stimmen singen*' (When airwaves swing/Distant voices sing'). This sense of wonder at modern, everyday technology was unique within popular music. For Kraftwerk, the everyday was an endless source of inspiration.

After a musical intermission, and a piece of *musique concrète* with the cross-talk of radio news comes the vocodorised 'The Voice Of Energy', an electrical generator brought to life that speaks to us: '*Ich bin Ihr Diener und Ihr Herr zugleich/Deshalb hütet mich gut Mich/Mich, den Genius der Energie den Genius der Energie*' ('I am your servant and lord at the same time/Therefore guard me well/ Me, the Genius of Energy'). There is something simultaneously comical and threatening about the anthropomorphism in 'The Voice Of Energy', electricity given a voice, inanimate objects shown to have feelings. This is the start of Kraftwerk's fixation with the boundaries between the human and the non-human, between flesh and bone and diodes and wires. 'Antenna' is the closest thing to pop on the LP, but it's still very odd. Ralf's spooked vocal, processed with an analogue delay, similar to the tape delay used in early rock- 'n'-roll vocals, depicts not emotional but electronic connection: 'I'm the Antenna/Catching vibration/You're the transmitter/Give information!'

'Radio Stars' is not, as one might anticipate, about pop music at all, but is the LP's centrepiece of weirdness. Less a song, more a sound collage, it recreates the noise of pulsars and quasars from deep space with an insistent synth pulse, whilst Florian repeats the word 'Stern' ('Star') in a sonic mantra. Then comes 'Uranium', one of the signifiers of radioactive decay. The Mellotron-like wash or choral sound courtesy of the Vako Orchestron is again deployed to eerie effect. The sound would appear again, either copied or sampled, much later in New Order's 'Blue Monday'.

Following this highpoint of abstraction, the penultimate track, 'Transistor', has a stately, classical flow, and predicts the next album's 'Europe Endless', before we come to the end, 'Ohm Sweet

Ohm'. Its quaint melody begins at a snail's pace, as if played on a Stylophone by a five year old, before building, quickening, with a stately grace. So ends this unique, ground-breaking album, a complete sonic adventure in a world of its own, a paean to the beauty of transistorised melody and the wonder of decaying particles.

3.4 'My Eureka Moment'

It is September 11, 1975 and 16-year-old Andy McCluskey's world is about to change. Kraftwerk have come to town. The Empire Theatre, Liverpool, was the sixth concert on their UK tour to promote the soon-to-be-released *Radio-Activity* LP. A neoclassical building built in 1925, it had staged shows by the Beatles, Judy Garland, Laurel & Hardy, Bing Crosby, Julie Andrews, not forgetting Roy Rogers & Trigger. But never had the theatre witnessed anything quite like this. And for some, it wasn't to their liking.

'The place must have been a quarter full,' remembers Andy. 'The theatre holds 2,300, and I would guess that downstairs was half empty, and I imagine in the balcony there was barely anyone in. In fact there was a large row of girls a few rows in front of me who half-way through "Autobahn" kind of said, "Why has this gone on for so long? I thought it was only supposed to be three minutes" – they got up and walked out!'

But Andy was transfixed: 'Basically the day that I went to see them play in September 1975 and sat in seat Q36 was my eureka moment, my road to Damascus moment, the first day of the rest of my life. Not only did they sound totally different, but they themselves looked and dressed so completely differently to all other musicians. To see them on stage in '75 at the height of long hair, lead guitar solo, flared denim-wearing grubby rockers; these guys came out in suits with ties, short hair, two of them playing what looked like tea-trolley trays with electronic knitting needles, their name in neon and projections behind them. Even in those early days it was a multi-media show, but rock 'n' roll it was not.'

Three days later, Malcolm Garrett saw Kraftwerk play the Free Trade Hall in Manchester. 'It was amazing. It was just the four guys on stage. I don't remember any projections, any visuals, but there might have been some. The back of the stage they had a semi-circle of florescent lights which were in a rainbow pattern at floor level, the four guys in the classic line-up, with the two drummers in the middle facing the audience and Ralf and Florian, stage left and stage right facing in on the stage, and each of them with his neon name in front of them. In my memory, they just played in darkness apart from these lights.'

So much has been made of defining concerts in British pop music, concerts which stopped people in their tracks, and made them want to be rock stars themselves. The number of people who claim to have seen the Sex Pistols' *Anarchy* tour must now be in the millions, whilst the Stone Roses' Spike Island gig of 1990 seems to have attracted half the adult population of Northern England and a good proportion of their children as well. Yet this, Kraftwerk's at times sparsely attended first UK tour, converted, either through direct contact or by the hubbub and chatter which ensued, a significant proportion of aspiring young musicians to the joys of all things electronic. Seen from the perspective of today, with rock and alternative music so marginalised and generally unloved, and with so few worthwhile new rock bands on the touring circuit, one could make a claim that the almost contemporaneous incendiary appearance of the Sex Pistols in 1976, or the much later Madchester love-in of 1990, ultimately lead to a dead end.

The set list for the tour included two new songs, yet to be recorded. 'Showroom Dummies' showed off the band's deadpan humour – a song written in response to critics who chided Kraftwerk for their stationary act. Included too was a very early version of the piece which would provide the title to their next LP, 'Trans-Europe Express'. The tour would also debut a significant new piece of musical kit, the Synthanorma Sequencer, designed in Bonn by Hajo Wiechers. Difficult to keep from going in and out of time, it was, nevertheless, an essential new component of Kraftwerk's sound.

Another odd feature of the performance was Wolfgang's *Lichtschranke* [light barrier], constructed in cube form out of metal. This was an early example of the same mechanism now used to detect moving objects, such as intruders, or in the design of doors that open automatically as a person approaches. This photocell design was here constructed so that Wolfgang, by cutting through the light beam with various hand gestures, could play various electronic drums. Lower frequencies played the bass drum, higher, the snare. 'Nobody got it,' remarks Karl Bartos. 'It was way ahead of its time, and also we only used it on a few gigs as it didn't work, it was unreliable!'

Wolfgang himself found his role in the band to be limited at this time. Additionally, he found the mood of the *Radio-Activity* album itself too downbeat. 'For my part it was too melancholic. I was not so happy with the rhythms I had to play. I came in to the studio, and the lyrics and melodies were already there. The little part which I played in that cube, in that frame, with the light cells, without sticks, was the most important and difficult thing to manage.' But it was this very sense of melancholy that hooked people and drew them in to Kraftwerk's world.

'*Radio-Activity* was *the* album,' enthuses Andy McCluskey. 'We liked *Autobahn*, but *Radio-Activity* was our bible. That was the one that me and Paul [Humphreys, co-founder of OMD] listened to for two years non-stop. The charm of Kraftwerk was that it had a melancholy to it. It had a tension created by the lyrics, those beautiful choir sounds that they would use and the melodies. Even Ralf's vocal deliveries sometimes had a naïve charm to them.'

'The LP has a musty scent of Old Europe,' writes *Uncut*'s David Cavanagh, 'and it retains a blood-chilling, Wagnerian quality even now.'

The synth Futurists, Ultravox, OMD, Human League [Mark 1], Visage, John Foxx and Gary Numan, would all, to a greater or lesser degree, look to an untrammelled Europeanism as the well-spring for a new direction which was elegant yet darkly emotive. Wolfgang Flür: 'The British jumped on that train and we had that new wave of synth acts suddenly coming up after our *Radio-Activity* tour. There were so many groups that saw us and they threw away their guitars and went out and bought synthesizers the next day,' says Wolfgang, with a hint of over-simplification but more than a grain of truth.

Despite *Radio-Activity*'s obvious impact, it had sold comparatively poorly in the territories which had taken *Autobahn* to their hearts. In Germany, the album reached number 22. In the USA it peaked at number 140, and in the UK it appears not to have charted at all. However, the album was huge in France, reaching number one and receiving a gold record for sales of 100,000 units, along with *Autobahn*, in 1977.

3.5 'Tomorrow Belongs To Those Who Can Hear It Coming'*

It wasn't just young would-be musicians who were listening either. The old guard were listening too. In 1975, modern music's most important icon, David Bowie, was listening hard to Kraftwerk. Receiving an endorsement from Bowie, at the time the most innovative and critically lauded rock star on the planet, was a big deal. It's hard now to imagine how influential David Bowie was in the seventies and early eighties. Far and away the most sought after interviewee by the UK music press, his every move was scrutinised, his every word picked over by an adoring audience.

Not that 1975 was personally a good year for Bowie. Commercially, he had never been more popular. 'Fame', an unlikely collaboration with John Lennon, became his first US number one, and a re-released 'Space Oddity' from 1969 would top the UK charts later that autumn. But physically and emotionally, Bowie was a man of shellac, ready to shatter into pieces, addicted to cocaine and obsessed with the occult. However, amongst the non-sequiturs and ridiculous assertions in his interviews, Bowie was, once again, picking up on a massive shift within modern music. He felt that rock, as a statement, was over. His music of the time, dubbed by its creator 'plastic soul', was his first attempt to break free from rock cliché. His second attempt, more fully realised, and much more artistically successful, would be just around the corner. 'Rock 'n' roll certainly hasn't fulfilled its original promise,' he told Anthony O'Grady in August of that year. 'The original aim of rock 'n' roll when it first came out was to establish an alternative media speak voice for people who had neither the power nor advantage to infiltrate any other media or carry any weight, and cornily enough, people really needed rock 'n' roll. And what we said was that we were only using rock 'n' roll to express our vehement arguments against the conditions we find ourselves in, and we promise that we will do something to change the world from how it was. We will use

---

* Strapline used to promote Bowie's "*Heroes*" album in 1977. There is also a German echo. 'Tomorrow Belongs To Me', written by John Kander and Fred Ebb for the stage show *Cabaret*, was imported into the film version where, chillingly, the families gathered around their lunch tables pick up the song in adulation of the Nazi ideal.

rock 'n' roll as a springboard.' Bowie continues: 'But it's just become one more whirling deity, right? Going round that never-decreasing circle. And rock 'n' roll is dead ... It's a toothless old woman. It's really embarrassing.'

Bowie picked up on the ennui that many felt at the time. Glam rock was over, and there seemed nothing new to replace it with. One solution came from punk. But Bowie's solution was to look not to New York's CBGBs or to Malcolm McLaren's Sex fashion emporium, but to Continental Europe, and to Germany. The first inkling of Bowie's new direction, at first a powerful mixture of hard, neurotic funk with brash synthesizers, came in January 1976. The title track to his *Station To Station* album began not with a piano chord progression (as had *Hunky Dory*), a drum figure (*Ziggy Stardust*), a power chord (*Aladdin Sane*), a theatrical canine yelp (*Diamond Dogs*) or a swinging Latino drum beat (*Young Americans*), but with a carefully faded-in wash of white noise which ran from speaker to speaker. The listener was truly ambushed. This was not rock music; this was not pop music. The Doppler effect of a speeding train gave way to a slow, mesmeric pulse, an incantation, a spell as a disturbing refrain repeated with a demonic intensity. Bowie's vocal, when indeed it came – but not until a third of the way through this nine-minute experimental piece – was now so excessively overwrought as to remind us not of rock at all, but of theatre, of electro-cabaret.

Paul Buckmaster recalls Bowie playing him Kraftwerk's music in LA when the two were working on the soundtrack to the Nic Roeg film *The Man Who Fell To Earth* in the late autumn of 1975: 'We listened a lot to the Kraftwerk albums, *Autobahn* and *Radio-Activity*. We also listened to some classical stuff, including Richard Strauss (not *Also Sprach Zarathustra!*).' 'I was fascinated and tickled and amused by them,' continues Buckmaster. 'We both enjoyed their records very much indeed. We kind of took them seriously, but we kind of laughed as well. Not at it, but because the music had a kind of innocent quality which was very fetching, and a deadpan humour as well.'

Bowie's 1976 *Station To Station* tour confirmed the Europeanisation of his muse. Known by fans as the 'White Light' tour, Bowie lit the stage in varying intensities of white light. Bowie himself was dressed in austere monochrome, the only flash of colour his swept back red hair and a glimpse of the pale blue packet of

French Gitanes cigarettes that he kept in the pocket of his black waistcoat. 'The staging of the performance was inspired,' wrote Michael Watts in *Melody Maker*. 'Using an overhead bank of neon lights, and the auxiliary power of Klieg, he exposed the stage in a brilliant glare of black and white expressionism that emphasised the harshness of the music and reflected upon his own image as a white-shirted, black-suited creature of Herr Ishyvoo's cabaret. It was, I think, the most imaginative lighting of a rock concert I have ever seen.'

The support slot for the tour had been offered to, and turned down by, Kraftwerk, thus beginning a pattern of saying 'No' which has continued to this day. Kraftwerk, as we will see, have said no to so many ideas, to so many people, and for so long, that rejection, dismissal and moving forward only through a process of rejection is without question their guiding philosophy. Wolfgang Flür: 'It is easy to understand why they turned him down. It is the same policy that they use today, to be absolutely on their own. No mixing with enemy cultures; not "enemy", but *foreign* cultures. Nothing completely influenced by other music styles, cultures, instruments, sounds or countries ... We had to be on our own, self-referential. That was their decision.' Kraftwerk had missed the chance of playing to hundreds of thousands of fans in Europe and America. It would, in all probability, have broken Kraftwerk globally.

Bowie, in effect, still used Kraftwerk as tour support. As the crowds entered the arenas – among them, in Detroit, on March 1, 1976, a 17-year-old Michigan girl called Madonna Louise Ciccone – selections from their latest record, *Radio-Activity*, were played at concert-level volume to accompany Luis Bunuel's silent twenties classic film, *Un Chien Andalou*, which was projected on to a screen at the rear of the stage. The sight of a scalpel slicing through an eyeball, accompanied by the eerie new music from West Germany, provided exactly the right sort of feelings of dissociation in the audience before Bowie's (literally and aesthetically) blinding performance.

It's hard to decide which influenced Madonna more: Bowie's stunningly visual show or the unrelenting rhythmic pulse of Kraftwerk's introductory music. Either way, both would become key elements in the work of the most commercially successful female singer of all time.

3.6 'Five-Minute Standing Ovation'

Bowie and Iggy Pop toured America and Europe in the spring of 1976, and Bowie introduced Kraftwerk and a very Kraftwerkian song to his friend. 'The big one for me was *Radio-Activity*,' remembers Iggy Pop of his 28-year-old self (then an almost unthinkably old age for a rock star to be). 'I would go to sleep at night listening to "Geiger Counter".' Bowie had written a new song, 'Calling Sister Midnight' which, with typical Bowie largesse, he gave to Iggy. Perhaps more than any of the other songs Bowie was writing at the time, this was the one most influenced by Kraftwerk – it was slow, jarring, a mix of the freedom of funk and the robotic discipline of the synth. 'Sound as texture, rather than sound as music. Producing noise records seems pretty logical to me,' Bowie told *Rolling Stone*. 'My favourite group is a German band called Kraftwerk – it plays noise music to "increase productivity". I like that idea, if you have to play music.'

Maxime Schmidt, the manager of Kraftwerk's French record label and friend of the band, recalled one oft-quoted meeting between Ralf and Florian and Bowie and Iggy: 'It was in Paris, after one of Bowie's concerts,' he told writer Pascal Bussy. 'He had hired the L'Ange Bleu nightclub on the Champs-Elysées for a private party. When we arrived there was Bowie, Iggy Pop and their court, and when Ralf and Florian walked in they received a five-minute standing ovation. Iggy Pop was gazing devotedly at them, he completely adored them. Both he and Bowie were transfixed, Bowie was saying to Iggy Pop, 'Look how they are, they are fantastic!"'

Not that the band were unappreciative of Bowie's support. 'That was very important for us, because it linked what we were doing with the rock mainstream,' said Ralf in 1991. 'Bowie used to tell everyone that we were his favourite group, and in the mid-seventies the rock press used to hang on every word from his mouth like tablets of stone. We met him when he played Düsseldorf on one of his first European tours. He was travelling by Mercedes, listening to nothing but *Autobahn* all the time."

Wolfgang claims that Bowie was even keen to record with Kraftwerk. 'He was so fanatical about it, wanting to do a record with us, to co-produce with us. We should co-produce with just him [Wolfgang says this as if it was the clear message they were getting from Bowie at that time]. He wanted to produce his next album with

Kraftwerk. That was the reason that he was in Düsseldorf sometimes. I was not invited to these meetings: it was Ralf's thing, Florian's thing – they are the masters of Kraftwerk. In the end, finally, they decided against co-productions; and they have their reasons. We loved him [David Bowie], and he loved us. He is a very mild man, he is an educated man. He has a very good aura, fantastic.'

Karl Bartos, however, remembers differently: 'Yes, Hütter and Schneider did meet up with Bowie and Iggy in Düsseldorf but I can honestly say that I have no recollection that a collaboration was at any time intended, although we all worshipped Iggy Pop and David Bowie. We went to Frankfurt to see the *Station To Station* tour. It was so super-good with the wall of neon lights.'

In a 1995 interview, Bowie denied there was ever a serious intention to record with Kraftwerk. 'We met a few times socially but that was as far as it went,' he said before explaining how different his own modus operandi was to theirs: 'My attention had been swung back to Europe with the release of Kraftwerk's *Autobahn* in 1974. The preponderance of electronic instruments convinced me that this was an area that I had to investigate a little further. Much has been made of Kraftwerk's influence on our Berlin albums. Most of it lazy analyses I believe. Kraftwerk's approach to music had in itself little place in my scheme. Theirs was a controlled, robotic, extremely measured series of compositions, almost a parody of minimalism. One had the feeling that Florian and Ralf were completely in charge of their environment, and that their compositions were well prepared and honed before entering the studio. My work tended to expressionist mood pieces, the protagonist (myself) abandoning himself to the "Zeitgeist", with little or no control over his life. The music was spontaneous for the most part and created in the studio.'

And so, we don't know if there was ever a serious meeting of minds. What is known is that the Bowie camp and the Kraftwerk camp were on friendly terms. Iggy Pop was Bowie's travelling companion during the 1976 tour, and the two would tour again in early 1977, this time with Bowie playing piano in Iggy's band: 'I went shopping once for asparagus with Florian Schneider! I met the two of them, and he suggested, 'If you like, it is the asparagus season and I am going to the market to select some asparagus, would you like to come along, and I said, 'Yes, I would. We had a very nice time doing that!'

88

'I like them as people very much, Florian in particular. Very dry,' said Bowie in 1978. 'When I go to Düsseldorf they take me to cake shops, and we have huge pastries. They wear their suits. A bit like Gilbert and George, actually, God, whatever happened to those two? I used to really like them... When I came over to Europe – cause it was the first tour I ever did of Europe, the last time – I got myself a Mercedes to drive myself around in, cause I still wasn't flying at that time, and Florian saw it... He said, "What a wonderful car", and I said, "Yes, it used to belong to some Iranian prince, and he was assassinated and the car went on the market, and I got it for the tour." And Florian said, "Ja, car always lasts longer." With him it all has that edge. His whole cold emotion/warm emotion, I responded to that. Folk music of the factories.'

3.7 In Motion

Watching Can playing 'I Want More' on *Top Of The Pops* in August 1976 goes down as one of those rub-your-eyes-in-disbelief pop moments. True, Can were entitled to perform as their song was in the Top 30, but with Elton and Kiki Dee at number one, the sun shining with almost obscene vigour during the Drought Year, and Michael Holding sending English stumps clattering at the Oval, the appearance of Can, pushing 40, with their strange beats and no lead singer, on a mainstream pop programme before punk had partly democratised the show's set list, stands as a little piece of cherished pop history, two worlds colliding. Can were the first, and last, Krautrock group to appear on the show.

By the mid-seventies it wasn't just Kraftwerk who were resetting the co-ordinates of modern pop music. Can would have a massive impact on many maverick musicians. John Lydon famously wanted to join the band as lead singer. For Krautrock expert Henning Dedekind, Can were the standout group from the scene. 'Being a guitar player myself, I love Can because it's got this acid sound. This very hard and aggressive sound.'

What marked out the music of Can, Kraftwerk and, most importantly, Neu!, was the sense of a music in motion – *Motorik*. According to Henning Dedekind, the term is a combination of 'motor' and 'music'. You can hear this beat, a beat which sonically encodes a propulsion towards the future, a sensation of motion, travel and adventure, in early Kraftwerk pieces, most notably 'Ruckzuck'. The defining moment though comes with the first Neu! album in the insistent beat and jabbing guitar of 'Hallogallo', and, on *Neu 75*, 'E-Musik' and 'Hero'. Brian Eno said: 'There were three great beats in the 1970s: Fela Kuti's Afrobeat, James Brown's funk and Klaus Dinger's Neu! beat.'[*]

John Doran, writing for *The Quietus*, gives a further exegesis: '[*Motorik*] … literally means "motor skill" in German, [and] was originally coined by journalists to describe the minimal yet propulsive 4/4 beat that underpins just a small amount of the music from this time and place. However, if this non-existent genre has anything approaching a definable quality, then this beat is it. It was a hallmark of Klaus Dinger's drumming for Neu!, although he rejected the term, preferring to call the rhythm the "Apache beat". This metronome was first used in this context by Kraftwerk on tracks such as "Ruckzuck", and Can on the blistering "Mother Sky".' He continues: 'This beat was the war drum of modernity, pushing the listener forwards into the future. It is often associated with the great transport networks of Germany, the railway lines and the autobahns. In fact the rhythm even mimics that of a car speeding along the open road or a train clattering along the rails: fast, measured, travel never ending. It was the rock beat stripped back to a glittering chassis. It was the minimalist framework on which improvisation could take place.'

'Anyone who's listened past the first track of a Neu! album will know that they were nothing if not eclectic,' writes Lee Arizuno, again for *The Quietus*.[†] 'They played proto just about everything, from industrial to introspective lo-fi to straight-ahead punk to

---

* Sadly, there was no room in Professor Eno's schema for beats the general public actually listened to, such as Leicester's Showaddywaddy three-thud bass drum kick in 'Hey Rock And Roll' (1974), or the earlier football-terrace plod and call-and-response glam sing-song which was Gary Glitter's 'Rock And Roll (Parts 1&2) (1972)'!

† *The Quietus*, undoubtedly the best magazine, online or otherwise, to give Kraftwerk and their contemporaries coverage, produced a list of the definitive *Motorik* songs. This included David Bowie – 'Red Sails' (1978), Human League – 'Seconds' (1981), Ultravox – 'Dancing With Tears In My Eyes' (1984), The Fall – 'Touch Sensitive' (1999) and The Horrors – 'Sea Within A Sea' (2009)

ambient electronica. But playing the bass drum in the way a learner drummer would the hi-hat (eight beats to the bar) was their rhythmic ident: pummelling and relentless, yet precise and energising, what could at first sound almost like mockery of rudimentary trad-rock drumming turned out to be an inversion that helped found a new modernity in pop.'

Michael Rother has no clear view on where the term *Motorik* came from: 'I can't remember when it first turned up. It wasn't used by Klaus. It wasn't used by me. Actually, we hardly ever used any words to explain the music. I never discussed this with Florian Schneider or with Klaus or with my Harmonia colleagues. It was just obvious. Everybody was trying to create something that was not an echo of somebody else's ideas. I still feel this amazement when I listen to "Hallogallo". How it turned out, that was the result of the quality, I guess, of course, of the three individuals. You shouldn't forget Conny Plank's contribution, and also of some lucky circumstances, and, you know, the magic of the moment that was with us.'

With all the theorising, it may come as something of a shock to discover that the origins of the beat may have rather more quotidian origins. According to Michael Rother, during his time in Kraftwerk, their favourite pastime was playing football. 'I'm not sure that we thought it had anything to do with transport. I remember that Klaus and I never really talked a lot about theories; we just both really enjoyed playing soccer. You know football, running up and down and everything. We even had a very good team with me and Klaus and Florian [Schneider, Kraftwerk] – he could run very fast. I remember on one tour there were some British bands there at a festival and we met them on the field. I remember we played against Family [UK hippy blues rock band from Leicester] at one festival. We all loved to run fast and this feeling about running fast and fast movement, forward movement, rushing forwards that was something that we all had in common and the joy of fast movement is what or part of what we were trying to express in Neu!' In this respect Rother's love of Little Richard was certainly an influence, though a prime impulse for the creation of one of the most mythic beats in rock history could have been a West Germany versus England re-run of the 1966 World Cup Final, Krautrock versus Blues Rock, a precursor to Monty Python's *The Philosophers' Football Match* of 1972, filmed at the Sechzger Stadion in Munich, pitting the likes of Archimedes and Socrates against Nietzsche and Kant. And, in a strange way, Kraftwerk versus Family was some sort of philosophical meeting of two very different schools of thought.

Unlike Ralf and Florian, who were temperamentally close, Michael Rother and Klaus Dinger were polar opposites, providing a necessary if ultimately destructive edge to their music. As David Bowie put it, '[Neu! were] Kraftwerk's wayward, anarchistic brothers.' Wolfgang Flür: 'Dinger was such a crazy personality. He was rather malicious. I was afraid of this person. He could change his mood in an instant. He was unreliable. More than that. He could have been on drugs – heavy drugs – already, at that time. That may be the only way to explain it. I didn't want to be near such a person. But there was no problem, because I never worked with him.'

'To put Neu! into words,' says Iggy Pop, 'the drummer was playing in a way that, when you listen to it, allowed your thoughts to flow, allowed emotions to come from within, and occupy the active parts of your mind, I thought. It allowed beauty to get there. The guy had somehow found a way to free himself from the tyranny of stupid blues, rock, of all conventions that I had ever heard of. Some sort of pastoral pyschedelicism.'

Motion, speed, flow. These were already ideas being spoken about and worked on by contemporary German artists. For Kraftwerk's next sonic adventure, they would provide us with the definitive statement on getting from A to B. And the experiments took place in their Kling Klang Studio in Düsseldorf.

3.8 Inside The Musical Laboratory

Seldom has a locus in popular music history been granted such iconic status as the band's Kling Klang Studio situated in a Fifties building at Mintropstrasse 16 near the main railway station in Düsseldorf. Unlike, say, the Abbey Road studio in London, it's a pretty unprepossessing building in a rather faceless and slightly rundown area. There are a few café bars. A sex shop serves as a reminder that we are close to the red-light district.

Kling Klang has become akin to a mythic space, representing something much greater than is obvious to the eye. In the same way that Liverpool Football Club's boot room, a small, cramped space, where the Liverpool management team would discuss tactics and invite opposition managers over to post-match inquests, became totemic of a dynasty of footballing genius, with each manager judged by his adherence to the principles of the boot room tradition, so Kling Klang, itself no more than a functional set of buildings in a not-terribly nice area of a middle-sized German city, became something much more than a recording studio. It became the site not only of greatness, but of some sort of pop alchemic power, and the source of endless rumours and conjecture.

It has been reported that girlfriends were banned from visiting Kling Klang. In fact, this is not so. Although visits were not that common, girlfriends did hang out. However, Kling Klang was primarily a studio and place of work. 'It was like an English gentleman's club, but with a German twist!' says Karl.

According to Ralf, Kling Klang ran along rigid lines. 'Our daily schedule of work lasts some 8–10 hours in the studio. We don't regard ourselves just as musicians but as *Musik-Arbeiter* (musical workers), and we designed and built up our complete portable studio set that includes the stage backdrops, curtains, lighting, frames, staging and stereo PA system as well as the instrument equipment stands. Multi-wired cable looms are used for quick dismantling of each section of the movable instrument frames. The players stand on metal box staging that hides the mass of wiring. Fortunately, we are all about the same stature, so each of the four players' sections of the instrument gear is built to be suitable for any of us. All the instrument racks are standard 19″ width and pack away into cases for transit.'

Ralf revealed in 1981: 'During the week, we work from 5 p.m. until 1 or 2 at night. During other times in the day we do the administration for Kraftwerk and liaise with our engineers and visitors.' Ralf refers to the studio as his 'electronic garden'.

However, according to Wolfgang, the working pattern at the studio was such that, by the late-seventies, the band members would meet up at Kling Klang around eight in the evening. 'We were no *Arbeiter* [workers],' Wolfgang maintains. 'It's so nice to build that picture for the people, you know. We had a lot of hobbies and interests besides that. I would have much preferred all the time to have had meetings in the day, because it was like a job for me. I wanted to be at home in the evening: I had a girlfriend, and other interests, so it was not necessary. The others, especially Ralf, used to sleep until noon or early afternoon.'

93

Wolfgang provides us with a description of the layout of the studio. 'As you go in, on the left, there was a work room, a workshop, where I worked on re-furbishing the instruments, to make them look like metal and so on. And you pass through that work room, and then there were two intermediate rooms, a toilet and a little kitchen with a sink and two hot plates. From that kitchen you could go up to another little floor; and then there was a small hall and a huge living room. There was a big couch and a big TV, and a big bookcase. We put in carpets, dark grey and black and white. Those were our colours, just white, black, and grey – like the whole studio. The recording studio was on the left as you entered the main entrance towards the back yard of the house. The *Elektro-Müller* company was on the first floor and we used the same stair-well.'

Work would often begin after time spent watching TV, and would go on into the night, often into the small hours. Meals were taken out in the local restaurants. Coffee was mandatory. 'We all drank coffee; Ralf a bit more than the others,' says Wolfgang. 'Everyone loves coffee.' There were the occasional sweet treats. 'We had some ice cream sometimes. Sometimes Florian would put quark, cream and frozen raspberries into a bowl, with sugar and vanilla. He whipped it and put it into the fridge. It was a fantastic dessert.'

So, Kling Klang, although a place of work, was also somewhere four twenty-something men could hang out. A stylish bachelor pad it perhaps wasn't, but the atmosphere was, obviously, male, convivial.

Kling Klang was integral to Kraftwerk. It provided a space, outside the mainstream music industry, which was theirs and theirs alone. As such, Kraftwerk were highly unusual. Not for them the globe-trotting recording sprees of many Anglo-American musicians keen to try out new studios, new cities or simply get away from the domesticity of home. Every part of the creative process would be dealt with 'in-house' with as little as possible outside interference in the quest to provide the listener with a pure, unmediated music. 'We have always been producing our own records, writing our own compositions, and also the words. We have established since 1970 our studio,' said Ralf. 'First we started out with some old cassette recorders and some old speaker cabinets and from there over the years, we have been building from there. We call our studio also some kind of electronic garden, where we have some kind of biological biofeedback with the machines. And through the time they have been growing and getting more and more complex and been growing different stages, and we have since we started out, complete control over all our material. In Germany we have our own record label, Kling Klang Records, and this is very important politically, we are completely anarchic and have total control over what we do. But we started out very basic. And I think it's just, if you don't let yourself be confused over the mechanisms of today's society, then you can have some really very creative aspects to your life, and this was really what we set out to do, to live out our fantasies, at least try, and get those things communicated with other people.'

In many ways, Kling Klang hermetically sealed the four members of Kraftwerk off from the outside world. In the same way a writer might have a shed in the garden in which to write, or a painter a loft, Kraftwerk had an area that was virtually cut off from the 'real' world. Karl Bartos: 'We only had contact with the record companies when absolutely necessary. For years we did not even have a telephone in the studio. Later on, people could leave a message on the answering machine.'

Ralf was keen, in interviews, to stress that Kling Klang was less a traditional recording studio, and more like a musical laboratory: 'We consider ourselves not so much entertainers as scientists,' he said in 1976. 'The idea of the scientist or mad scientist finding something that is true within its definition. We work on our studio/laboratories and we find something, we put it on a tape, it is there and we present it. We find that many people like the way we work.'

Much later, when the technological possibilities at Kling Klang seemed to have become almost limitless, Ralf told *Mojo* magazine: 'We play the machines, but the machines also play us. The machines should not do only slave work, we try to treat them as colleagues so they exchange energies with us.... We feel that the synthesizer is an acoustic mirror, a brain analyser that is super-sensitive to the human element in ways previous instruments were not, so it is really better suited to expose the human psychology than the piano or guitar.'

95

In the eyes of Ralf Hütter, Kling Klang was almost alive, a complete technoid environment, a place where man and machine could become one. Their next two LPs would develop this theme to devastating effect.

VIER
EUROPA
1976 – 1977

4.1 'Sekt? Korrekt!'

AROUND 1976 and 1977 something odd happened to Kraftwerk. For a short time, and only in the area around Düsseldorf, they became celebrities. Unlikely as it may seem, they indulged in the usual rock star habits, night clubs, girls, and expensive cars – the stuff of celebrity, to be sure.

Florian bought expensive Mercedes cars in this period. Wolfgang Flür describes Florian's choice: 'It wasn't just a big Mercedes: it was *the* big Mercedes 600. Dark blue. Diplomat Blue! It was the President's car. The biggest politician in Germany, our President, drove that car. There were two versions, the normal version and the Pullman version. The Pullman version is much longer and had a special compartment inside. Florian paid DM 25,000 for a used car! There was a big dealer here in Düsseldorf, Auto Becker. It was a huge place. He had everything from small cars to luxury ones, every style, all second-hand. Florian went in with a plastic carrier bag containing DM 25,000 in cash, the proceeds from ticket sales in Germany. He put it on the counter. He had to count it .... 5, 10, 20 ... until he got to 25,000; and off he went with the car. It was huge. It could seat seven, I think, comfortably. It had air conditioning. In the seventies such cars were very expensive to drive, real petrol-guzzlers. They had a battery inside under the bonnet and two light engines. It used so much electricity for all the luxury add-ons. Everything worked without electric motors. It was powered by oil pressure and was absolutely silent. You couldn't hear any electro-motor inside. Everything went with hydraulic. When you opened a window it was almost silent. It was so strong that if you had your hand in the gap at the top of the window, it would almost cut it. It was dangerous! I drove the 600 a lot. Florian lent me the car as often as I wanted.'

Florian was, by all accounts, a very dangerous driver. 'He was rude. Not bad, rude!' remembers Wolfgang. 'He was crazy: he drove too fast, too close to the car in front. He started with a cold engine straight away. And he had to pay for it, because apart from the Pullman he bought another one, a Mercedes coupé, a 1973 280 S, an early seventies model, eight-cylinder, 300 horse-power, in concrete grey. This was an elegant car, dark grey outside, dark grey leather inside. Once, only once, we drove to Spa in Belgium for a Formula One race, just to see, just for fun. We just wanted to hear the pressure, the sound. We – Ralf and Karl and I – took Ralf's smaller car, also a luxury one, and Florian was on his own. He set off an hour before us. We were on a country road in Belgium and ahead of us we could see in the distance a big black cloud coming up. There must have been an accident, we thought. Hopefully nothing serious. As we got closer, we could see the police and the emergency vehicles and so on. We thought, "Oh no, this looks like absolute shit." You know what it was? It was Florian. His car was standing there, boot open, black smoke coming out. Florian was standing next to it talking to a policeman. We passed by, opened the window and said, "Hello, Florian! Did you start with a cold engine this morning?" He blew his motor, it was completely broken.'

The teenage Ralf Dörper remembers seeing the band around town in Düsseldorf. 'There was a sort of "pop star" period they had, quite a flamboyant lifestyle. They were quite recognisable in the middle of Düsseldorf. They had a clique. The people around them, they all looked the same, because they all dressed the same way and mostly in black. Kraftwerk always wore these sharp and tight sixties-style clothes. They weren't hippies in the way, let's say, that La Düsseldorf or even Neu! were hippies. A lot of the younger people were still walking around wearing flares, with long hair, beards and parkas and stuff. Kraftwerk simply looked "korrekt."'

German punk, as Dörper describes, was just starting in Düsseldorf. There was a scene for new music at a new club in the city, the Ratinger Hof. 'I started to go there around 1976/77. It was a place where a lot of new bands started to evolve. It was like in New York, at CBGBs. We had this place, and the Deutsch Amerikanische Freundschaft (DAF) and Liaisons Dangereuses, amongst others, evolved from there, as well as a few other bands that weren't electronic but were more or less the front-runners of punk rock and new wave in Germany. That was not far from the Düsseldorf Academy (headed by Beuys at that time). So you had a strange mixture in Ratinger Hof of artists and wild young people.' Düsseldorf was an important stopping off point for the major acts of the day such as Roxy Music and David Bowie. The city had links with style, design, and the fashion world: 'The best clubs at that time in Germany, let's say in the mid-seventies, were in Munich and Düsseldorf. Malesh was a popular club in Königsallee. The other very famous one was Sheila (later Matchmoore) in the Altstadt. Düsseldorf was about the rich and beautiful people, in a way. I think that is very important to know about that particular environment for Kraftwerk, because they used to go out, to night clubs, and this is something that is reflected in their music, I believe.'

Dörper would see Ralf relatively often, if initially only from afar. On his street was a car park which had been constructed on an old bombed-out part of the city. 'I lived on Jahnstrasse, with my parents. At that time, Ralf actually had a Bentley. At that time only very few Germans drove flashy English cars, like a Jag, a Spitfire or a Mini-Cooper, because they were so unreliable (i.e. not Volkswagens). But on the street where I lived there was a car mechanic who specialised in English cars – and they were all parked there, even Rolls-Royces

– and Hütter's Bentley – waiting to be fixed. On the block there was also a small club, in the mid-seventies. I think it was called Café TV or Peppermint; At the time I saw the 'Jungs' [the boys] quite often. They had also a long Pullman car, a stretch limo Mercedes 600. That left quite an impression on me, because I often saw the car pulling into this parking lot. There were members of Kraftwerk, their friends, and their girlfriends. The robots had very cool girlfriends – and a very cool car, which made them real pop stars in Düsseldorf. I was pretty impressed (and probably impressionable). I thought "Chapeau", this had style.'

On stage, the haircuts and clothes that Kraftwerk wore became central to their image. Karl Bartos, for one, was never completely convinced that they pulled it off: 'The initial image came from Ralf,' he told Kraftwerk biographer Pascal Bussy. 'He wanted to make it clear that Kraftwerk was different from any other group and he wanted this image of a string ensemble. I didn't like it that much; I thought I always looked like a banker.' Crucially, the members of Kraftwerk maintained the same rather dignified image when they were off duty. Ralf Dörper: 'They wore tight trousers and jackets. Even then they had connections with some people in Paris who made quite futuristic clothes. So they looked just how you imagine a pop star should look, with style. The way the girls were dressed, that was already sort of pre-new wave because of the way they walked and their attitude. There was a whole group of people who were linked to the Kraftwerk camp.'

Equally important to the Kraftwerk look, of course, were the haircuts. At the time, very few rock stars had short hair that was parted in the traditional way. Peter Gabriel, perhaps with some significance, had his hair cut comparatively short for the 1974–1975 *The Lamb Lies Down On Broadway* Genesis tour. It was as if he was rejecting the accepted images that surrounded progressive rock, a statement to his band members that he was ready to move on. Bowie too, by 1975, had relatively short hair – the wedge – which would be copied for the next 10 years and more. There was still a flamboyance to Bowie's hair, particularly in its colouring, but in early 1974 he had ditched the glam-era costumes for suits and a new style, as had Bryan Ferry, perhaps the originator of the rock star as faded Hollywood icon or world-weary playboy. By the end of 1976, many on the punk scene had converted from long hair with a centre parting to the ragged, spiky, orange cuts that would be their trademark. However, Kraftwerk were singularly different. Their hair would be elegant, yet highly conservative, a throwback to the pre-rock'n'roll era.

It should not be understated how radical this was. Kraftwerk had the sort of haircuts your bourgeois dad requested from a barber who advertised his services with a time-honoured red and white striped pole over the door of his shop. They had made the straight world hip. Overturning the notion that to dress down was to express some sort of generational displeasure, now, dressing up, and dressing smart, was the key. 'There was a very old hairdresser, Herr Rindlaub, who I think was way over 60,' says Ralf Dörper. 'He was an old, traditional guy who lived in a very small shop with his wife. Kraftwerk went there, and also some of the Ratinger Hof punk people. You got the best haircut in town. The way Kraftwerk was styled was very sixties, or even late fifties, with regard to "short back and sides". That was actually where most of the Kraftwerk guys – maybe not Wolfgang because he always had longer hair – went for their haircut. It was really funny because later on, when he got featured in the local papers, and the more trendy people came, the old guy actually charged them double because he knew they were just coming because he was in the paper!'

In Britain, the well-dressed, short-coiffured look became an almost instant hit. It didn't matter that Kraftwerk were, by and large, well-heeled. This was a look which could be instantly repeated with high street clothes. 'I was largely unaware of their social backgrounds,' Andy McCluskey remembers. 'I think in the early days, even when I became aware of it, it made absolutely no difference to me at all, because what they were doing was more important than who they were. I certainly didn't get into Kraftwerk because they were working class heroes. I wasn't looking for that in Kraftwerk, so I had no problem about them, whether they came from money or not. I rather liked the fact that they all wore suits and ties or black and that they drove around in black Mercedes. I bought into the whole lifestyle thing. I just thought it was great, even though at the time I still had an afro and dressed like fucking Tom Baker from *Doctor Who.*'

It was in the clubs, and the discos, that Kraftwerk the socialites would pick up new musical ideas. Their favourite clubs were Mora's [in the Altstadt] and later on the Malesh. Wolfgang Flür reports that he, Ralf and Florian frequented the Düsseldorf club scene but that Karl Bartos rarely joined in. 'You could mostly see Florian, Ralf and me. Karl was not much of a clubber. Sometimes he was with us, but mostly not. We drank some wine sometimes with dinner but we didn't drink alcohol just for fun. We had to drink alcohol when we were in discotheques, because you had to. It was in order: you walk in, you get your glass, being asked in a rhetorical manner: "Sekt? Korrrrrrekt!" [Champagne? Corrrrrr-rect!]* This is the thing we recorded [for the German lyrics to 'The Model']; we invited that man in our recording, the man from the Mora, the famous discotheque in Düsseldorf. The head waiter, he served everyone a glass of champagne when they came in. He asked 15 Deutschmarks for it – for the entrance and for one glass of champagne. In fact it was not genuine champagne, it was *Sekt* – sparkling white wine. These were elegant discotheques, with beautiful girls and boys, "Schickimickis"†, with their nose up in the air, and sometimes a punk from a rich family who had gone astray – a fashion-punk.'

Good-looking, highly sexualised, and with an easy charm, Wolfgang, by his own admission, was in demand and attracted women effortlessly. Not so Ralf. 'With girls it was a big problem for him; he was not much of a ladies' man. He was a lonely boy in his flat in Krefeld. He used to ask me what I would be doing at the weekend, if we could go out together, because I was very successful with the girls. Because I was very handsome in those days, he hoped that, maybe, he could get a little bit from those girls who were always around me. It was easy for me. I didn't have to do anything; the girls did it. Ralf was close to me, and sometimes it worked, although not often. I felt sorry that it didn't work out so well for him with the girls. He often seemed pretty lonely to me, and quite sad about it. He was very, very nice to me at that time, so we had a good relationship.'

One thing that was never part of Kraftwerk's lifestyle was drugs, at least not hard drugs. There would be no such health-

---

* In my interview with him, Wolfgang imitates the words, spoken as a kind of challenge, by the headwaiter, and with the heavy intonation in which it would be said. In fact Sekt is a German sparkling wine similar to champagne. As we all know, only wines from the Champagne region can actually be called as such.
† German word for someone ostentatiously trendy.

destroying substances as cocaine or heroin in the Kraftwerk camp. Another recreational 'drug' would come to dominate two members of the band later in the eighties, but more of that anon.

4.2 Cool Germania

The UK in the mid-seventies gave out confusing messages about Germany. The rise of the National Front, a neo-Nazi, whites-only political party, although deeply troubling at the time, had the paradoxical effect of inspiring the beginnings of a genuinely multicultural ethos, particularly amongst Britain's youth. The sight of white men, draped in the red, white and blue of the co-opted and corrupted Union Flag marching under slogans such as 'Defend Rights For Whites' sickened many. One response was Rock Against Racism, a multicultural and multiethnic movement, a celebration of diversity through unity. Rock, pop and punk artists joined forces with reggae from 1976 onwards to combat the threat of white supremacists.

In 1976 two major white rock stars seemingly aligned themselves with the enemy. An onstage, alcohol-fuelled rant by Eric Clapton warned that Britain had 'become overcrowded' and was in danger of becoming a 'black colony'. He is reported to have told his audience that we should 'get the foreigners out, get the wogs out, get the coons out' before repeatedly shouting the National Front slogan 'Keep Britain White'. Coming from a man steeped in the blues tradition, this was not just alarming but also idiotic.*

A more artistic, if misguided, theatricalisation of Nazism came from David Bowie, whose onstage persona at that time, The Thin White Duke, 'flashing no colour' was 'making sure, white stains'. In interviews he called Adolf Hitler 'the first rock 'n' roll star', perhaps not without a degree of accuracy in terms of the staging and magnetism of many a Nazi rally. It is now written as fact that in May 1976 at Victoria Station Bowie gave a Nazi *Sieg Heil* salute to his fans, although film footage of the incident renders the evidence

---

* Some other members of the rock aristocracy were into Nazi chic. Led Zeppelin's Jimmy Page wore jackboots and what looked like an SS hat on stage. Ex-Stooge Ron Asheton was also photographed in full Nazi regalia stamping on the blood-stained torso of Iggy Pop in 1974.

inconclusive at best and Bowie's assertion that a still photograph, which shows him stiffer of arm than common decency would dictate, merely caught him mid-wave may indeed be true.* That said, Bowie, in interviews, was certainly not helping his position: 'As I see it, I am the only alternative for the premier in England. I believe Britain could benefit from a Fascist leader. After all, Fascism is really Nationalism.' By way of excuse, too much Bolivian marching powder was later attributed by Bowie for his interest in the Far Right, along with the occult. And in no way could Bowie be deemed to be racist. His then current band included two black musicians and a Latino, whilst he would later go on to marry a Somalian supermodel of colour.

Additionally there were those who dared to see the funny side of Nazism. Monty Python placed Hitler's inner circle, including 'Mr Bimmler', 'Mr Boering' and 'Mr Ron Vibbentrop', in a Minehead bed and breakfast plotting the invasion of Stalingrad, while former Python John Cleese and Connie Booth's 'The Germans' episode of *Fawlty Towers* is famous for the lines: 'Listen, don't mention the war! I mentioned it once, but I think I got away with it, all right.' And later, when a concussed Basil takes dinner orders, he blunders on: 'So! It's all forgotten now, and let's hear no more about it. So, that's two egg mayonnaise, a prawn Goebbels, a Hermann Goering, and four Colditz salads'. Whatever the message that the sketch might have conveyed, the episode was a huge success and was even aired in Germany with subtitles. What was worrying was that many people didn't realise that Cleese and Booth were sending up British attitudes towards the war rather than Germany and the Germans, in the same way that it was also worrying that people laughed with Johnny Speight's bigot Alf Garnett in *Till Death Do Us Part*, and not at him. In 1970, Viv Stanshall from the Bonzo Dog Band and Who drummer Keith Moon were photographed together by Barrie Wentzell in full Nazi regalia for a promotional shot. Stanshall had, of course, hysterically lampooned Hitler in the 1967 send-up 'The Intro And Outro', which featured such notional

---

* Gary Numan, then Gary Webb, and a huge Bowie fan at the time, was at Victoria Station and told me, in an interview for my book on David Bowie, *Strange Fascination*, that Bowie did not give a Nazi salute. Indeed, if he had, it was not reported in any of the national or local press in the immediate aftermath of any such incident.

performers as UK Prime Minister Harold Wilson on violin, John Wayne on xylophone, and 'looking very relaxed, Adolf Hitler on vibes'. Keith Moon occasionally wore a Hitler moustache and adopted the Führer's mannerisms, but he simply liked to dress up, often also as Long John Silver or a humble vicar, and was neither a racist nor an anti-Semite. Probably the greatest rock drummer of all time, he was also, however, totally barking mad. Other Hitler impersonations from the era and a little later came from Huyton-born comedian, singer and impersonator Freddie Starr and, most surreally, by ex-Goon Spike Milligan*, whose wartime memoirs were best sellers.

There were also those who neither applauded nor mocked Nazism. Rather, they decontextualized it, detached it from its historical significance, and used it merely for its shock value. Driven in part by the sale of bondage, leather and taboo items in Malcolm McLaren and Vivienne Westwood's Sex shop in London, some of the original punks, including Jordan and Siouxsie Sioux, wore swastikas as a blank symbol of hatred and separation, although it must be said that the original punk T-shirts were just as likely to feature other images of provocation such as Marx, anarchists, rapists and porn. Originally, punk was all about shock and awe, of disturbing the complacency of mid-seventies culture, and the wearing of the swastika was about the most provocative symbol of its kind.

Although in the seventies some of the media, most notably the tabloid press, pandered to what it believed to be British sentiment by maintaining an agenda that carried more than a hint of anti-German feeling, a new generation looked to Germany with fresh, un-judging eyes. Pre-Nazi Germany, the Germany of the Bauhaus school, of experimental filmmaking, of radical literature, was a well-spring of elegance and endeavour. 'I realised that Germany simply had to reinvent itself and reconnect with the untainted parts of its own culture after the Second World War – and it was the young people, the new post-war generation, who were busy doing this, and were all very conscious of the job in hand,' says John Foxx, who first visited Germany with his band Ultravox! around this time.

---

* In his 1982 series, *There's A Lot Of It About*, he impersonates Hitler singing *Deutschland Über Alles* and having a custard pie thrown in his face.

'When we arrived in 1976/77 we were unwittingly accessing all that massive, determined creative energy. England seemed sadly moribund in comparison. Kraftwerk seemed determined not to go the way of everyone else in adopting hippy American/British modes derived from the psychedelic era, particularly the Pink Floyd and the "Tomorrow Never Knows"-era Beatles. They wanted to rediscover and reinvent the culture of Germany through their own respectable, middle-class, educated, intellectual, unpresumptuous, rigorous and pleasantly melodic music. Just the kind of music the Germans had always loved. Ironically, Germany seemed to dislike them at first, perhaps because all this seemed to take them too close, too quickly, to the immediate past. I think they didn't get the irony and the humour and the wry elimination of outside clichés in favour of local ones. Yet the French loved it, I think perhaps because of its stylistic elegance – the style chimed completely with the intellectual and sartorial Paris fashion of the time. I think they also enjoyed the irony and wry humour of these stylised Germans, too, the French being great critics of stereotypical Germanic traits. So Kraftwerk's first major success happened in France. (It also helped that there were people in charge of radio quotas who liked them, and allowed them a great deal of airtime).'

Germany was now cool. Bowie and Iggy went to live there in the autumn of 1976. When the 18-year-old Gary Webb was looking for a stage name, he chose 'Numan' because he thought it sounded German. In fact, it was Dutch, but no matter. By now, that supreme arbiter of good taste in the UK, broadcaster John Peel, had made a Tangerine Dream album his record of the year, which helped to promote not only that band but, by association, other Krautrock bands to a UK audience. Neu!, Harmonia, Can, Cluster and La Düsseldorf albums would be bought simply because they were German. Malcolm Garrett recalls his first encounters with Krautrock: 'Some of the reasons I got into it are three things that happened simultaneously: a friend of a friend had been to Germany and had brought some music back, specifically Tangerine Dream; secondly, John Peel was playing stuff on the radio, so I was discovering the first Klaus Schulze album, still one of my favourites, *Irrlicht*; and thirdly, *Melody Maker* ran a huge article on what they called 'Krautrock'. So I was introduced to Can, Kluster, Faust, Neu!. There was one record shop in Manchester called Rare Records which was on John Dalton Street. Downstairs they had listening booths, and occasionally I would take the day off school and go into Manchester and listen to this stuff. So I listened to and bought the first Neu! album. There were so many bands and they were all so different from anything else and all different from each other. I loved *Tago Mago*, I loved the first Neu! album, I loved the first Klaus Schulze album and I loved Kraftwerk; but you couldn't put them side by side and say these guys were coming from the same place musically. They were all so different from each other. Amon Düül was an easier proposition, given their connections with Hawkwind. I was totally into Hawkwind, because they were the crossover point, if you like, they still had guitars and sounded like rock music, albeit a bizarre rock music. But, all the others were just like, where the hell are these guys coming from? Alpha Centauri? It was like outsider's music, for the outsider that wanted to belong to some kind of special group of people who "knew" something other people didn't.'

While these more adventurous and open-minded UK fans lapped up Krautrock, the reality for the young musicians living in Germany was rather different. The groups eulogised above failed to make headway commercially. The massively influential Can, for example, had just one hit single, 'Spoon', back in 1972. Rather, in 1976, the German charts were still dominated by the *Schlager* and its scions. The best-selling singles were from the likes of Harpo ('Movie Star'), Pussycat ('Mississippi') and Abba ('Fernando'), all songs your grandmother would be happy to sing along to. The revolution in German music was to all intents and purposes not happening in Germany at all. It was happening in Britain.

4.3 Electronic Autons

For many British children born in the sixties, one of their earliest memories would be sitting down in front of the TV to be scared. Every Saturday night from September through to May, *Dr Who*, then a snappy 25 minutes long, was essential viewing. In January 1970 it went colour; a new Doctor, veteran comedy actor Jon Pertwee, and a new adversary, the Autons. What made the Autons frightening, truly frightening at least to anyone under 10, was the fact that they *looked* real, but weren't. They would announce themselves by their normality, as shop-window mannequins in clothes stores. But they would animate, start moving, smash through the window, and walk towards us, smart-suited, in ties, but with a face that looked like diseased plastic, their wrists revealing a space gun. They kill, indiscriminately, a line of commuters at a bus stop. All the time, their faces remain frozen, totally without movement; dead.

By some strange pop alchemy, Kraftwerk would reflect this scene in a new song, 'Showroom Dummies' [*Schaufensterpuppen*].* The song itself was written by Ralf and performed on their 1975 tour, and would be released as a single, in edited form, in 1982. The association for the original *Dr Who* generation was unmistakable, although Kraftwerk themselves claim not to have seen the British TV programme at the time.†

In many ways, 'Showroom Dummies' is a pivotal song in the Kraftwerk story. It does not contain the best Kraftwerk melody (although it's wonderful enough), nor was it a major hit single, but it is the first Kraftwerk song you can dance to. The accompanying promotional film for the track features four bald mannequins who, at various stages, replace the band and play drums, robotically. Kraftwerk themselves appear and at one stage freeze, striking robotic poses. The end of the promo sees the band dancing in a night club, first throwing mannered, mechanical shapes, before the final few seconds sees them as they really are – four young men at a disco.

One of the ideas behind 'Showroom Dummies' was that the artificial carries with it a certain elegance, beauty, even. Duran Duran's John Taylor: 'It was a really important track for them. It was like a very cool, very chic, dancefloor filler. They're on show. Maybe they walked past a store-room, a store window, and the window was in the process of being re-dressed, so the mannequins were there without clothes on. I think I'm right in saying that Germany has the

---

* One fan was the American producer Tony Visconti. In his early thirties, he was already a veteran producer of Marc Bolan, Bowie and Paul McCartney. 'All I can say about Kraftwerk is that I only heard them in German first and I loved them. I was shocked when I heard a song called "Showroom Dummies" that sounded remarkably like "*Schaufensterpuppen*."'
† An effective video montage, matching the Auton invasion on a London high street with the track, was posted on *YouTube* several years ago, but now appears to have been withdrawn.

most beautiful mannequins in the world." '"Showroom Dummies" fitted with our meaning of elegance,' confirms Wolfgang. 'We were from Düsseldorf, and Düsseldorf is always full of showroom models and dummies because of the big fashion industry and the big fashion fair. We always had a strong affinity to elegance and fashion, and to *gutes Benehmen* ["good manners"].'

The mannequins are also, of course, dressed, posed and ordered, a theme which would be developed throughout the rest of Kraftwerk's career with their, or perhaps more accurately, Ralf's, fascination/obsession with robots. 'The four robots are also models,' says Wolfgang. 'They are workers, they are soldiers and also robots. They get their orders and showroom dummies also. They need orders to look like this. They show clothes and fashion. That's how we liked it. We didn't want to be on stage like the rock bands. We were shy, we wouldn't move and dance.'

Ralf confirms the idea of the dummies as alter egos, replacements, which the band, as mere humans, with human weaknesses, might hide behind. In a later interview he said, 'With a camera, a person is shot to death. That's why I wrote "Showroom Dummies" and that's why we had physical dummies, replicas of ourselves made. They are plastic and more resistant to photographs. We don't do photo sessions now because of experiences we've had of people coming at us and trying to kill us with their cameras. They don't realise what they're doing. Now the dummies do the photo sessions and as a result we have almost an overflow of energy for our own lives' (Mark Cooper).

So, the dummies were, in fact, Kraftwerk's avatars. David Bowie had famously created a succession of alter egos (Ziggy Stardust, The Thin White Duke) as an artistic exercise. He would play them on stage, rather than be himself (although fiction and reality would, in the end, meld together with troubling psychic results). Kraftwerk take this idea, if not one step further, then undoubtedly more literally. Dummies and robots would, in an ideal scenario,

---

* Duran Duran did a live cover version of 'Showroom Dummies' at a concert on their *Red Carpet Massacre* tour as a tribute to the band. The usually energetic Duran played the song as they imagined Kraftwerk would, standing four in a row, still. Joe Black reports that when Ralf Hütter saw it, he said: "See, I told you it was difficult to stand completely still."'

replace the originals. Ralf also points to the depersonalisation of the camera.* In the eighties and nineties, the paparazzi became the bugbear of the rich and feted. Happy to have their faces in a tabloid newspaper when it suited them, and on *their* own terms to promote a record, a film, or even a marriage or a new-born baby, celebrities would often become unhinged when photographed 'off-duty', leading to all manner of unseemly scuffles and litigious threats. Kraftwerk, very clearly, and comparatively earlier in their careers, decided that they were private individuals. They were not, and are not, hypocrites. They are not media stars, and have based a career on not being known. Uniquely for a group with chart aspirations, between 1981 and 1991 not a single promotional photograph of them was released for publication.

There is also a degree of self-awareness and humour (of an unintentional kind) on 'Showroom Dummies'. Kraftwerk's concert performances had been criticised in the media for their stiffness. They were, so one critic pointed out, like shop dummies. In an era in which rock and pop performers were meant at least to move, having four men standing rigidly, as if at a classical concert, just looked wrong. Additionally, a mistranslation by Ralf of the original German lyric in the very first line has given native-English speakers cause for much mirth for decades: 'We are standing here/ Exposing ourselves/We are showroom dummies.' The song also memorably starts with Ralf counting the band in, '1, 2, 3, 4', in a swipe, doubtless affectionate, at the likes of the punks and the Ramones in particular. The dummies thus liberated, they end the evening as surprise guests: 'We go into a club/And there we start to dance/We are showroom dummies.' In reality, Ralf's jerky, robo-dance on stage, and on the accompanying promotional film for the song, was something of an influence three years later on the post-punk club scene. Even Roxy Music, with their 1979 comeback album, *Manifesto*, designed the album artwork as a party or club scene populated by garishly attired mannequins. We would then enter an era of mannequin-like pop performers, some more mannered and annoying than others.

---

* Interestingly, and to confirm the parallel here between Kraftwerk and Bowie, the famous video for Bowie's 1980 UK number one 'Ashes To Ashes' sees a photographer take a photograph of Bowie only for him to clutch his arm as if shot by a bullet.

4.4 'In Vienna We Sit In A Late-Night Café'

*Trans-Europe Express**, produced by Ralf and Florian, and recorded at the Kling Klang Studios in 1976, is not just a perfect album musically, but also an album, in places, intriguingly out of kilter with the times. It is a complete experience, a journey, a reclamation of the romance and beauty of middle Europe at a time when West Germany itself was convulsed by change, fear and violence.

A nightmare which haunted the seventies in West Germany was the RAF or Red Army Faction, commonly known as the Baader-Meinhof group. Founded in 1970 as an 'urban guerrilla concept' by Andreas Baader, Ulrike Meinhof and two others, the RAF was not finally dissolved until 1998. Marxist-Leninist in ideology, it began a programme of terrorist attacks in 1971, with two police officers killed, in separate incidents, that year. In May 1972, however, 13 people were wounded in its first serious attack – the bombing of a US Army barracks in Frankfurt-am-Main. Many young West Germans, if only secretly, shared the objectives of the Baader-Meinhof group, if not their methods, in the same way that many British knew that mainland interference in Ireland was counterproductive, and that the objections and objectives of the Irish Republican Army (IRA), if not their terrorist methods, were also not without merit. In West Germany, there was still a huge sense of injustice that so many of the captains of industry, so much of the hierarchy of big business, was still, in effect, under the control of a generation who had fought for, and supported, Nazism. There was a deep mistrust of their parents' generation and a distrust of patterns of authority, both of which combined to create a revolutionary spirit in the youth of the country. According to the author of the book *The Baader-Meinhof Complex*, later successfully turned into a 2008 film, 'A poll at the time showed that a quarter of West Germans under 40 felt sympathy for the gang and one-tenth said they would hide a gang member from the police. Prominent intellectuals spoke up

---

* The idea for *Trans-Europe Express* did not, so it would seem, originate with Ralf and Florian themselves but with their friend Paul Alessandrini. According to Pascal Bussy he commented to Ralf and Florian, 'With the kind of music you do, which is kind of like an electronic blues, railway stations and trains are very important in your universe, you should do a song about the Trans-Europe Express.'

for the gang's righteousness (as) Germany even into the seventies was still a guilt-ridden society.'

By the mid-seventies, attacks were becoming more numerous, more bloody and more astutely targeted. Four people (among them two members of the gang) were killed in the siege of the West German embassy in Stockholm in April 1975. Then, in 1977, they targeted the federal prosecutor-general, a director of Dresdner Bank and the chairman of the German Employers' Organisation (all killed, in separate incidents).

Ralf Hütter gave a somewhat enigmatic reply when asked about his own political beliefs. 'We strongly believe in anarchy and self-rule,' he said. Quizzed about the Baader-Meinhof group he replied: 'It's not anarchist. When I say "anarchy", I mean no outside rule. I don't rule you, you don't rule me. I rule myself. These people are not using the term anarchy correctly. They are pressing, putting pressure.'

In his autobiography, Wolfgang Flür tells of an incident which, although not caused by the RAF/Baader-Meinhof gang, made him think automatically of that group: '...We were brunching on the Champs-Elysées... we were sitting on the terrace of the Café de Paris opposite the drugstore... when a violent bang suddenly thundered through the city... a billion tiny fragments from countless shattered windowpanes of the US TWA offices came flying towards us....' This, it turned out, was an attack by the Algerian OAS movement. However, it could have happened in London as a result of an IRA or in Frankfurt where the RAF mounted several attacks in the seventies.

In addition to the threat of terrorist activity, not completely confined to the RAF, there was the canker of a divided nation. 'There was a special atmosphere in West Berlin because of the menace from the East,' says journalist and broadcaster Jakob Mayr. 'You never knew how long Berlin would remain a free city. Under pressure cultures evolve even quicker than normal with newer ideas, fresher ideas. The morbid character of the city fascinated artists and musicians. Many buildings were devastated during the war and this devastation would still have been visible in the seventies. On the other hand there were still many older buildings left, including buildings built in the Nazi era. You feel this atmosphere even now.' Quizzed if Kraftwerk had visited the East, Ralf replied, 'It's very difficult. We have been once. We would like to play there, but there's no chance.' 'We get fan mail from there,' Florian added.

Despite the political problems of the West German state, there was also a huge optimism. The major shift emerging from the seventies in West Germany was its closer entanglement with, and interdependence with, the rest of the Western world, and in particular with the European Economic Community, later to become the European Union. The *Wirtschaftswunder* ['economic miracle'] had brought West Germany to its position as the leading economy in Western Europe. The fact that Kraftwerk strode on to the world stage in the mid-seventies would not be regarded, in itself, as a noteworthy event in national terms by most Germans. It was only those Britons and Americans who were ignorant in terms of national perceptions that regarded Kraftwerk's German identity as something meriting derision.

Against this backdrop of fear, yet of self-confidence, *Trans-Europe Express* first of all spoke of the beauty of Europe, and of Germany in particular. To this day, many Brits are astonished by the beauty of certain parts of Germany, its forests and lakes, castles and cathedrals, cafés and beer gardens.

One instantly recognisable shift on *Trans-Europe Express* is the foregrounding of vocal parts. On previous albums, Ralf's voice had either been largely absent or had been so heavily treated as to sound de-humanised. Now, however, his voice is higher in the mix. Five of the album's seven tracks have words. 'For nine years we were afraid to put our voice on tape,' said Ralf, talking of what he called 'tape paranoia'. For the first time, Ralf recorded his vocals in both English and German for different versions of the LP.

The album's two centrepieces are the opening piece 'Europe Endless' and the title track. The two present a conceptual unity more powerful than anything on either *Autobahn* or *Radio-Activity*. The album's repetitive structures were made easier through the use of the Synthanorma Sequenzer. 'Europe Endless' begins with a glistening, pristine, and slow-paced fade in, a synth refrain almost classical in its structure. As on *Radio-Activity*, Kraftwerk's use of the Vako Orchestron lent a charming choir-like quality to the treated voices. It's a melody every bit as good as that of any of the great European classical masters of Central Europe in the Romantic Period and one anticipates this was exactly Kraftwerk's intention. 'Europe endless/Endless endless endless endless/Europe endless/Endless endless endless endless/Life is timeless/Europe endless.' As the beautiful melody repeats, and the words repeat, the antiquity of Europeanism as a *Zeitgeist*, and as a future project, is reinforced with Germanic pride. 'Parks, hotels and palaces/Europe endless', continues Ralf – simple descriptions, a trademark of his style of writing – but possessed with a rare power: 'Promenades and avenues/Europe endless/Real life and postcard views/Europe endless.' This is Europe as an idea, expressed as an endless infinity loop.

'We travelled all over Europe, and especially after a tour in the States, we realised that Europe is mostly parks and old hotels… "promenades and avenues",' Florian told journalist and friend Paul Alessandrini in a 1976 interview with the magazine *Rock And Folk*. 'Real life, but in a world of postcards. Europe, when back from the States, it's only a succession of postcards…'

Back in the seventies, Britain, as now, was a reluctant European bedfellow. Having been taken into Europe by the Conservative Heath Government in 1973, a 1975 referendum ratified the UK's membership in the teeth of opposition from both elements of the Right and the Left, the latter led by socialist Tony Benn. Having been blocked from the European club for decades by the veto of Gaullist France, Britain was belatedly part of the club. But although Britain has always contained a pro/pan-European faction, a mistrust of Europe and particularly European bureaucracy has always existed. Taken with the populist tabloid coverage of Germany that whipped up jingoistic feeling during football World Cups and suchlike, positive images of Europe, let alone Germany, were in short supply. To be confronted, therefore, with a song such as 'Europe Endless' was something of a shock. A song which delighted in the European project, European history, and which, in its simple words and electro-retroism, made the European Project seem like some sort of utopian vision.

However, it is the title track which would go down in Kraftwerk-lore as the most influential possibly in their entire career. Driven by the rhythm of a train's clatter on a track, but tweaked so to make the beat danceable, the song's ominous seven-note ascending synth melody then gives way to Ralf's heavily vocodorised mantra, 'Trans-Europe Express'. But whereas 'Europe Endless' is regal, romantic, the music on the title track seems foreboding: 'Rendezvous on Champs-Elysées/Leave Paris in the morning on T.E.E./Trans-Europe Express.' The lyrics, however, are a celebration of travel, speed, and ever-changing vistas of European humanity: 'In Vienna we sit in a late-night café/Straight connection, T.E.E./Trans-Europe Express.'

The Trans-Europe Express network had begun in 1957. At its height it would connect 130 different cities throughout Western Europe. It was constructed as a rich man's pleasure, with only first-class pricing, and a supplement paid on top of that according to the distance travelled. Aimed squarely at the businessman (this was not yet the age of the businessperson), it offered luxury and elegance for those whose work took them across national borders. With fine dining on board, and only short delays at border points (customs officials came on board to check passports), it made travel a wonderful new experience.

For Wolfgang Flür, the piece captures perfectly the romance of travelling along the Rhine. 'This is my neighbourhood. This is where I lived ... with all the nice castles and sloping vineyards. My great-grandfather was a famous architect from Frankfurt, Josef Rindsfüsser [Mr Cow's Foot],* who built a lot of the big villas for the rich industrial people who lived on either side of the Rhine. And if you go by train today, you can see, besides the famous castles, the wonderful villas which he built for them. The TEE had the panorama carriage where you could sit and look out all around. You could see everything, the panorama on both sides of the Rhine. This is the TEE, the Trans-Europe Express. It doesn't exist any more. Sad!'

Today, many of us are no longer enthralled. Travel has lost much of its magic through its availability. We travel all the time; maybe too much. The world is a smaller place, so we are told, but at what cost? The elegance of the TEE, the finery of an expensive luxury car, has been replaced by the bargain-basement herding techniques of budget airlines, and being sardined on the underground. Travel has become perfunctory in its ubiquity. Kraftwerk's monumental title track captures a time before travel came to be seen as a God-given right, before a foreign holiday was the norm for the working

---

* "Rindsfüsser" does not actually mean "cow's foot", but sounds very like it.

class, and certainly before the 'Gap Year' phenomenon, and the massive expansion of the business class for whom the two-day trip to the Italian office in Milan just has to be scheduled in (on expenses, of course).

4.5 The German Gilbert & George

'Trans-Europe Express' also famously name-checks two new friends of Ralf and Florian's. With Bowie's 'Station To Station', recorded in the autumn of 1975 and released in January 1976, fresh in the memory, it is common wisdom that Bowie had been an influence on Kraftwerk, and this might indeed be so: but according to Karl Bartos a version of 'Trans-Europe Express' was being played by Kraftwerk on their 1975 tour. Although not a song about train travel at all (Bowie's 'Station To Station' refers to the Kabbalah and the 'Stations of the Cross'), that track did begin with a musical pun – heavily treated washes of white noise shaped into the sound of an oncoming steam train complete with Doppler effect, and the clatter of wheels and carriages on track. Kraftwerk deliberately allude to Bowie in 'Trans-Europe Express': 'From station to station/back to Düsseldorf City/Meet Iggy Pop and David Bowie/Trans-Europe Express', describing the band's meeting with Bowie and Iggy at the Paris party on the 1976 Bowie tour.

Kraftwerk's name-checking is not an expression of vanity but of genuine appreciation. In fact, a theme which emerges on the LP is a deep suspicion of the star-making machinery. 'The whole ego aspect of music is boring. It doesn't interest us,' opined Ralf. 'In Germany in the Thirties we had a system of superstardom with Mr Adolf from Austria and so there is no interest for me in this "cult of personality". It has to do with placing things so far away from you that they get out of touch. That's another way of condemning you to inactivity. With all these superstars you are just watching them. But we do DIY and that's what we're suggesting other people should do. Maybe EMI Records wouldn't like to hear this.'

'Hall Of Mirrors', a song which took fame, and its distorting effect on the personality, as its theme, is a hidden Kraftwerk classic. The historic Hall of Mirrors at the Palace of Versailles is here replaced by the looking glass of vanity, multiple versions of oneself looking back at the frightened gaze of the 'greatest stars', who 'dislike themselves'. It's hard not to listen to the song without thinking of David Bowie, and his quixotic personality and changes/crises, although the song might also refer to the career of Ralf and Florian themselves, and their journey from obscurity into the public domain. The walking-pace of the song's beat, deliberate, measured, the synth melody, eerie, uneasy with nostalgia, all go to create one of Kraftwerk's most unsettling psychic moments: 'Sometimes he saw his real face/And sometimes a stranger at his place.' The Bowie-esque nature of one of the song's most resonant lines is unmistakable: 'He made up the person he wanted to be/And changed into a new personality/Even the greatest stars change themselves in the looking glass.'

Again, a whiff of the old Europe and of upper-class manners is suggested. The use of the term 'looking glass' avoids the repetition of 'mirror' and would also have fitted in perfectly with Nancy Mitford's 1954 typology of 'U' (versus 'non-U'). The allusion to the Versailles Palace itself is significant. During the previous century it was one of the most famous and beautiful buildings in the world, and of great historical significance being the venue for the treaty which saw Bismarck victorious at the conclusion of the Franco-Prussian War in 1871, and also for the victorious French Prime Minister Clemenceau in 1919 to sign the peace treaty which formally ended World War 1.

The LP closes with the instrumental 'Franz Schubert' (which then closes with an echo of the opening track, 'Endless Endless', in instrumental form). It would appear to be a deliberate attempt to link Kraftwerk to the grand tradition of German classical composition, and it is simply beautiful. 'One of the things that I would like to have seen Kraftwerk expand upon is the direction of the track "Franz Schubert" from the end of *Trans-Europe Express*,' says Peter Saville. 'This quotes classical music, but in an ironically synthetic way. I found that very interesting. Similarly I think it would be great for them to do a requiem.'

A promotional film was made for the title track. Although primitive by the standards set in the MTV era of the next decade, the film is wonderfully evocative of time and place. Shot in black and white, it mixes still photography (including an image of Iggy Pop and David Bowie, of course) with actual footage of the band aboard a train, looking suavely debonair, much influenced by film noir but with the added twist of being heavily made-up. In interviews, Kraftwerk often spoke of 'retro futurism' as a guiding aesthetic, and nowhere is this idea better developed than in this short film – the soundtrack is astonishingly ground-breaking. That the music and beats date from early 1977 is startling, even today, and set against these neon-lit shots of railway stations, platforms and the train travel, it evokes a feeling of the past colliding headlong with the future in a cultural derailment which seems to place the music outside of pop time. Few musicians working in 1977 had this simultaneous connection with their cultural past and futures.

The film was made by Günter Fröhling, who had trained at the DEFA studios in East Berlin. 'He was a fantastic man. He always filmed with that big Arriflex, a film camera, not a video,' remembers Wolfgang. 'When we sat in the train, he was lying in one of the luggage racks. We helped him up there, with his big camera. He was handicapped; he had a hunched back, and he was so funny. We "folded" him in, he wanted us to do it. He must have needed an angle to look at us in the compartment. So there he was, lying in the luggage compartment, and we gave him the camera. Don't ask me how he handled it, filming us at an angle from up there. He did photos and films. He was just an artist himself. He used to film the small model trains and railways made by Märklin. We built all of that on a big table, with all the tunnels and the countryside scenes and the cities that the special train went through. The train was an old one, the silver one with the propeller on the back. The Nazis designed that train, and you could have that as a model, you know.'

Equally striking as the promo was the album art work.[*] The original UK cover showed the band as the 'electronic quartet'. A photograph taken by J Stara in Paris was heavily retouched to resemble a painting: Ralf and Florian wear matching grey suits and white shirts; Florian smiles, Mona Lisa-like, Ralf, in profile, looks dominant, assertive; Karl and Wolfgang again enigmatically avoid our gaze. The formality of the composition, the sepia tones, the lighting, make the photo montage almost timeless. It was constructed in the seventies, but it might easily have dated from any point in the preceding 40 years.

---

[*] The original cover, later rejected, was very different, and took its cue from the song 'Hall Of Mirrors'. Ralf said in 1976: 'The sleeve will be made from a set of mirrors reflecting our pictures.'

The German version of the LP sleeve has a different photograph, one of the photos taken by Seymour Stein in 1975 adapted by Emil Schult. Schult, born in Dessau in 1946, was an important part of Kraftwerk's success at the time. Not only did he design many of the iconic sleeves for the band, but as a lyricist too, his contribution to both 'Hall Of Mirrors' and 'Trans-Europe Express' was significant. He was, according to Wolfgang Flür, 'a very self-conscious, good-looking lad with brown curls and soft, blue-grey eyes'. Schult's work was perfect for Kraftwerk – enigmatic, economical, it was oddly blank, almost like a German version of Warhol. 'He is our medium. He writes lyrics, takes care of the lights,' said Ralf in a 1976 interview. 'When I met Emil, and when he showed his comics to me, I thought they looked like our music,' added Florian.

The most striking image is in the original centrefold. Schult takes a 1975 photograph by Seymour Stein, lifts the figures and places them seated around a table draped in a tablecloth. This time, Kraftwerk look towards us, smiles playing around the corners of their mouths. Bartos, classically trained, wears formal evening wear including black dicky bow. Wolfgang is less formal in cord jacket, white shirt and tie, Ralf in stylish grey pinstripes, Florian in a formal suit with waistcoat. Behind them, Schult has painted an archetypal scene of rural Germania. The four sit as if ready to picnic under the shade of a tall oak, and in the distance are the lakes and the rolling green hills of the countryside. 'The poses were very studied,' says Jon Savage, in 1977 a young music journalist writing for *Sounds*. 'The whole mood was very kind of Art Deco, camp. It was almost like a German version of Gilbert & George.'

'I enjoyed the *Trans-Europe Express* art work,' says John Foxx. 'They used a beautifully archaic form of photographic family portraiture that involved stylised retouching by hand. It all seemed to chime with their European/urban music very well – stylised, perfected, and knowingly and charmingly naïve.'

The expressionless, enigmatic quality of the way in which Ralf and Florian are posed, the attention to sartorial detail, the conservatism of (often matching) attire, did mirror the work of Gilbert & George. One of the very few unashamedly right-leaning artists working in Britain, Gilbert & George were a couple on and off duty, and artists on and off duty too. They were self-proclaimed 'living sculptures' who today dress only in tweed, are almost never

119

seen in public separately and who 'made a big point not to become friends of anybody'. They came to the art world's attention in 1970 with their art work. *The Singing Sculpture*, sprayed with metallic coloured powders and singing the 1931 Flanagan & Allen song 'Underneath The Arches'. The parallels with Ralf and Florian are certainly there to be made: the elitism, the assertion of no real demarcation between being on and off duty, the *Gesamtkunstwerk* ethos, perhaps even a mildly misanthropic mistrust of others.

Most importantly, like Gilbert & George, Kraftwerk set themselves apart from the mainstream of the medium in which they worked. They had deliberately positioned themselves as outsiders and, as intended, this had become a key element in their modus operandi.

4.6 Metallic KO

Success in France led to a promotional event organised by Maxime Schmitt, the manager of Kraftwerk's French label, on the release of *Trans-Europe Express*. Journalists were invited to join the band in restored carriages on an Orient Express train from the Gare du Nord in Paris to the city of Reims, and the new album was played continually over loudspeakers during the journey. Wolfgang Flür describes in his autobiography how everyone was transferred, on arrival at Reims, into waiting buses, to transport them to the vineyard of Moët et Chandon.

Like *Radio-Activity*, the LP sold strongly in France, reaching number two, and was Top 10 in Italy. Yet Germany, once again, was reluctant to commit, the LP reaching no higher than number 32, while in the UK, a number 49 highest chart placing hardly indicated that Kraftwerk were a commercial act. In the USA, it failed completely to break into the Top 100.

Success, however, can be measured in several ways. Today, the LP is regarded, with complete critical consensus, as a classic. Outside the Holy Trinity of those-who-must-not-be-criticised – the Beatles, the Stones, and Dylan – it must be one of the very few LPs made in an artist's prime to be awarded (if only retrospectively on re-issue) five-star commendations from the three major British monthly music magazines, *Q*, *Mojo*, and *Uncut*. 'In my opinion,' wrote Wolfgang Flür in his autobiography, '*Trans-Europe Express* is the best and most melodic album that we ever recorded'. It's an opinion echoed by many. Ex-member Eberhard Kranemann: 'Most of the later music is, for me, dead music. It doesn't live. It is not interesting. There's only one thing I like very much, and that's *Trans-Europe Express*. There is a very deep impression and very deep feeling in it.'

'I think my big conversion to Kraftwerk came with *Trans-Europe Express*,' says Jon Savage. 'I was obsessed with Franz Schubert, and I really liked those pretty brutal and simple synthesized melodies. But they also had kind of a lot of space in them. I would now define it as a kind of European romanticism. That's what I liked about it. It was like psychedelia had been in the late-sixties. It seemed to offer mental and physical space.'

The really impressive thing about *Trans-Europe Express* is the playing, given the technology at the time. 'When I first bought it, it seemed so precise, so mechanical. Only now do I realise that it was all done by hand,' says Andy McCluskey. 'Those drums are sometimes flat and don't land right. There was a human element in the band, certainly up to and including *Trans-Europe Express*. *Trans-Europe Express* for me was probably the zenith. That was the ultimate piece where they distilled their theory, but they were still delivering it in a very human way – in the same way that OMD had that melancholy sound created by the juxtaposition of the electronic and human. Kraftwerk were doing that. It is funny because it really wasn't touched on at the time. But actually, the charm of Kraftwerk was that it had a melancholy to it. It had a tension created by the lyrics, those beautiful choir sounds that they would use and the melodies. Even Ralf's vocal deliveries sometimes had a naïve charm to them. "Europe Endless" and "Radio-Activity" are side by side, they're my Gemini of shining stars in my life. The songs are just glorious. The way "Europe Endless" just wanders in with that sequencer. You know the drums are coming, you know the drums are just coming, you know the drums are coming, and finally it lands... and Ralf just announcing... "Europe [pause] endless". I just love that song.'

Trans-Europe Express' enchanting melodies would have a direct influence on a new breed of British synth acts. However, it would be the section 'Metal On Metal', the instrumental section which led on from the title track, which would, five years later, have an even more profound legacy. One of the inspirations behind 'Trans-Europe Express', and perhaps particularly the 'Metal On Metal' section, must have been the 1948 composition *Étude aux chemins de fer* by the French composer Pierre Schaeffer. Schaeffer's piece, part of his *Cinq études de bruits* (Five Studies of Noises) used recordings of trains (whistles, the rattling of carriages on the track) married with electro-acoustic techniques to form what he termed *musique concrète*. '*Musique concrète* is music made of raw sounds: thunderstorms, steam-engines, waterfalls, steel foundries', is how the critic Tim Hodgkinson put it. 'The sounds are not produced by traditional acoustic musical instruments. They are captured on tape (originally, before tape, on disk) and manipulated to form sound-structures. The work method is therefore empirical. It starts from the concrete sounds and moves towards a structure. In contrast, traditional classical music starts from an abstract musical schema.'

The 'Metal On Metal' sequence was recorded quite simply by hitting a hammer on a metal pipe. Karl Bartos: 'Eventually Hütter and Schneider went to train bridges and were listening to the sound the train would actually produce: and by using the final rhythm it was just a little faint because a train doesn't actually sound like this! Because on a train you have two wheels, and then the next wagon is starting with another two wheels and if you cross the gap on the rails it makes the sound "da-dum-da-dum; da-dum-da-dum" but of course you wouldn't be able to dance to that! So we changed it slightly.'

'Metal On Metal' was an early form of industrial music to be developed, in the eighties, by acts such as West Berlin's Einstürzende Neubauten. It would also be the section of music which, later, in 1982, would help launch hip-hop as a global phenomenon.

4.7 It's So Good, It's So Good, It's So Good...'

In the seventies, all roads led to David Bowie. Or so it seems today. In the early summer of 1977, Bowie is holed up at the Hansa Tonstudio in West Berlin recording *"Heroes"* which would become, like almost all David Bowie records at the time, an important album from the day it was released. Bowie ducked the crossfire of punk by removing himself physically to West Germany and, musically, into soundscapes which, to this day, disturb and haunt. The primal disquiet of 'Sense Of Doubt', the ambient-inventing Zen quietude of 'Moss Garden', the East-meets-West alienation of 'Neuköln'; Bowie was reimagining what it was that pop stars did after they first became famous. Like John Lennon and Scott Walker in the sixties, they moved into the margins. It's a trick many major rock stars have attempted subsequently, from U2 and Prince in the eighties, Radiohead in the nineties, to Coldplay and Kate Bush in more recent years. It's not an easy trick to pull off.

'Since my teenage years I had obsessed on the "Angst-ridden", emotional work of the expressionists, both artists and film makers, and Berlin had been their spiritual home. This was the nub of *Die Brücke* movement, Max Reinhardt, Brecht and was where *Metropolis* and *Caligari* had originated. It was an art form that mirrored life not by event but by mood.' This was how Bowie put it in an interview with *Uncut* magazine in the mid-nineties. 'This was where I felt my work was going. My attention had been swung back to Europe with the release of Kraftwerk's *Autobahn* in 1974. The preponderance of electronic instruments convinced me that this was an area that I had to investigate a little further.'

Bowie, however, is keen to point out that his own music owed little, in fact, to the work of Kraftwerk. What he admired about the band was their rejection of the musical lingua franca which was American rock. 'Kraftwerk's approach to music had in itself little place in my scheme. Theirs was a controlled, robotic, extremely measured series of compositions, almost a parody of minimalism. One had the feeling that Florian and Ralf were completely in charge of their environment, and that their compositions were well prepared and honed before entering the studio. My work tended to expressionist mood pieces, the protagonist (myself) abandoning himself to the "zeitgeist", with little or no control over his life. The music was spontaneous for the most part and created in the studio. In substance too, we were poles apart. Kraftwerk's percussion sound was produced electronically, rigid in tempo, unmoving. Ours was the mangled treatment of a powerfully emotive drummer, Dennis Davis ...What I was passionate about in relation to Kraftwerk was their singular determination to stand apart from stereotypical American chord sequences and their wholehearted embrace of a European sensibility displayed through their music. This was their very important influence on me.' One of the tracks on *"Heroes"* showed that Bowie was certainly close to Kraftwerk. 'V-2 Schneider' was a tribute to Florian, although, perhaps, a rather double-edged one in that it linked his name to that of a Nazi-era Luftwaffe missile.

Although Bowie admired greatly the work of Neu! and others, he states in the *Uncut* interview that he was keen to keep a degree of distance from the German musicians. 'I knew Edgar Froese [from Tangerine Dream] and his wife socially but I never met the others as I had no real inclination to go to Düsseldorf as I was very single-minded about what I needed to do in the studio in Berlin. I took it upon myself to introduce Eno to the Düsseldorf sound with which he was very taken, Conny Plank et al (also to Devo btw, who in turn had been introduced to me by Iggy) and Brian eventually made it up there to record with some of them.'

So we have Iggy, Eno and Bowie (not forgetting other collaborators at the time such as producer Tony Visconti, and musicians such as Carlos Alomar and Robert Fripp) all fired up by new music, all keen to introduce friends and colleagues to new sounds. It would not be unreasonable to suggest that there might have been some rivalry, some competition amongst them about who had the best, and most up-to-date musical references – the 'My Record Collection Is Cooler Than Yours' syndrome. One of the songs which certainly impacted greatly in the summer of 1977 was a song which sounded as if Kraftwerk had gone potty and recruited a bona fide American soul singer. In fact, it wasn't Kraftwerk, but Italian musician and producer Giorgio Moroder. 'One day in Berlin,' says Bowie, 'Eno came running in and said, "I have heard the sound of the future." ... He puts on "I Feel Love", by Donna Summer ... He said, "This is it, look no further. This single is going to change the sound of club music for the next 15 years." Which was more or less right.'

No one had heard anything like this before – a totally synthetic piece of pop, with a beautiful soul voice over the top. There was no conventionally good singer in Kraftwerk, or for that matter in any of the Krautrock bands. This was a game-changing move, and would, as Eno and Bowie predicted, provide the template for music in discos and clubs for years. So began the era of electronic music with 'proper' singers, firstly Phil Oakey and the Human League, and, four or five years later, groups such as the Eurythmics and Yazoo, with female vocalists and great sets of pipes.

In the same interview, Bowie reveals that his first choice for lead guitarist on *Low*, the album he made before *"Heroes"*, was

'Michael Dinger' [he meant Michael Rother] from Neu!, a band musically and artistically much closer to Bowie than Kraftwerk were. Bowie claims that he received a diplomatic 'No' from Rother at the time. Rother himself remembers things rather differently: 'The story is this: David Bowie and I were obviously tricked into believing that the other had changed his mind about our collaboration in 1977. I was surprised to read an interview with Bowie in a British magazine some years ago in which he said that I had declined to work with him. This isn't true. David called me in summer 1977, invited me to join him and Brian Eno in the studio in Berlin. We were both absolutely eager to do recordings together. However, some days after our conversation I received a phone call from somebody speaking for David (it may have been his management, I can't say for sure), telling me that he had changed his mind about our collaboration and that I needn't come to Berlin. And David was obviously told that I had changed my mind. We only found out about this trickery when we exchanged emails in 2001. It's up to speculation why somebody didn't want our collaboration to happen, but it is known that David Bowie's more experimental albums in the seventies didn't do so well commercially back then. Anyway, the short answer to your question is: I didn't turn David Bowie down at all.'

While it is intriguing to speculate that someone with an interest in steering Bowie towards more commercial music might have sabotaged the collaboration, Kraftwerk and Bowie would continue to stalk one another from a respectful distance, each mindful that they were pushing at boundaries, illuminating an electronic future as yet unmapped.

4.8 The One-Fingered Revolution

While Kraftwerk and Bowie were working in West Germany, punk rock was exploding in Britain. *Sniffin' Glue*, Britain's leading punk fanzine edited by Mark Perry and featuring a young Danny Baker and Kris Needs, preached the mantra of simplicity. A famous punk T-shirt with scrawled guitar tabs proclaimed: 'This is a chord. This is another. This is a third. Now form a band.'*

---

* This famous punk drawing originates not from *Sniffin' Glue* but from the January 1977 edition of *Sideburns*. It was later reprinted in *Strangled*, the official Stranglers magazine.

'Punk was the politicised pop experience again,' is Peter Saville's assessment. 'It was for a generation for whom the established music scene wasn't working... by the time you are floating helium balloons over Battersea Power Station you are not speaking for 15 year olds on housing estates. Pop had lost its authenticity and punk was super-authentic. Punk was the band standing next to you having a drink at the bar rather than ultra-beings that you queued up with three thousand others to watch. Suddenly music was part of your reality again.'

What punk was against was never altogether clear, however. John Lydon himself was a self-proclaimed fan of Can and Van der Graaf Generator. Secretly, many punks were in love with Genesis and Pink Floyd, but to say that in an interview would have been the end of a bright career. And, even more secretly, several punks could also play many more than the three chords their press releases claimed was all they could muster on a good day, with a fair wind, and a can of Special Brew.

What punk was *really* against wasn't, perhaps, the intricate lead guitar of a Steve Hackett, or the romantic piano flourishes of a Tony Banks, but 'cock rock'. This was a term coined with some intellectual brilliance back in 1978 by Simon Frith (now Professor Simon Frith, and Chair of the Mercury Music Prize committee) and sociologist Angela McRobbie. Cock rock was music with a bell-end on it. This was music sung by hetero men, with long hair, in tight trousers. This was 'authentic' music, with loud, piercing guitars, thudding bass and drums and even louder high-pitched vocals; it was the dead-headed march of the untouchable rock God stadium superstars whose lead singer's head was choked back in a rictus of feigned orgasmic pleasure as he bawled about doing it "all night long". But it was Kraftwerk – suited like posh bank managers, barely moving on stage, dealing with any sexual themes (if they arose at all) in a totally detached manner – who were the real slayers of cock rock, not the punks. This was music with no guitars at all, no indebtedness to the blues, no appeal to any of the basic motivations behind so much pop music such as who to love, and, essentially, no frontman for the audience to identify with. This wasn't so much an attack on the status quo, or even an attack on Status Quo, as a complete theoretical annihilation of most of the precedents and tenets on which modern rock music was based. Those who walked alongside Kraftwerk in the seventies, and in the eighties, were the true apostates.

Ralf would later say that Kraftwerk's music and the music of punk did share a common aim: to de-clutter music. Asked in 2003 if he could see similarities between his music and punk, he replied, 'In a way, yes. Also the simplicity, minimalistic attitude, definitely.'

Punk was important: but it was a Beta version, a dry run, because punk, in the end, was too much like that which it sought to replace. For every genuine talent there would be hundreds of no-marks, band-wagon-jumpers of no-fixed talent. The fact that punk created the space for amateur musicians to attempt their 15 minutes of fame was lionised at the time, and still is by sections of the media. The reality, however, was conformity, a flow of derivation. The Sex Pistols might have sounded radical: but the imitators of the imitators of the imitators certainly did not, as punk split into Power Pop (yawn), Oi (no thank you), or retreated like a wounded meerkat in a fake TV commercial battle to patch up a scratch wound, and to return as Pub Rock, Mark 2 (definitely no thank you).

The true destroyers of the fat, bloated, conceited mid-seventies rock turned out not to be the punks at all, although many had been amongst their ranks initially. It would be a second wave of musicians for whom even the technical ability to play three chords on a guitar would be beyond them. It would come from those who couldn't play an instrument at all.

By the end of 1977, bands in Sheffield (Human League, Cabaret Voltaire), in London (Ultravox!), in Hull (Throbbing Gristle) and on the Wirral (VCL XI, later OMD) were hatching a new future for music. 'The key to the Human League was that we didn't have to play it,' is how Phil Oakey puts it. 'We could think it out, plan it, and get it played somehow. Then we'd piece it together. But the key was that we couldn't play well enough to do it.' It was the beginning of 'virtual' pop music, a tape machine taking the place on stage traditionally reserved for the drummer. And, in all this, Kraftwerk were key. 'The day I joined the group, Martyn Ware walked into my house carrying "I Feel Love" by Donna Summer in one hand, and *Trans-Europe Express* in the other,' said Phil Oakey.

FÜNF
MECHANIK
1977 – 1979

5.1 How To Be A Robot*

FORTY YEARS ago in the UK, colour television was reaching the homes of ordinary people. With three channels, and much of the morning and afternoon schedules empty, trade test colour films were what passed for daytime television programming. From 1968 until 1972, one such film was aired on the BBC, with an exotica soundtrack with some jokey synthesized sections by Jaap Hofland and the Moonliners, and no commentary. It bemused and intrigued many a pre-school child. Made by Philips to promote Evoluon, the newly built, flying saucer-shaped science museum in Eindhoven,

---

* With apologies to Caitlin Moran.

it showed a world of almost incomprehensible modernity. Visitors would be filmed looking intrigued by an array of interactive features including a talking frog ('Ik ben de Kicker')*, a human being sculptured in wire, a robot head inspired, perhaps, by the 1927 film *Metropolis*, and, most bizarrely, a talking coffee machine whose voice sounded remarkably like one of the voice simulator programmes later used by Kraftwerk. Indeed, the entire exhibition was a celebration of a very Kraftwerkian theme: the usefulness of automation and mechanisation.

It is either the longest-running gag in pop music, or Ralf Hütter genuinely believes that humankind and machine-kind form a symbiotic unity. The history of Kraftwerk from 1978 to the present has been dominated by this idea. For their next LP, the first to have co-songwriting credits for Karl Bartos, Kraftwerk, in just over 36 minutes of music, examined the relationship between the human and non-human.

In a 1978 interview, Florian was keen to stress that the machines were neither master nor servant. 'It's rather a more sophisticated relationship. There is an interaction. Interaction on both sides. The machine helps the man, and the man admires the machine. [Showing the Sony tape recorder] This is the extension of your brain. It helps you remembering. It's the third man sitting at this table. As for ourselves, we love our machines. We have an erotic relationship with them.'

Machine love? Eroticism? Was this more of Florian's trademark droll quippery, more mischief, or a hint at something more, as if a man's best friend was no longer his dog, or his car, or even his wife, but his synthesizer and his computer? A British 2011 TV ad for ADT burglary alarm systems asked the question, 'What means most to you in the world?' The reply from one man was 'my wife, my kids [then a guilty smirk]... my home cinema', whilst an actor playing a student replied, 'my laptop'. The Kraftwerkian future in which men prized machines over people had become a reality.

Expressionless and statuesque, Kraftwerk initiated a completely new performance idiom, and building on 'Showroom Dummies' from the previous album, their reinvention as robots was logical. It paved the way for a new wave of pop performers who

---

* In English, 'I am the kicker.'

130

would affect an air of emotional dislocation, staring blankly out on an audience to be neither greeted nor even acknowledged.* It was as far removed from the smug platitudes of many rock acts with their 'Hello London, lemme see your hands!' as one could get.

The key track to the new album *The Man-Machine* was its opening shot, 'The Robots' [*'die Roboter'*]. Beginning with a series of bleeps and pulses, we can imagine a robotised Ralf becoming activated, the sizzling lifeblood of electricity coursing through his veins. This is the human condition booted into action not through flesh and blood but by electrochemical cells. 'We're charging our own battery/and now we're full of energy' sings a suitably heavily vocodarised Ralf, before announcing, 'We are the robots!'

It was not an altogether new idea within pop music. 'Doing The Robotic' had been a style of dancing developed synchronically by the Jackson 5, and Michael's stage performances of the 1974 song 'Dancing Machine'. Much later, in the eighties, Styx would score a US hit with 'Mr Roboto'. All it needs are a blank stare, a jangling frame, jerky movements, and a sense of self-mockery. English footballer Peter Crouch, famous for his robotic dance for club and country, fitted the brief perfectly over 30 years later. However, there seemed to be a seriousness to Kraftwerk's cyborg manifesto. 'Ja tvoi sluga, [I'm your slave'] 'ja tvoi Rabotnik' ['I'm your worker'] intones the robot voice in Russian.

Three more tracks on the album dealt with the trans-human. The title track, 'The Man-Machine' [*Die Mensch Maschine*], is a genuinely eerie composition. Like 'The Robots' it builds from a simple synth refrain which repeats throughout the track before another cyborg voice intones: 'Man-Machine, super human being'. The song's title is then repeated eight times, each time working its way up an octave before a final 'MA-CHINE' in a style memorably described by critic Simon Reynolds as 'android doo-wop'. Like much of Kraftwerk's oeuvre, this locks us into the past whilst predicting the future. A strand of German intellectual thought has always been shaped by the idea of an *Übermensch*, a philosophy which, in

---

* I attended a Gary Numan concert in Liverpool in 1988 during which Gary didn't speak a single word to the audience. When I reminded him of this in an interview in 2011 he quipped: 'I probably didn't have anything to say!'

a twisted and abhorrent form, underpinned the vile Aryanism of the Nazis and its obsession with purity. 'The Man Machine' revisits the original idea that mankind can be improved but posits the idea that this can only be achieved through a marriage with the non-human.

'The Model' ['Das Modell'], at the time not even deemed worthy of release as a single in the UK, is now, along with 'Autobahn', one of the band's best-known tracks. Unusually for Kraftwerk, it's a short, narrative song, which depicts a strange fascination for a supermodel, a star of fashion magazines and a catwalk beauty who drinks 'just champagne'. Ralf, showing his carnal side, 'would like to take her home, that's understood'. Behind this song of deadpan sexuality, however, is the linking theme of how we objectify, and therefore depersonalise, human beings, making them commodities to exploit. 'We are not macho or anything, we are more androgynous,' said Ralf. 'A lot of the music around is pap, with the same values as pornography. Those are the values that turn "The Model" into a robot. Is there a music beyond pornography? That's the question we're asking. And we've taken some small steps in that direction.'

'Metropolis', although essentially an instrumental, also references the Fritz Lang film of the same name. The music is pulsing, dark, but, as ever, graced with memorable synth melodies; however, is there the very first hint of the masters copying the followers? The second instrumental on the record, the equally inventive 'Spacelab', was also singled out by reviewers at the time as being close to the Moroder template. An *NME* piece from December 1978 called Moroder the 'Munich Mensch Maschine' and stated: '"Spacelab" runs Moroder's sound so close a second it's hard to resist implying plagiarism on the part of the Düsseldorf Dynamen.' The music certainly has the same sort of Euro-Disco pulse as some of Giorgio Moroder's singles of the time. It is difficult to ascribe influence, though. Florian was convinced that Giorgio was stealing the Kraftwerk sound. *Rock & Folk* magazine asked: 'What do you think of Giorgio Moroder? "From Here To Eternity" is quite close to what you are...' Florian replied: 'Yes. In Germany, some people asked me if it was our new record.'

'From Here To Eternity' had been a hit in the autumn of 1977. A Kraftwerk influence is apparent on the 'Trans-Europe Express'-like melody refrain which appears along with the vocodorised vocal. However, the sequenced music is considerably more brazen in its wish to fill the dancefloor, and the song, unlike the vast majority of Kraftwerk's, is sexual, and knows it. The album of the same name has been cited by many musicians in the eighties as an influence on house music.

By 1977, Moroder was already something of a music business veteran. Born in 1940 in Urtijëi in the South Tyrol region of Italy, he had written 'Son Of My Father' with British lyricist Pete Bellotte. Recorded by an unremarkable glam quartet from Kent called Chicory Tip, it became a UK number one in 1972, and the first British chart-topper to feature a synthesizer as its main instrument, in this case a Moog played by producer Chris Thomas. Moroder worked out of the Musicland Studios in the basement of the Arabella Tower in the *Bogenhausen* district of Munich. 'I Feel Love', the song that sounded like a woman making love to a machine, in turn, made him. Apart from his own work, as producer and as solo artist, Moroder himself would prove to be as unlike Kraftwerk as one can imagine in that he loved to share the spotlight with other major pop and rock luminaries. Moroder would go on to work with David Bowie on the single 'Cat People (Putting Out Fire)'* and Phil Oakey from the Human League on the Euro smash 'Together In Electric Dreams'.† Unlike Kling Klang, Musicland was open to all-comers, and would be used by Led Zeppelin, the Electric Light Orchestra, Queen, Deep Purple and Elton John.

Perhaps the comparison is unduly harsh on Kraftwerk. Ralf and Florian never sought to be producers of works by others. Maybe through a lack of self-confidence, diffidence, or, as we have been told by Ralf in interview after interview, Kraftwerk, for them, is a daily job of work, and, to quote from a line from Dickens' *A Christmas Carol* uttered by that perennial Yuletide miser Ebenezer Scrooge: 'mine occupies me constantly'. Moroder had a more simplistic, and maybe more realistic, even more honest take on the music he made. 'The disco sound, you must see, is not art or anything so serious. Disco is music for dancing, and I know that the people will always

---

* A minor hit for Bowie in 1982, re-recorded for his multi-Platinum album *Let's Dance* the year after, but known to a new generation in its original and superior Moroderesque glory as part of the soundtrack to the Quentin Tarantino movie *Inglourious Basterds* (2009).

† In recent years apopted by the Human League as not only their song, but the ending of their live set.

want to dance.' In the same 1978 interview, *NME* opined, 'The producer of Donna Summer, Roberta Kelly, the Munich Machine and, most recently, Sparks, Moroder has unwittingly – or so it seems – precipitated a veritable flash-flood of madcap-modernisms and pseudo-sociological static.' It is certainly true to say that the 'Moroder Sound' was a huge hit with a new generation of musicians looking to build on punk's ground-zero guitar-based music. The likes of the Human League, and later Duran Duran, were Moroder admirers. *NME* again: 'Moroder is, the radical chic surfers of the disco wave inform us, as crucial to the developing of the new "disko" aesthetic as are, say, Kraftwerk, Bowie, Eno, Amanda Lear, the Baader Meinhof and Devo.'

The crucial difference between Kraftwerk and Moroder was that six letter word. Kraftwerk had last sneakily used the G-U-I-T-A-R on the title track of 'Autobahn' (although everyone seems to have missed it). But for Moroder, there were no such self-denying ordinances: 'In the studio these days you generally change the sound of natural instruments – but then, if you are not careful, you get just another synthesized sound. I am looking for ways of changing natural sounds in other directions, away from pure electronic treatments. The synthesizer has limitless sounds to give you, but I am again really too much of a commercial composer to be able to make full use of its possibilities. I would want to, although I accept I will probably not have the time or ability to do so. As it happens, I am not a very good keyboards player anyway. In fact, I am a lousy keyboards player...'

In 1977 and 1978, Kraftwerk had been without a major hit in either Britain or America for three years, whereas Moroder, either as a solo act or as a producer, seemed to be able to provide them effortlessly. Of Kraftwerk, Moroder said: 'I like their sounds very much because they are very clean, but I don't particularly like the songs. They are sometimes a little too easy in their music...' By 'easy', Moroder seemed to suggest that he thought their melodies 'facile' or 'under-developed'. They certainly lacked the fairy dust production of a Moroder dancefloor hit. As if in partial acknowledgement of this, *The Man-Machine* although made at Kling Klang would actually be co-mixed, and mastered, by Leanard Jackson, who had worked with ex-Motown writer and producer Norman Whitfield. 'Well, I think they thought that they must start selling more,' says Moroder. 'I guess they are making a simple mistake. They still reckon that with an easy melody and a synthesizer they can have a hit.'

5.2 The 'New Musick'

Moroder was the most important figure in an emergent genre of what could be called 'electro-disco'. This was music designed to be played in discos, and music which was either totally, or mostly, synthesizer-based, and which in this respect differed from earlier disco music that featured not only guitar, drum and bass, but also lavish string arrangements too. Opinion was split on the merits of the two styles. However, between 1977 and 1979 a good few 'serious' acts bolted a disco sensibility onto their music. Talking Heads, by now possibly the coolest American group on the planet, and born out of the same attitudinal amniotic fluid as Television and the Ramones, used disco-inspired bass-lines on otherwise impeccably new wave tracks such as 'Warning Sign'. Blondie, originally also a punk-ish act, albeit one without Talking Heads' artistic pretensions, were also soon to use disco, and synths, as major constituents of their music.

Then came Devo, an astonishing act from Akron, Ohio. Devo were the supreme American ironists of the new wave. A version of Devo had, in fact, been operating as far back as 1972, but by the late seventies the band had stabilised into the classic line-up of Gerald Casale, Mark Mothersbaugh, Bob Mothersbaugh (or Bob 1), Bob Casale (or Bob 2) and Alan Myers on drums. Their film, *The Truth About De-Evolution*, won plaudits at the Ann Arbor Film Festival and, crucially, was seen by Iggy Pop and David Bowie. Bowie toyed fleetingly with producing the group before his then collaborator Brian Eno took on the task of working with Devo on their debut album at Conny Plank's studio outside Cologne.

Their big idea, that mankind, far from evolving, was in fact regressing, formed the basis of their all-encompassing theory of de-evolution (from which they took their name). They saw all around them a bland, homogenised popular culture, a herd mentality, a society which extinguished individuality. They lampooned it all mercilessly and perfectly. In this they were the Janus face of Kraftwerk. Whereas Kraftwerk predicted, if not progress or improvement, then an inevitable alliance between mankind and the robotic, Devo saw regression everywhere. But both Devo and Kraftwerk appeared to see humans as drones, as replacements or replicas, lacking individuality. Devo's iconography echoed Kraftwerk's in its drilled uniform style. Whether it be taking to the stage dressed in baggy anti-radiation workers' gear, or with absurd flower-pot styled hats, or being cartooned as potatoes with human faces, Devo presented, like Kraftwerk, an instantly memorable identity.

Back in Europe, France was also energised by electronics. Jean-Michel Jarre, son of the eminent composer Maurice, was in the UK Top 5 with an edited version of 'Oxygène' from his four-part classic album of the same name, a single which was again completely instrumental, and a totally wonderful piece of early electronica that straddled the uncomfortable divide between classical/progressive on one side, and cool pop on the other. Also in the summer of 1977, an instrumental, 'Magic Fly', by the group Space, saying a big bonjour from Marseilles, reached number two in the UK. It seems as if Daft Punk have long-lost parents after all.

A group of young writers on *Sounds* would be bewitched, looking for something better than the fag-end of punk. 'The Pistols had just done "Holiday In The Sun', and, you know, the death knells were already there,' says Jon Savage. 'We came up with this idea of doing a couple of issues of *Sounds* around tribal electronic synthetic cut-up music. I think Vivien Goldman had a lot to do with it, and so did Dave Fudger, who were both senior editors on *Sounds* at the time. Jane Suck and I wrote the intros. We were both obsessed by 'Magic Fly' and 'I Feel Love', which was a huge record and was the record that made all of us punk rock snobs say "Oh, my God, disco is fantastic", you know, electronics are the way forward. A year before then, Joe Strummer of the Clash had been on telly saying, we don't have synthesizers in our group, so synthesizers were seen as kind of punk rock nightmares. It was Bowie's Berlin period, *Low* and *"Heroes"* that changed things. *"Heroes"* was fantastic, particularly the second side.'

The 'New Musick' columns in *Sounds* were genuinely agenda-setting pieces of writing. *Sounds* was the first British music weekly to realise that punk was exhausted and a dead end. As Jon Savage recalls, the term "New Musick" was coined to describe what perhaps now might be dubbed post-punk music, or at least a subsection of

136

it. 'The term originates from a big two-issue article that we did at *Sounds* on November 27, 1977 and December 3, 1977. Alan Lewis had asked his punk correspondents – myself, Jane Suck, Sandy Robertson and features editor Viv Goldman – to do an "Images of the New Wave" part 3. Having already decided that punk was old hat, we collectively came up with the idea of celebrating the new electronic and futuristic music that seemed much more interesting than old pub rockers banging out three chords. Jane Suck and I did the editorial in the first issue. Over the two weeks, Steven Lavers wrote about Kraftwerk, Viv about dub and Siouxsie, Davitt Sigerson wrote about disco, Sandy Robertson wrote about Throbbing Gristle, and I wrote about Devo and the Residents. Obviously Bowie and Eno were a big reference, cited in the editorials.'

For Jon Savage, electronic music offered a genuine alternative to the preachiness of punk: 'Punk had become very claustrophobic, London had become very claustrophobic, at that particular point, and that's why all the synthesizer music was such a boon, really, because it offered a way out. I'm not positing it as a total solution to the problems of the UK in 1977/'78. But then there is the argument, which of course Eno would have stated very, very lucidly at that time, which was that pop music should not get involved with politics and social issues beyond a certain point.'

Popular music, for the first time, was catching up with Kraftwerk, or so it seemed. Along with the 'New Musick' and Moroder came, comparatively quickly, pop songs which appeared to have distilled the intellectual import of Kraftwerk, and turned it into pure pop. 'Automatic Lover', by Munich-based 24-year-old Dee D. Jackson, and produced by Moroder, was a sizeable hit in spring 1978 in the UK. With a programmed synth pattern, Jackson, not without a certain allure*, sang: 'See me, feel me, hear me, love me, touch', while a robotic male voice claimed: 'I am your automatic lover'. Later in 1978 came Cerrone, and 'Supernature'. Marc Cerrone, born in 1952 in Vitry-sur-Seine, near Paris, was again, an important, if largely forgotten, begetter of the Nineties DJ cult. This was the first wave of music influenced by Kraftwerk. Like Elvis, like the Beatles, the Stones, the Velvet Underground, Bowie, the Sex Pistols, Chic,

---

* I plead diminished responsibility in that I was 13 at the time of the song's release. However, I must confess: I still love the record.

Michael Jackson, they were inspiring imitators not when they were finished and dead, but while still living and recording.

Cerrone's hit, actually an edited version of a 1977 album track, included the lines: 'Once upon a time/Science opened up the door/We would feed the hungry fields/Till they couldn't eat no more/But the potion that we made/Touched the creatures down below/And they grow up in a way/That we'd never seen before/Supernature.'

Automatic lovers? Supernature? Had the pack caught up with Kraftwerk?

5.3 The Uncanny Valley

The Man-Machine was launched in April 1978 in Paris. It is not often that a press invitation stipulates a dress code; but in this instance the Fourth Estate was kindly requested to wear something red. 'The crimson tide of Euro hackdom have another surprise in store,' writes *Mojo*'s Danny Eccleston in an online tribute to the band. 'Instead of Ralf Hütter, Florian Schneider, Karl Bartos and Wolfgang Flür – the musicians of Kraftwerk – they encounter four dummies onstage. Red shirts, black trousers, black ties, Subbuteo hair, the faces eerily approximating those of the group's human members. "Ralf" to the left in three-quarter profile; "Florian" cradling a flute, to the right; "Karl" and "Wolfgang" in the middle "playing" synth and electronic drums. As one of the band's new songs beeps over the PA, a vocodered voice intones "We are the robots."'

'The Fritz Lang film *Metropolis* was on a loop whilst the album was playing,' remembers Karl Bartos. 'The dummies were on stage posing with intruments looking super-cool. We just stood there with a glass of champagne, stayed an hour and then left. I seem to rememeber that we dined as always at La Coupole and had a great meal. I do remember one time we ate there, the Ramones came to our table just to say hello!'

'We went to Munich to a company called Obermaier which made dolls, puppets, and mannequins,' says Wolfgang. 'The old owner of the company formed our faces from plasticine. Then he made our heads from plastic, and they were then sprayed with colours and hair, and glass eyes were added. He photographed everything; he knew exactly the colour of our skin. It was all hand-made, fantastic and extremely expensive. I think they cost DM 4,000. Each!'

138

The replicas were undoubtedly uncanny in their likeness. A promotional film for the single, 'The Robots', showed the real Kraftwerk performing with the stiff, programmed mien of robots intercut with close-ups of the robots themselves. Both real and fake Kraftwerks were dressed in grey trousers, red long-sleeved shirts and black ties. At the end of the film, Karl, Wolfgang, Florian and Ralf stand in front of their *Doppelgängers*. Throughout the film, the real Kraftwerk are such convincing dummies that it makes for unnerving viewing indeed.

The themes and discoveries of *The Man-Machine* both summarise and predict. The iconography of the robot, the man-built simulacrum in human form, dates back to the twenties. A totemic reference point for Kraftwerk was the work of Fritz Lang, particularly his film masterpiece *Metropolis*, turned into musical form on the album, featuring Maria, the robot. Science-fiction writers such as the academic Isaac Asimov propounded the 'Three Laws of Robotics' in the early forties, writing best-selling science-fiction novels and short stories about the possibilities of cyborg life. In the fifties, *The Day The Earth Stood Still* (1951) and *Forbidden Planet* (1956) starred the robots Gort and Robbie The Robot, respectively. Such technoid-humans were often depicted as slaves, drones, apparatchiks with a semblance of humanity but, in essence, creatures to serve. Indeed the etymology of the word 'robot' comes from the Czech word *'robota'*, which means 'work' or 'labour' or in the figurative sense, 'drudgery'. This idea of a non-human-humanoid was conceived as a powerful emblem of man's mastery over technology. Such artificial constructions did the mundane jobs men and women found arduous or repetitive. The idea of artificial intelligence, as a serious academic discipline, was, by the sixties and seventies, much discussed in universities. And by the eighties the automobile industry was partially automated with machines building cars. But there was always a more sinister side to the idea of the robotic. The dehumanisation inherent in the concept shadowed the rise of dehumanisation in reality, on a wide scale, as Nazi Germany, Communist Russia, and other totalitarian regimes of the mid-twentieth century either classified and/or treated certain ethnic groups as sub-human, disposable drones.

Kraftwerk take the concept a stage further, predicting, even welcoming, an interface between man and machine. Florian spoke of his brain as 'blank tape', a microphone for each ear. Ralf spoke of 'the duplicate'. 'We were born biologically from a moment of hazard … But we were born in ourselves. We have an internal duplicate.' As ever with Kraftwerk, there's always a level of irony and humour in the depiction, perhaps a further swipe at those British and American journalists who saw the earlier Kraftwerk shows and mocked their statuesque stage presence. However, the topics introduced in *The Man-Machine*, the idea of the 'demi-human being', now seem eerily predictive. Over the following 30 years, mankind has merged with technology on several levels.

For the severely handicapped, the seriously injured, those with degenerative illnesses of various sorts, or for a variety of people with heart and lung conditions, the interjection of technology, whether it be through speech-recognition technologies, implants of various sorts, or a range of prosthetics, has prolonged life where in centuries past, it would have ended. However, the range and extent of this intervention has led to cries from the unconvinced that man is 'playing God'. Where would it all end? A human being supported almost completely by prosthetics, a nightmarish vision of future-kind as cyborgs? It's a vision skilfully dramatised in science-fiction, most chillingly (for British audiences at least) in *Dr Who*, whose Cybermen, unlike the more famous Daleks, are a more believable and accurate piece of projection in terms of the horrors of what might happen if mankind fused completely with technology.

And, in our everyday life, we increasingly function in tandem with machines. Back when Kraftwerk recorded *The Man-Machine*, our everyday 'machines' in affluent Western societies would include a telephone (for most), a TV set, a variety of household electrical appliances, maybe even the odd sex toy. Today, many people under the age of 70 would find it difficult to function at all without an internet connection and a mobile phone. We cannot now conceive of writing a document or communicating with friends and work colleagues without the use of the sort of sophisticated technology which would have seemed deeply strange to someone living in the seventies. Social networking, dating, even sex can now be practised solely by proxy, by an interface between man (and woman) and machine. We can now read a book without having a physical book, and play tennis in front of our Xbox and television without ever thinking of packing a racquet and heading off to a tennis court. Our lives have become a tangled mix of the real and the simulated.

Perhaps on a more obvious level, the projection of the four Germans as four robots is yet another manifestation of the performer hiding behind a mask. But there is something camp about the Kraftwerk robots which undercuts, if only slightly, the real menace many find in the robotic. Watching the *Man-Machine*-era Kraftwerk, and the relatively life-like *Doppelgängers*, we are certainly puzzled, disquieted, if not frightened. An explanation for this lies in the theory of the 'uncanny valley', first used by robotics professor Masahiro Mori. In a graphical representation of empathy (and the lack of it) with humanoid figures, the hypothesis states that the more human a robot looks, the more empathy we will have for it. And so, the creations in the last decade, of robots which look strikingly lifelike, tend not to frighten as such. In the same way, robots who look like Meccano kits, or are made out of junk with car hubcaps for eyes, do not frighten us either, as their form is sufficiently un-human as to be decoded as false, even comical, or childlike.

However, it's the liminal state, the 'uncanny valley', which frightens us, the stage before a robot becomes 98% human-like that sends shivers down the spine. In a controlled experiment conducted at the University of California, San Diego, 20 subjects aged between 20 and 36 were shown three different sequences of images of a robot made at Osaka University. This especially lifelike robot was shown, along with the real-life human model, and then the robot stripped of any lifelike prosthetic, essentially a metal frame. The results were startling: 'The subjects were shown each of the videos and were informed about which was a robot and which human,' wrote Mark Brown in 2011. 'Then, the subjects' brains were scanned in an MRI machine. When viewing the real human and the metallic robot, the brains showed very typical reactions. But when presented with the uncanny android, the brain "lit up" like a Christmas tree. When viewing the android, the parietal cortex – and specifically the areas that connect the part of the brain's visual cortex that processes bodily movements with the section of the motor cortex thought to contain mirror (or empathy) neurons – saw high levels of activity. It suggests that the brain couldn't compute the incongruity between the android's human-like appearance and its robotic motion. In the other experiments – when the onscreen performer looks human and moves likes a human, or looks like a robot and moves like a robot – our brains are fine. But when the two states are in conflict, trouble arises.'

This is why we are frightened of ghosts, zombies, Frankenstein's monster, and, perhaps also, in real life, corpses; they are sufficiently within our frames of reference relating to what a human being should look like, but grotesquely framed at that, and so elicit responses of confusion and, ultimately, fear. Kraftwerk's walking mannequins are just sufficiently real-life to remain unthreatening to most. But only just. There's still something which strikes us at not quite right about the man machines.

What Kraftwerk were conscious of, on the level of theory, was that they were making music at a time when the Western world was heavily industrialised, rationalised, and organised under a completely new set of rules. 'The point of view of the nineteenth century is over,' proclaimed Ralf. 'The myth of the important artist has been overexploited. It doesn't fit any more with the standards of modern society. Today, mass production rules.' Kraftwerk were, in part, satirising these new rules of production and consumption. By turning themselves into robots, they were linked into the current mode of production very clearly. The successful West German car manufacturer Audi may have proclaimed '*Vorsprung durch Technik*' ('advancement through technology') in its adverts from the late seventies onwards, but it would be hard to find a better sales pitch for Kraftwerk too. With one's high-tech cars being built by robots, it was only fitting that the music you heard when you drove them out of the showroom was made by robots too.

5.4 Military Cabaret In Red, White And Black

Films such as *Star Wars, Close Encounters Of The Third Kind* and *Saturday Night Fever* might have been the big box office successes of the late-seventies, but these mainstream films were not usually the sort watched by young men and women with pretentions of the artistic kind. Tortured left-field French-language art-house films were likely to be favoured, along with many a silent classic from pre-Nazi Germany such as *The Cabinet Of Dr Cagliari, Nosferatu,* and *Metropolis.* Having unusual, interesting frames of reference outside the mainstream was not simply a modish affectation (although it probably was for some). It was part of a quest to find material with which to enrich the mainstream, part of a questing spirit which sought to break down the barriers between the arts.

Ralf Dörper outlines how movies were – for him, at least, as a teenager in the late-seventies – more important than music: 'For me, they were, or could be, more radical or multi-dimensional than music before punk and industrial. One of my favourites was John Carpenter. It was not just the picture or the storyline, however. The music played a big part. So a lot of music that I thought was pretty interesting came from the movies, and a lot of this music was electronic. It probably first started with *Clockwork Orange*.' Ralf Hütter commented in 1978, 'I think the records are, to us, like film. We call our music acoustical films, and actually when we perform in concert there's the volume factor and also the reverb and the echo of the hall where we play, because the volume of the music really is only to be there when we perform live, and the presence of people in the room changes the music.'

When *The Man-Machine* was released, attention was lavished on the album artwork which depicted the band dressed in grey trousers, red shirts and black ties, wearing red lipstick, their hair smartly combed and cut uniformly short, and posing in a drilled military order facing left, arms on hips.* It immediately resonated with its public, perhaps in ways which were unintended. The imagery was consciously indebted to the expressionist black-and-white films of the interwar period with the use of thick make-up and bold contrasting monochrome. However, many fans and critics read into the imagery darker shadings, as if Kraftwerk had turned themselves into some sort of parody of gay storm troopers.

'That red and black of *The Man-Machine* included lipstick for the lads,' says John Foxx. 'I think there's a more serious cabaret angle in Germany. In Britain, it's all *Dad's Army* and panto; very different.' 'In the German films of the twenties, men were covered in make-up just like women,' says Wolfgang, 'with their red lips and powder everywhere, there were some very sweet-looking men from this time.'

---

* To this day, one can see men and women at Kraftwerk concerts dressed in red shirt and black tie, and extremely cool they look too.

That said, the colours of *The Man-Machine* – red, white, and black – are exactly those of the Nazi flag, with its black swastika circled in white and framed in red. Karl, however, is at pains to point out that any similarity is totally accidental: 'Black and white and red and grey just work perfectly well together as a colour language.'

What was incontrovertible was that the sleeve design by Karl Klefisch drew heavily on, even pastiched, the work of Russian Constructivist artist El Lissitzky (to such an extent that he is credited in the sleeve notes), and specifically his art work in *For The Voice* (1924). Andy McCluskey on *The Man-Machine* album cover: 'The styling of it definitely has that kind of Russian modernist look. They are standing on the staircase, the kind which you find all over Germany and which were rebuilt in the forties and fifties. And, yes, they are wearing that stark red and black, and the red lipstick (whether that was painted on afterwards or not). It is quite disturbing. One of the things that I always liked about Kraftwerk is that they were not afraid to wear... not their heart on their sleeve... but their 'art' on their sleeve, to wear their brains on their sleeve.' Ralf Dörper comments: 'I remember seeing the artwork for *Man-Machine* and thinking that everything was really perfect. The photographs, the way they were designed, that for me was perfection in a record.'

The Man-Machine sold impressively if not spectacularly, reaching the Top 20 in Germany, France (where it sold 200,000 copies), Austria and Italy. In the UK, a highest chart placing of nine brought a gold disc. In the USA, however, the album, like its two predecessors, failed to break through. Reviews, particularly in the UK, were on the warm side of glowing. In *NME* Andy Gill wrote: 'The scarcity of the lyrics leaves the emphasis squarely on those robot rhythms, chilling tones and exquisite melodies. The mastery with which Kraftwerk handle these aspects results in the most extraordinary unification of science and art, turning on its head the commonly accepted Kantian split between the classical and the romantic.' He goes on: 'This is a bitch of a dance record; but its complexity of construction (there's a lot more than electronic percussion in there) makes it just as enjoyable for those with broken legs... *The Man-Machine* stands as one of the pinnacles of seventies rock music, and one which... I doubt Kraftwerk will ever surpass. You will buy it, or you will be deemed mentally unstable.'

144

Today, *The Man-Machine* has entered into critical immortality. It has also been, like its three predecessors, a major source of inspiration for aspiring musicians. 'It was really *The Man-Machine* that bought me into Kraftwerk properly,' says Gary Numan. 'Kraftwerk seemed to be totally technology-driven. It had to be machine-made. I was much, much less of a pioneer than they ever were. They were streets ahead of pretty much everybody. And most of the people that followed, me included, just took elements of it, really, and added it to something else. They were genuinely pioneering.' 'It had roots almost in a type of German cabaret,' says Duran Duran's John Taylor. 'It all feels like Marlene Dietrich is not too far away, and you've got that decadence of twenties Berlin, you've got *Metropolis* in there.'

There's one track from the album we haven't yet mentioned. It would be unique within the Kraftwerk canon, a song which was, indeed, the first electro-ballad, and a song full of love... for the city.

5.5 The City As Beauty

Kraftwerk have repeatedly fallen foul of two lazy pieces of criticism. The first is that their music 'all sounds the same', which simply betrays ignorance or some sort of music-deafness, and the second is that it sounds cold and detached. The first criticism often seems to come from listeners so wedded to the idea that a song should have traditional instrumentation, the comfort of a verse, chorus, middle-eight structure, and a 'proper' lead singer, that any sort of pop music which challenges these basic premises is somehow not music but noise. The second criticism exposes an aesthetic sensibility that for a pop song to work on an emotional level it must either come from the soul or blues tradition, or be some sort of *X-Factor*-styled over-emoted piece of fluff. 'Florian [is] very annoyed at how Kraftwerk are sometimes perceived,' says friend Uwe Schmidt. 'He's very annoyed about the type of musicians who say they're inspired by Kraftwerk when they lack entirely this romantic aspect which for them was very important.' 'Neon Lights' from *The Man-Machine* is a sonic refutation of the allegations that Kraftwerk had no soul.

Finding joy in the bright lights of the city, 'Neon Lights' is a love song for the modern world, a world of coffee bars, night clubs, and light all around. 'I thought "Neon Lights" was strikingly beautiful. Sinatra should have covered it,' says John Foxx. 'It's tantalising too, because it also seems to represent a direction they never took. That was one beautiful, dignified, romantic song. I felt they'd managed to attain a certain elusive new poise just perfectly, then that was it.'

Kraftwerk felt themselves as musicians of and for the city, and for the industrial, the modern. Ralf Hütter: 'Living in this industrial zone where the Rhine and the Ruhr cross… it's the biggest industrial zone in Europe, it stretches out over 100 km and there's like 20 million people, so when we were touring all the time, we went from Düsseldorf, Dortmund, Essen, all the cities and factories and… since we were into noise anyway, and we kind of liked industrial production and we had this vision of our music being like the voice of this industrial product. Germany has no popular music.'

The sublime attraction for the city was felt by other electronic artists in the UK too, in the wake of Kraftwerk's initial statement. The Human League, from the northern industrial city of Sheffield, were one. On their debut album, *Reproduction*, released in 1979, they sang, in response to the Sex Pistols' nihilism of 'God Save The Queen', and the existential miserabilism and negaholicism of the Manchester scene: 'No future they say/But must it be that way?/ Now is calling/The city is human', and then later, with an eye cast backwards to their fathers' generation who had endured mass poverty and world war, 'We've had it easy, we should be glad/High-rise living's not so bad.'

If for the Human League the city represented optimism and a certain allure, for an artist like John Foxx, equally obsessed with the urban, it related to something rather different. Foxx had a sublime attraction to the city, in parts thrilled, in parts repelled, even frightened. As leader of Ultravox, Foxx had engaged with similar themes before the release of *The Man-Machine*, and claims that Kraftwerk's fascination with the city had many precedents within popular culture. 'Sinatra for instance built his career on singing songs that were a phone call from a neon bar in some great city. Chuck Berry was the terminal zone automobile poet, and Bob Dylan had rerouted everything on the list (but transhumanism) into his music by 1968. So there were lots of others parked up close,' said Foxx in 2009. 'Most of us are living in cities now, we're still figuring out how best to do it, and what effects that environment – plus its allied technological and psychological ecologies – is having on us. I guess we're all interested, because we all have to deal with it on a daily basis. Also, I was writing from that perspective some time before I'd seriously listened to Kraftwerk ('I Want To Be A Machine' for instance, was written in 1975 and recorded in 1976, and released a year or so before *The Man-Machine*). I believe that these overlaps are a result of something more generalised. In this case, there are a couple of recent generations of musicians, filmmakers, writers and artists who draw on a very similar set of themes – how to live in a city, its mystery, fear and beauty, the possibilities of the modern city as new myth-land, how cities will alter us. Among these I'd number Ballard, Burroughs, Sinclair, Auster, Ishiguro, David Lynch, Gilbert and George. These shade off at some outer edges into Roxy and Bowie, and at others into film noir and French cinema – Resnais particularly, then at others into artists such as Duchamp and Rauschenberg and Factory-period Warhol, even back to Fluxus and the Situationists.'

'Neon Lights', released as a single from the LP, would fail to chart inside the UK Top 40. However, it would be covered by OMD in 1991 on their *Sugar Tax* album, and would have the odd distinction of also being recorded by those twin giants of eighties stadium rock, Simple Minds and U2, although much later in their careers. It suggested a warmth and wonder at odds with so much of *The Man-Machine* itself, which rather begs the question, what were Ralf, Florian, Wolfgang and Karl being when they were just, well, being?

5.6 'RFWK'*

Behind the carefully constructed carapace of *The Man-Machine*, Kraftwerk were, of course, four young men. Sometimes Kraftwerk are spoken of as if they were abstractions, divorced from everyday life, a chimera largely created by Ralf and Florian who would rather we all see them as worker bees serving the Queen bee that was Kling Klang. Not so.

The dynamic within the band was important. Some members of Kraftwerk were more equal than others. By the late seventies, Ralf

---

* The title of a tribute to Kraftwerk from OMD, and found on their 2010 CD *History Of Modern*.

had emerged as the undisputed leader of Kraftwerk. Wolfgang and Karl certainly did not feel in the same league as Ralf. Karl thought of himself always as the younger brother, and although, technically, he was more proficient musically than Ralf, he demurred in many other areas. Ralf had been educated in a Waldorf school, guided by the intellectual programme of Austrian philosopher Rudolf Steiner. This humanist schooling helped students fulfil their 'unique destiny'. What effect this schooling had on Ralf is, of course, open to conjecture, although one critique of those who have gone through the system is that it produces children who believe themselves to be members of an elite; and detractors of Steiner schools also point to something approaching educational quackery behind the educational plan. Ralf was, without question, extremely bright. He could speak English and French fluently and was an unconventionally brilliant musician.

Ralf was, however, somebody who felt isolated, different. 'How can a man like him find love? And a good partnership, that's most difficult,' says Wolfgang. 'The girls he had, as far as I know, in the 14 years I was in the band with him, he would try to change their personality so they were how he wanted them to be. This would work a little while until the moment the girl realised what was happening and left him. It was always the same. So he had no long-term relationship, ever.'

Ralf liked to give the impression that he was always on duty. He was driven, and even lapses into idleness and boredom would not be admitted readily. 'In our society, everything is geared towards leisure and holidays. You can put people into slavery for 10 months by promising them fulfilment on their holidays. This separation between work and holidays doesn't interest us,' he said a little later in 1982. 'You don't get out of slavery by going on holidays. We don't need to go on holiday. I wouldn't know what to do. We are suggesting that people re-think their whole working situation, co-operate with one another and become productive. This is how work should be whether you are a musician, a journalist or a dentist.'

In an interview with Glenn O'Brien from 1977, we get a snapshot of the human side of Ralf. He would be somebody, using the parlance of the time, who might have been called an 'odd-bod'. We learn that he has no pets: 'We are not fond of animals. We like humans. Most people have animals as a substitute for human

148

contact.' He gets up around noon and goes to bed around 4 a.m. He runs to keep fit, although 'Florian races bicycles'. He likes toast with apricot jam and cake. He drinks coffee. 'We don't drink beer. It makes your brain go slow.' We learn that Ralf's favourite composers are Schubert and Wagner and that he doesn't like flying, likes trains, but likes cars most of all. Asked about his looks and if he likes them, he replies, revealingly, only 'sometimes', and that he plans on changing them but 'it's a gradual process'. In the same interview, we also learn that Florian is a lover of cheesecake, and that 'we drink a little champagne, not hard liquors'. And finally, we hear that Florian's nickname is 'V2', and Ralf's 'Doktor'! Finally, O'Brien elicits a response which is perhaps the most revealing of all. 'Do your parents like what you do?' 'No, they would like to prevent us from doing what we do,' replies Ralf, reminding us that it was a major act of rebellion not to conform to their parents' view of what one should become in a moneyed society. 'We are doing business, but we should be doing office business.'

Karl's impression of Ralf and Florian was of two young men who were, to a certain degree, young fogeys. 'At one of our first meetings, I recall that they opened the car boot, and there were golf clubs and golf shoes with spikes. They impressed on me the virtues of fresh air and walking in the countryside. They said it was good for the mind, and contemplation. I am not sure if they ever took golf seriously, but it was certainly the kind of activity with which they wished to be associated. I also remember Ralf's niece had a dog, and his then girlfriend also had a dog too. He loved dogs! Schneider, like Hütter, was really in control, although slightly less so. I never saw Ralf or Florian drunk in 15 years. Florian had his principles but he could change them; he was more flexible. He would say that he was a vegetarian unless, of course, there was the possibility of eating some ham with his asparagus! He would claim he didn't drink beer until he had two or three beers in a restaurant during a break from our Kling Klang work, our "late-night lunch!". We had a fantastic time together, all four of us.'

Ralf Hütter and Florian Schneider were interviewed by Ralf Dörper in or around the year 1980. 'I was already in Die Krupps,' says Ralf Dörper, 'and I was also working for the music pages of a German programme magazine called *Überblick*, which was Düsseldorf's answer to *Time Out*. I decided to do an article on them.

That led to a direct meeting. Ralf was a very nice guy – we even exchanged records: "The Model" for "Wahre Arbeit Wahrer Lohn". He really had a vision for Kraftwerk and he was really living that vision. If you look at him, whatever he says, you end up by saying, that's "Kraftwerk". He couldn't be something else.'

According to Ralf Dörper, 'Florian was also, in a way, undeniably Kraftwerk. He was the one who even could *be* Kraftwerk in the short period when Ralf was not around, the period when he was working with Michael Rother. For me, it was always Ralf and Florian, but for me it was Florian who was always the "robotnik". I think he's great! If you had wanted to cast characters in a movie in the thirties or even the sixties about German mad professors or people working on strange inventions, he would have been perfect. He would be a perfect Dr. Mabuse as well. But essentially, for me he is very much the face of Kraftwerk. When I meet him I always think he is great, because he is in a way also strange.'

'Florian could be absolutely charming and nice to everyone,' remembers Wolfgang, 'but it could change from one second to the next. He could be completely different and have a split personality. But he could be generous, also financially generous. He always paid when we went to restaurants. I don't think I paid for one meal in all the 14 years that I was with them. It was easy for them to pay. They knew that they paid us lousy, so they paid for our meals.' It was probably down to Florian that Kraftwerk did not tour regularly. 'Florian wanted to stay at home,' is how Wolfgang puts it, and that says a lot about the secretive nature which was Kraftwerk's received media image. Confident and with a quirky humour, Florian was not someone to have role models. 'He never spoke about anybody else's music, or anyone who might be his hero,' continues Wolfgang. 'He was his own hero!'

Florian's girlfriend in the mid-seventies, Barbara Niemöller, is described by Wolfgang Flür in *I Was A Robot*: 'Barbara Niemöller was Florian's girlfriend, although she obviously liked Emil a lot. She was a quiet girl and was very delicate, almost spiritual. She appeared almost translucent, with her pale skin and pale blue eyes. Her thin body seemed to sway as she walked. She wasn't a very lively person, though, and was absolutely androgynous.' After Barbara came Sandhia Whaley, an American, who gave the entire band yoga classes.

Wolfgang, Karl and Emil Schult lived together in a large apartment, originally rented by Ralf, in Bergerallee 9 in Düsseldorf: three fanciable young men in a stylish bachelor pad and with enough money. 'At the time, we didn't actually have bank accounts, or, if we did, they had no money in them,' says Karl. 'Money for us wasn't the main objective. During this period, I was also working as a classical musician, playing with different orchestras in the Düsseldorf region.' Wolfgang also supplemented his income by working as a drummer with various local dance bands. Wolfgang and Karl became close friends. 'Karl's personality was completely different to that of Ralf and Florian,' says Wolfgang. 'He is very generous, and he has a sense of humour which is extraordinary. Karl is very, very special.'

'Wolfgang was fun to be with,' says Karl. 'Always a good laugh. We got along very, very well! I always thought that he would have been a good actor, if he'd had the chance to get into a circle of filmmakers.' Emil, the band's collaborator as co-lyricist and graphic artist, made up the triumvirate of hormonally charged young men. 'He was a nice guy. He is sensitive. He is an artist, very interested in nature and the countryside,' remembers Wolfgang. 'We had a very good friendship.' On Sundays, Wolfgang would often drive out with Emil into the surrounding countryside in his blue, 6-cylinder 1964 Mercedes. Like Florian, Emil was apparently not someone you would willingly get into a car with if they were at the wheel.

Life was rather good. 'The apartment was maybe 200 square metres with parquet flooring and a two-room cellar,' says Karl. 'We had a washing machine and a small rehearsal room there. Emil and Wolfgang built our own speaker systems in the cellar room. Upstairs we had a view of a small lake and a park. It was beautiful. It was very close to the Mannesmann skyscraper building, one of the first built in Germany after the war, built incidentally by Paul Schneider-Esleben! It is still part of the skyline. From the flat we were within walking distance of the Kling Klang Studio and the Altstadt where all the clubs were.

'We were a kind of family. We cooked together sometimes. And sometimes we didn't see each other for two weeks,' adds Wolfgang, looking back with obvious affection. 'We each had our own special circle of friends, who had nothing to do with music, people from other levels, with other interests. Sometimes we held big parties in the flat. It was fantastic for partying. We had more than a hundred people. A lot of wine went down our throats! We had a lot of girls there, as well. It was a fantastic time. It was before HIV. We didn't need to be afraid of going to bed with a girl. We didn't need to be afraid of anything.'

5.7 The Working Man's Kraftwerk

In 1979 and 1980, Kraftwerk were still far from being an overground success. None of the singles from *The Man-Machine* had in fact charted in the UK Top 40, and although they remained much quoted in the press, the public as a whole needed persuading. John Foxx is adamant that, after the initial push from Bowie, the patronage of British musicians kept Kraftwerk current. 'Kraftwerk actually benefitted greatly from the success of British bands and artists, from being lionised by Bowie and Iggy, and acknowledged as a source influence by the next generation of bands. At the time they weren't too popular in Germany, Britain, most of Europe, or mainstream America – only France seemed to take to them. It was British bands who really put them on the map. The Brit bands demonstrated how you could create a new form of popular music from an (initially) non-pop, non-song, largely experimental blueprint. Britain added pop songs to the mix – and that was what cracked it for everyone. It's what we're good at.'

Foxx continues: 'We lived in big, dirty, post-industrial, out-of-control cities. Punk was a sort of one-dimensional jumpstart to dealing with that, but everyone was well beyond being angry all the time. That was just spitting your dummy out of the pram. Fun, but useless. There was a great need for something far more capable of conveying all the wonder, fear, beauty, romance, bravado, hope and inadequacy that everyone felt. Synthesizers were capable of that. More sonic range than a guitar, and you only needed one finger to play them – or none, if you sequenced. They arrived – in their cheap versions – at just the right time to equip a generation ready and waiting for some method of assembling their own particular grammar of the cities. So that generation got to work – just as every generation does – assembling their particular civilisation from all the flotsam and wreckage and worn-out discarded stuff lying around. You simply incorporate everything that chimes – disco, film noir, pop songs, rock, cheap sci-fi, pulp fiction, comics, avant-garde

152

art, haircuts, certain specific forms of sex and violence, authors who hurt – Ballard, Burroughs, and films and music that do the same – Kubrick, Carlos. Cool stances of all kinds ... Kraftwerk were only one element, but they were a significant one, partly because they defined themselves directly against conventional pop and rock, not by being in any way oppositional, but by simply omitting the clichéd posturing involving guitars and tight pants. We'd all had enough of that.

'Their music had the power to operate well through a club sound system, in fact better than any music other than disco – but with none of the clichés of disco. They simply understood and used the potential of disco's remorselessly repetitive and powerful new bass drum and percussion sonics, via club sound systems. And the sounds they made were imaginative – detached and fierce at the same time. The clubs were the place where a generation waiting to be patterned were sifting everything for just the right design. They recognised Kraftwerk as the significant prototype, just as the Rolling Stones and Beatles generation had recognised Chuck Berry or John Lee Hooker. So the generation of Gary Numan, the Human League, Soft Cell, Depeche Mode, Visage etc., had arrived. I remember a sort of pinball effect – when you walk into a room, there's a series of moments of recognition – ping – where the lights go on as like minds spot each other by some sort of inherent, instantaneous recognition process, more electrical than chemical. Most importantly, the Brits had that innate ability to make good pop songs and have fun with images and stances of all kinds. That was what we added to European electronics. We are better at that than anyone. We've got plenty of time, because it's raining outside, there are reasonable welfare and educational systems, and no job to go to.'

The first group to accept fully the principles of Kraftwerk were the Human League, based in Sheffield. 'It was a kind of manifesto that we weren't going to use anything but electronic equipment, even though that was actually quite debilitating in a way,' says Ian Craig Marsh, one of the group's co-founders. 'Kraftwerk also definitely had that view that they were an electronic outfit. In fact, all the new German bands had the view that this was a new age, and, on principle, you shouldn't be using old instrumentation. It's like the new folk music, moving forward in a purely electronic medium.'

153

What struck the Human League were two things. Firstly, that Kraftwerk did not have a natural singer among their ranks and they quickly identified a sonic gap here. In recruiting Phil Oakey as lead singer they had found a frontman with an instantly recognisable baritone and also someone with commanding good looks. And secondly, the Human League understood something that many people missed about Kraftwerk: that their music was visceral. Played at high volume it hit the solar plexus just as brutally as any guitar solo. The Human League's first two albums, and their most inventive, *Reproduction* (1979) and *Travelogue* (1980), explored this potential on ground-breaking tracks such as 'Being Boiled', and particularly 'The Black Hit Of Space', a song which began with such an overload of synth sonics it sounded as if the mixing console was blowing up.

Up and down the UK, people were now listening hard. Gary Numan would be the first electronic star. Today, Numan concedes that there was a lot of good fortune involved, and is also quick to point out that although he is thankful for the tag 'the world's first electronic superstar', many of his early classic singles were either written on the guitar or had guitars and drums all over them. When 'Are "Friends" Electric?' reached number one in the early summer of 1979 it marked a sea change in modern music. It was from this point on that a completely new pop aesthetic swept through and lit a tinderbox of talent up and down the country.

In Basildon, Essex, a bunch of teenagers soon to become Depeche Mode were also listening, and so were another group of teenagers based in Birmingham. It was in this period (around 1978) that John Taylor and his friend Nick Rhodes started making music, a development which would lead to the formation of one of the biggest bands of the next decade, Duran Duran. 'We sort of set up shop together in 1978. We were already friends before that. It was 1978 when we decided we were going to form a band together. We decided to get a synthesizer, because we liked the way things were going, we liked the rhythmic things that were happening in the synthesizer world. I'd have to say that Kraftwerk were a part of that.' Looking back, John muses: 'The Human League were like the working man's Kraftwerk, in a way!'

The lineage from Bowie and glam, through punk, then Kraftwerk and British electronica, and, by the end of the eighties, house music, is nowhere better demonstrated than through the personal biography of Mark Moore, whose band S-Express would score a massive mainstream hit in 1988 with 'Theme From S-Express'. 'I was a punk rocker. I started going to gigs, first one I saw was the Damned... I met this girl at a punk party called Bowie Teresa, who looked exactly like David Bowie as he did in *Man Who Fell To Earth*. ... And she said, "We're going to go to this great club, which is full of weirdoes, freaks and rent boys and prostitutes. It's called Billy's. It's a Bowie night and they play Bowie, Roxy Music, Kraftwerk." I went there and it was Steve Strange's first club with Rusty Egan DJing.'

For Moore, Rusty Egan was crucial to the burgeoning early eighties club scene. 'Rusty was definitely – along with John Peel and also this girl called Mandy who played at the Marquee – they were very influential for me. John Peel for the variety, but also Rusty Egan. Very underrated. The Blitz opened up and we'd be going to the Blitz, but also another club opened up by Rusty Egan and Steve Strange: Hell, which was in Covent Garden, just in the place round the corner from the Rock Garden. They opened that one because Blitz was becoming quite well known, a bit like the Blitz but more elitist, I suppose. Even though the Blitz was quite elitist!... We'd come back from clubs like Blitz, lay mattresses out on the floor and crash out there and listen to Kraftwerk and Psychedelic Furs' first album.'

A glance now at the Blitz Club set list is a reminder of a time when being modernist, rejecting the blues along with most soul and rock, the Beatles and the Stones and most punk too, was a mission statement. It is also a snapshot, had we known it, of possibly the very last time in British pop culture when recycling the past, the long, dead past, wasn't in the minds of the scenesters. Just two years later, the dominating force on the horizon was indie music with its obvious connections, both musically and temperamentally, with the sixties and early seventies. As a portal into a time when everything seemed modern, the set list makes emotive reading – Bowie tops the list of contributions with six songs regularly on rotation (all from the then recent albums – *Low*, *"Heroes"*, *Lodger* and *Scary Monsters*), along with the electronic glare of early Ultravox, Neu!'s ground-breaking 'E-Musik', Roxy Music's recent cool pop, Simple Minds at their early experimental best and, of course, Kraftwerk. There would

155

even be slots for Vangelis, Jeff Wayne and the mournfully addictive 'Magic Fly' by Space.*

---

* Blitz Club Playlist: Don Armando – Deputy of Love (12″ full length version) 1979, Blondie – Heart Of Glass (7″ edit) 1978, David Bowie – Always Crashing in the Same Car (from the album *Low*) 1977, David Bowie – Be My Wife 1977, David Bowie – Helden (German 7″ version) 1977, David Bowie – Sound & Vision 1977, David Bowie – D.J. (7″ edit) 1979, David Bowie – Ashes To Ashes (7″ edit) 1980, Cabaret Voltaire – Nag Nag Nag 1979, Wendy Carlos – Theme From A Clockwork Orange (Beethoviana) 1972, Cerrone – Supernature (12″ full length version) 1977, Billy Cobham – Storm (from the album *Crosswinds*) 1974, Barry De Vorzon – Theme from *The Warriors* (from the soundtrack to *The Warriors*) 1979, Alice Cooper – Eighteen 1971, Cowboys International – Thrash 1979, Holger Czukay – Hollywood Symphony (from the album *Movies*) 1979, Sheila and B. Devotion – Spacer (12″ full length version) 1979, Brian Eno – No One Receiving (from the album *Before And After Science*) 1977, Brian Eno – King's Lead Hat 1978, Brian Eno and Snatch – RAF (b-side to King's Lead Hat 7″) 1978, Eno, Moebius, Roedelius – Broken Head (from the album *After the Heat*) 1978, Fad Gadget – Ricky's Hand 1980, Marianne Faithfull – Broken English (12″ long version) 1979, Flying Lizards – Money (7″ edit) 1979, John Foxx – No One Driving (7″ remix) 1980, Peter Gabriel – Games without Frontiers (7″ edit) 1980, Nina Hagen Band – TV Glotzer (White Punks on Dope) 1979, Human League – Being Boiled (from the 7″ EP *Holiday '80* and *Travelogue* album) 1980, Japan – Life in Tokyo (original 7″ short version) 1979, Jean Michel Jarre – Equinoxe 4 (French 12″ remix) 1978, Grace Jones – La Vie en Rose (7″ edit) 1977, Joy Division – Atmosphere 1980, Kraftwerk – Radioactivity (7″ edit) 1976, Kraftwerk – Trans Europe Express (7″ edit) 1977, Kraftwerk – The Robots (original 7″ edit) 1978, Kraftwerk – The Model 1978, La Düsseldorf – La Düsseldorf (from the album *La Düsseldorf*) 1976, La Düsseldorf – Geld (from the album *Viva*) 1978, Landscape – U2XME1X2MUCH 1977, Landscape – European Man (7″ version) 1980, Thomas Leer and Robert Rental – Day Breaks, Night Heals (from the album *The Bridge*) 1979, Lori and the Chameleons – Touch 1979, M – M Factor (UK version, b-side to Pop Muzik 7″) 1979, Magazine – Touch And Go 1978, Mahler – Adagio from the 5th Symphony (from the soundtrack *Death In Venice*) 1971, Patrick D. Martin – I Like 'Lectric Motors 1979, Giorgio Moroder – The Chase (12″ full length version) 1978, Ennio Morricone – 60 Seconds To What (La Resa Dei Conti) (from the soundtrack *For A Few Dollars More*) 1965, Mott the Hoople – All The Young Dudes 1972, Neu! – E-Musik (from the album *Neu!,75*) 1975, The Normal – Warm Leatherette (b-side to T.V.O.D. 7″) 1978, Gary Numan & Tubeway Army – Down In The Park 1978, Gary Numan – Cars 1979, OMD – Electricity (7″ re-recorded version) 1979, Iggy Pop – The Passenger (from the album *Lust For Life*) 1977, Iggy Pop

156

After the punk wars, and the recidivism of pub rock and power pop, the Blitz scene was a haven for fun and frivolity, as well as serious agenda-setting moves. 'It was sort of happy, fun,' remembers Billy Currie of Ultravox and Visage. 'When Rusty invited me round to Billy's Club, which was just over from the Marquee, they were just playing music; and it was lovely to hear this music because we were all a bit sick of the punk vibe. Ultravox had wasted a lot of its energy trying to participate in that, really. We were always getting gobbed on and there was fighting and all that shit and so we were sick of

---

– Nightclubbing (from the album *The Idiot*) 1977, The Psychedelic Furs – Sister Europe 1980, Lou Reed – Perfect Day 1972, Lou Reed – Vicious 1972, Lou Reed – Walk On The Wild Side (unedited album version) 1972, Rinder & Lewis – Willie And The Hand Jive 1979, Rockets – Space Rock (12″ full length version) 1977, Michael Rother – Zyklodrom (from the album *Flammende Herzen*) 1977, Roxy Music – Do The Strand 1973, Roxy Music – Trash 1979, Roxy Music – Dance Away 1979, Roxy Music – Angel Eyes (7″ remix) 1979, Shock – R.E.R.B. (b-side to Angel Face 7″) 1980, Simple Minds – Changeling (original 7″ version) 1980, Simple Minds – I Travel (7″ edit) 1980, Siouxsie & the Banshees – Hong Kong Garden 1978, Sister Sledge – Lost In Music 1979, Space – Magic Fly 1977, Space – Carry On, Turn Me On (from the album *Magic Fly*) 1977, Spandau Ballet – To Cut A Long Story Short (12″ extended version) 1980, Sparks – Number 1 Song In Heaven (7″ edit) 1979, Donna Summer – I Feel Love (7″ edit) 1977, Talking Heads – Psycho Killer 1977, Television – Little Johnny Jewel (Part 1 – 7″ version) 1975, Television – Marquee Moon (album version) 1977, Telex – Moskow Diskow (12″ Maxi version, French vocal) 1979, Throbbing Gristle – Hot On The Heels Of Love (from the deceptively named album *20 Jazz Funk Greats*) 1979, Harry Thumann – Underwater (12″ version) 1979, Ultravox – Hiroshima Mon Amour (re-recording from the album *Ha! Ha! Ha!*) 1977, Ultravox – Slow Motion 1978, Ultravox – Dislocation 1978, Ultravox – Quiet Men (12″ full length version) 1978, Ultravox – Sleepwalk 1980, Vangelis – Pulstar 1976, The Velvet Underground – I'm Waiting For The Man 1973, Vice Versa – New Girls Neutrons (from the 7″ EP 4 Music) 1979, Visage – Tar (original 7″ mix) 1979, Visage – Frequency 7 (original version, b-side to Tar 7″) 1979, Visage – Fade to Grey (12″ extended version) 1980, Jeff Wayne – Eve Of The War (7″ edit) 1978, Wire – I Am The Fly 1978, Gina X – No GDM (7″ edit) 1979, Yello – Bimbo 1979, Yello – I.T. Splash (full length Swiss 7″ version) 1979, Yellow Magic Orchestra – Computer Game (Theme from The Invaders) 1979, Yellow Magic Orchestra – Behind The Mask 1980, (*Solid State Survivor*)
© The Blitz Club 2011 http://www.theblitzclub.com/music.php.

it. It was nice to hear Rusty play Kraftwerk, Bowie and it was easy, quite fun.'

One crucial difference between the new electro pack and Kraftwerk was their attitude to stardom and celebrity. Steve Redhead, author, journalist and expert on youth culture, has some interesting insights into Kraftwerk's influence: 'The anti-celebrity, the anti-media thing, wasn't necessarily taken on by the people who copied Kraftwerk, and Numan's a great example, and a lot of the other people who became singers/pop stars, they certainly took their legacy from Kraftwerk; but actually what they wanted was just to be famous.'

If a new era of dressing up, play, fun was emerging, then a perhaps more fundamental shift was occurring too. Kraftwerk had shown that rock authenticity was outmoded. No guitars, a democracy on stage with no lead singer. And the next step was a logical one. Thomas Dolby: 'Hearing Kraftwerk made me realise that I didn't need to join a band to make pop records, I could do it all myself.'

5.8 Factories And Refineries

There were some, however, who took the Kraftwerk blueprint more literally. Perhaps the most direct, and, most extreme, piece of artistry in the Kraftwerk mould came in 1980, on *Organisation*, the second album by OMD. '"Stanlow" is directly inspired by a working relationship with industry,' records Peter Saville, who worked on the album as designer. 'It uses sounds recorded in the oil refinery in Stanlow [in Ellesmere Port, Cheshire] as its inspiration. That led eventually, 25 years later, to having a tentative approach at combining motion image and ambient recording, which is *The Energy Suite*. Andy ends up writing a love song, a hymn to an oil refinery. It's very much a McCluskey romantic piece. The lyrics to "Stanlow" open "Eternally, this field remains Stanlow. We set you down to care for us, a million hearts to warm".

'His father worked at Stanlow for a while, and there were some issues of labour relations that are interwoven into his lyrics for "Stanlow". The sounds are the sounds of the machinery in the oil refinery. Andy managed to get his father to make some recordings of the industrial equipment. And the result is the opening sounds of "Stanlow".'

158

'We felt entirely comfortable about the fact that oil refineries, aeroplanes and telephone boxes were legitimate subjects,' says Andy from OMD. 'Also the fact that I refused to let us use the word "love" in a song until our third album, because I considered it to be a rock/pop cliché word that was to be avoided at all costs. I am sure that that was a leftover Kraftwerk mentality. The most important thing that we derived from our Kraftwerk inspiration is, as I said previously, the fact that we weren't aware of it. And maybe Kraftwerk weren't aware of it at the time. It is this tension between architecture and morality. We didn't consciously analyse Kraftwerk and say, "Oh, that's what we want to do. We want to inhabit that space. We want to mine the ground between machinery and humanity where that tension lies." We just happened on it. I think, also, that we were trying to be experimental. What we abandoned, the afros and the flares, the last thing that we changed was actually the way that we looked. It was Peter Saville who said, "You don't have to look like Kraftwerk, but you have to look like the music you make. You look like a pair of hippies, how can you be making the music of the future?" We were like "Oh, I guess so", and that is when we got our hair cut and changed our clothes.'

OMD, although essentially a synth act, made certain grudging concessions in how their sound was constructed: 'The fact that, in the early days, when we finally decided we were going to expand and let more people in, we weren't going to let Malcolm [Holmes] have a drum kit, because that was sloppy, messy rock 'n' roll. We wanted him to play an electronic kit with no cymbals so that we could have clarity of sound. We built our own electronic kit and it broke down after the first two gigs. Malcolm said if he couldn't have his own kit back he was going to leave the band. When we recorded things like "Messages", "Souvenir", "Maid Of Orleans", "Electricity" and "Enola Gay", Malcolm was never allowed to play his kit. He had to put down the bass drum, then the snare drum, then the hi hat. We recorded each individual instrument individually to get clean, separated sounds. We didn't want that loose organic spillage.'

What OMD did was to take music which sounded at the time 'completely alien', and give it a more recognisable form. 'We unconsciously distilled Kraftwerk down to three and a half minutes and unconsciously added an early seventies glam, pop catchiness.

The other reason that OMD was huge was because Kraftwerk don't like choruses, the melody is the chorus.' Live on stage, while Paul Humphreys would be mainly static, only occasionally taking centre stage to sing, Andy, with bass guitar strapped and played upside-down, would be an uncommon whirl of adrenaline. His angular, arching dancing is a feature of OMD performances to this day. While Ralf and Florian left the stage at the end of the concert literally not having broken sweat, sweat is all Andy is by the end of an OMD gig.

Perhaps not unsurprisingly, Kraftwerk were big in Northern Britain's urban conurbations, in Liverpool, in Sheffield, and also, crucially, in Manchester. 'The really interesting influence was Joy Division,' says Steve Redhead. 'I've always been a big fan of Joy Division and New Order, and they did learn from Kraftwerk's anti-media and anti-celebrity thing. They watched that European style of dress, synth-pop and all the rest, and they did learn I think that they're an example, actually, of how you disappear within the media.' As for Joy Division, 'It was a general European style that they were after, I think, in post-industrial Manchester in the seventies, and they definitely, individually, were Kraftwerk fans, even in their style of dress. They liked those narrow ties and all that sort of thing. It was a pervasive influence, it seems to me, in music, fashion, style and so on, and they took so much which eventually came out more and more in the actual music that they made as New Order.'

Redhead adds: 'This sleek European style, which is what impressed Joy Division so much, leads to a sleeker kind of modernism which obviously comes through in all Kraftwerk's designs, and then Factory Records' designs. There's so much which links Kraftwerk and Factory, this kind of desire for what I would call European modernity, which I think Kraftwerk represent, at a time when basically you have this kind of flabby, end-of-hippy, post-industrial Manchester, or perhaps Britain, but I think Manchester fits beautifully. Somehow Kraftwerk, Joy Division and New Order were brilliant at the time at making this music which fitted then but also fits now. I call it post-futurism. William Gibson said something like: "The future's here, but it's just unevenly distributed." And they understood it then, as I say. They got it in terms of musical style, fashion style and an ability to transcend this post-industrialism. I think Kraftwerk, New Order and Joy Division are great examples of that, but you could go on: Human League and Sheffield, Cabaret Voltaire, and so on, and there's lots of others. But I think Kraftwerk and New Order are the best examples of it, and that's why their music from then – and now – sounds just absolutely contemporary. What a trick to pull off!'

Peter Saville, the artist and designer at Tony Wilson's Factory Records, has explained the impact of Kraftwerk on his thinking and personal development: 'My own aesthetic point of view is highly influenced by Kraftwerk, in ways that I know and also in ways that I barely even know. I am very influenced by Kraftwerk: they shaped my understanding of the possibilities of contemporary music, and that shapes my understanding of a visual language that can be associated with it. The almost industrial notion of 'going to work', but in the context of contemporary culture, was a kind of art/ philosophical idea that I acquired more from Kraftwerk at that point in my life than from anywhere else. The whole Factory numbering system which pretty much comes from discussions between me and Malcolm Garrett, the appreciation of a number, as opposed to a title, was the kind of idea that Malcolm and I shared as students. This obsession with the catalogue number is a very kind of seventies conceptual art notion, which is very German and very Kraftwerk. The culture of Factory is highly informed by Kraftwerk: and it's Factory that pretty much defines Manchester culturally in the late 20th century.'

Although, as the writer Paul Morley put it, 'there was nothing wooden about Kraftwerk... If it didn't have a button, it wasn't worth pushing', many of the musicians they influenced were willing to use conventional rock instruments. In a way, this was liberating. As Karl Bartos himself reveals, 'The fact that a song is composed on a synth or on a guitar doesn't make any difference. It's the quality that counts. Although, if you compose on piano, guitar, flute, drums or sequencer you will more or less generate different results because each instrument supports certain techniques and/ or concepts of writing music. The media always influences the content.'

Almost every electronica act, from Depeche Mode, OMD and the Human League in the early eighties to the second wave of synth acts such as the Pet Shop Boys and Erasure later in the decade

161

would eventually use non-synth instruments. There would be only one major group who stuck to their guns in banishing conventional instrumentation, and that would be Kraftwerk. Their next LP, the very distillation of a career's worth of knowledge, concepts, and ideas, would be their definitive statement.

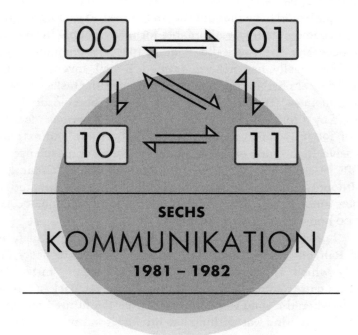

SECHS

KOMMUNIKATION

1981 – 1982

6.1 'Beam Myself Into The Future'

AT ITS highest level, popular music can take on a seer-like quality. Those musicians blessed with a keen sense of perception are able to detect the faintest vibrations of a possible future then express it through music. Back in 1970, the Who's principal writer, Pete Townshend, developed a rock opera, *Lifehouse*, so difficult to realise in its complexity that, faced with the bewilderment of his band mates, he abandoned it altogether amidst a nervous breakdown. One of the ideas in the opera was 'the grid', a matrix which could be plugged into and which could connect individuals from across the globe. It was the sort of idea Tim Berners-Lee would develop 20 years later in reality.

Computer World, Kraftwerk's eighth album, was written by people who appeared to be able to see the world in 1990 and beyond. Few people would have thought that in the next 10 years, computers would become not simply affordable for many people in the West, but a necessity. Kraftwerk did. Back in 1980, the computer age, at least domestically, had not yet dawned. E-mail, invented in 1965, was used by almost no-one outside certain specific tasks performed by big business (the first major rock tour to be co-ordinated on the road by a form of e-mail was David Bowie's *Serious Moonlight* tour of 1983). Home computers were cumbersome and extremely expensive. In the early eighties, models made for domestic use were the BBC Micro, Sinclair ZX Spectrum, Atari 800XL and Commodore 64, although market penetration was still low. It was estimated that, in 1982, among the USA's population of around 226,000,000, only 621,000 home computers were in use.

'I program my home computer/beam myself into the future,' sings Ralf on 'Home Computer,' against a two-note descending melody which appears ominous and forewarning, rather than welcoming us to some electronic Elysium. And yet, back in the early eighties when the song was composed, what the future held for the world of computing was nothing like the way it was portrayed by the media. In the sixties and seventies, when computers were seen on TV at all, they tended to be associated either with science fantasy programmes or with real-life space-age dramas such as the scene inside mission control in Houston, Texas from where the Apollo moon landings were being co-ordinated. Also, they were enormous, occupying entire rooms with rack after rack of what looked like tape-to-tape recording machines, all spinning at wildly different speeds, stopping and starting at will while lights flashed and scrolls of seemingly random numbers appeared on illuminated screens.

Most predictions for domestic computer use were fanciful and posited a future of a fully automated home in which machines would perform tedious everyday tasks and thus leave the occupiers free to enjoy greater amounts of leisure time. Indeed, back in 1969, Honeywell had produced a kitchen computer which was offered for an eye-watering $10,000 and weighed a hundred pounds. It was designed as a labour-saving device as it could store recipes, meaning the lady of the house – inevitably the lady in 1969 – would never be at a loss for a new recipe for the hubby and kids. There is no hard evidence that any of these items were actually sold. Indeed, fully automated houses of the future have been a standard feature of many trade fairs over the years, but almost all the predictions (domestic robots to take out the trash, anyone?) have all proved to be the stuff of the imaginary. And yet, the home computer, or rather home computers, have assumed a central role today that few would have predicted 30 years ago. From seven to 70, we use computers to shop online, to archive our memories, to organise our finances, and to communicate.* The handwritten letter is an antique.

But along with freedoms came rights and responsibilities, also the opportunity for states to monitor activity and collect the personal data of their inhabitants. Kraftwerk make no fanciful claims on *Computer World*. They do not predict a robotised, sci-fi future. However, they do predict, with complete accuracy, that our modern-day lives will be revolutionised: '*Automat und Telespiel/Leiten heute die Zukunft ein/Computer für den Kleinbetrieb/Computer für das eigene Heim.*' ['Automat and tele-game†/Introduce us to the future/ Computer for the small business/computer for the home.'] And, most tellingly, they predict accurately that surveillance culture is here to stay. They announce this without any supporting comment, but rather as an indisputable and possibly necessary component of modern global society for the developed West. Here, the band's ethos might position them in opposition to those in the then West Germany, who regarded the centralised collection of personal data as an infringement of civil liberties. Unlike the UK, Germany requires all its inhabitants to carry an ID card. The German-language version of 'Computer World' contains lyrics missing from the English version: '*Interpol und Deutsche Bank, FBI und Scotland Yard/Flensburg und das BKA, haben unsere Daten da.*' '[Interpol and Deutsche Bank, FBI and Scotland Yard/Flensburg‡ and the Federal

---

* It should, however, be pointed out that as of today, only around 7% of the global population have access to the Internet, a salutary reminder that the majority of humankind are living very different lives to us.

† The forerunner of the computer game and the wonders of the PlayStation and Xbox, back in the mid-to-late seventies, a generation of children were entertained by playing tennis, football, and shooting on the TV with ludicrously basic graphics.

‡ Flensburg is the equivalent of the UK Driver and Vehicle Licensing Agency (DVLA) situated in Swansea.

Criminal Police Office all have our details]. 'Now that it has been penetrated by micro-electronics our whole society is computerised, and each one of us is stored into some point of information by some company or organisation, all stored by numbers,' said Hütter in a 1981 interview. 'When you get into Germany at a border, they place your passport into a machine connected to the *Bundeskriminalamt* [the BKA, Federal Criminal Police Office] in Wiesbaden so they can check whether you can enter or leave, for various reasons other than whether your passport is correct.'

That Kraftwerk were ahead of the curve was further evidenced, in the UK at least, when, in January 1982, the BBC launched the BBC Micro. This was the first time that most of the UK population had seen a computer which looked as if it just might become part of the household. The two studio presenters were Ian McNaught-Davis and Chris Searle, who was then best known for a stint on the consumer choice programme *That's Life*. 'Mac' showed us the delights of simple programming, while Searle played the role of uncomprehending layman. The title music was Kraftwerk's 'Computer World', released six months earlier, Mac showing Searle some of the rudimentary basics of computer operation and BASIC programming.

The music of 'Computer World' was perfect for the programme, indeed, perfect for the new age it predicted. The track began with an insistent, quick tempoed beat, like computer code being punched out uniformly and incessantly before the track's main four-note melody, repeated with an upward modulation as if suggesting a techno triumphalism. Ralf's vocals, the eerie, claustrophobic, mini-transistorised voice, condense the modern world into a sociological mantra: 'Numbers/Money/People/Time/Travel/Communication/ Entertainment'. The entire Western world, all its stresses, needs and desires, is perfectly captured in these seven words. What psychologist Oliver James many years later would call 'affluenza' is the contagion which can grow, unchecked, within this modern mantra. Again, Kraftwerk make no moral judgement, no prescription for change. The modern world is what it is, a world of capitalism, in our own making.

It was, however, another track on *Computer World* which, musically at least, pointed directly to the future. With its minimalistic and almost brutal beats, 'Numbers' basically invented a large part of the eighties and nineties. Hip-hop, techno and trance would all be indebted to this track. The beat itself was written by Karl Bartos. However, a drum pattern, like an arrangement, cannot be copyrighted; and so Bartos himself, although proud to see his invention take hold so completely in so much music, maintains a certain bittersweet feeling about a piece of music over which he had lost control. 'You might recognise the influence that Karl, and, before him, Michael Rother might have had in Kraftwerk,' says Ralf Dörper. 'Both had studied classical percussion. If you study classical percussion, you play not only drums, but also stuff like marimba and xylophone. The way that it's structured, it's very much like a sequencer. So you recognise somebody who is playing a marimba, he could very well do some sequence programming, because that's the way these kinds of instruments work.' The beat, a five-note sequence, is overlaid by what sounds like a sonic typewriter, a fast-tempoed sequence of itchy, shard-like sounds created on the Minimoog which pop and explode with no resonance or maturity, almost like the noise of an electronic bowl of Rice Krispies.

Heavily treated and vocodorised voices count up to eight in German ('Eins', 'Zwei', 'Drei', 'Vier', 'Fünf', 'Sechs', 'Sieben', 'Acht') and are interwoven with similar numerical sequences in English, French, Italian, Japanese and Russian.* On one level, this merely restates Kraftwerk's appeal to children, a generation of youngsters brought up on *Sesame Street* and Big Bird telling us the basics of maths. But then something sinister happens. The refrain from 'Computer World' returns, and the syncopated rhythms of counting break down to a simultaneous babble of noise, the counting resembling a crossfire of computer code, an anarchy of binary code. Unchecked, the future would be technological overload. The song dissolves into some sort of frightening new space, perhaps something akin to what the novelist William Gibson would a year later name 'cyberspace'.

'Numbers' is also significant in continuing Kraftwerk's agenda to break free from the tyranny of the English language by using Japanese. 'The Western world is dominated by Anglo-

---

* A much earlier attempt to construct a song around a repeating arithmetical pattern came in 1952 with Frank Loesser's 'Inchworm', performed in 1952 by Danny Kaye. 'I thought it was an extraordinary thing to use numbers as backing vocals', said David Bowie in 1979.

167

American speech,' Ralf told Tommy Vance in a Radio 1 interview. 'And us being German, we had to use other languages, and then we discovered the special psychological context of different languages. Because we sometimes record our songs in different languages: French, and now on the last album we did for the first time Japanese. We feel that changes our music completely, so we have different variations of our music, and some of the languages go even better sometimes with our music than others.'

The supreme irony of the album was that Kraftwerk had no computers in the Kling Klang Studio during the making of the record. Of the band members themselves, only Florian actually had a home computer. Ralf, speaking in 2008: 'Definitely, we've been very lucky that the technology developed in our direction [laughs]. This is what we envisaged in the late seventies when we worked with mostly analogue [equipment] of course. Then we composed the concept of [the album] *Computer World* coming out in '81 and we didn't even have computers at that time. So that was more like a visionary album. We only got that technology, a small PC, around the tour of that album and we used one on stage just writing letters.'

6.2 Digital Love

Although Kraftwerk were clearly imagined as a band in the thrall of the incipient computer age, this did not necessarily sit well with the more traditional branches of music, be they serious or popular. There were even those who were actually afraid of – or at the very least felt threatened by – the new technology. Ralf Hütter has gone on record as stating that in the seventies and early eighties Kraftwerk were refused permission to enter the Eastern Bloc with their computers. 'They thought that they were tools of war,' he said.

This technophobia would be replicated within pockets of the music business as well. Kraftwerk were a direct challenge, specifically to rock music in general but also, on a wider scale, to the grand tradition of music itself. Electronic music, so the detractors' line went, was 'machine music'. It was somehow invalid, a form of non-music, at best a gimmick, a novelty, at worst a direct affront not just to the romance of rock but to the grand narrative tradition of dead, white, male, classical greats. Music was meant to be made by and performed by real people using real instrumentation, wasn't it?

Electronic music, in their eyes, lacked this validity. Not surprisingly the UK's Musicians' Union, an institution historically opposed to innovation of any kind, demanded that the use of electronic music be restricted, even banned, as it was seen as a danger to the livelihoods of its members. The pomp-rock band Queen proudly displayed on their album sleeves the words 'No Synthesizers', as if such a disclaimer was a badge of honour, of quality and authenticity, up until their eighth album, *The Game*, in 1980. When the Human League released their second album, *Travelogue*, in 1980, they retaliated, wittily, with the legend 'Synthesizers and vocals only'.

Kraftwerk had no allegiance whatsoever to musical authenticity. Ralf Hütter: 'When we select an instrument sound, we don't worry if, for example, the strings are not authentic – we simply take the sounds we like!' Kraftwerk's music, like so much music which was to follow, was interested above all in sonics. It was the timbre* of the individual notes, their tone colour, their resonance which mattered more than anything else: 'We aim to create a total sound, not to make music in the traditional sense with complex harmony. A minimalistic approach is more important for us. We spend a month on the sound and five minutes on the chord changes! Germany has no predominant pop-music scene, unlike England, so we have a thriving communication between electronic music listeners and performers.'

The sound of *Computer World* is brighter, cleaner and more clinical than any of Kraftwerk's previous records. In part, this can be explained by technological advancements in the three years since *The Man-Machine* was recorded. However, there's also a much changed musical aesthetic at work. The beats were pared down with no spillage. Everything is played perfectly. On 'Home Computer' the middle section, with its upwardly spiralling repeats like bubbles in a jacuzzi made of sound, is trippy, almost a full decade before Acid House. Electro-pop pioneer Thomas Dolby described the sonic shift like this: 'With *The Man-Machine*, Kraftwerk had defined the gritty sound of analogue electronics, and it had a dark, farty, fuzz-pedal sound to it. When they first released *Computer World*, it was shockingly clean. It took a few years for public tastes to catch up, for

---

* Differences in timbre are what make a middle C played on a piano very different from the same note played on a violin.

our collective ears to adapt. Also, at the time, computers seemed too insignificant to be worthy of having an album title devoted to them! It was actually 10 years before pop culture was really impacted by computers and the Internet, yet Kraftwerk were highly attuned to it.'

The *Computer World* album was preceded by 'Pocket Calculator', a single that was just a little bit silly – a playful song on a topic that hardly anyone else could think worthy of enshrining in music. By 1981, pocket calculators were becoming an essential part of the school-child's armoury. No longer prohibitively expensive but increasingly compact, they were gradually being accepted as an important part of the maths class, although there was still resistance to the pocket machine by those who claimed it legitimised 'cheating'. And now they were immortalised for the very helpful things that they were and had their very own little song. One of the funniest songs ever written, its typically addictive melody line makes it one of Kraftwerk's' very few sing-along songs too. 'I'm the operator with my pocket calculator,' sings Ralf almost in monotone before a seemingly random three-note line, the sort of child-like noise a seven-year-old might have made on a cheap Casio. He follows this with an almost camp detachment: 'By pressing down this special key, it plays a little melody', before another short section of randomly generated synth notes.

'Pocket Calculator' poked fun at rock music subtly but devastatingly. Rock music was traditionally all about the electric guitar, about neat fretwork, power chords, and the masturbatory excesses of the solo. It was *manly*. On 'Pocket Calculator', Ralf shows how electronica has dispelled all the sweaty guff and ludicrous posturing of the cock rockers because the star of the show now isn't even a real instrument. It's a battery-powered hand-held abacus which can sound a jingle and is operated not played. The German-language version of the song, 'Taschenrechner', carried a slightly different lyric, but was still as droll: *'Ich bin der Musikant mit Taschenrechner in der Hand.'* ['I am the musician with a pocket calculator in my hand.'] This was, as Karl Bartos remembers, a trademark piece of lyric writing by Emil Schult: 'Emil had a good sense of the English – or shall I say American – language since he spent some time at high school in the USA. He could easily come up with simple lines in German which were catchy and witty at the same time. He contributed a great deal to the Kraftwerk lyrics. Listen to 'Autobahn', 'Trans-Europe Express', 'Radio-Activity', 'Computer World', 'Pocket Calculator', 'The Model' – just to name a few.'

However, the LP's most haunting melody, and perhaps Kraftwerk's best-ever pop single, was 'Computer Love'. Today, the melody to 'Computer Love' is known to a new generation having been sampled and reworked in the Coldplay song 'Talk'. It was composed in a flash of inspiration a year earlier in the Kling Klang Studio by Karl Bartos; Ralf then put the bass line over which the words 'another lonely night, lonely night' would eventually be sung. 'A melody makes no sense. We experience a wonder,' said Karl in 2007. 'Physical frequencies turn into a feeling. Nobody knows how it happens.' There has been some discussion whether the English-language versions of Kraftwerk's songs have somehow dumbed down the original German; but on 'Computer Love', the title of the song scans much better in English than in the German: the four syllables of 'Computer Love' fit the music better than the five of '*Komputer Liebe*.'

As the second single off the album, it initially fared little better than 'Pocket Calculator', reaching three places higher in the UK Top 40 at number 36. But it stands, for many people, as Kraftwerk's most perfect pop song. A nine-note synth melody introduces a tale of a 'lonely night, a lonely night'. The repetition works to build up a sense of tension, of frustration. The words are simple, like everyday dialogue, and therefore a perfect fit for the song. 'I don't know what to do, what to do/I need a rendezvous, rendezvous.' At the time, 'Computer Love' seemed to describe a scenario of a man needing a woman, and possibly being in the position to pay for that service. But today, the song has taken on a very different character. It seems to predict, however obliquely, social networking and matchmaking sites.

One of the world's first online dating services, Match.com, began in 1995, making 'Computer Love' itself startling in its predictive insight. A relatively high percentage of relationships are formed through online dating of whatever form. It has been estimated that by 2002 one in five new relationships were formed on the net. In November of that year the US magazine *Wired* said: 'Twenty years from now, the idea that someone looking for love won't look for it online will be silly, akin to skipping the card catalogue to instead wander the stacks because the right books are found only

171

by accident. We will be charmed, but helpless to point out that the approach isn't very pragmatic. After all, how likely is it that the book of your dreams will just fall off the shelf and into your arms?'

Ian Harrison at *Mojo* points out: 'Ralf brings a lot of heart to Kraftwerk. "Computer Love" – melancholic, human – is not like cold machine music at all...' It is stunning in its purity and simplicity: 'I have this tendency that if I can't remember it from memory then maybe that music is not worth doing', is how Ralf puts it, revealing one of the secrets of Kraftwerk's approach to songwriting.

6.3 The Infinity Loop

Computer World was released in May 1981 and would be supported by a world tour. Its impact, commercially, would be far outweighed by its massive critical success in future years. The album broke the Top 10 in Germany; in Britain, it reached number 15 and was awarded a silver disc. In America, it charted inside the *Billboard* top 100, the first Kraftwerk album so to do since *Autobahn* six years earlier. However, with the notable exception of 'Pocket Calculator' and a number two placing in the Italian charts, the record, once again, was a moderate rather than massive success.

The pop world of 1981 was very different from that of the mid-seventies when Kraftwerk had last toured extensively. Then, they were regarded by many as either an annoying novelty act or, worse, as harbingers of doom and the end of 'real music'. But now, in Britain at least, Kraftwerk saw the double helix of their musical DNA everywhere. 'At the moment we feel very much encouraged to hear that there's a lot of energy in electronic music happening in England, because the last time we came here – six years ago – we were attacked for what we were doing at that time,' was Ralf's assessment in a Radio 1 interview from May, 1981. 'And I think now there's so much energy coming back to us from all the people and the young industrial bands. I think we feel very much encouraged by this whole movement. It's our life to communicate and to record and make these things happen, and therefore we don't feel ripped off that way.'

In 1981 electro-pop took over the mainstream. The early months saw Visage's 'Fade To Grey' became a massive hit across Europe, reaching number eight in the UK, Top 5 in France and

Italy, and number one in Germany. Ultravox's 'Vienna', its very title a reminder of the Kraftwerk lyric from 'Trans-Europe Express', began its ascent to number two in the UK charts in January of that year, four years on from Kraftwerk's romance of 'parks, hotels and palaces'. The video for 'Vienna', directed by Australian Russell Mulcahy, captured the New Romantic scene as perfectly as any cultural moment: epic, *Third Man*-inspired noir drama battled with cinematic Gothic sweeps, intercut with the arty world of the post-punk club scene. Filmmaker Julien Temple can be spotted briefly with a tarantula crawling across his face. The video, shot mainly in venues in London including the Gaumont State Theatre in Kilburn and Searcy's near Harrods did, however, contain some hastily filmed shots in Vienna itself. 'We bombed round Vienna in a taxi and shot bits when we saw them,' says Chris Cross of their day trip to Austria. 'None of us knew Vienna. We just had a guide book we got from the library!'

In the spring of 1981, the Human League, now re-modelled as a pop band with the addition of two teenage girls to dance and sing, finally broke into the UK Top 20 with the Martin Rushent-produced 'Sound Of The Crowd'. They would be followed by electro pop's biggest ever success, Depeche Mode. Their first hit, 'New Life', was a premium slice of bouncy electronica; its follow-up, 'Just Can't Get Enough', is now the sing-along stuff of football terrace chanting. The oddest and still mildly incomprehensible moment came in the autumn, when performance artist Laurie Anderson reached number two with 'O Superman'. Part recitation, part confession, Anderson's vocal was dominated by the backing vocal, or rather, background sound: a jarring repetition of 'Ha', which was programmed on a loop. It was close to the sort of wordless vocal experiments of the likes of Philip Glass in his mid-seventies work. Anderson's half-spoken vocodorised vocals instantly reminded us of Ralf's *Sprechgesang* for Kraftwerk.

As Britain entered the eighties against a backdrop of rising unemployment, double-digit inflation, weekly closures of factories and collieries, tax breaks for the rich and massive pay increases for society's uniformed services – the police and the armed forces – Britain's inner cities became gloomier and more radicalised. Pop culture's response to the brutal miasma of Thatcherism was an escape into the self. The new rock stars weren't straightforward rock stars at all. They were, like Bowie, Roxy and Kraftwerk, multi- and mixed-media tableaux. Music was only part of it. Spandau Ballet, Duran Duran, the Human League, Ultravox, and Depeche Mode all broke big in a six-month period between October 1980 and April 1981, and all were self-consciously arty, and radically self-made. In 1981, Adam Ant became the first pop star to trademark his look. Like Bowie, and like Kraftwerk, pop stars became small businesses, with fingers in all the pies from merchandise and marketing to styling and promotion. Pop was now a very serious business.

Critics will offer up the example of the Velvet Underground and the sales figures of their first album, repeating Brian Eno's[*] assessment that: 'The first Velvet Underground album only sold 10,000 copies, but everyone who bought it formed a band.' According to this ratio, Kraftwerk = VU^2. 'For me,' says Karl Bartos, '*The Man-Machine* and *Computer World* are the two most important albums. The *Gestaltung* [concept] is of a consistently high level on both.'

'*The Man-Machine* was a tough act to follow: and I think it took them three years,' says John Taylor. 'But it's a fantastic album and I think rhythmically I was hearing so much stuff, thinking, God, I've heard that so many times, it's got to be one of the most sampled albums, it's got a dance and techno and hip-hop groove.'

Computer World was perfect, agrees Ralf Dörper. 'It was perfect because of the fact that there was nothing on it that was filler. It is also quite short, a similar length to all the punk albums of the time, when nothing was longer than 40 minutes. On many LPs you say what you have to say and then fill it up; but not on *Computer Word*. That's why, really, I think it was absolutely perfect.'

Some Kraftwerk fans were, however, if not disappointed, then aware that a new sort of Kraftwerk was emerging. There appeared to be something very clinical, almost abstract about *Computer World*. Replacing the banks of mellotron-like choirs, fragile vocals, and percussion which seemed, on occasion, not to be totally perfectly played, came music which was almost harsh in its perfection, no sound misplaced, no beat unnecessary. 'I thought that the real turning point was *Computer World*,' is Andy McCluskey's opinion. 'I think they did lose the human element.'

---

[*] Some claim that R.E.M.'s Peter Buck was in fact the originator of this aphorism, and not Brian Eno.

For Peter Saville, *Computer World*, in both form and content, is a finishing point. 'The total work, the *Gesamtkunstwerk*, of Kraftwerk, the process of being Kraftwerk, probably found its own conclusion. And I would suggest that it found its conclusion in *Computer World*. It is in a way the ultimate conclusion of their own sort of path.

'It concludes in itself. *Computer World* is like an infinity loop, the simplest, most coherent loop of one melody. It is like the television image that disappears into a dot. They had digitised the canon, allowing the past, the present and the future to run simultaneously. For me Kraftwerk were the bridging point, in a way, between canonical culture and pop culture. They did that by allowing the fragments of history to run alongside our industrial technology. They literally do it through allowing the influences of classical music to become pop. My saying that I tried Mozart because of Kraftwerk is a perfect example of it. Kraftwerk were the portal that endorsed history for me. I cannot listen to Kraftwerk without thinking of an autobahn and Cologne Cathedral, one in the same. That, in a way, is the end of the journey. I have a worrying perception of a digitised culture where our history has been atomised. We have gone from an analogue (logical) stream to a digital one that then fragments and becomes ultimately atomised. You can see it in the way that things are done today. The digital stream allows for everything simultaneously and history no longer has a logic to it. Kraftwerk are avatars through their work. They both describe and determine the world around them. In a way *Computer World* is almost a logical conclusion of the Kraftwerk project.'

Kraftwerk were working in what theorists later in the eighties would call a postmodern culture. In this culture, all that existed was now, not tomorrow, or yesterday, a 'depthless present'. At the end of the eighties, theorists of youth culture would begin talking about pop moving from 'linear' to 'circular' time. Instead of progressing and innovating, popular music would run in a series of re-inventions of musical idioms. No longer would a musical idiom replace an outmoded one, but all types of music would now run in sequence. What Peter Saville senses about *Computer World* is the very first suggestion of popular music folding in on itself, a music which literally goes round in circles. For Kraftwerk, everything could be music, the splutter of a car engine, the noise of a train clattering along a track, the faintest sound of a distant star, the chatter and bustle of computer code, the randomised series of notes played on a pocket calculator. Music, non-stop.

6.4 'a', 'au', 'o', 'u'

The *Computer World* tour, the first major world tour of the band's career, and their first live performances since the autumn of 1976, took three years to plan, and even then the first gig of the tour had to be postponed because the set wasn't ready: 'The paint was literally just drying off as the items were packed,' said Ralf.

In 1981 Kraftwerk played more than 80 concerts in Europe, America, Australia and Japan. Dressed in either all black, or red shirt, black trousers and black tie of the *Man-Machine* era, their look soon became iconic, and much imitated by fans up to this day. 'So many people move or even jump around on stage these days, and it's important for our music that we do not do this – our rather static performance is also necessary for emphasising the "robotic" aspect of our music,' said Ralf in 1981. 'We have been building the set for the last three years (since *The Man-Machine* album), whilst composing the music and preparing the video graphics.'

As was the norm, the new V-shaped stage design positioned Ralf, Karl, Wolfgang and Florian from left to right, their names again lit in neon, but this time with four-metre-wide video screens custom built by Sony in Japan behind them. Although rudimentary from today's perspective, it set the standard back in 1981. 'Everybody seems to limit themselves by saying "I'm an instrument player" but we like to "play pictures" as well as share the instruments available,' said Ralf in a 1981 interview. 'Günter Spachtholz is the video and lighting engineer handling all the visuals and he sits on the left hand side of the stage (viewed from the audience). On the other side of the performers is the sound engineer (we call him our dB man!), Joachim Dehmann. Although he makes the final balance of the total sound output, each player mixes his instruments separately from up to eight sound sources.'

The set was drawn almost exclusively from their most recent four albums, the opener 'Numbers' ('Nummern') a powerful somatic attack. Kraftwerk would take to the stage from the right with a brisk walk led out by Ralf, followed by Karl, Wolfgang and Florian. Ralf and

Florian wore headsets, and Ralf sang with his distinctively unusual style, right hand cupped against his face mic, dancing robotically to the rhythm. 'In normal singing you can work loudness by moving the mic nearer and closer. I can't do that, as it's fixed to my head, so I use my hand to emphasise what I'm singing,' said Ralf in 2006. 'On *Computer World*, lines like "Interpol and Deutsche Bank", it makes it louder, gives the words a bit more room ambience, reverb. My hand is a small resonance chamber, intimate but enabling me to proclaim without a loudhailer. The figure in Edvard Munch's *The Scream* is like 'Aaaaaaargh!', but I'm more 'aaaaaah', whispering in your ear.'

There was a dark and driving version of 'Metropolis', a suite of songs from *Radio-Activity* and, of course, 'Autobahn', at this point far and away their most well-known composition. There would be the odd glitch, proving that electronic music did have its human side. Ralf Dörper: 'There could be faults in the set-up, and I've seen at least one concert where they had to interrupt the show because something went wrong. I think they said they had to re-programme the computer.' Each track would be accompanied by its own visuals, either computer graphics or a film. By the standards of the early eighties, this was a radical departure but not one wholly unprecedented. In progressive rock, Genesis had attempted to turn their *Lamb Lies Down On Broadway* tour of 1974–75 into something of a mixed-media event with the use of slide projections, while Pink Floyd had used graphics of one form or another, often projected on to a large circular screen behind the band, since their popular breakthrough with *Dark Side Of The Moon* in 1973. While light shows accompanying rock concerts can be traced back to Bill Graham's Fillmore West in San Francisco, perhaps more relevantly the Human League had a non-playing band member, Adrian Wright, who was in complete charge of the band's visuals. In real time, he would change slides to reflect, often with bizarrely surreal results, their equally bizarre all-electronic repertoire. Their lead singer, Phil Oakey: 'As soon as we did the shows with Adrian, showing pictures of people's heads blowing up, or Jesus crying on an early woodcut, the gigs started to go well!'

Kraftwerk's visuals, however, were often literal and economical rather than excessive or surreal. Numbers appeared on the banks of screens during the song 'Numbers', a radio antenna for

'Radio-Activity', and a black and white movie of an autobahn, along with the white on blue motorway sign for 'Autobahn', and again the use of black-and-white imagery for the imaginary train journey that would be 'Trans-Europe Express', and some film of glamourpusses from the post-Second World War era for 'The Model'. Both these films featured a meld of futurism and studied nostalgia, and were edited sections of promotional films for the tracks.

A highlight of the show was 'Pocket Calculator', which ended the set proper before the encores. Here, the four members of the band left their consoles and, at the front of the stage, played hand-held instruments, Ralf with a tiny Bee Gee rhythm machine mini- keyboard, Karl with a Stylophone, Wolfgang, keeping the beat with a miniature drum pad he built himself, with what looked like a small baton rather than a drum stick, and Florian, always with a keen interest in voice modulation, with a Casio calculator module which played beeping noises and burping cyborg vocal effects: 'a', 'au', 'o', 'u'. 'We found the instruments in a department store last Christmas, so we took everyday items into our music from "street level",' revealed Ralf. 'We both agreed the way musical equipment is designed in the future could be as an extension from the human being, with suitable feedback between machine and man. The emphasis on keyboards could turn to instruments, controlled by some part of the body, using piezo pick-ups, special electrodes and heat-sensitive elements. Even 10 years ago, I used to rub a contact microphone on my clothes and skin to produce different sounds that would change at each performance.' Ralf and Florian would solo, in a parody of the guitar solo, handing over their instruments to the audience to play. The result was an entertaining self-parody, and an amusing assault on core rock values. They say that a German joke is no laughing matter, but this was one of the funniest moments ever seen at a pop concert.

This tour would also see the first appearance of the custom-built robots on stage. Dressed identically to their human counterparts, they came on stage during the encore, 'The Robots', with 10 flashing diodes on their ties, taking up positions next to their real-life counterparts. Andy Warhol had commented in the seventies, 'I want everybody to think alike. I think everybody should be a machine', and there was certainly a pop art influence to Kraftwerk's robots. Like Warhol they were blank, lifeless, and just slightly creepy. Warhol also quipped: 'I love Los Angeles. I love Hollywood. They're beautiful. Everybody's plastic, but I love plastic. I want to be plastic.' Shortly before his death, he got his wish. An Andy Warhol robot was designed by Alvaro Villa for use in a stage show entitled 'Andy Warhol: a No Man Show'. 'Andy loved this idea,' said Bob Colacello, editor of Warhol's *Interview* magazine. 'He loved the fact that there was going to be this Andy Warhol robot that he could send on lecture tours. It could do talk shows for him. The idea was that the show, if it was successful in New York, could then also simultaneously be running in London, Los Angeles, Tokyo, with cloned robots. And people would actually be able to ask questions of the robot, which would be programmed with a variety of answers. The whole thing was so Warholian and so perfect.'

Warhol's black humour would not be lost on Ralf. As Kraftwerk's career developed, the human side would be increasingly marginalised. The music would become even more refined, distilled, abstract. For the next 10 years, the only promotional shots of the band would be of their robot selves.

6.5 Life In The Looking Glass

Sometimes, even the participants in an event know instinctively that now is a time which cannot be bettered. Even as it was happening, there was the sense that the 1981 tour was the highpoint, the culmination of 10 years' work, the moment when Kraftwerk resonated the clearest and radiated the strongest in terms of their musical impact. For Karl Bartos, the tour was his happiest time as a member of the band. 'London, New York, LA, 1981 – I was still quite young and naive. Life stretched out endlessly before me, the mood in the band was good, sometimes even euphoric, and the response from the audience overwhelming. Was it a case of "eternal adolescence", I wonder? Or maybe we were just a bunch of arrogant kids? No idea. But we had a really good time.'

Touring was not, however, without its tensions. 'Sometimes we were really frustrated,' reveals Wolfgang. 'We were often in small or mid-size towns. We were always alone, and there were no nice clubs to go to so we went back to the hotel.'

Wolfgang was certainly not without admirers. 'He is lovely. He was basically electronic music's sex symbol for years,' says Andy from OMD. 'He was the sexiest man in electronic music, a very good-looking man. When he was younger he was very good-looking indeed.' On tour, Wolfgang did not go short. One night in New York lingers long in the memory. Kraftwerk played at the Ritz Club in early August. 'I was grabbed by a beautiful slim black girl after the gig, Michelle was her name. We played two concerts that night. I found her on the balcony, looking down. There was a little pause, and I went through the hall and stood next to her and also looked down to the stage. The audience had gone, and I said "You are still there? You want to see the second concert?" And she said, "Yes, I have already bought a ticket for the second show." Then she said, "What are you doing afterwards?" And I said, "If you are asking me so nicely, I have no idea, maybe you ..." And she said, "I have an idea. I invite you, if you like." And I liked. And she was wonderful. When the second concert was over she asked me, "Shall we go to a restaurant?" But I don't eat so late. It was hot and steaming. So, we went to her place. She had a lot of fans around her big bed. She had a round bed. I had never seen that before. She brought me straight to her bedroom! She put all the fans on and started to get undressed and show me her body. I sat there. She couldn't wait to get me, to grab me. Ha ha ha. That was New York! This is why I always have this nice memory of New York. The concerts, both of them, were brilliant. The audience was standing on the other side of the street. So many people were standing to get a ticket.'

Not every venue was as welcoming. One might have expected that they could be assured a warm reception on their home turf. Not so. A December concert at the Philipshalle in Düsseldorf was a dispiriting experience. 'I must tell you, it was half empty,' says Wolfgang. 'That didn't look nice. When we were in Cologne at the Sartorysaal, or in Dortmund, at the Westfalenhalle, 40 kilometres away, it was crowded. The Düsseldorf audience, and the Düsseldorf people, are very special people – arrogant, and noses up in the air. And they cannot even applaud if something is done well. We played in Cologne just before Düsseldorf and we played twice in one evening; there were so many people there that we said, "OK, we'll do a midnight concert as well, straight afterwards, we will start again from the beginning." It was something like the Roundhouse in London. It had a balcony, and it was one of the nicest concerts.'

The *Computer World* tour played almost 100 concerts, and took in 16 countries. In suitably Kraftwerkian style, the tour did a loop, beginning and ending in Europe, with North America, Hong Kong, Japan, Australia and India, as well as two Eastern Bloc countries, Hungary and Poland in the middle section. Kraftwerk were continually travelling from May to September, with a seven-week break before the tour resumed in November back in Europe. Being away from creature comforts was not something Florian took to readily. In fact, it all became too much for Florian by September when they reached Australia, where he famously went missing from the Princess Theatre in Melbourne at a critical moment. The rest of Kraftwerk had convened backstage but there was no sign of Florian. Peering through the stage curtain, Emil Schult saw him sitting in the first row, apparently unrecognised by the rest of the audience. Emil told Florian in no uncertain terms that if he didn't get backstage right now and prepare for the concert that not only would the tour end, but Kraftwerk would too. Florian relented and took to the stage on time, but it was the closest of shaves: '*Ihr braucht mich ja gar nicht*', ['you don't really need me'] he is reported as saying.

As early as 1981 Florian was finding the regimen of hotel, flight, concert, energy-snapping and unfulfilling, and in this he is not alone. Kate Bush has toured just once in her entire career, and that was restricted to the UK. XTC abandoned live shows completely as the whole process made lead singer Andy Partridge suffer stage fright so badly it made him ill. Florian's reluctance to tour would be an important factor in the history of Kraftwerk from 1981 onwards.

6.6 Flat Batteries

The last date of the *Computer World* tour was in Bremen on December 14, 1981. 'We were so happy, when it was stopped,' says Wolfgang. 'It was dark, it was cold; it was winter in Germany. We didn't want to be on stage any more. It was unbelievable. We couldn't imagine doing anything like it in the future again, such a tour. We were just finished physically.' At the end of the tour, Kraftwerk were not in the mood to jump back on the road anytime soon. Astonishingly, it would be nine years before they would play live again. No tours, no concerts, no television appearances, nothing.

The end of the tour brought about changes in the domestic circumstances for certain members of the band. Florian lived in an elegant flat in a building inherited from his father, and Ralf lived in the house in which he grew up, his parents having bought a modern bungalow and moved into that; but Wolfgang, Karl and Emil were vulnerable to the whim of their landlord. While still on tour in India, they received a letter from the owners of their flat saying that they had been served notice and would have to move out of their home at Bergerallee 9 in the 'old town' of Düsseldorf. The property was owned by Mannesmann, the Düsseldorf-based steel company, and the 10-year lease had run out. It seemed, at least to Wolfgang, that an important part of the social glue that kept Kraftwerk together was being washed away. They had been happy there. 'When we had to leave, we gave the order to a lawyer. The lawyer said "There is no problem. You don't have to leave immediately." He dealt with them so that we had nine more months; and that bought us time. We could properly finish our tour, and everyone looked for a new flat.'

Looking back, for Wolfgang at least, the end of the tour, combined with the need to move house, was the tipping point. 'Our peak was over. We split from living together. We split from working together. Ralf and Florian became more and more interested in cycling.' Wolfgang, by now 34 years old, was also looking for a steady relationship. He would find a new girlfriend – Constanze – with whom he settled down: 'A beautiful girl, intelligent, educated and with a wonderful aura.'

Although he played an important role in Kraftwerk's live presentation and, behind the scenes, in building instrumentation and the various onstage units, Wolfgang was the least important member of the band as far as composing the music was concerned. The 2008 reissue of *Computer World* doesn't even credit him with playing on the album. He is listed in the CD credits, along with the other members, as contributing 'software', whatever that means. For Wolfgang, Kraftwerk was only viable when the group played live, where he could demonstrate his undoubted prowess as an electronic drummer.

Around this time, Karl met his future wife, Bettina Michael. 'I met Bettina in August 1977,' says Karl. 'The name of the club was the Peppermint Club, later Rocking Eagles, on Talstrasse in Düsseldorf. Yes, we're still married and in love.'

'I don't miss the seventies,' reflects Wolfgang today. 'I grew older; and today I don't need to have this time, to try everything out. By the time of HIV and AIDS, I had already settled down with my steady girlfriend Constanze.' Neither Wolfgang nor Karl wanted any children.*

On tour that winter were OMD, now one of the biggest new acts in Europe. Their first single, 'Electricity', owed a debt to Kraftwerk's 'Radio-Activity'. Clearly influenced by Kraftwerk, their music betrayed an affectionate steal here, a sonic tribute there. In the autumn of 1981 came their hit single 'Souvenir', which had the sort of choral quality found on 'Radio-Activity' and 'Europe Endless'. Their new album, *Architecture And Morality,* would sell over three million copies worldwide, and its third single, 'Maid Of Orleans (The Waltz Joan Of Arc)', would top the German charts, its artwork co-designed by fellow Kraftwerk fan Peter Saville. From a purely commercial standpoint, by early 1982 OMD were bigger than Kraftwerk.

OMD were playing a gig at the Zeche Club in Bochum that February. 'I can remember Malcolm [Holmes, OMD's drummer] and Martin [Cooper, their keyboard player] came backstage ready to do the gig; and they were "Hey, guess who we have seen out there on the balcony?" "Who?" "Kraftwerk!" Paul and I just basically shat ourselves. I have never been so nervous on stage in my entire life. All I can remember is that I spent the whole gig gazing up at these four black-clothed figures in the balcony. I was just thinking to myself, "I wonder what they think, I wonder what they think, I wonder what they think?" Very fortunately, after the show we did get a chance to meet them. I was so, so nervous. It was one of those "I am not worthy" moments. All I wanted to do, really, was to get down and praise them and pray at their feet. So I couldn't think of anything more interesting to say than "What speakers were you using in Kling Klang Studio?" Of all the things that you may have ever wanted to say to your ultimate heroes... that was what came out of my mouth.'

Paul Humphreys also recalls the moment when the servants met the masters: 'I've met so many megastars over the years, but I've only ever been lost for words when I met them. I shook their hands and it was like meeting God. I mean, what do you say, "I love you,

---

* Thereby dashing any hopes of 'Kraftwerk, the Next Generation'.

you're great"? They were totally on a pedestal for us.' According to Andy, they were very complimentary about OMD in general, and Andy's live pièce de résistance in particular. 'I think that it was either Karl or Wolfgang who said that I danced like a whirling dervish in "Maid of Orleans". They thought it was great.'

It was the adoration of fellow musicians, almost entirely in the UK, which helped to create the Kraftwerk myth, kept them in the music papers, and ensured that their name would always be synonymous with something cool, new, agenda-setting. Their records sold in pockets, unevenly. In 1982, without Kraftwerk doing anything at all, everything would change; coming up, the biggest validation of their career.

6.7 The Most Important Number One Ever

1982 began with the Human League. 'Don't You Want Me', the fourth single off their third album, *Dare!*, was by now on its way to clocking up sales in excess of a million copies in the UK alone. It was a phenomenal breakthrough for a band that, just a year earlier, had largely been seen as write-offs after the departure of two of their members to form Heaven 17. The song wasn't even meant to be a single – at least half of the group, including lead singer Phil Oakey, were against releasing it at all. 'Don't You Want Me' was made with no conventional instruments, a pure piece of synth heaven.

Six months earlier, in the summer of 1981, the second single off *Computer World*, 'Computer Love', had been a minor UK hit. However, in the increasingly radicalised climate of pure synth pop, as the autumn of 1981 turned to the winter of 1982, and with the Human League so dominant, DJs began playing the B-side, 'The Model', a track that was now almost four years old. In 1978 it sounded odd. In 1981, it sounded, finally, of its time. 'Computer Love' and 'The Model' were then officially rebranded as a double A-sided single, not uncommon at the time, and the former B-side was playlisted across the UK in the run-up to Christmas*. There was, of course, no promotion whatsoever

---

* A friend of mine, not by any stretch of the imagination a Kraftwerk fan it must be added, thought 'The Model' actually was a Human League song when it reached number one and was surprised to find out, many years later, it was written by a band he hated.

184

by the band, but a four-year-old video of them was shown on British television. By the New Year, the single was speeding up the charts. By January 9 it was number 21, and by the week ending January 16 it had reached number 10. The next week it was number two, and although the single dropped a place the week after, by the release of the chart week ending February 6, mainly due to a chart abnormality whereby songs promoted on *Top Of The Pops* on the Thursday had their sales counted not in the week of the broadcast but the week after, it reached number one in the UK charts.[*] It was astonishing that a cult band such as Kraftwerk had reached the top of the charts. They had truly moved from the margins into the mainstream and had achieved something that the Who, Bob Dylan, Depeche Mode, R.E.M., Nirvana and Bob Marley & The Wailers had never been able to put on their C.V., a UK number one single.

Apart from *Top Of The Pops*, the promotional film for 'The Model' also made its way onto some unlikely areas of daytime scheduling, including the anarchic children's programme *Tiswas*, ITV's answer to the rather more sedate BBC Saturday morning children's shows of the time. 'I do remember seeing "The Model" on *Tiswas*,' says Ian Harrison of *Mojo*. 'It was the video, which they are still using on the live show to this day on the screens. I remember thinking this is something quite different, although it was a "pop" record.' Kraftwerk on *Tiswas* was a strange thing indeed, although perhaps not so strange as one might think, given that this was the show on which a bucket of cold water was poured over Mike Oldfield, and Phil Collins and Mike Rutherford of Genesis were covered in green gunge.

In February 1982, Ralf was called upon to promote Kraftwerk's first major hit single since 'Autobahn' six years earlier. He spoke to the chart-fixated *Record Mirror*, the only weekly publication aimed at the youth market that carried the official charts. 'Ralf Hütter is the voice of Kraftwerk,' wrote Mark Cooper in his scene-setting description of the Kraftwerk supremo. 'He writes the words and gives the interviews, talking in the kind of perfect English which no English person can manage. This afternoon he is in London, helping

---

[*] The author heard the chart rundown, and Kraftwerk's enthronement at number one, in the school common room on a portable radio. The author cheered when the opening bars were played!

to promote Kraftwerk's first big hit since "Autobahn", all those years ago. Ralf is small and precise, giving an overwhelming impression of neatness. Like Kraftwerk, he likes a joke. Bad puns are his favourite and he underlines them with his eyebrows as if to explain. "I make joke."' He goes on: '"There's a certain black humour because we all wear black," explains Ralf. This tickles him. Polite and shy, Ralf is extremely reasonable and pleasantly ponderous – like German bread.'

Although conforming to the logic of what makes a great hit single, being under four minutes, and on the subject of love, of sorts, 'The Model' was still an oddball guest on any disco's playlist. 'The quintessential line where you feel it must be ironic is "I'm posing for consumer products now and then",' says Peter Saville. 'That has got to be ironic. It cannot be a "lost in translation" moment. And I always sensed that the translation was a clever and ironic use of English. No model would ever say they are "posing for consumer products". Models don't use the word "consumer". It is not in their dictionary.'

Up until the success of 'The Model', the accepted line of thought was that the appeal of the band was rather unisexual. Songs about cars, pulsars, trains, robots and computers seemed to confirm the rather male obsessions of the authors. The success of 'The Model' was a turning point. 'Evidently our fans now preferred to have romantic melodies and human lyrics, and it showed that women were possibly buying our records, too,' is Wolfgang's assessment in his autobiography, perhaps revealing his own taste for more romantic melodies and human themes. 'Women are normally less inclined towards electronic music or technical subjects, and our music was often too cold for them.'

On a personal level, Wolfgang had mixed feelings when the single became such a success. 'It was fantastic! But I got nothing from it, because I did not get a share from radio play, as an artist or a composer. But I found it nice to be with my band at number one.'

'Ralf Hütter called me on the phone one night. It was unexpected, yes, but I was not carried away by it,' was how Karl remembers hearing the news. 'I think I said something like "cool, great, nice one – thanks for the information. And what are we going to do next?" At the time my life was exciting anyway and the hit single did not change anything for me. You know, we'd not been part of the music industry. Nobody around me was overexcited, I seem to remember.'

The most important UK number one single? Well, that is open to debate. Fans of Elvis, the Beatles and the Stones in the rock era will doubtless argue that earlier hits sparked off social revolutions, changed the way people thought, dressed, lived and loved. However, 'The Model' at number one, just 11 and a half years after Woodstock, sounded as if it had been made 111 and a half years after the music featured at that particular concert. No front-of-stage lead singer, no traditional rock instrumentation and no hippy ideals to betray. This was *New Musick*, music for a post-industrial computer age, music for the future. Its significance would not be lost on a future generation of forward-thinking broadcasters and radio people when the UK's *6 Music* devoted an entire day's worth of scheduling in February 2012 to this singular event. It was the moment the world finally caught up with Kraftwerk.

6.8 Planet Kraftwerk

'In a disco the lights are coming on you and then on me, but if you go to see a band or a group, all the lights are on the stage which is a very fascist sort of situation. Everybody is in the dark and the spotlight is on the stage whereas in the disco, the spotlight is on everybody.' Ralf was alive to the inequality of even his own concerts. In a rock concert, lead singer dominant, ultra-powerful, the gap between musician and audience is largely unbridgeable. At his own concerts, there was a more democratic feel. What Ralf and Kraftwerk were edging towards was something very modern; a new way of enjoying music whereby the fan becomes the performer, and the performer becomes the fan.

Kraftwerk always felt comfortable in clubs, and always liked to dance. Not for them standing at a gig for two hours, followed by a *Currywurst* and a *Helles Bier* or two. In their view, an evening's musical entertainment required more variation, more sophistication and élan, and less slumming it with the crowd. Ralf Hütter: 'Living in Germany we would never go out and listen to a band like you do in America. It's boring. Why spend two hours listening to one band when you can spend two hours listening to a hundred records?' He added, 'We were always very rhythmical. We always hated "electronic" music whose connotations were intellectual only. We introduced the body to electronic music...

Discos to me are like your own public living room. In Düsseldorf today you can't afford a large apartment, so if you want to see your friends, you go to the disco.'

Therein lies the kernel of one of the most astonishing developments in popular music history. Music made in West Germany in the seventies and early eighties by four young men had such a seismic impact on black and Hispanic musicians working in America that, within a dozen years, it would change modern music for all time. Back in the seventies, however, Ralf Hütter could sense that Kraftwerk's music had already won acceptance in the underground. 'We always had a strongly favourable reaction from black audiences in America, even before house and techno,' he would later say. 'I remember somebody took me to a club in about '76 or '77, when *Trans-Europe Express* was out, and it was some loft club in New York, after hours, just as the DJ culture was starting, when the DJs began making their own records, their own grooves. And they took sections from "Metal On Metal" on *Trans-Europe Express*, and when I went in it was going "boom-crash – boom-crash", so I thought, "Oh, they're playing the new album." But it went on for 10 minutes! And I thought, "What's happening?" That track is only like two or three minutes! And later I went to ask the DJ and he had two copies of the record and he was mixing the two, and of course it could go on as long as people were dancing... This was a real development, because in those days you fixed a certain time on the record, under 20 minutes a side in order to get the print into vinyl. It was a technological decision to say how long the song would last. We always used to play different timings live, but there we were in this after-hours club, and it was 10 minutes, 20 minutes of the recording, because the vibe was there.'

Karl Bartos also remembers vividly how their music was almost immediately assimilated into underground Amercian culture. The roots of this acceptance took hold earlier than many people think: 'It happened not too long after my first encounter with Ralf and Florian. In 1975 we went over the Atlantic and spent 10 weeks on the road. We went from coast to coast and then to Canada. And all the black cities like Detroit or Chicago, they embraced us. It was good fun. In a way apparently they saw some sort of very strange comic figures in us I guess but also they didn't miss the beats. I grew up with the funky beats of James Brown and I brought

188

them in more and more. Not during *Autobahn* or *Radio-Activity*, but more and more during the late seventies.'

Bartos again: 'Well it happened actually when we were in New York and we were in the street and we saw a record shop full of our records and black people stood in front of them making jokes about the covers and about how strange we looked, but people were making loops out of "Metal On Metal" and dancing to it. These loops were going on forever! Made from just these heavy metal sounds! They were breakdancing to it. Then we were aware that we had access to this culture.'

A new generation born in the sixties were simply bored with rock music, with its canon of 'greats'. 'Maybe it's just that we were so completely different,' says Wolfgang, looking back on the early eighties, and still trying to find answers why their music translated so well into the US club scene. 'After all these guitars, since 50, 60 years only this guitar music. The Americans are tired of hearing always this Nashville sound, *Die Schlager von Amerika*, country music, and on the other side, rock and heavy metal. There was nothing in between. So we filled a very good space there, with our music.'

Listening very hard in a certain nowhere suburb of Nothingsville was 16-year-old Richard Melville Hall, the future platinum-selling electro and rock artist better known as Moby. 'In almost every town there's, like, the cool kids who get the records before anyone else. In the small town I grew up in just outside of New York, called Darien, Connecticut, the cool kid in my town, whose name was John Farnesworth, had somehow got a copy of *Autobahn*. I think his dad might have even brought it back from Germany. We were all nerds, so we were all science fiction-obsessed, and honestly, when I first heard electronic music, what appealed to us was that it sounded like the soundtrack to science fiction movies, it sounded futuristic, it reflected a completely different world to that of provincial suburban Darien, Connecticut. And that to me was the huge appeal of Kraftwerk, these strange half-man, half-machine Germans making this sort of very mannered electronic music, driving round the autobahns at 3 a.m. bathed in the light of their Mercedes and BMWs. It was as far from provincial Darien, Connecticut as you could get.'

Being a music-obsessed nerd in early-eighties America was a singular, occasionally hazardous position and one likely to lead to

189

a certain degree of opprobrium. 'The town I grew up in, you were allowed to like classic rock. You were allowed to like the Doors, and the Kinks, and Jimi Hendrix, Led Zeppelin, but basically there was like a statute of limitations. The 'cool'/popular kids in our school wouldn't listen to any music made after 1974. So, my friends and I, having been ostracised and rejected by the popular kids, decided we would only listen to music made after 1974! And whereas the popular kids in our school would only listen to music made by people with long hair, we decided we would only listen to music made by people with short hair. And so Kraftwerk fitted that perfectly. Kraftwerk because they were German, had short hair, and didn't use guitars, was about as far from classic rock as you could get. They were this perfect amalgam of science fiction, disco, and classical music. When I listened to Kraftwerk, it might seem like stating the obvious, but it didn't sound like anything I'd heard before. And I'd heard other synthesizer music, whether it be Jean-Michel Jarre, or Tangerine Dream, even the first couple of Suicide records, but with Kraftwerk, their ability to create complete and comprehensive worlds in each record was unique. When I bought other records, it felt like I was buying a bunch of nice songs with an artistic vision, but when you bought a Kraftwerk album it was like you were buying an entire world.'

Kraftwerk, like an internet meme or, to the non-fan, a dangerous new virus, were spreading, multiplying, reacting, diverging and reassembling. In Britain, the new wave of synth-pop acts was now well-established and would continue to dominate British music. However, it is to America where the focus now shifts as DJs and musicians, skilled in the new art of sound bricolage, and, a little later, sampling, would use Kraftwerk's incendiary beats to create a musical manifesto which would take over the world.

SIEBEN

BOING!

1982 – 1990

7.1 Viral Kraftwerk

THE YEAR 1983 bore witness to the end of the history of modern; 'SYNTH-POP, 1977–1983 R.I.P.' It was, as Andy McCluskey would later say, 'the last great populist movement of modernism'. There would be great music made after 1983, of course, but, with the arguable exception of jungle in the nineties, all the major movements to come would be 'sounds-like' music. It would be music that was essentially an extension, or a revival, of what had gone before. Rare was the day when we would hear a piece of music and think, 'I have never heard anything like this in my life before.' Music now sounded 'a bit like Motown', 'a bit synthy', 'a bit Stonesey', 'a bit like the Beatles', 'a bit like the Kinks', 'a bit like Michael Jackson'. Music would have a 'glam stomp', 'a James Brown funky drummer beat', 'punk's attitudinal swagger', or would be 'angular', like post-punk (whatever 'angular' was ever supposed to mean). After the mid-eighties, it was difficult to find a review of a new artist that didn't compare them to something that had come before. Like the Jesus And Mary Chain? Then, you'll like the Velvet Underground. Keen on the Pet Shop Boys? Better check out Sparks too. For a while *Q* magazine acknowledged this, perhaps subconsciously, by adding such helpful information to the end of their album reviews.

The Kraftwerk story ends now too; or rather, the story becomes a series of related stories, all running in parallel and at different speeds.* Kraftwerk would return to Kling Klang; but that wave of creativity which had resulted in eight LPs in 11 years was over. What happened was something almost unprecedented within modern music: the sounds they created became, with what appeared to be an ever-accelerating pace, part of the fabric of popular culture. As each year passed, the music Kraftwerk would hear in the clubs and on the radio would sound like theirs. Wave after wave of musicians, from across the globe, would make music that first imitated, then built on, then sampled, and finally paid tribute to Kraftwerk in a deluge of covers, steals, pastiches and parodies. For the four musicians involved, especially Ralf, it must have been unnerving and disorientating to listen to a future that had so speedily become nostalgic.

In 1982, Afrika Bambaataa and the Soul Sonic Force released their album *Planet Rock*. Its title track, released as a 12-inch single, was not a big hit, but its status is legendary. With its TR-808 drum-machine-generated beats† and Fairlight synthesizer, the single blew apart the idea that a song should have a single point of origin, or that authorship indeed mattered. The writers of the song included producers Arthur Baker and John Robie, the named act on the record, Afrika Bambaataa and the Soul Sonic Force, but also a certain

---

* This book cannot list all the samples by other artists of Kraftwerk, nor can it deal extensively with Kraftwerk's influence on dance music from 1990 onwards. To do so would require another book-length study.
† Made by Roland, the earliest users of this still quite primitive drum machine were the Yellow Magic Orchestra. It was also used by Marvin Gaye on his 1982 hit 'Sexual Healing', and also by Phil Collins.

Ralf Hütter and Florian Schneider. Incorporating the melody from Kraftwerk's 'Trans-Europe Express'* and the Bartos-inspired beat of *Computer World*'s 'Numbers', this was a dance track which predicted the remix and the mash-up, and it was one of the first pieces of music to indicate that popular music was moving towards a 'curator culture', whereby the canon could be cut up, reassembled, and digitally displaced from its historical contexts. The legacy is a mixed one. Today, music has become so decontextualised from its moment of production, so scrambled temporarily by the randomisation of the iPod's shuffle facility, the miasma of pathetic cover versions on 'talent' TV shows, and the not-so-clever or arty borrows from older songs by musicians with no imagination, that one might regard the advent of sampling as the beginning of popular music's obsession with its past. Yet, at the time, and for a good many years, these post-modern bricoleurs seemed ironic and clever. Pop may have been eating itself, but the sonic reflux was strangely tasty, at least at the beginning.

Born in the South Bronx in 1957 to New York parents but of Caribbean descent, Afrika (birth name unknown) had been throwing street parties before he was a teenager, soundtracked by the likes of Sly Stone and James Brown. Even before that, he was a pre-teen Stax and Motown junkie. In the seventies, gang-life predominated, leading to the sort of factionalism and sense of disempowerment to be captured by Grandmaster Flash & The Furious Five's 1982 crossover hit, 'The Message'. Bambaataa, however, appeared to be a one-man walking music library. He would host sessions with various 'pools' of people, all addicted to music. One day, he hit them with 'Trans-Europe Express'. 'I thought it was some weird shit. Some funky mechanical crazy shit,' he said in a 1998 interview. 'And more and more as I kept listening to it, I said, they some funky white guys. Where they from? Start reading all the... I always read labels yunno, want to see what it says on the back, who wrote what. I went digging more into their history so I got into *Autobahn*, their dub album, and once I got into Rock Pool, and they told me other things to check

---

* The Kraftwerk record which would have helped popularise the band in the clubs of New York at the time would be one of the world's first 12 inch singles. 'Kraftwerk – Disco Best' was a rare promo with just four tracks: 'The Robots', 'Showroom Dummies', 'Neon Lights' and, crucially, 'Trans-Europe Express'.

out, and I was checking *Radio-Activity*, and the more stuff I was checking and playing to my audience.'

The result was 'Planet Rock', although the track itself was a cut-up of other non-Kraftwerk references too. Bambaataa wanted the Soul Sonic Force to be the 'the first black electronic group. After Kraftwerk put "Numbers" out, and I always was into "Trans-Europe Express", I said "I wonder if I can combine them two into something real funky with a hard bass and beat." So we combined them. But I didn't want people to think it was just Kraftwerk, so we added a track called "Super Sporm", by Captain Sky. The breakdown as the synthesizer's going up, that's the "Super Sporm" beat. And then we added 'The Mexican' by Babe Ruth, another rock group, and we speeded it up.' 'At the time the sound was fresh and clean – the 808 drumbox was not known by the audience in the club,' says Karl Bartos. 'And the vocals had that "party feeling". No other record sounded like it.'

It would be wrong, however, to claim that the flow of electronic music which followed in the next decade, hip-hop, house, ambient, big beat, was influenced only by Kraftwerk. 'I used to look for weird covers,' remembers Bambaataa of his trawl round the record stores of his youth. 'I might have seen Yellow Magic Orchestra and thought, that's a weird lookin' cover, let me pick this up. Then it was something called "Firecracker". I said, "Hmm, I could play with this..."'

Yellow Magic Orchestra were the second crucial influence and came not from Europe or even America, but from Japan. They were formed in 1977 by Haruomi Hosono (bass, keyboards and vocals), Yukihiro Takahashi (drums and lead vocals), who had toured Britain supporting Roxy Music as part of the Sadistic Mika Band, and the classically trained Ryuichi Sakamoto (keyboards and vocals). They were so like Kraftwerk, and yet in another way so unlike them.

Japan, like West Germany, had suffered terribly at the hands of the Allies. The destruction of two of its cities, Hiroshima and Nagasaki, by US atomic bombs in 1945 was, in the eyes of many, the cruellest and most shocking event in World War II. It might have brought a conclusion to the war in the East closer by a few months, but at a terrible cost. From that moment on, those who claimed that nuclear weapons were a military necessity because their presence kept a balance between East and West and thus acted as a deterrent, seemed misguided, given that the world's new superpower, the USA, had dropped two atomic bombs itself. The members of the Yellow Magic Orchestra (or YMO for short), slightly younger on average than Kraftwerk, were nevertheless operating in a similar cultural atmosphere to post-war Germany. Like Kraftwerk, they wished to reassert a national identity, not slavishly copy Western musical imports.

In some crucial areas, YMO were just as innovative as Kraftwerk, even though the group's lead singer, the supremely photogenic Ryuichi Sakamoto, admits that they were heavily influenced by them. Sakamoto, a Krautrock fan, converted the rest of the band and, in a fashion that also mirrors elements of Kraftwerk, they strove to create an indigenous music. 'We were tired of being told the Japanese were copying everything – the cars and TVs – at that time. So we thought it was time to make something very original from Japan. Because everything else was very much an imitation of the West at that time. Kind of coincidentally, when YMO came out, the Japanese cars and TVs also came out and it was very controversial. Some American workers were destroying Japanese cars. [Laughs] It was an interesting time.' He goes on, 'We are still amazed by the strong concepts behind Kraftwerk – their visuals, logos, live presentation, everything. It's very, very formalised. We thought that was very German and we knew we couldn't do that. So, instead, in Japan we have everything. We have Japanese traditions and heavy Western influences on everything like music and food and architecture – everything. So it's kind of chaotic, Japanese culture. That was something we wanted to reflect in our music – that chaos, that everything. So instead of reducing and purifying one's style (as Kraftwerk did on their technopop albums) we did the opposite. We let in everything: techno, but a little bit of jazz and classical. Asian, Western, American... Hawaiian, even!'

There is a playfulness to YMO. The sound on their breakthrough hit single 'Computer Games' is, in fact, a re-recording and melding together of two YMO songs, the original 'Computer Games', which sampled arcade games, *Space Invaders* and *Circus*, and a second song, 'Firecracker', a 1959 Exotica composition from Martin Denny which YMO re-wrote with catchy Asian melodies and beats in what is almost a parody of a pastiche of orientalism. 'Tong Poo', also from their eponymously titled debut album, was

195

perhaps the first techno record ever made, while a synth line of 'La Femme Chinoise' would be later recreated by OMD for their 1983 hit 'Genetic Engineering'. This was all two years before *Computer World*'s release.

Sakamoto, in a solo outing which would become part of YMO's tour set, produced another track widely held to be a crucial influence on the development of hip-hop and techno: 'Riot In Lagos'. Its juddery beats and oriental motifs appear, as *The Guardian* critic Richard Vine put it, to 'seem constantly on the edge of falling apart'. This was music that sounded deconstructed from its point of departure.

YMO became huge in their home country. The Japanese loved innovation and technology and so rather than being viewed, as Kraftwerk sometimes were, as harbingers of a new desensitised age, YMO chimed perfectly with Japan's love of the robotic. Shintoism, Japan's old religion, did not make a strict separation between the animate and the inanimate. In a culture thus programmed, the appearance of a robotic dog was looked upon not with bafflement but with amusement.* Their second album, *Solid State Survivor*, released in 1979, would go on to sell two million copies worldwide. 'Technopolis', announced with Sakamoto's vocodorised salvo of 'Tokyo! Tokyo', a new-wave slab of synth-crunch, might have been indebted, in the title at least, to Kraftwerk's own 'Metropolis', but future techno artists regarded it as the originator of the style. Perhaps the most internationally well-known YMO song, recorded in 1978 for a Seiko advert and included on *Solid State Survivor*, is 'Behind The Mask'. The YMO version is the best with its wonderful melody and lyric by the British lyricist Chris Mosdell, a collaborator on many of YMO's songs. It is one of electronica's greatest songs. 'There's nothing in your eyes/That marks where you cried/All is blank/All is blind', sings Sakamoto in this enigmatic tale of identity-revelation/hiding, a Kabuki mask brought to life in a pop song.

---

* 'Japan was the first to have created Tamagotchi, a little mechanical gadget that in a very short time has become the dearest pet for children all over the world. Japanese people feel comfortable in a robot's company and that is mostly because they have been portrayed as friendly, helpful devices, designed to make their lives easier. That's contrasting with the Western vision, fed by the science fiction literature, characterized by the fear of a great robotic invasion over the human race.' http://www.japaneserobots.net/

Kraftwerk had their own masks too, of course: their robots. Michael Jackson would record a version of 'Behind the Mask' with new lyrics for *Thriller*, but a dispute with YMO's publishers meant release would have to wait until after Jackson's death when it was considered the highlight of the posthumously released *Michael* CD. Michael too, allegedly, had his imaginary friends; his Neverland ranch was, reportedly, filled with life-sized mannequins to keep him company. The song would, however, be covered by Greg Phillinganes in its rewritten form, and then introduced to Eric Clapton by Phillinganes when he became part of EC's touring band. Clapton included a rock version of the song on his 1986 album *August*. Later versions would include a remix by the dance act Orbital on an album of YMO mixes and re-versions entitled *Hi-Tech/No Crime*, and a collaboration between YMO and the Human League in 1993.

Unlike Kraftwerk, YMO included 'conventional' elements in their sound – pianos, drums, saxophone – although the main thrust of the music was always the synth. They really could play, unlike the UK's 'one-fingered revolutionists', and rather than dealing exclusively with ominous themes of de-humanisation, their music was often zany and poppy. They did playful cover versions such as the Beatles' 'Day Tripper' and 'Tighten Up (Japanese Gentlemen Stand Up Please)', a cover version of Archie Bell & the Drells' 1968 *Billboard* number one hit; and unlike Kraftwerk, YMO became media stars. In a moment as wonderfully incongruous as Kraftwerk's appearance on *Midnight Special* playing 'Autobahn' five years earlier, YMO were invited onto the top-rating and iconic *Soul Train* programme to perform the single 'Computer Games' in December 1980, introduced by Don Cornelius, creator and host of the show, and a veteran journalist of the Civil Rights movement in the troubled America of the sixties. 'Everyone went mad,' Haruomi "Harry" Hosono, YMO's bassist told John Lewis of *The Guardian* in 2008. 'They were breakdancing and bodypopping,' says the band's drummer and lead singer, Yukihiro Takahashi. 'We'd never seen anything like it.'

YMO became bone fide pop stars. The band can recall Beatles-esque moments, of being mobbed and girls ripping their clothes off as they were chased down the street, and the unwanted intrusion of the paparazzi. Their tale in this respect is as unlike the story of the notoriously media-shy Kraftwerk as one can imagine. It all led, in 1983, to the band announcing a *sankai* or 'fan-out'. YMO would take a ten-year sabbatical.

Another influence on the incipient US hip-hop scene came from one of the most maligned musicians in British popular music. In 1982 Gary Numan was something of a figure of fun, castigated in the mainly left-wing music press for his honest (if, as many people thought, misguided) support for Margaret Thatcher's Tory government, and dismissed by many as a Bowie clone. But with two major UK number ones, and a dedicated tribe of fans, the Numanoids, Gary connected with a stream of early-eighties disaffection in youth culture, that constituency which wasn't necessarily interested in fighting the state, but was much more interested in Numanoid themes of alienation and disconnection, where there's 'no one to love'. For Kraftwerk, the autobahn represented freedom, the car a status symbol; for Numan it was simply the place where this man, barely into his twenties, felt 'safest of all'.

Numan himself would claim that Kraftwerk was not a huge influence on his music at the time, which seems odd. Given Numan's honesty in interviews, however, there should be no reason to doubt this statement: but there surely has to be some Kraftwerk influence in those swooping synths, frozen stare and technological themes? 'Kraftwerk to me have always been clever little ideas,' says Numan. 'They have never had that same level of songwriting and production attached to them. Some of the other people I really admire. I admire Kraftwerk because they were at the beginning, because they were completely technological in a way; and it really was ahead of its time. None of that can be taken away from them, but I think that, in the history of great songwriting, I don't think they would ever feature in it.' That this alienated, bleached and very English electronic music became so big in the American underground scene is almost as remarkable as Kraftwerk's future market saturation. Numan became one of the most sampled artists of all time, providing the melodies for massive hits for the Sugagbabes and Bassment Jaxx in the early years of the 21st century.

By 1982, Kraftwerk's music was adored by blacks, Hispanics and gays, played in the coolest nightclubs and was a huge influence on the incipient DJ scene. Faced with an evening of stop/start three-minute vinyl records, as one dancefloor hit followed the next, MCs in the mid-seventies had developed new techniques to extend their favourite records, either by making their own longer versions of songs through an editing process that involved seamlessly repeating bar after bar, or extending the groove by using two record decks to play discs in sequence so they flowed together without the slightest hint of a break between them. By the late seventies, the industry had caught up with the ingenuity of the DJs by servicing the disco scene with extended edits, instrumental versions and 12-inch remixes, and in so doing created a new function for those studio engineers who cottoned on to what was happening and grasped the opportunity to become celebrated 'remixers' in their own right. Kraftwerk's music – repetitious, yet danceable, and often, crucially, developed over six, seven, eight minutes or more – had many of the right credentials. Their music had always been rigid, disciplined and taut.

Perhaps the most Kraftwerkian single of all time however would be 'Blue Monday', released in early 1983 by Manchester's New Order, which would become the world's biggest-selling 12-inch single. 'Kraftwerk had significantly informed the scene or the circumstances that created Factory Records,' says Peter Saville. 'Without a doubt they were an influence on Joy Division and even more evidently on New Order, because of the circumstances, post-Ian, for Bernard, Stephen and Hooky. They had to find themselves. The band had to find itself when Ian died. So, they found themselves in, let's say, a rhythms-based sound, to compensate for the absence of a writer, a writer of words. So they go, in a way, from poetry to beats, in the transition from Joy Division to New Order. So, in a way, the Kraftwerk influence is, I would say, even more significant in New Order than in Joy Division. The dial of importance is turned up a little bit more as they try to find themselves as New Order. 'Blue Monday' which, it's commonly said, is the publicly defining moment of New Order, is a very Kraftwerk-inspired or Kraftwerk-informed possibility. You can't fully understand 'Blue Monday' without sounding ideas epitomised by Kraftwerk. 'Blue Monday' was intended as a number that they played for encores, because they didn't like playing encores. They almost set out to find a piece that the equipment could play. That was one of the stated objectives around 'Blue Monday' – is there something that our equipment can play, so we don't have to? If that is not a Kraftwerk-related idea, I don't know what is. So Kraftwerk were incredibly important to them. If we understand Joy Division and New Order as the very foundation block of Factory and without them there is no Factory, and without Kraftwerk, there is no Joy Division or New Order, the way they turned out.'

New Order came up with the rhythm when they were experimenting with a new Oberheim DMX drum machine they had purchased. In *The Guardian* of February 24, 2006, Peter Hook explained: 'Bernard [Sumner] and Stephen [Morris] were the instigators. It was their enthusiasm for new technology. The drum pattern was ripped off from a Donna Summer B-side. We'd finished the drum pattern and we were really happy, then Steve accidentally kicked out the drum machine lead so we had to start from scratch and it was never as good. The technology was forever breaking down and the studio was really archaic. Kraftwerk booked it after us because they wanted to emulate 'Blue Monday'. They gave up after four or five days. It was a collection of sound bites – it sort of grew and grew. When we got to the end I went in and jammed the bass; I stole a riff from Ennio Morricone. Bernard went in and jammed the vocals. They're not about Ian Curtis; we wanted it to be vague. I was reading about Fats Domino. He had a song called 'Blue Monday' and it was a Monday and we were all miserable so I thought, "Oh that's quite apt."'

There were many others, but 'Blue Monday' was undoubtedly the most important product of 'viral Kraftwerk'. The song itself contained either a sample, or a very faithful reconstruction, of a section of *Radio-Activity*'s 'Uranium' in its wordless choral section. And with each reissue ('Blue Monday' would go on to chart in the UK on three separate occasions), it was a sonic reminder of what Kraftwerk were. Kraftwerk themselves were publicly silent, and had been for two years, yet their imprimatur on modern music by 1983 was everywhere. But they were working, or, at least, some of the time...

7.2 Fitter, Happier...

There is something compulsive about cycling; and this is not simply based on anecdotal evidence. Although there are the dangers of breathing in petrol fumes, or being knocked over by car fanatics who regard cyclists as little more than mobile organ-donors*, the advantages are manifold: fresh air, exercise, saving money on a bus ticket, reducing one's carbon footprint (seldom a priority for the populist Right), and getting to wear slightly pervy trousers (if one takes the exercise seriously). Although statistics are extremely hard to draw firm conclusions from, given that many people own bikes they hardly use, and some enthusiasts own more than one and ride them almost every day, what is true is that production of bicycles far exceeds that of automobiles in terms of units. In 2003 bike production had climbed to over 100 million per year compared with 42 million cars.† Almost half the world's bikes are to be found in China. Interestingly, in 1996, Germany was estimated to have a total of 62 million – over three times the number in the UK at the time.

The Tour de France is, of course, the world's premier cycle race, taking place every July and August and covering over 2,200 miles which, as the crow flies, would be a bit like cycling from Paris to Mosul in Iraq. For the uninitiated, its charms are hard to fathom, but for aficionados the Tour is much more than simply a race. The award of yellow, green, polka-dot and white jerseys for various disciplines or achievements signifies that it is a team event that also incorporates various individual competitions, and for many it is addictive viewing, for to ride a stage of the Tour is to compete in a major feat of endurance. Like Formula One motor racing, the lead cyclist of any given team appears to be 'allowed' to win various stages by team mates if in competition for the coveted yellow jersey. The Tour has also been subject to scandals of the doping variety, and even drug-induced deaths, although the regulations to stop unfair advantage are now among the most stringent in sport. At their very best, cyclists appear almost superhumanly fit, totally in synch with their machines, an unstoppable meld of flesh, blood, and titanium. In 2012, William Fotheringham's biography of Eddy Merckx, five-time winner of the Tour, and always a welcome 'get out of jail free' card when asked to name three famous Belgians, was entitled *Merckx: Half Man, Half Bike*. By the mid-eighties, such a

---

* Media celebrity Jeremy Clarkson on cyclists: 'They do not pay road tax and therefore have no right to be on the road, some of them even believe they are going fast enough to not be an obstruction. Run them down to prove them wrong.'

† Source http://www.worldometers.info/bicycles/

sobriquet would have fitted Ralf Hütter perfectly too, as the man machine became the human bicycle.

There is no denying that cycling was, and indeed still is, very important for Ralf Hütter. With plenty of fresh air, exercise and camaraderie, it's a healthy hobby to pursue and on the face of it certainly less harmful to body and soul than the headline-grabbing recreational activities of many other rock stars, the promiscuity, alcohol abuse and penchant for pharmaceutical experimentation. But cycling isn't rock 'n' roll. In the same way that Cliff Richard has been ridiculed for his love of tennis, or Alice Cooper and Iggy Pop for the joys of golf, cycling, with its aerobic severity, male nerdiness, and comical racing attire, lends itself to accusations of geekiness.

Ralf was no dilettante. Indeed, it is probably inaccurate to describe his passion for cycling as a hobby. As the eighties progressed, it became more like a second (unpaid) job. It was, however, Florian who bought the first Kling Klang racing bike. 'It came from Florian,' Wolfgang remembers. 'He sometimes rode on a racing bicycle from his home in northern Düsseldorf to the city centre, because he didn't like driving then. It was much too crowded, and it was faster on a racing bike. Ralf took his bike once, I think it was in the late seventies, and he liked it straight away. It was easy to ride. It was so lightweight, and it was good technically... it made a wonderful sound with the chain and gears.'

The introduction of cycling into the Kraftwerk camp came at a time when fitness and health became the editorial focus of several newly launched men's lifestyle magazines. As the kilos fell from Ralf's frame, a new self-confidence took over. 'Suddenly he felt that he had a body,' Wolfgang Flür diagnosed. 'He felt blood in his veins: he felt his muscles growing, the tendons working, drawing and pulling and everything. And this was the impact it had on him, because, for the first time, he felt attractive.' Florian was also a willing and committed cyclist, as, initially, was Karl. 'Actually, I was more into running,' remembers Karl. 'I ran a marathon and I timed myself. Wolfgang was lazy, though, he wasn't into keeping fit.' The main problem with the new, strict, fitness regime was, firstly, it took a huge chunk out of the conventional working day, and secondly, the effect of the work-out on the motivation of the individual. 'After being on your bike for five to six hours you return to Kling Klang with your heartbeat at 60. All you want to do is eat something, relax, and watch TV! You don't want to work.'

As Ralf's fitness levels increased, he began attempting harder and harder climbs, longer and longer routes. In a 2003 interview, Ralf revealed the true extent of his cycling bug. 'In the spring I cycled the Amstel Gold Race for cycling amateurs. I also never skip Liège-Bastogne-Liège, and each year there are some trips through the Pyrénées and Alps on my programme....' He then lets slip that he had climbed Alpe d'Huez, 'several times. The whole ride: Col de la Madeleine, Col de la Croix-de-Fer, Col de l'Alpe d'Huez, Luz Ardiden also and the Tourmalet ... I did Paris-Roubaix a few times, but for that you need an old bike, because on these cobblestone strips you will certainly break something. I did also the Tour of Flanders a few times: also very difficult.' Ralf estimated that, at his peak, he was cycling around 200 kilometres a day. It has been reported that on occasion on Kraftwerk tours, the bus would drop him off around 100 kilometres from the venue, and he would complete the final stretch on his bike.

It was perhaps no surprise that the band's first new product since *Computer World* was the single 'Tour De France'. Surprisingly, a slap bass sound was re-created electronically and used throughout. The song itself was a celebration of the joys of that most famous of professional cycling competitions, the wonder of the terrain ('Les Alpes et les Pyrénées'), and the consolations of male bonding ('Camarades et amitié'). Hütter's vocal would then give way to the gasps for oxygen of a cyclist on a long climb, rhythmically incorporated into the electronic beat of the song. One can almost feel the lactic acid building up in one's legs as the song unfolds. Despite the quality of the song, for the first time in Kraftwerk's oeuvre, it sounded as if the band were reacting rather than setting the pace. The music doffed a cap to the pulsating proto-techno beats coming out of New York and Detroit of the early eighties.

For the promotional film, Wolfgang had to buy a bike and practise: 'Yes, yes, I bought one. For a little while it was fun. It was a beautiful one in dark grey with a chrome frame. A Raleigh – that was the make. I practised alongside the Rhine, on my own, to get fit for the riding, for the filming. If you see the video today, you can see that I am the one who rode worst, you know. I was not as stable as the others, even though I was mostly at the front when we are coming towards the camera.'

203

The single's sleeve, the four members of the group on racing bikes in a paceline superimposed over the middle white section of the French tricoleur, has become another iconic Kraftwerk image. The song would prove to be a moderate hit for Kraftwerk, reaching number 22 in the UK charts, and, in a remixed form in 1984 for the film *Breakin'* (or *Breakdance* as it was known internationally), the song charted once more, its highest position number 24 in the UK charts.

But there was still no new album from Kraftwerk. *Computer World* was now three years old, the long world tour a fading memory. 'Tour De France' itself had been written to form part of a new album, *Techno Pop*. Karl Bartos: 'Coming from Japan in 1981 we had the idea of a genre which was supposed to be called technopop. "Tour De France" was just one track off this record. The original front cover of the four of us riding bicycles eventually became the cover to "Tour De France". According to Wolfgang, however, the original name for the album was something entirely different: 'As I remember, Ralf and Florian couldn't really decide which name to take. The *Techno Pop* album was initially going to be called *Technicolor*. But the problem was with the American movie company, Technicolor, who had the copyright on it. We were not allowed to use it, as I remember; so then it was meant to be *Techno Pop* ... and then? ...'

Nothing happened. According to Bartos, the LP was pretty much finished: 'The record was almost finished and Ralf went to New York for a mixing session and he brought the final tape with him but we didn't put it out.' Tracks included 'The Telephone Call' and 'Sex Object', the riff for which Bartos had written on a sound check on the 1981 tour in London and which originally had an almost rock feel to it. The cover was the cover of the 'Tour De France' single. But then Ralf said 'nein'.

This was not the first time, of course, that Kraftwerk had decided against a plan of action already committed to, or, indeed, that they had turned people down. In fact, in 1982, Kraftwerk turned down the chance to work with Michael Jackson. Then aged 25, Jackson was a major star, a successful soul and disco singer, but yet to become the self-styled 'King Of Pop'. 'Michael Jackson's management contacted us,' confirms Wolfgang. 'Michael was fanatical about electro-music when we had the *Man-Machine* album out and he wanted us to produce his next album. But we gave him

'Ralfbot' in animated mode: the robotised Kraftwerk. TIM JARVIS/RETNA PICTURES

Ralf and his mannequin self, at The Ritz in New York City, 1981. LAURA LEVINE/CORBIS

Wolfgang and Florian (with trademark wide smile) on stage at The Ritz in New York City, 1981. LAURA LEVINE/CORBIS

Kraftwerk play 'Pocket Calculator' at The Ritz, New York City, 1981. LAURA LEVINE/CORBIS

Karl and Wolfgang with their Doppelgängers at The Ritz, New York City, 1981. LAURA LEVINE/CORBIS

Mannequins of Kraftwerk on display to promote *Man-Machine*, 1978. EBET ROBERTS/REDFERNS

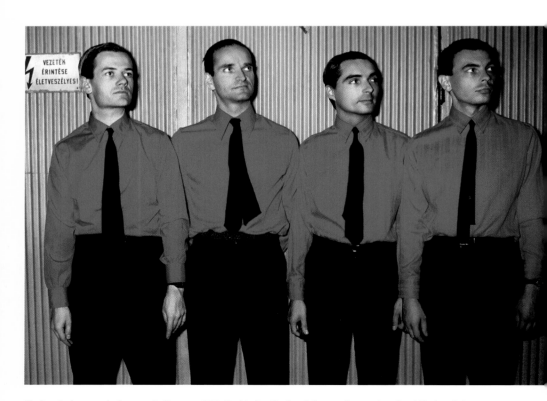

Kraftwerk photographed on tour in Hungary, 1981. To this day, Kraftwerk fans can be seen in red and black at their concerts.
GETTY IMAGES

lorian and Ralf pose at a party. EBET ROBERTS/REDFERNS

Florian on stage in Helsinki, February 5, 2004. JAAKONAHO / REX FEATURES

Michael Rother on stage with Hallogallo at the Edge Festival, The Picture House, Edinburgh, Scotland, August 17, 2010.
MARC MARNIE/REDFERNS

Wolfgang outside Kling Klang, November 2010. Karl Bartos: 'He was always a good laugh. I always thought that he would have been a good actor.' DAVID BUCKLEY

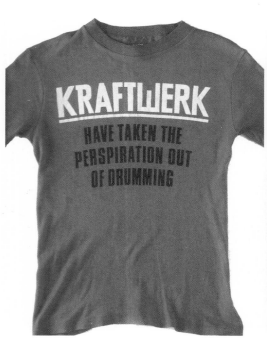

Kraftwerk T-Shirt.

Karl Bartos attends the BMI Awards at the Dorchester Hotel, London, October 2007. BRIAN RASIC/REX FEATURES

Ralf Hütter, Henning Schmitz, Fritz Hilpert and Stefan Pfaffe of Kraftwerk perform during the Kraftwerk Retrospective at the New York City Museum of Modern Art, April 10, 2012. MIKE COPPOLA/GETTY IMAGES

Kraftwerk on stage during the Global Gathering Festival, at the Hordern Pavilion, Sydney, Australia, November 30, 2008. WENDELL TEODORO/WIREIMAGE

Later period Kraftwerk members Fritz Hilpert (left) and Stefan Pfaffe at the Kraftwerk Retrospective, New York City Museum of Modern April 10, 2012. MIKE COPPOLA/GETTY IMAGES

the brush-off. That's why he went to producer Quincy Jones instead, and did the *Thriller* album. It was a good decision for him [laughs].'

Karl Bartos, however, remembers events differently: 'I was under the impression – although you must remember that I wasn't actually involved in any of the discussions – that Michael Jackson's people contacted EMI because Michael wanted to use the multi-tracks of *The Man-Machine* album in the production of what would have been Janet Jackson's *Control* album. I would have jumped at the chance of working with someone like Michael Jackson, so young and ambitious, but Ralf and Florian, quite rightly, were hesitant. They thought that if they worked with Michel Jackson they would lose their musical identity. They did not want to be swallowed up by him, or any other successful artist. But I have no evidence; it's just something that has stuck at the back of my mind.'

Other suitors reportedly destined to be disappointed were Beatles buddy Klaus Voorman, the inventor of the Blue Meanies in their animated film *Yellow Submarine,* and the Italian filmmaker Dario Argento. It was also rumoured that Elton John contacted the band to discuss a collaboration. 'It is the same politics that they use today, to be absolutely on their own,' says Wolfgang. 'No mixing with enemy cultures. Not "enemy", but *foreign* cultures, you know. Nothing completely influenced by other music styles, cultures, instruments and sounds, countries... We had to be on our own, "*Selbstreferentiel*" [guided only by oneself]. That was their decision.'

Ralf was distracted and suffered a loss of confidence. Option paralysis of a sort set in. By 1983, the international music scene seemed to be full of what then sounded like great pop productions using synths, productions which were busy and sounded great on a dancefloor as well as on AM and FM radio: Arthur Baker's production of Freeez's early house classic, 'I.O.U.', Depeche Mode's move towards a more industrial sound on 'Everything Counts', New Order's 'Blue Monday' and 'Confusion'. Ralf, in particular, started chasing the latest sounds, the ZTT productions – ABC, the Art Of Noise, Frankie Goes To Hollywood – in London and Nile Rodgers' productions – Chic, Madonna, David Bowie – in New York. There appears to have been a loss of nerve. They suddenly felt their sound needed a radical updating to compete. 'Trevor Horn's influence was everywhere,' recalls Karl Bartos. 'With the Synclavier and the Fairlight it was the advent of digital music. Up until *Computer World,* remember, everything was played using analogue synthesizers and we recorded on 16-track, quarter-inch tape. That mid-eighties stuff, it sounded cool and new then. Now it sounds crap!'

And so, *Techopop* was pulled from the schedule. Regular bike rides, however, were not.

7.3 'Is My Bike OK?'

You're fairly young, you're very rich, you're not sure what to do next musically, you've already written your page in the annals of rock 'n' roll lore. Most musicians in that position get lazy, or release substandard records which tarnish their legacy, or become actors; or all three.

Ralf Dörper, by then a recording musician in his own right with the groups Die Krupps and Propaganda, was also a keen cyclist in the eighties but insists no one was in Kraftwerk's league. 'The only chance to meet any of Kraftwerk outside of, say, a coffee shop that was near to Kling Klang, would have been at one of these cycling shops. But then they got more and more into it, and they went to the really specialist shops outside of Düsseldorf which really sell equipment for professionals. That is something I think Wolfgang didn't take part in, and I guess Karl not too much either. They would probably easily do 50 to 100 kilometres a day. And I thought, very well, I'd cycle, but OK, I'm working, so there's a time limit. But normally I wouldn't do much more than 20 to 30 a day, so they were in a completely different league!'

By the mid-eighties there would be a group of riders who would cycle with Ralf and Florian. 'They had a crew which became bigger and bigger. They used the weekends to be in the countryside in the hills in the surrounding area,' remembers Wolfgang. 'There was an architect friend of ours, Volker Albus, and an orthopaedic professor, Willy Klein.* Then there was the barber who always cut our hair in those days, he was such a nice guy. All in all, there would be five or six men cycling off into the hilly country, the wonderful "bergisches Land" around Solingen and Remscheid. I like it there too, but I prefer to go walking there, with my wife.'

---

* Dear reader: absolutely no sniggers, in this instance, of the 'Biggus Dickus' Python variety please!

206

Wolfgang for one could see Kraftwerk's focus shifting away from music. He was becoming increasingly dissatisfied, marginalised. As a non-writer, he needed to keep working, and touring. 'The side-effect of this was that they were not in the studio. Ralf felt his muscles shaping up, his body growing. His face took on a kind of beauty which I can't describe. If you see the riders on the Tour de France or other high-tech bikers or sportsmen generally, the look in their eyes when they just finished a fight or a race, they are so enthusiastic, even ecstatic. I'm looking for another word which was on the tip of my tongue: "fanatics", or even better: "insane"! This is what I realised and I don't like it. I don't like fanaticism at all, especially not in politics, religion or sport. Speaking for me and for Karl, the result was that they didn't go to work enough, and they gave us even more bad feelings because the studio was always full of piles of bicycle chains, tyres, biking clothes stinking of sweat. We had a little workshop where I used to build things for studio design, stage design. It became more and more a workshop for preparing and repairing bicycles. That's the reason why I went there less and less, because I couldn't stand it. It had nothing to do with music any more for me.'

Wolfgang is convinced that cycling went far beyond being a hobby, certainly for Ralf if not Florian as well. He believes it became an addiction. In fact, cyclists, like runners, can become 'cardioholics'. Today's obsessive cyclists blog about how they feel too tired to get to work in the mornings *unless* they cycle there, and that cycling is like alcohol, or nicotine to them. Runners speak of a state of peace, an almost trance-like state which can be attained during prolonged, extreme physical exercise; maybe even a state of grace. 'He wanted it more and more. It was a kind of drug for him,' says Wolfgang. 'The bike-riding, the racing, feeling nature, the wind, everything, not sitting in a car on the autobahn, sterile inside. Now his body was feeling everything, and he became just like Goethe's sorcerer's apprentice, who could not stop doing what he was told to do. Cycling was the master, it was the sorcerer who told him what to do, and he couldn't stop it any more. That is why I say "sorcerer's apprentice". It was a kind of magic. Karl and I realised that he was never going to stop with that. He couldn't come back as the musician he was before, with all that passion and zeal and music-making and sound-creating and travelling and music-presenting with us as his friends.'

Was this wrong of Ralf? What was bad about being fit and cycling with chums? Should he have had a responsibility, particularly to Wolfgang, to keep touring? It should be remembered that Kraftwerk was his and Florian's original concept and in their eyes, on a level above personal likes and dislikes, personal friendships or animosities, Kraftwerk was a business which they ran on business-like lines. Ralf and Florian created the music when, and if, they wanted. Ralf had become someone who was deeply committed to cycling. He wanted to be healthy. What, in a sense, was wrong with that?

There was another shift within Kraftwerk's inner workings; the increasing importance of Karl Bartos. Recruited for the 1974 tour, he had been a credited co-composer on the last two Kraftwerk records. A glance at the credits of *The Man-Machine* and *Computer World* indicates that Bartos had written a not inconsiderable part. Karl and Wolfgang had to keep playing and performing to live (in the manner to which they were accustomed, of course). In 1984 and 1985, such discontents were shared privately but not publicly. But this would change. If not a catalyst, then certainly a step toward the next stage of the Kraftwerk saga – the inaction that befell them in the eighties – was a serious cycling accident suffered by Ralf.

'I wasn't actually with him, so I can only tell you what I was told,' says Wolfgang. 'They were on the left bank of the Rhine, on a path off a dyke with a hard surface covered in gravel. They didn't ride with helmets: and they had reached a high speed. They were riding in Indian file, and Ralf – "I want to be the best, I want to be the first" – sped up and went faster and faster and let his front wheel touch the rear wheel of the rider in front of him, rubber against rubber. He fell and landed on his head on the concrete, without a helmet. He was immediately knocked unconscious; he didn't react, so I've heard. His cycling friends tried to wake him up but he didn't wake up, and there was blood flowing out of his ear. So then they were very afraid. They managed to stop a car. I don't know how they managed to get an ambulance, because the road wasn't open to traffic. They drove him to Krefeld, to hospital, where he spent four days, I think, in a coma. The doctors said it was very serious. We and his family thought he wouldn't get up again. But he regained consciousness, and the first thing he asked was, "Is my bike OK? What happened to my bike?" That's really true! Everyone tells me that. There is no reason for them to lie. We know how fanatical he was. He was in hospital for two, maybe three weeks, but he was back on a bike soon afterwards, I think.'

Although in later interviews Ralf was either cryptic about, or keen to downplay, the severity of his accident – 'No. It was just a very normal fall and a couple days in the hospital. It was nothing to worry about... I just forgot my helmet. That's the real story', is one such matter-of-fact reply – the truth seems to be that Hütter was in a coma and dangerously ill for a period of days. Nevertheless, Ralf is adamant that the seriousness of his accident has been blown up out of all proportion in the telling. In 2009 he told John Harris, 'It didn't affect me. I got a new head, and I'm fine. It was a few days in hospital, and that's it. A very normal accident. It's one of those things where somebody tells a story, and the next guy adds another story, and in the end ... like I say, I got a new operation, and I got a new head. I just forgot my helmet, and I was in hospital for three or four days.'

This is one part of the Kraftwerk story which seems destined to remain clouded by conflicting testimony. 'It might sound pretentious to say today but after the bike accident Hütter was not the same,' says Karl Bartos. 'He changed.'

7.4 'For Those Who Heed The Call Of The Machine, We Salute You....'*

By 1985, electronic pop, machine music, robo-pop, whatever one wants to call it, had taken over, and to such an extent that synths seemed to be appearing everywhere, and in some extremely unlikely areas.

A raft of hoary old rock acts were now incorporating synths within their sound palette. Examples are legion. Yes had recruited Trevor Horn, who remodelled this most committed of prog groups with synths and samples, helping them to score a US number one with 'Owner Of A Lonely Heart' in early 1984. This was followed three weeks later by soft-metal stadium rockers Van Halen with their massive single 'Jump', a song introduced by a synth melody played on an Oberheim OB-Xa. Neil Young had already perplexed his fanbase and record company with the vocodorised synth-pop of

---

* ZTT, Propaganda, *A Secret Wish*, sleeve notes.

Trans. Queen, who famously boasted their antipathy towards synths in the seventies, scored a worldwide hit with the almost all-synth singles, 'Radio Ga Ga' and 'I Want To Break Free'.

In a parallel development, those original synth groups formed in the wake of Kraftwerk's initial breakthrough appeared to be losing confidence and moving towards more conventional terrain. There was a collective groan of disappointment when the Human League released a single, 'The Lebanon', with guitars all over it. OMD were moving into their 'Hollywood Era', the weirdness of their first four records now reined back in favour of lush, radio-friendly pop ballads. Gary Numan's star had been waning for several years, with each new record exposing his discomfort at trying to write commercial hits. Depeche Mode, the runts of the litter back in 1981, were now the unlikely pedigree breed. Album by album, tour by tour, their fanbase grew steadily outside the UK, into continental Europe, America and Japan. As their music became darker, more industrial, less radio-friendly, indeed more akin to rock than the original synth prototype, so their commercial status soared.

Pure electronic music in the UK charts would now be championed by two duos: the Pet Shop Boys, who paired stylishly literate pop journalist Neil Tennant with synth boffin Chris Lowe, and Erasure, Vince Clarke's fourth pop experiment in five years, this time alongside the almost operatic vocals of Andy Bell. Neither group had an obvious link to Kraftwerk. However, the biggest new pop star of 1984 and 1985 was Madonna, who in her first incarnation took Bowie's gender-confusion and musical and image rebrands as a base. The first concert she ever attended was a Bowie show: 'He blew my mind,' she told *Q*'s Paul Du Noyer in 1994. 'Ziggy Stardust in Detroit. What he did on stage was so inspiring, because he was so theatrical. He really played with ideas, iconography and imagery and his work was provocative. He's a brilliant man.' In the same interview she talked of the post-punk scene and revealed: 'One group I saw around that time who blew me away was Kraftwerk, they were amazing.' Madonna's music on early tracks such as 'Holiday' and 'Into The Grove', while not directly like Kraftwerk, certainly had a mechanical, repetitious, electro quality. By 2000, and her international hit 'Music', the Kraftwerk influence was so strong that it sounded like Madge singing over a Kling Klang backing track from *Trans-Europe Express*.

210

Kraftwerk, now no longer pioneers so much as the first settlers in the new electro-hinterland, took their new LP to François Kevorkian and Ron St. Germain at Right Track Studio in New York. This was the first time that they had worked extensively outside their Kling Klang comfort zone for years. By now, the album had been retitled *Electric Café*.

When the LP was finally released, in November 1986, the moment had passed. Had it been released when it was originally ready, in 1983, it might have been more kindly regarded, but with so many delays, rethinks and tinkering, the LP sounded oddly sterile to many ears. Though at the time it was released *Electric Café* seemed to lack melodic content and sounded brash and mechanical, few would disagree that the passing years have been kind to the record. Today, it sounds oddly ahead of its time. The fact that Kraftwerk had pared everything down to the most essential beats and melodies gives the LP a beguiling, abstract quality. The centrepiece of the album, 'Musique Non-Stop', was a collision of industrial beats overlaid by an almost comical, and now iconic, 'Boing, Boom, Tschack!' with a 'Ping!' thrown in on alternate lines. It was as if Kraftwerk had become the electronic Neanderthals, unable even to speak in words, and forced into talking homophonic signifiers of the sounds they made. This was an aspect picked up by Biba Kopf's *NME* review at the time. 'This record has been soft-machine tested over and over and round and round the dance halls of Düsseldorf until its beats have been thoroughly perfected, forcing the listener to respond to its imperatives. In the process, every ounce of excess is removed, reducing the group character to its barest essences. Its economy is as stunning as it ever was... K's great ability is to reduce words to a weightlessness that places the onus of meaning on the listener. You can invest in them as much or as little sense as you want. The economy of Kraftwerk's expression has become their signature. In a world given over to the illegible scrawls of B-Boy Braggards, their modest autograph is something to be cherished.'

As Karl concedes, Florian was not just an excellent producer of music but also the group member most interested in the area of speech synthesis. He was well-connected to people working in this field and was often able to procure prototype inventions before they were readily available on the open market. 'Sometimes Florian would be given a speech computer that sounded very human, and we'd modify it to sound robotic, more technoid,' Ralf told Simon Witter in 1991. 'The trick was to be able to inspire somebody with artistic ideas, and persuade them to work on the weekend, create that interest in making something that would be different from office work.'

The critics' uneven response to *Electric Café* was partly justified disappointment, but also part sacred-cow slaying. In the mid-to-late eighties, few rock or pop artists of any stature escaped 'death by two-star review'. Andy Gill in *Q*, under the tag-line 'TIRED: Kraftwerk's robo-pop in need of an overhaul,' pulled no punches: 'All of a sudden, a group so pioneering and innovatory they could alter the course of black American dance music has been reduced to ignominious self-parody.' The truth was that *Electric Café* was Kraftwerk's most minimal and most abstract-sounding record. Twenty-five years after its release, it is by no means the cold cup of instant many thought at the time. 'It was always said that *Electric Café* was not worth the wage, it was sort of sterile,' says Kristoff Tilkin, then a teenage Kraftwerk fan, now a journalist for the Belgian magazine *Humo*. 'When I listen to it again I always hear a real beautiful melancholy in it, there are some really amazing melodies there.'

The catchy orchestral-synth of 'Sex Object' (itself an odd title for such a sex-less project as Kraftwerk) drew this slightly withering comment from Wolfgang: 'Why has Ralf written that song on the *Electric Café* album? – "I don't want to be your sex object." Of course he wanted to be!' What was more surprising was the use of a synth which sounded like a slap bass guitar. It was as if Kraftwerk were slowly falling into the same trap many American musicians had at the time – trying to create exactly the same sounds on a synth they could easily have made on a 'real' instrument. The best pop song on the album was 'The Telephone Call' sung by Karl (the only Kraftwerk song so to be). 'The song starts with the engaged tone,' says Karl, 'then a collage of an old-fashioned rotary dial telephone being dialled, together with a newer digital version before the Moog kicks in overlaid by a clever riff based on the international "number unobtainable" sound. 'The number you have reached, has been disconnected,' says the female operator. It possesses a trademark melancholy: 'You're so close but far away/I call you up all night and day.' In the middle of the song, there's a break, an improvisation of riffling dialling tones and the hurry-scurry of the rotary dial from speaker to speaker. But the mood of the piece seemed dislocated. Life seemed wrong for Kraftwerk. The phone lines were down, disconnected or engaged, the calls unanswered.

The 2009 Kling Klang reissue of *Electric Café*, released under its original title, *Techno Pop*, includes the instrumental 'House Call'. Essentially an extemporisation of the musical themes of 'Telephone Call', it is in the tradition of 'Metal On Metal', 'It's More Fun To Compute' and the entire second half of the LP version of 'Computer Love'. Ralf and Karl were interested in electronic music which built on, riffed on, and restated the main body of the song. 'We didn't look too close to home when we were looking for inspiration,' says Bartos. 'We were, for example, very interested in songs like 'Summer Breeze' and 'Harvest For The World' by the Isley Brothers. These were songs which were self-contained pop songs in the first half, and then went off on an improvisatory journey in the second part, with solos and a re-structuring of the song's main motifs. This is what we're trying to do in Kraftwerk on many of the songs.'

A video for the single edit shows the classic line-up for the last time. For Wolfgang it makes for uneasy viewing. 'If you watch it closely, you can see how far apart we were from one another: emotionless faces, as always, but this time even more so. Everyone facing in different directions. It was so cold at that time. My heart was cold. I was freezing when we met up.'

Another aspect of *Electric Café* which might also lead to some sort of reappraisal is the title song itself. Musically, its unmemorable melody is disappointingly derivative of 'Trans-Europe Express'. Conceptually, it is significantly more interesting. Although the idea is not clearly stated, did Kraftwerk, however obliquely, tangentially, subconsciously even, have some sort of inkling of what the nineties would bring, the explosion of electric cafés all round the world in the form of the internet café?

Wolfgang and Karl, though, were dissatisfied. 'I didn't like this record too much,' Flür remarks. 'It was half-hearted.' For Karl, the main problem was a loss of confidence. Ralf began listening to the competition, chasing sounds. 'Ralf was unsure of his mixing ability,' says Karl. The rules of the game had changed fundamentally since *Computer World* five years earlier. Pop music had become programmed, the use of the Fairlight and Synclavier a commonplace.

213

Ralf Dörper was disappointed in the result, once *Electric Café* was finished: 'It was funny because I had heard some early stuff from what would have been *Techno Pop* in this Cologne discotheque, Morocco, where they tested it. And the DJ played I believe "Sex Object" back-to-back to "Zauberstab" by Zaza – and the latter made a better impression on me even then. But it wasn't released, it was delayed. And that is strange as I know that the artwork was already prepared. It's quite funny because Jürgen [Engler of Die Krupps] used to work at that time at a sort of printers – and that was in the early eighties – and he got the designs in for *Techno Pop*, and then they withdrew it. I think they had to withdraw it because they were not satisfied with the result, so it took, I think, a further three years or so. At the time we had a lot more electronic music in the clubs, and it mixed well, but it was not, shall we say, outstanding. But at the same time you had all this new electronic stuff from the Human League and Heaven 17. So in a way it was not unique any more to have a Kraftwerk song played in a discotheque. If somebody had played, let's say, "Dignity Of Labour" by Human League or some of *Music For Stowaways*, the instrumental B.E.F. stuff, I think some people might have thought, "Oh, something by Kraftwerk!" It was all coming closer together. There was also a technological step-up coming, the digital step, but that did not necessarily mean better music, in my opinion especially not for *Electric Café*. It was their move from analogue to digital, because they decided to record it using Synclavier, but they re-recorded what they had made earlier. At that time I thought The Art of Noise were more Kraftwerkian than Kraftwerk.'

Electric Café might have met with a muted response from both the public and critics, but it was released at a time when the imprimatur of Kraftwerk was as strong as ever in American club-land. Chicago had now become the epicentre of the house music scene, another hybridisation of seventies American soul, late seventies disco, early eighties techno, dance and hi-NRG. For a brief moment, the clubs of America and Britain would be populated by young things who would 'rather jack, than Fleetwood Mac'. In suburban Detroit, Derrick May, Carl Craig, Kevin Saunderson and Juan Atkins were music fanatics into disco, electro and Kraftwerk. Their new construction, techno, was described by May as 'George Clinton meeting Kraftwerk in an elevator'. Again, as in the hip-hop explosion earlier in the decade, the lineage set in motion by

European electronica was crucial to the style too. Writing in *NME* in August 1986, the critic Stuart Cosgrove proclaimed: 'House music is as new as the microchip and as old as the hills. It danced through every inner city, finally settling in Chicago, "the city of broad shoulders": the home of jacking bodies... House music is the sound of the moment. J.M. Silk's "Music Is The Key" reputedly sold 100,000 copies without any help from a major label, record companies are at war trying to sign the best of Chicago, imports are flooding back into Britain on the crest of another new club sound, and like flies around the proverbial hot shit, British journalists have been flying to America daily to track down the sound.' But house music was no pure American sound, as Cosgrove pointed out. 'Chicago has some of the biggest import record shops in America and every house musician will tell you that European music is one of the biggest single factors in the emergence of the sound: Bowie, New Order, Kraftwerk, Human League, Heaven 17, The Art Of Noise, Italian disco, the Munich Sound... The list is endless, sometimes embarrassing, always cosmopolitan and a reminder that house is neither precious about its 'black' identity nor parochial in its taste.'

By the end of the eighties, the media were rife with the idea of the 'end of music', and the 'death of rock'. Sampling technology had both democratised and de-contextualised music. In Britain, the indie-dance band Pop Will Eat Itself embodied this new aesthetic perfectly. Building on the earlier pioneering work of Big Audio Dynamite, their music was a raucous tripped-out collage of chants, noise and samples. It was the beginning of an era where one's ability to forge and counterfeit music was more important than to craft it afresh. Music, in its now pure postmodern phase, was curated rather than created. Here is Stuart Cosgrove again, writing in 1987: 'In the sixties ripping off the riffs of R&B was an amoral crime. Pop tolerated full-scale exploitation as black American music was systematically pillaged by white performers. Modern theft is democratic, a two-way process in a desegregated dance-hall: hip-hop steals from heavy metal, house music steals from Europop and British indie bands steal from their own latter-day heroes. Trouble Funk steal from Kraftwerk, JM Silk steal from Depeche Mode and the Age of Chance steal from everyone. Unlike punk, which kicked against the statues of decadent rock, hip-hop, house and sonic theft have waged war on the laws of property.'

7.5 Robotic Upgrades

'Musique Non-Stop', the first single off *Electric Café*, might have sold unimpressively on release, but its promotional video has been a mainstay of music television ever since. The complex and, for the time, state-of-the-art video was made by Rebecca Allen.

Back in the mid-eighties, Allen – now an internationally renowned artist and academic – was a young multimedia-fixated artist, a professional working in the field, who was contacted by Kraftwerk. Initially based on the East Coast of the US and having studied at Massachusetts Institute of Technology and Rhode Island School of Design, Rebecca is nowadays based in Southern California where she is a media art professor at UCLA. 'Kraftwerk came to me because I was specifically working on human motion, simulation and facial animation for 3-D animation,' she says. 'This was great in the early days, because nobody was doing anything like that.'

Allen was employed at The Computer Graphics Laboratory in New York, where staff were engaged in creating the first computer-generated characters for TV shows and movies. Among the ideas that Allen's team presented at a technical conference was a computer-generated news presenter. 'That inspired Max Headroom,' she recalls. 'We were leading that whole movement and creating, really creating, this field of computer graphics, painting programmes, 2-D animation programmes and 3-D modelling and animation. I had wanted to get human motion and a human character in the computer as it was all very geometric and mathematical-looking at that time. So I worked hard to get a 3-D model of a human character to move and come to life. Ed Catmull, who is now head of Pixar was at our lab. He had developed the first human model, and we had to figure out how to make her move.'

Allen's work came to the attention of Twyla Tharp, the choreographer, who was producing a film called *The Catherine Wheel*, a dance film with a soundtrack by David Byrne and Brian Eno. 'We were very ambitious,' says Allen, 'trying to do the first computer-generated character and TV shows and movies. I was passionate about the idea of art and technology and I was really plugged into music, too. Besides loving Kraftwerk's music it was clear that they were artists. They were experimenting, and they refused to use any kind of analogue instruments. It was all about being digital. I completely connected with that because that was my mission – to explore and invent new digital technology to make art and to understand how art could be part of this. Because my interest was in doing motion pieces and animated pieces, sound was always a big part of that too. As a visual artist exploring digital technology I loved connecting. It was very exciting in the early days because nobody was doing anything like that.'

Working with Kraftwerk was, according to Rebecca, 'all fun, just constant amusement and laughing and jokes. It was so different; I would see them in public or on stage and see a look that was very strict, non-smiling. I read a lot of the press when I was starting work on this, and it was all about them being Nazi robots and emotionless, just because they were working with computers and that meant they were taking all the emotion out of everything. It was just mechanistic, and then I meet these funny guys who were playful and humorous. It was quite clear that so many of their songs had an irony and a sense of humour to them.'

The collaboration with Kraftwerk began more than two years before the final record came out. 'Florian was my main link,' continues Rebecca. 'I talked to him on the phone initially about where we might go with this idea and then to work out how to start working together. We decided to meet when Florian and Ralf were going to be in Paris for a bicycle race. So I said "OK, why don't I meet you in Paris and then we could drive to Germany?" which is what we did.'

During their time in Paris, Ralf and Florian met Afrika Bambaataa socially in a club. The meeting was cordial, and full of mutual respect, and seemed to follow the same pattern as when Kraftwerk had been asked about their influence on the Chicago house scene. They were flattered and fascinated that their music was being used (and also keen that they, as the artists sampled, were given their due credit and recompense of course). Ralf and Florian regarded it as a kind of information flow, an opportunity for exchange and feedback. From this stage in their careers onwards, Kraftwerk were happy to 'quote' the music of their original imitators.

In Düsseldorf Rebecca Allen discussed in more detail the sort of imagery they required. The conversation took a theoretical turn. 'There was that statement "Look, we have these digital instruments; and here we are, performers, and we're doing the same thing every time we perform. Maybe we could just have robots do this." That was a very strong statement, maybe humans can just be replaced by robots. I think they were just trying to make that point, and to say that, one day, there can possibly be robots of ourselves... I think that, more and more, society is beginning to understand what that might mean, with avatars and other things, too. So then they'd say, "That way, we don't have to perform all the time." I never heard them say that was a goal, that they would actually not perform at all. It always seemed to be this mix, where they would perform sometimes; and then the robots would perform sometimes. It's hard to remember today that, back in the sixties and seventies especially, society was really afraid of computers, because people assumed computers were much smarter and better than they really were. There was this fear that computers were going to take over everything, that they would take away everybody's jobs. That was a real fear during that time. It probably went on until the personal computer became familiar in the mid-eighties. And now we've seen how computers aren't so smart, and, yes, computers have taken over tons of jobs. On the other hand, they've made certain parts of life easier. These were the kind of deeper messages that Kraftwerk and I were both exploring.'

Allen looked at the existing Kraftwerk robots, modelled faces on top of a basic bodily structure and decided, for the video for 'Musique Non-Stop', to go down a different, more challenging, and, as history has shown, much more ground-breaking route. 'I said to them "We don't need physical robots. What I want to do is create virtual characters, in a way to create virtual robots. But I want to make virtual representations of you", which today doesn't sound like any big deal. But I said, "We're going to model your bodies, and we're going to model your heads. And we're going to bring these characters to life." Back then, it was an incredibly hard, technical problem, to animate faces and bodies. The way I did that was I had them ship me the mannequin heads that they used for their robots, rather than to digitise from their real faces. I started from their mannequin heads, which were already a kind of artistic representation of them. I also shot video of them live, from different angles. So I could mix the look of the mannequin heads with some of the characteristics of their live images. In the video, I intentionally showed computer artefacts, intentionally showing wire frame version, rather than all-solid, rendered, realistic, faces.

I called it a kind of cubistic look, rather than smooth, very realistic faces. I really wanted to develop a computer art aesthetic, in the same way that they were taking computer music instruments and making a computer, digital aesthetic to music. The reason I got into computers as an artist was to create a whole new aesthetic, not to try to use computers so it looks completely like a photograph would look. We really treated this as a collaboration. They wanted to learn things through this process. I wanted to learn things from them. In fact the "Musique Non-Stop" – that's a simulation of my voice. They'd say, "You're building computer models of us physically so we're building a model of your voice." So it was a kind of trade-off. They simulate my voice. I'm simulating their visual look.'

Whereas most musicians, indeed most artists, produce their work through a steady process of accruement, Rebecca was intrigued to discover that Kraftwerk worked in reverse. 'I remember Florian saying to me, "We start with a lot," because they work and work and work. They would put one layer upon another, upon another, but then they'd start taking things away. That process was really interesting. People say, "They take forever to make an album." But the process was to explore all sorts of things and then look for the simplicity of it, to take it away to the essence.' She soon got a feel for the dynamics of the group. 'I got the sense that Ralf was perhaps leading the group, but that Florian had a lot of input in just the feeling of the music, how the vocals were going, the overall sense of it.'

7.6 Miss Kling Klang

Rebecca Allen occupies a unique position within the Kraftwerk story. She was the first woman since 1973[*] to work with Kraftwerk. Kling Klang was 'part of their mystique,' says Rebecca. 'It wasn't as if the space itself was so special. It was their private chamber. I think as they started to become more famous, and people wanted to infiltrate all parts of their lives, they realised they had to put up this kind of wall of privacy if they wanted to keep their private lives and their private space. But I didn't realise even family members

---

[*] Florian's then girlfriend Barbara took the photograph of Ralf and Florian featured in the gatefold sleeve of the album *Ralf And Florian*.

weren't allowed in. I guess it was the way that they took their work so seriously. When they were working in Kling Klang that was what they wanted to be doing there, and they didn't want to mix it with families coming in, and girlfriends hanging out, and things like that.'

Rather than being stiff, or serious, working at Kling Klang was fun. Allen had little direct contact with Wolfgang and Karl, at that time not the confident English speakers they are today, but she spoke freely with Ralf and Florian, who would, in turn, chat amongst themselves in German discussing the various technical aspects of matching beats and sound with Rebecca's planned robotic upgrades. 'I remember having a lot of fun with them, laughing and jokes. So, it wasn't at all like their public image. They seemed very friendly, very polite, accommodating, but also really serious about their work. When it came to the work it was very serious, but socially we had a lot of fun. With the beats they spent quite a lot of time on all aspects of it. I remember them working with the percussion side and on how to get it right, not just the beats themselves, but the tone and the equalisation around it, to get just the right kind of feeling. So the beats have this kind of trance-like effect. I went there initially partly to get the sense of how they worked, and how the music was evolving. But also, because I was making computer models of them, and getting them to come alive and animate, I just wanted to see how they behaved, to examine them as people, too, just to try to include in the animation a sense of who they were as people.' In addition to the voice "Musique-non-stop, techno pop", Rebecca's voice can be heard saying "Yes, No, Maybe, Perhaps ..." for the track 'Sex Object'. 'That was for me a great example of collaboration, where, again, I had made visual representations of them, and they had made an audio representation of me.'

The design for the *Electric Café* album cover was carefully prepared: 'I designed the album cover image to be a classic kind of portrait of the guys to get an expression with their computer models which would relate to the personality of each of them. If you look at the album I was actually trying to show the process of putting this together. So you had the front. If you looked at the back of the album, it was actually their heads. So it was showing this sense that they were truly models. On the sleeve you had wire-frame versions, to emphasise the "techie", computer look, the wire frame look of them front, and also back. There were also beautiful images of their physical mannequin heads covered with thin black tape that was used for the digitizing process. And I think we had pictures of the musical notes. I really liked the album art presentation. When you open it up, you see the process to make their heads. The process was really tedious in those days, but it was very artistic.'

Kraftwerk shipped their mannequin heads to Allen in New York where she collected them from the customs office. 'Customs said, "You're going to have to come down here",' she recalls. 'They opened up this container; and there were these four heads staring out! I had to somehow explain what the idea was and tried to explain this as an artistic project we were working on.'

It was an elaborate process for Allen to prepare and shoot the heads. 'I had to input all of them into the computer and put them all together to result in 3D computer models of each of them. It was a huge ordeal. When the head models were built as wire-frames we then used models that had been done for another commercial piece that we did at our lab, because, again, building human figures was a really hard problem as well. The human body models were modified so they were more to the body style of Kraftwerk (they were originally modelled to be football players). Then we used those models and put the heads on top of them.'

Rebecca was guided by her love of the style of artist of Tamara Lempicka: 'The idea of stripping things away, to expose the digital quality, the digital aesthetic of the tools, I stayed with this kind of cubistic look, which again is influenced a little bit by Lempicka's work, as was the colouring of the face. For me the red – they used red a lot in their uniforms and other albums – made me think of the Bauhaus, with this black, white, grey, and then red, it's a colour that's pulled in. So, I used red, for the lips, not so much to make them look as if they had lipstick on, but as part of this colour tone. They had the subdued blue, almost purple, kind of faces, and then the strong red for the lips. I intentionally made the eyes to be the most realistic part of the face, to add a sense of life.'

'In the video, I used minimal movements, again I was trying to keep with the minimalism. I looked at their past performance, when they toured and how they performed, they are intentionally very minimal in their movements, very robotic. In a way they are making a statement that, if you have a guitar and drums, you will be flailing all over the place, your arms will be going crazy and you'll

221

be running around the stage, but they had chosen to have these electronic instruments and just stood there. In the video, when I'd show faces, it would just be like a little look of the eye, or a look in a certain direction that would be typical of how they might be glancing into space. It was really thoughtful, each step of the way, very different from the way things are usually done, where you have "Hurry, hurry, quick, quick, get the thing done...." And this was done in a similar way to the way they would "craft" each part of the music. I was looking for that kind of craftsmanship as I was putting something also intangible like this digital technology together, but to get the subtlety that would express the sense of a digital aesthetic.'

In 1986 when, after a considerable delay, the video and album were completed and the launch about to take place, Rebecca Allen was able to see for herself the inner workings of Kraftwerk's relationship with their record label. 'Kraftwerk had an unusual arrangement – I don't know if they still do – with their record company, where they had control over their video, their artwork, their music... So [Kraftwerk] couldn't have people coming in saying, "Hey, we want you to do this, this way. We want an album that looks like this, a video that looks like this ..." which for me was great, because it meant I was working direct with them.'

Kraftwerk had evidently decided that Allen's work would extend to the promotion of the record, too. Never happy with the usual promotional chores of being interviewed and photographed, the group took the whole enterprise to its natural conclusion. 'They didn't want photographs of themselves, they just wanted to use the computer-generated models I had made,' says Allen. 'Unfortunately the record company didn't promote the video, though it became very popular on its own. Perhaps that was the downside of not involving the record company in the process. No one knew that I was the one behind it except people who already knew my work, but the general public wouldn't necessarily know who did it. It was the same with the photographs that were computer-generated. It made the press and the marketing people not want to get so involved.'

For Rebecca Allen, it was a landmark period: 'For me this video was a high point in my work, because it addressed some of the things I was trying to do as an artist. Working with them very much influenced my work, and it was a unique opportunity for me to be able to experiment in that way and to work with musicians who were trying to do similar things to what I was trying to accomplish.'

7.7 'They Stopped, And Stood There…'

Wolfgang Flür's heart was no longer in Kraftwerk. He began spending less and less time at Kling Klang, waiting and hoping for the creative ball to start rolling again. As the only non-composing member of the group, his role as electronic percussionist couldn't even begin until the songs themselves were formed. Each day, each week, the wait went on. When Flür was at Kling Klang, he would find Hütter and Schneider almost always out. They would return in the late afternoon drenched in sweat after another lengthy cycle ride.

The credits for both *Computer World* and *Electric Café* do not mention Wolfgang Flür as an actual instrumentalist. It seemed that Wolfgang was now reduced to the role of a Kling Klang factotum, his undeniable skills in design wasted on beavering away at non-pressing parts of the live Kraftwerk set-up. 'During the time I was with Kraftwerk I was deficient in self-awareness. I was regarded as a good drummer, that was all. Everything that I told them musically, about melody, was met with the same response: *"Ja, ja, Wolfgang, ja, ja. Machen wir vielleicht. Eine ganz gute Idee"* ["Yeah, yeah, Wolfgang, we might do that. It's a really good idea."]. It was a bit arrogant, and if you are always handled like that your self-confidence, self-awareness, self-esteem goes further and further down. It would end up by you saying nothing more about the music, just obeying the instructions to come to a recording session or go on tour. The last few years were like that. They were always in the hills on their bicycles. The studio was empty, just Karl and me, we waited for hours for them to come back. It was endlessly frustrating. Karl will tell you the same. He was the only one who was working. He made his own studio at home where he lived and prepared music for the few rare meetings we had then. And when he showed it to them and said, "Can we not make this, or this?", they behaved as they had done with Konrad Plank, saying, "Yeah, it sounds good. We'll take this but not this", then "Bye-bye" until the next meeting. Karl worked so much then on the important and main records.'

Eventually, Wolfgang simply stopped coming into Kling Klang. There seems to have been no recognition from either Ralf or

Florian of the fact that he was unhappy and upset, nor any attempt to persuade him to come back. 'The love became cold, as between partners. When you change your mood, direction and interests, people split and go in different directions. So that was the reason. I didn't fit into the band any more. I changed, it wasn't Kraftwerk that had changed. They stopped and stood there and didn't develop. Nothing has developed, even up to today, I tell you, this is my opinion. They are just reproducing their old stuff, again, and again, and again.'

The psychological effect all this had on Wolfgang was, by his own admission, long-lasting and damaging. 'Yes. 1986 and 1987 was the time when I didn't go there. I went to the furniture design studio where I worked with two other design colleagues. They had their bicycles. I had my furniture room, with new friends, new colleagues. It was cold between us. I didn't want to go back into the Kling Klang studio any more. It was finished. There was a time in between, for some years, when I had no vision for doing anything. It became very depressing for me. I had bad dreams in the night, "*Alpträume*", nightmares. It was a burden for my friendship with Constanze also. As a man you want to show your partner what you are, what you can do, what you will be in the future. I had no future. I didn't know what to do. I discussed it very often with my girlfriend, and I didn't know what I could offer her. For me that's a little bit ... it's not enough. It was a problem for me, a really big problem for some years, until I was so happy to meet these other two guys, and we made this new project. We even gave it a name. It was called GAF-Atelier – Gerick, Altfeld, Flür [Atelier is the German word, derived from the French, for a workshop or studio]. We were pretty successful as furniture designers and builders. We made a lot of set buildings for photographers here in Düsseldorf. They had big budgets from the advertising companies here, especially in the fashion industry.'

According to Wolfgang, Ralf and Florian were 'no longer interested in their own company. As you would say if they were directors of a producing company, of a consumer product, as music is, generally, as well. Nothing else, it's a product. And you can sell it well, if it's a good product, like the new Mercedes, the new Kraftwerk album. Everyone would run for it, if there was one, like the new Mercedes "S" Class.'

224

'They might not have been interested in Kling Klang being musically productive,' says Karl. 'But as a business, it was running brilliantly; the money from royalties and licensing was coming in in huge amounts, especially for Ralf and Florian.'

Although Wolfgang certainly had issues, as his autobiography makes clear he is ultimately proud to have been part of such an important band; the resentment he felt towards the way his colleagues in Kraftwerk treated him has softened with the passing years. 'I am not angry today about any of these things,' Wolfgang says of his departure from the band. 'I compare everything with the good fortune I had with the whole 14 years until the bad end for me. OK, it ended in depression for me, of course, because there was no more work, and I had no more future in my profession. But in conclusion most of those years were fantastic, and I always think today what good fortune I had to be with them. It gave an entrée for me to find my own artistic style and my own music project, Yamo, as a lyricist, composer, writer, and later book author. They would never have believed that I could have brought something on my own, with melodies, with lyrics. So, I needed 10 years for it. Most of those years were fantastic, and I always think today what good fortune I had in being with them all over the whole world – journeys that I couldn't afford as a normal young man; and this is the main thing for me.'

7.8 The Jumbo Jet That Never Takes Off

Electric Café had taken four years to make, and Hütter was now free to embark on another long-term project, digitalising and overhauling the Kling Klang Studio. In the process, he decided that the band's next album would be a collection of new, improved versions of many of their past glories. So began a painstaking process of transference, reinterpretation and, so Hütter hoped, improvement.

Bartos played a major role in this process, whilst also demoing ideas for new Kraftwerk songs. But Hütter was focused, some might say, fixated, on the remix album. As 1988 turned into 1989, work on the album was halted when Schneider was involved in a skiing accident, breaking both collar bones in a fall on the snow.

Working for four years cleaning up, digitalising and reworking one's own back catalogue was not a project with which Karl Bartos had a great deal of sympathy. 'First of all, the original idea was to make a *Best Of Kraftwerk*, putting all the classics onto one record and to go on tour again. This idea was very much appreciated by all four of us. But then, it was too normal a thing to do. A *Best Of* record somehow indicates the end of a career for an artist. And maybe for that reason, and maybe also for Dadaistic reasons, Ralf came up with the idea of the re-contextualisation of all the music we had done before ourselves. First of all you have to transfer all the multi-track magnetic tapes onto a digital storage media. Ralf bought a Synclavier which cost a fortune, and Fritz Hilpert, the new member of the band, had to get acquainted with the machine and do all the transferrals. Fritz is from Augsburg. He is a good engineer. You'd like to have him in the team. I knew Henning Schmitt from the Robert Schumann Institute and I actually asked him to join Kraftwerk, but he declined and suggested Fritz.'

Having developed into a major songwriting talent from *The Man-Machine* onwards, Bartos was left frustrated by Ralf and Florian's reluctance to record new material. Weeks, months, years would go by with them endlessly re-fashioning, distilling, purifying the past. 'It's like I have this jumbo jet in the garden, but it never takes off,' was how Bartos expressed his frustration. In fact, Bartos had been a key member in terms of songwriting, originating many of the hooks and melodies from the classic Kraftwerk period. By the time of *Electric Café*, he was taking a central role in lyric writing as well. 'My first official (music) copyright was for 'Metropolis' in 1978,' affirms Karl. 'I worked on the bass sequence and chords. Electronic percussion, it goes without saying. That was followed by all the tracks on *Mensch Maschine*, *Computer Welt*, the 'Tour De France' single, *Electric Café* (alias *Techno Pop*). On the *Techno Pop* album I have copyright for parts of both the music and the lyrics. I suppose it's what you would call "co-authoring"; there were usually two or three writers involved in composing each track.' It would not be unreasonable to suspect that, in purely musical terms, Bartos was now very important indeed to the band. He was, first of all, the most musically proficient in terms of technical ability and, secondly, he had become the group's chief melody writer.

Sick and tired of sitting around doing very little, the overriding emotion for Bartos was – like Wolfgang before him – one of massive frustration. 'All those people who wanted to work with us, and we never even did a soundtrack. We could have crossed over, become a big, big selling band,' Karl told Kraftwerk biographer Pascal Bussy. 'But there was never any management, not even on a small level, like two or three people. There was no telephone, no fax, nothing. And in this business, if you need five years to put out a record, then people forget about you.'

In a world in which pop stars are pressured by their record companies into touring to promote their work, encouraged to give access to the media, and even legally bound to produce new music at designated intervals, Kraftwerk had simply become a law unto themselves. 'The telephone is an antiquity – you never know who is calling, there is no image, it is an outmoded product which constantly disrupts work,' Ralf said in a 1991 interview. They had total control over what they did, and when they did it, but the decision-making process was now almost entirely in the hands of Ralf. In this way, as the years went by, Kraftwerk became less and less connected to the music business. They were essentially self-managed, un-managed, perhaps even un-manageable. Their relationship to the wider media became a labyrinthine network of official and unofficial band supporters in the music business, promoters, lawyers, and a select few at their record label, EMI, whom they strongly trusted. With the possible exception of the equally media-phobic Kate Bush, hardly any other artists working in the field of popular music acted with such apparent disdain for the usual obligations and constraints that the music business demanded. Ralf and Florian had long ago realised that their most potent weapon was silence.

In the summer of 1990, Karl challenged Ralf. 'I remember it clearly; we were sitting eating *Pflaumenkuchen* in a café close to Kling Klang and the railway station.' Bartos suggested leaving Florian at home, a bit like what happened with Brian Wilson and the Beach Boys, as Florian disliked touring so much, the schedules, and the mechanics of touring, the whole travelling party. Karl wanted a clear plan for his future in music in the band. 'We talked for an hour or two. I got the impression from this conversation, and also from other conversations we had around this time, that Hütter felt that that wouldn't work. Hütter said that Florian Schneider was a major presence on stage. People wanted to see him, and Kraftwerk would not be complete if he was not there. By this stage, me and Ralf Hütter had written some of Kraftwerk's biggest songs and I wanted to continue. But Hütter acted like a straight businessman and turned me down. It was a good, clear and amicable conversation, and I understood and respected his reasoning. I know now, however, 22 years later, that this would have been the best thing Hütter could have done, to leave Florian Schneider at home and tour without him. We could have made two or three great records, with Schneider still in the band. But Hütter impressed upon me that he was married to Schneider.'

By 'married', Ralf was speaking figuratively, of course. It should be assumed that Ralf and Florian were a unit; the implications in terms of their business partnership would have been profound. They simply had too many obligations, too many contracts which they had signed together.

And so, shortly afterwards, Bartos left the band, just a matter of months before the release of *The Mix*, an album on which he had worked extensively but in whose sleeve notes he remains uncredited. His last appearance on stage with the band would be on February 11, 1990, at the Psycho Club, Genoa, Italy*.

'Karl is very down to earth, with a very, very wicked sense of humour, actually,' says OMD's Andy McCluskey. 'He is a very talented musician, he can play anything. Obviously he went to the conservatoire or wherever it was. He was very young when he joined Kraftwerk, he was basically straight out of the music conservatory. I got the impression from Wolfgang and Karl that they left just because, by 1990, it was patently obvious that they weren't doing anything. They would be going to the studio every day, but nothing was getting released. It was like Ralf had already hit the wall. They were just really frustrated. Nothing was happening.'

There are those who still see Kraftwerk's main work as having been written by Ralf and Florian in a similar relationship to Lennon and McCartney in the Beatles, and this was certainly the case for the band's first six albums. Florian remained a contributor and an excellent editor and producer of ideas in the studio, but it was Karl who emerged as an important melody writer in the band. Karl had, in fact, copyright on every song from 1978 onwards.

As Kraftwerk entered the nineties, and middle age, there was, perhaps, another reason for the group's apparent reluctance to speak. The triumvirate of game-changing albums, *Trans-Europe*

---

* A tremendous, anarchic version of 'Musique Non-Stop' from these final Italian gigs can be found on *YouTube*.

Express, The Man-Machine, and *Computer World,* were now over a decade old. Some critics (and maybe some of their fans too) regarded Kraftwerk as a unique case in popular music. Their records were so ground-breaking, so ahead of their time, and so perfect, that to add to the canon was fraught with danger. So how could Ralf and Florian, now in their forties, set out a genuinely new vision for music in the nineties?

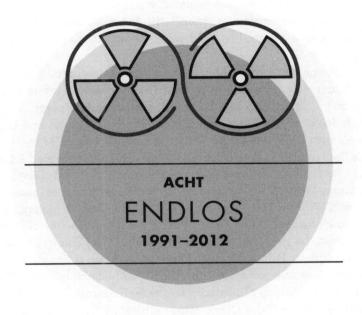

ACHT
ENDLOS
1991–2012

8.1 Mix It Up And Start Again

POP WILL eat itself; not only the name of a band, but a comment about music in the bright young postmodern world. Pop music in the early nineties was less about how good you were at originating than how skilled you were at re-assembling the past and quoting from it. In January 1991, the band Enigma reached number one with 'Sadeness Part 1'. The track was 'written' by Michael Cretu, F. Gregorian and David Fairstein. In fact it was assembled from Latin and French texts and included a quotation from Psalm 24. The Gregorian chants were mostly sampled from the 1976 album *Paschale Mysterium* by the German choir Capella Antiqua München, illegally, until compensation was agreed in 1994. In the UK the CD single included a 'Radio Edit', 'Extended Trance Mix', 'Meditation Mix' and a 'Violent US Remix'. The trend towards mixing and remixing which began in the early eighties was, a decade later, keeping a whole raft of people in business, and in constant demand. Was this giving the customer more choice? Was it playing around with notions of authenticity and originality in a clever, liberated way? Or was it simply exploiting music fans?

That same month the UK Top 40 charts included the Farm's 'Altogether Now' (its descending chord melody heavily influenced by German Baroque composer Johann Pachelbel and his piece *Canon*), Vanilla Ice's 'Ice Ice Baby' (bass line taken from Queen and David Bowie's 1981 UK number one 'Under Pressure'), Snap's 'Mary Had A Little Boy' (melody taken from the nursery rhyme 'Mary Had A Little Lamb' by Sarah Josepha Hale), the extremely dubious delights of 'The Crazy Party Mixes' by Jive Bunny & the Mastermixes (sampling Rossini's *William Tell Orchestra* Part 2), 'The Grease Megamix' by John Travolta and Olivia Newton John (a cheesy medley of cheesy songs from the 1978 film), 'Mercy Mercy Me (The Ecology) – I Want You', by Robert Palmer (a fusing together of two different Marvin Gaye songs as one cover version), EMF's 'Unbelievable' (containing samples from 'Ashley's Roachclip' by the Soul Searchers, and 'Mother Goose' by Andrew Dice Clay), 'Hippy Chick' by Soho (sampling the disturbing riff of 'How Soon Is Now?' by the Smiths), 'Always The Sun (Remix)' by the Stranglers (a remix of their fairly recent 1986 hit), 'Justify My Love' by Madonna (sampling the then two-year-old Public Enemy track 'Security Of The First World'), 'Can I Kick It?' by A Tribe Called Quest (sampling Dr. Buzzard's Original Savannah Band's 1976 song 'Sunshower'), The Dream Warriors' 'My Definition Of A Bombastic Jazz Style (sampling 'Soul Bossa Nova' by Quincy Jones), MC Hammer's 'Pray' (sampling Prince's 'When Doves Cry') and, lastly, 'X, Y and Z' by Pop Will Eat Itself with, fittingly and most radically, a whopping five samples ('For What It's Worth' by Buffalo Springfield, 'Slim Jenkins' Place' by Booker T. & the MG's , 'The Pusher' by Steppenwolf, 'I'm Gonna Love You Just A Little More Baby' by Barry White and, finally, the 1978 UK number one 'Uptown Top Ranking' by Althea & Donna).

This list of songs made up of other songs was also supplemented by the reappearance of ancient hits by Patsy Cline ('Crazy') and the Righteous Brothers ('You've Lost That Loving

Feeling'), as well as covers of Earth Wind And Fire's 'Fantasy' by Black Box, 'It Takes Two' by Rod Stewart and Tina Turner, 'King Of The Road' by the Proclaimers, a segue of hits from Status Quo called 'Anniversary Waltz Part 2' and, finally, a cover of the 1975 10cc number one 'I'm Not In Love' by Will To Power. And all this is without even counting the Top 20 placing for Yazoo's 1983 song 'Situation', originally a US-only release but now a UK hit eight years after its creation, and '(I've Had) The Time of My Life' by Bill Medley and Jennifer Warnes, a hit again, four years after its original appearance in the charts due to the fact the film *Dirty Dancing*, in which it featured, had been given exposure on terrestrial TV.

The fact that Kraftwerk, eight months later, would bring out an album called *The Mix*, was, on first inspection, an unimaginative thing to do. Ten years after *Computer World*'s accurate crystal-ball gazing, came a 'new' product which seemed to be desperately chasing current trends.

This knee-jerk reaction to the new *Kling Klang Produkt* would not, however, be totally accurate. The resultant album, on first listen, was obviously confusingly titled, since the songs, technically speaking, were new versions of the originals, not mixes, or really even remixes. The 11 tracks on the album were essentially re-recordings, the originals transferred onto Kling Klang's now fully digitalised mainframe, and then laboriously worked on, improved, with new sections, new vocals, new ideas. Unintentionally, though essentially a tribute album to themselves, it had taken four years to make, when, it could be argued, a greatest hits package could have taken four months to prepare. It is to Ralf and Florian's credit that they regarded a compilation of previously released tracks to be short-changing the fans, and one suspects there would be very little by way of unused material to flesh out any compilation package. No pre-1974 material was included on the album.

Some of the 're-meddled' songs sounded very similar to the originals in many respects, but all were given a new production sheen. A new version of 'The Robots' was released as a single and reached number 20 in the UK charts: Kraftwerk's calling card, 'Autobahn', now swung gently with a trip-hoppy rhythm, whilst 'Computer Love' was extended with a blistering brand new opening section. With beats per minute (bpm) speeded up, and bright if thin new digital sounds, *The Mix* sounded of its time. The biggest surprise was the new version of 'Radio-Activity', now re-titled 'Radioactivity'. It came with a new vocal introduction warning of the potential horrors of a radioactive leak and nuclear war with the cyborg recitation: 'Sellafield', 'Harrisburg', 'Chernobyl', with each of the last words' final letter stressed and repeated in a chilling echo, before the final landmark of horror in the quartet, 'HIROSHIMA', intoned over an increasingly urgent beat. What made the words so powerful was that the deliberate attack on Hiroshima was put alongside the appalling accidents at three 'safe' nuclear reactors. Live, the band projected the 'Radioactive' trefoil symbol across a bank of video screens. It made the hairs on the back of your neck stand up.

The new 'Radioactivity' made for powerful listening, and, to this date, remains a highpoint in their live set, its sentiment very much an expression of the antinuclear stance evident in Germany to this day. The badge *'Atomkraft? Nein Danke'* is worn with pride by Greens. In fact, so strong has the anti-nuclear lobby become that Germany, the most important economy in the Eurozone, is committed to the decommissioning of all nuclear power stations by 2022, a pledge made by the CDU Chancellor Angela Merkel after the Fukushima disaster in 2011.[*]

When *The Mix* was released, Germany was the greenest country in Western Europe. Emerging from the pro-ecology movement of earlier decades, the German Green Party (*die Grünen*) was founded in January 1980 in Karlsruhe, West Germany. Industrial and agricultural pollution were among the main concerns of the activists; and West Germany's espousal of nuclear power was a main issue, too. It is this issue which has been seized upon by many Kraftwerk fans (who can now be seen at any of their gigs, dressed in white protective suits, all-enveloping helmets and heavy white boots). The party's breakthrough came in the 1983 federal election when they exceeded the magic 5% barrier into the Bundestag, winning thereby 27 seats, reportedly through hostile reaction to the deployment of NATO and US Pershing and cruise missiles on

---

[*] Along with lobbying from the Greens and the Left, economics also played a role. This was the realisation that nuclear had high levels of (mainly concealed) financing subsidy and uncertain decommissioning liabilities stretching centuries ahead, not only in Germany but in other developed economies, too.

234

FRG soil. The Chernobyl disaster of 1986 added momentum to the movement, largely because acid rain carried by a south-easterly wind – fall-out from Ukraine – fell on German forests. Under the label 'Green' a wide range of campaigning issues are embraced. Gay, lesbian and trans-gender-friendly policies, for example, are promoted. The German Greens have been front-runners for green movements worldwide, being the first to join coalition governments at national level in a major developed industrial country.

Kraftwerk's commitment to the antinuclear cause was reinforced in 1992 when they took part, along with U2, Public Enemy and Big Audio Dynmanite II, in the 'Stop Sellafield' concert organised by Greenpeace that summer. Sellafield, a nuclear reprocessing plant in Cumbria, UK, was built on the site of Windscale, the notoriously unsafe power plant. One section of Sellafield, Building B30, in an *Observer* report of 2009, was called 'the most hazardous industrial building in Western Europe' by George Beveridge, Sellafield's deputy managing director. The building next door, B38, was called 'the second most hazardous industrial building in Europe' by the same man. The same report quoted Greenpeace as describing the disused plutonium reactors as a 'slow-motion Chernobyl', and put a price tag of £50 billion over the next century to clean the place up.* Live versions of 'Radioactivity' would contain a new opening section, a macabre warning: 'Sellafield 2 will release the same amount of radioactivity/ Into the environment as Chernobyl every four, five years.'

Kraftwerk took to the road and performed a major world tour for the first time since the heady days of *Computer World* back in 1981. It must have been galling for Wolfgang and Karl when the unpleasant irony of a re-activated live Kraftwerk hit home. Wolfgang had been replaced on the few 1990 Italian live dates by Fritz Hilpert, who had worked at Kling Klang on *The Mix*. The recently departed Bartos would be replaced by the only non-German ever to perform with Kraftwerk, Fernando Abrantes from Portugal. His tenure would not last long. Hired for the entire European tour, Abrantes' services were dispensed with after the UK leg. Rumour has it that his animated stage performances (that is, he can actually be seen dancing to the music as he played it) were regarded as some sort of

---

* http://www.guardian.co.uk/environment/2009/apr/19/sellafield-nuclear-plant-cumbria-hazards.

breach of the unofficial Kraftwerk code of non-mobility. However, another reason, discussed on fan forums, was apparently Abrantes' 'liberal' interpretation of the set's closing piece, 'Musique Non-Stop' at a concert at the Sheffield City Hall. Footage exists on *YouTube*, and whilst it cannot be ascertained with complete certainty just who is playing what, it does sound as if Abrantes had fiddled with the pre-recorded vocal parts in the manner of a live DJ mix. It sounded fabulous, so, if this was the reason for his sacking then it is mystifying. Abrantes would be replaced by studio engineer Henning Schmitz, and this line-up of Hütter/Schneider/Hilpert/Schmitz would endure for the next 17 years.

In 1991 British fans had the opportunity to see the band in concert for first time in a decade, and although half of the classic line-up had been sloughed off, it was still credible and valid. 'I saw them at Brixton Academy. It was packed, sold out,' says John Foxx. 'Very enthusiastic, very hip audience – all generations represented. Excellent sound. Good projections. Great to see them accepted at last. I enjoyed the jolly percussion section at the end. But I came away with a question mark about it being better to see them live or listen to the records through a good sound system. I still have an early music paper review that stated that these "German mathematicians" were "nothing to do with rock music". As I put the cutting away in the drawer, I thought "Let's leave it a few years and see, shall we?" Very satisfying.'

Andy McCluskey also saw them on tour: 'It was nice to see that they had expanded the production a bit more and got more films and things. Wolfgang and Karl had gone by then, but at least it was still Ralf and Florian. It was interesting to hear the band re-interpreting their songs, and it was interesting to hear the band changing their mind about "Radio-Activity" and making it more negative with all the references to Chernobyl and Harrisburg.'

This was the first time the author saw the band live. At the Liverpool Royal Court Theatre, pop luminaries such as Pete Wylie and Ian McCulloch were spotted, along with members of China Crisis and other local bands, thus confirming that Kraftwerk were very evidently a 'musician's band'. The set was almost the same as it had been in 1981, the highlight, for many, the appearance of the upgraded robots who performed their 'mechanical ballet' with the real-life Kraftwerk off stage. The robots inspired the biggest cheer

236

of the night, perhaps suggesting that the physical appearance of the real-life Kraftwerk was not as interesting as the appearance of their avatars?

With *The Mix*, and the subsequent tour, Kraftwerk now sounded completely of their times, which is not a criticism given how groups such as the Rolling Stones have done much the same thing throughout an entire career. There was nothing extraordinary, or puzzling, just a much-admired band basically playing a greatest hits package with élan. In a revealing interview at London's Rage club with long-time Kraftwerk-watcher Simon Witter, Ralf spoke of the current music scene as he watched the TV monitors and listened to the deafening electronic music in the club: 'You know... if people had been making a film about hell 20 years ago, they would have conjured up something like this... We were doing things like this early on... and one reviewer wrote that Kraftwerk is the death of music.'

In the same interview, he explains: 'Yes. We can always play with the computers, get into the programmes and change them, depending on the vibes of the situation. Nowadays the musical equipment is coming closer to what we always had in mind when we started out. There were always technical limitations before. Also we've replaced our percussionists Karl Bartos and Wolfgang Flür with an electronics engineer who always works with us in the studio and an additional musician. So now there is more sound, more electronics, programming and sound engineering going on.'

Ralf was keen to tell Witter that life and work went on and revealed some basic facts about their real selves. Both he and Florian were vegetarians. They chose their own stage clothes and have a regular barber. Ralf reveals he still goes dancing in clubs but has almost stopped buying new music, preferring to hear music 'environmentally', in the streets and in clubs. 'We make music all the time, then we sleep. It's a full time job.'

8.2 The Gathering Of The Tribes

So much music in the early nineties carried within it something of Kraftwerk's musical DNA. But although Kraftwerk were a huge inspiration, the music made by their original inspiration varied dramatically in worth. Important acts such as Orbital, Underworld, the Orb, the Prodigy and the Chemical Brothers were making music which was undeniably in the tradition set in train by Kraftwerk. But elsewhere, in mainstream pop, the subtleties of the Kraftwerk sound were being debased. The period 1990–95 saw the rise of a formulaic brand of techno – monosyllabic, populist, extremely successful, and almost completely without artistic merit. The 1992 clarion call of 'No no, no no, no no, no, no, no no, no no, there's no limit' set against a throbbing, basic, Euro beat, might have been enticing for the pre-teens or the musically brain dead, but it was an example of what could happen to electronica in the wrong hands. Kraftwerk were now being touted as the 'Godfathers of Techno'. But there were limits.

Valid practitioners of the dark arts of electronica had developed a new approach. The nineties saw the rise and rise of the festival. In the eighties, standing in a slurry of mud and being rained on all day was almost completely the preserve of the metal or hard rock fan with the continuing success of festivals at Donington Park, where the Monsters Of Rock events featured AC/DC, Iron Maiden and Ozzy, and probably the most entertaining of the lot, spoof metal band Bad News. The nineties, however, saw an almost exponential increase in the number and popularity of rock festivals. The early eighties had been a time when bands either didn't play live or wouldn't play live, and those that did played halls and arenas. Only the very biggest acts such as the Stones, U2, the Who, Springsteen, Bowie, Madonna, Michael Jackson or Genesis*, played open air gigs. However, with the advent of acid house, rave culture and the spontaneous, almost always illegal, warehouse party, dance music and dance culture espoused (with the help of copious numbers of illegal highs and uppers) a new sense of hedonistic freedom more akin to the sixties counterculture than the studied alienation of the original Brit-synth acts. It wasn't long before the 'dance tent' was an ever-present feature of the biggest open-air festivals.

By the early-to-mid nineties, a dance act such as Underworld had developed a Dionysian aesthetic; the electronic beats were euphoric. This was music which made you want to shout 'lager, lager,

---

* In 1987, Genesis filled Wembley Stadium on four nights, the same summer Madonna played three and Bowie, two, at the same venue.

lager', it was music that 'let light in'. Their music was about bliss, elation, a seething surge of serotonin and endorphins. Standing in an open field in the 15°C heat of an English summer in torrential rain no longer seemed to be so bad after all. When the doyen of good taste John Peel began reporting for the BBC from Glastonbury dressed in regulation wellies and fisherman's hat it was confirmation that festivals were now not only part of the fabric of popular culture again, but actually permissible to enjoy.

The next public appearance by Kraftwerk would come on May 24, 1997, at Tribal Gathering, a dance music festival that year staged at Luton Hoo in Bedfordshire. It seemed illogical that Kraftwerk, a project co-ordinated by two well-heeled middle-aged Germans, could headline such a festival, but the result was one of the best gigs ever played on British soil. Ralf and Florian had anonymously attended the previous year's event and, sufficiently convinced, agreed there and then to headline the next year. To an opening salvo of 'Numbers', 'Computer World' and 'Home Computer', Kraftwerk emerged from a five-year live hiatus wearing dazzling fluorescent suits. 'It was a phenomenal thing. It was verging on the unbelievable, actually,' says *Mojo*'s Ian Harrison. 'They closed the Detroit tent, so the Detroit people could go and see them.'

'It was a real calling of the faithful,' says Joe Black. 'I was crying, absolutely bowled over by the whole experience.' One fan posted on YouTube, 'I have been clubbing for 20 years and I swear I have never been in a tent quite so busy. A brick wall of people. We got lifted off our feet just by the motion of the crowd.'

'I think that the back catalogue was meant to come out then,' continues Ian Harrison. 'Then cassette promos were sent out, some of them have come out in foreign language with extra tracks on them. There was also a black box, which was a box of 12″ singles. There are four heavy 12″s, which were in a box that came out theoretically to promote the back catalogue. I think that was what it was for. It is a lovely item, which I still have, treasure. It has a couple of scuffs on it now, which is a shame. It came with a T-shirt as well, which I wore, probably shouldn't have done, but I still have it. It would be going for a lot of money.'

The gig was recorded by BBC Radio, but was aired, disappointingly, in edited form. The penultimate song performed on the night was, in fact, the first new song to have emerged from Kling Klang since 1986. Clocking in at five minutes 56 seconds, it was a fast-tempoed full-on techno instrumental track with a thudding beat and descending synth riff.

It is now that we run into problems because the song was never given an official title. It is known by bootleggers as 'Luton', or 'Tribal' which may or may not be an accurate title. However, what is certain is that the newly reactivated Kraftwerk were including new material in their one-off concert appearances. Later in 1997, in a gig in Karlsruhe, they played a second new song, possibly entitled 'Lichthof', again, an instrumental, but this time with the funkiest of bass lines and some astonishing electronic scat-like wordless vocals. A third new song, going by the name of 'Tango' was also performed in Karlsruhe. The new material seemed more energised than a good proportion of *Electric Café*, and yet none of these songs have ever been released.

Journalist Manfred Gillig-Degrave believes Kraftwerk did provide their publishers with music in the nineties, but that it didn't see the light of day: 'There's an album that has never been released. They played the tapes to EMI in Cologne, and were not happy about it because the reactions were not as enthusiastic as they had expected. That would have been sometime in the late nineties. And then they [Kraftwerk] took the tapes with them and said "OK, we'll work on it." They went to EMI London, to the headquarters, where they negotiated new contracts. I think they did this so Cologne couldn't tell them what to do any more. But they didn't come out with the album for EMI London. They were waiting for a new album and the rumours were going round: "Well they're almost finished, and we're waiting for their presentation in the company, and we're glad they will come up with a new album". But they never came up with it.' Gillig-Degrave concedes, though, that the tapes they presented to EMI may have been early versions of tracks they kept working on and may have released in some form or other later on.

8.3 Wolfgang Speaks, Then Is Silenced

In August 1999, Wolfgang's autobiography, *Kraftwerk – Ich War Ein Roboter* (English title *I Was A Robot*) was published by Hannibal Verlag. It had been over a decade since he had been a member of

Kraftwerk, and he felt the time was right to tell his story. In the meantime, Wolfgang had been tempted back to making music after a period when he was involved in furniture design. What brought him back to music was watching news reports from the Bosnian war. 'It was 1993. Suddenly I saw myself writing lyrics and melodies in my head for the orphans, the children of a *'Kinderheim'*, a children's home, in Sarajevo, shot at every day by snipers and Serbian troops. I couldn't stand it, couldn't believe what we saw on TV every evening. This was my chance to write about this, to work with music programmes, meeting young musicians in Düsseldorf and Cologne and recording some demos.'

Wolfgang's new musical project was Yamo. The resulting CD, *Time Pie*, a collaboration with Andi Toma of Düsseldorf's Mouse On Mars, was released in 1997. He had been tempted back into the music business but he couldn't be tempted back into Kraftwerk. 'He [Ralf] tried to "buy me back", for a big pile of money,' says Wolfgang of his meeting with Hütter in 1997. 'I told him all the things that I was not able to tell him in the years of my membership of the band. He offered me a big sum every year, just for being a member of Kraftwerk again.' The meeting took place 10 years after Wolfgang had left the band in Kaiserswerth, a northern area of Düsseldorf, under a chestnut tree where the two men ate *Pflaumenkuchen* (plum tart) together. Wolfgang felt able to speak frankly, unburdening himself of much of the resentment that had built up over the years. Phrases that Wolfgang can remember using are: *'Du hast alles kaputt gemacht'* ['You broke everything'] and 'You broke everything with your bicycle. You couldn't care less what happens to Karl and me.'

Despite the money that Ralf offered Wolfgang to rejoin the group, Wolfgang was not swayed. He told Ralf: '"You come today, after all that has happened, and use money to get what you want. Go and buy some dolls, go and buy some robots, but not me. Even if you were to tell me "A million!" today... the times have changed; so much has changed: you can't believe how much I have changed. But I think you haven't changed, and Kraftwerk as a whole hasn't changed.' For Wolfgang this encounter with Ralf was clearly a cathartic experience. What Wolfgang knew, and Ralf didn't, was that he had secured a recording contract of his own with EMI. This was, for Wolfgang, a game-changer in that he now had the opportunity to pursue a career outside the band which meant a great deal to him. He had a point to prove. He adds: 'They would never have believed that I could have made something on my own, with melodies, with lyrics.'

By now, Wolfgang's book was not the only one on Kraftwerk. Tim Barr's highly readable *Kraftwerk: From Düsseldorf To The Future (With Love)* was published by Ebury Press in 1998. Before that, in 1993, S.A.F. published *Kraftwerk: Man, Machine And Music* by the French journalist Pascal Bussy. Bussy had interviewed Ralf and Florian and had informed them he would be writing a book about Kraftwerk. He sent the manuscript to Kling Klang pre-publication in the hope that someone there might weed out any factual inaccuracies (an inevitable risk of writing about a band so cloaked in secrecy), but the package was returned unopened. After publication, late at night, Bussy received a phone call from a certain Mr Schneider. His first words were: 'Le livre, c'est la merde' ['Your book is shit']. We don't know Ralf's and Florian's true feelings. Perhaps they granted access to Bussy on the basis that he was an interested journalist and subsequently felt differently about the encounter when it became clear Bussy was intent on writing a book on the band without necessarily taking account of the inputs and views they considered necessary. Or maybe they genuinely didn't like the book? What seems certain is that Kraftwerk, like many major recording artists, adopt a degree of antipathy towards biographies they have not authorised, or at least not had an opportunity to censor. The reasons are fairly obvious.

Unauthorised biographies can ruffle a rock star's feathers in many ways, and not just because they are unlikely to have been written in the obsequiously flattering tone that is the hallmark of the 'authorised' book. The unauthorised book might also take the wind out of the sails of a scheduled autobiography for which any rival book is deemed a market nuisance, or disclose personal or business dealings on the part of the subject that might not necessarily show them in the best of lights. The objective critic can praise most of the music to high heaven, but in most cases even the mildest scintilla of criticism can immediately consign the writer to the status of persona non grata for refusing to be a yes-man or yes-woman. Anyone who feels a connection to any piece of art will naturally want to know the motivations behind the painting, the piece of music, the play or the film; it is inevitable that some details of the artist's life will shed light on this.

242

Both Bussy and Barr were obviously huge Kraftwerk fans. Their books would have recruited new fans to the Kraftwerk cause. Their tributes were, in effect, no threat to Kraftwerk. However, the publication of the memoirs of an ex-member was a great deal more threatening, and potentially embarrassing.

Wolfgang's book was readable and honest; perhaps too much so in that it revealed matters of an intimate nature not usually found in rock star memoirs. Much was made in the press of Wolfgang's description of himself as a normal guy with a healthy sexual appetite, as if this was in any way shocking. It would have been more shocking, and, indeed, much more remarkable, if Wolfgang had revealed that – in keeping with their mechanised image – the four members of Kraftwerk were completely celibate and really did find robots more of a turn-on than women. There was also the sense that, in the minds of many, Kraftwerk were mythic creatures; and to find out they were mere mortals, with human weaknesses, was either irrelevant or undignified.

Throughout the book, Wolfgang emerges as a kind, compassionate and sensitive man, at times surprised and dismayed by what he regards as coldness on the part of Ralf and Florian. Perhaps the memory of being a member of Kraftwerk, and the manner of his departure, was still too raw, too fresh in his mind, and the writing of the book was a form of catharsis.

The book had been on sale in Germany for two weeks and was selling well, 6,000 copies in the first two weeks after publication, when Hannibal received an unpleasant, if surely not wholly unanticipated, surprise: a letter from Ralf and Florian's solicitor, containing an '*einstweilige Verfügung*' [interim injunction].

The idea for the book had come from the American-based British music writer Dave Thompson, the author of many rock biographies since the mid-eighties. The task of editing the book had fallen to Manfred Gillig-Degrave, editor-in-chief of the Munich-based music industry magazine *MusikWoche*. 'I saw Wolfgang's book proposal and I told the publisher, "You've got to do it immediately. This is really interesting." Wolfgang's a nice guy, but he's not really an intellectual, so he sent some pieces, and I said "OK, I'll work on it", and put it into some form, but without destroying his special charm. He has his own style. He's not a professional writer, and he needed some tuning, but I thought it was interesting; and it was good. We worked together for six months or so. He was very happy with the finished manuscript.'

When it came to putting the photo section together, Manfred asked Wolfgang about the pictures. 'There were pictures included that were taken in Ralf's mother's garden, for instance,' says Manfred, 'when they smoked their spliffs, and things like that. There were also photos of band members naked under a shower. And he said, "Yes, I own them, I took them" and things like that, because I made the publisher aware that there's potential of having problems with publishing it. I also think we cut some things out of the text. I said "You'd better leave this out." There were some explicit things in it. I just said that "You had better leave it out because it makes your book better, you know."'

'The writs were delivered about three or four weeks after the book was published,' continues Manfred. 'It took them maybe two weeks to read it and check it, the lawyers. Then they sent about 30/40 pages. I didn't see it at that time because I was just a freelance editor, but I called the publisher up, Robert Azderball, and he said, "I stopped this book! I'm glad. All the 6,000 copies have been sold; but I'll give the rights back to Wolfgang Flür. He can have them back." So he really got scared, and this is… I wouldn't have done it like this because you could have changed some things, and the first print run was sold out anyway. So I would have done a second print run and would have granted what they wanted. But he was really afraid. I can understand him because he comes from a Jewish family, and all his family was murdered, and he really survived by hiding in a cave so he… and now he had a very big German law firm coming down on him with a very cold and uncompromising writ. He doesn't need troubles. The writ it was like a cease and desist demand… "Hannibal has to stop selling this book immediately, and if Hannibal sells another copy, it's an infringement of Ralf and Florian's rights and Hannibal will have to pay 500,000 marks penalty per copy!" and things like that. So Robert Azderball accepted their demands. If there had been a second print run, maybe altered things they wanted, he could have easily sold 40,000/50,000 copies in Germany. Then I told Wolfgang that he was free to have an English version because this writ was against the German edition only. And later on I also talked to his lawyer, Rüdiger Plegge. He was really fighting for Wolfgang when he had lawsuits brought on him by is former bandmates. The legal skirmishes dragged on for two or three years.' As well as the photographs, a key bone of contention was Wolfgang's claim that he had invented an electronic drum kit which became a major component of Kraftwerk's sound. 'But they [Ralf and Florian] seem to have a patent on it,' continues Manfred, 'so they said that's wrong, that he wrongfully claims [to having been] the inventor of this drum kit. That was something they [Ralf and Florian] wanted to have absolutely not in this book, because at least in America, Wolfgang Flür, if he had... [a] good lawyer... he could have claimed royalties from the patent.'

There were three hearings, two in Düsseldorf, one in Hamburg, all of which were attended by Wolfgang, Karl, Florian and Ralf. Wolfgang needed to collect details to refute a number of claims made by Ralf and Florian, including a denial that Wolfgang had played percussion on the *Autobahn* album, that he had not in fact designed and built the electronic drum kit used on stage, and also that he had not spoken to Ralf since leaving the band. Wolfgang disputed this latter claim by citing the 1997 meeting with Ralf when the attempt was made to bring him back into the group.

Since the litigation, Wolfgang has been in demand to give readings from the book. An English language edition, *Kraftwerk: I Was a Robot*, was published in the UK by Sanctuary Publishing in January 2001. This text had much of the offending material removed, but also now included several chapters about the lawsuit taken out against the publishers of the original German-language edition.

8.4 Adrenalin Endorphin

Waiting for a new Kraftwerk Produkt has always been a thankless task. 'I was speaking to a guy at EMI years ago,' says music consultant Joe Black, 'and I said, "What about Kraftwerk?" He said "No, no news." "What about Kate Bush?"* "Oh, yeah', he joked. 'They are producing her new album!"'

The first piece of new music from Kraftwerk came in late 1999, 13 years after *Electric Café*. It was, as journalists were quick to point out, a jingle. *Stern* magazine, interviewing Hütter in December 1999, asked directly: 'The Expo-Jingle, which was the basis for the 'Expo

---

* Kate Bush, also on EMI, took a full 12 years to produce *Aerial* (2005) after her previous record, *The Red Shoes* (1993).

2000' single, lasts 4 seconds. You got paid DM 400,000 for it. How long did it take to produce it?' 'You can't measure it in time. We don't work with a stop watch. But it was definitely longer than five seconds,' came back the reply.* †

That the band were sensitive to any criticism of the project was clear. The jingle was in fact part of an extended piece of music released as a CD single, and a chart hit in the UK and Germany. 'I wrote a short review of the "Expo 2000" single, saying how it took them all this time to come up with such a short piece, something like that – slightly ironic of course,' recalls magazine editor and publisher Manfred Gillig-Degrave. 'A few days later the review was in the magazine. A few days after that, I got a phone call from EMI in Cologne, from a friend I have there, Harald Engel. He is their press officer at EMI Cologne; and he's been working with Ralf and Florian for about 20 years. "We were not very amused about this thing you wrote about "Expo 2000."'

'Expo 2000' would later be rewritten and re-titled 'Planet Of Visions', and has now become a staple of Kraftwerk's live act: 'Detroit, Germany/We're so electric', sings Ralf. In interviews Ralf stresses that, for him, the feedback between influenced and influencer is a loop rather than unidirectional.

Since Karl Bartos' departure, therefore, Kraftwerk had released just one new piece of music. Karl, however, was creating a new musical identity. Having spent most of his adult life in Kraftwerk, his sudden arrival into the big wide world as a solo artist at the age of 38 required a period of readjustment. Freed from the self-imposed restraints of non-collaboration, Bartos embarked on a new musical career as a solo artist, university professor and as

---

* [Stern: Der EXPO-Jingle, aus dem später die Single "EXPO 2000" wurde, dauert vier Sekunden. Als Lohn dafür haben Sie 400.000 Mark bekommen. Wie lange haben Sie denn für die Herstellung gebraucht?
Hütter: Das ist in Zeit nicht zu messen. Wir arbeiten nicht mit der Stoppuhr. Es hat sicherlich länger gedauert als fünf Sekunden.]
† Kraftwerk were certainly not alone in providing 'jingles.' Brian Eno was commissioned to write the six-second start-up music-sound of the Windows 95 operating system. He was reportedly paid $35,000, and so came cheap. http://www.loosewireblog.com/2006/11/fripp_eno_and_t. html He wrote it on a Mac: 'I've never used a PC in my life; I don't like them.'

a collaborator. He was not short of willing takers. John Foxx, for example, tested the waters concerning a Foxx/Bartos team-up: 'I met up with Karl Bartos a few years ago; great musician, brilliant sound. We discussed doing something, but never managed to synchronise. He'd just left the band.'

There would be others too. 'I got to know Karl Bartos in the early nineties,' recalls Andy McCluskey, 'because I wanted clearance for doing "Neon Lights" [for OMD's 1991 *Sugar Tax* album], and I got no reply from Ralf and Florian, but I got a reply from Karl, so I went to Düsseldorf, and he came to Liverpool, and we did some work together. So when I was in Düsseldorf, I was very kindly invited to dinner at Wolfgang's apartment and met Karl there and Emil Schult, and that was wonderful, and I can remember standing in the hallway and seeing that Wolfgang had a gold record from France for *Radio-Activity*. I just happened to comment that, ah, "Radio-Activity", that was just the greatest song ever for us. Basically, "Electricity" [OMD's first single] was us just ripping off "Radio-Activity"; and they all said together "Yes, we knew!"'

Andy and Karl would go on to write songs for Karl's new project, Elektric Music: his first album, *Esperanto*, would be released in 1993. In 1996, Karl joined forces with Electronic, the group that featured former Smiths guitarist Johnny Marr and New Order's Bernard Sumner, co-writing six songs and contributing keyboards. For Bartos, the experience was both positive and liberating, with the result that his next release, the second and (almost) eponymous LP by Electric Music in 1998, was an exploration of sixties guitar pop – all made, impeccably, on computers, of course.

When Kraftwerk's new record was announced in the summer of 2003, there was very little warning. Entitled *Tour De France Soundtracks*, promo copies of the CD were distributed to the media very close to the release date of the actual record. The album was intended to commemorate the 100th anniversary of the Tour that July, but not even that deadline was met, and the album was given a worldwide release on August 4 over a week after the 2003 event had ended.

Although many media commentators assumed the album was commissioned by the Tour itself, in reality its origins went back to 1982 and 1983 when Ralf and Florian had been intending the follow-up to *Computer World* to be a thematic cycling album.

The idea was eventually dropped, and the new work (sans the song, 'Tour De France') would eventually be released as *Electric Café*. Ralf Hütter: 'In 1983 we were working on a concept for a feature film on Tour de France, so I wrote some lyrics and conceptual ideas for our album *Tour De France*. But then we just put out the single with the title song, so the album and script was put aside and we continued working other projects. So now when this world tour started, we came back to the idea to finish the album and work out all the concepts we had, like "Aerodynamik", and all these different compositions, for the 100th anniversary of the Tour de France.'

Some long-standing Kraftwerk-watchers were underwhelmed, and it is true that in places the synth sounds seemed mosquitoid compared to the burr of 'Autobahn' or the drama of 'Trans-Europe Express'. 'To me it just sounded like somebody who just got some sequencers and let it run,' says Andy McCluskey. 'There was nothing in it to me that really had any personality or focus,' continues Peter Saville. 'I would like *Tour De France Soundtracks* to have been more holistically organised. I imagined it to be the cycling version of *Trans-Europe Express*. It isn't: it is like a selection of snap shots.'

Others were more enthusiastic. 'If you still regard Kraftwerk as the deities that gave the world some of the most delightful and seminal electronica ever (and I do) you will take this record to your hearts,' wrote Chris Jones for the BBC, whilst there was also a four-star review in *Mojo*. Joe Black recalls what journalist Andy Gill had said when the album came out: '"It's really disappointing, they are covering old ground. All the new guard have caught up with them, and Kraftwerk are beginning to look a wee bit left behind". But, he said, "At the end of the day, even a mediocre Kraftwerk album is a work of sublime genius."'

Tour De France Soundtracks certainly had its standout moments. 'La Forme', late in the set, had one of those endearingly romantic melodies which harked back to the days of 'Neon Lights', this time with a suggestion of orientalism that broke new ground for Kraftwerk. There was humour, too. On 'Vitamin', Ralf, it seems, simply reads out the list of ingredients from a box of Centrum Multivitamin tablets: 'Kalium Kalzium/Eisen Magnesium/Mineral Biotin/Zink Selen L-Carnitin/Adrenalin Endorphin/Elektrolyt Co-Enzym/Carbo-Hydrat Protein/A-B-C-D Vitamin', tweaking the order in order to find a rhythm in the words. Ex-member Wolfgang remarked charitably that he liked a lot of the songs on the album, 'especially "Vitamin." I like that very much.' 'Sometimes we take supplements,' Ralf told Simon Witter. 'We have training programmes from cycling scientists, from East Germany of course. Through the sweating you lose a lot of water and vitamins, and we have cycling food products in our pockets, mineral drinks. Then there's diet. I'm a vegetarian and try to consume a lot of fresh food in order to do the long distances.'

On 'Titanium', Kraftwerk move from a song about nutrition to a homage to the extra strong, corrosion-resistant metal. Broadcaster and writer Andrew Collins asked Ralf if the song was actually about titanium. 'Yes that's very personal because our bikes are made out of titanium and we are using carbon parts, wheels, and aluminium elements on the bike, so this is very close material for us.'

Another highlight was 'Elektro Kardiogramm', written by Ralf and Fritz Hilpert, a sonic exploration of the unity between cyclist and bike, man and machine. 'The beat you hear in 'Elektro Kardiogramm' is my heartbeat during cycling ... You hear cycling noises, breathing, the chain which slides almost unhearable over the gear. You know, when cycling goes well, you hear almost nothing, only the environment, but on television you always get these disturbing comments. You know what you should do? Watch a ride through the mountains, switch off the sound and play our CD: you will be amazed.'

'On the *Tour De France Soundtracks* album we took medical tests I did over a couple of years, heartbeat recordings, pulse frequencies, lung volume tests, and used those tests on the album,' Ralf added. 'It's percussive and dynamic. We never feel there's nowhere left for us to go.'

Much of the first third of *Tour De France Soundtracks* glides along with echoes of house music, ambient and, fittingly, nineties trance music. 'The Tour is like life: a form of trance. And trance is based on repetition. Everybody is looking for trance in his life: in sex, pleasure, music, everywhere. Machines are perfect to create trance.' Here the timbres are soft, airy and smooth. 'Basically, it [cycling] sounds like nothing-silence, silence because when you're really cycling well, and your bicycle is functioning well, you don't hear the chain, you don't hear the wheels, you don't hear yourself, because you're in good shape and it's running smoothly,' Ralf told journalist Jim DeRogatis. 'That's one of the reasons we like it so much, to get away from the studio, always the musical sounds. The complete silence leaves space for concentration and imagination. When we worked on this album, we tried to incorporate the idea of very smooth, rolling, gliding.' Listening to the album, 'You can almost hear the sound of the wind in your face,' said DeRogatis. 'In German, it's called *fleischentonal* – space and soundscapes-landscapes, very open, wide sounds. So we tried to work in this spirit.'

The rest of the album is notable for the treatment of Ralf's voice. Only on the last track, an almost note-for-note reconstruction of the original 'Tour de France' single, do we hear Ralf's voice untreated. Florian, 'is very good at getting engineers from computer companies to work after hours and long nights to develop speech synthesis and things like that,' said Ralf. 'So we are using a lot of synthetic voices and all kinds of intonations.' In fact, Kraftwerk were the first artists to use the TC Helicon VoiceModeler for PowerCore, having received an exclusive pre-release copy. Promising 'Instant Vocal Transformation', the VoiceModeler claims it 'can be subtle or extreme: transform "male" into "female" voices, enhance dull-sounding voices by adding breath or a "throaty" sound or go beyond by creating unheard-of effect voices.'

'It is a great tool to transform voices completely,' said Fritz Hilpert in a rare interview. 'We used VoiceModeler to create these whispery voices in the chorus on the track "Elektro Kardiogramm."'

Very little is known about Florian's contribution to Kraftwerk at this time, and it is rumoured that, in terms of composition, his role had diminished. By allowing Ralf, near-perfect in English, to do all the interviews, Florian's appearances in the media were strictly limited. An electronic poem found on YouTube, and lasting just over 30 seconds, sees Florian Schneider, with the help of a Vocoder, pay homage to the Doepfer A100 modular synthesizer. The synth is 'technisch, logisch, funktionell' (technical, logical, functional) and 'leicht, kompakt und transportable' (lightweight, compact and portable), making it an object of desire for Florian.

Coincidentally, but not without a certain serendipitous advantage, Karl Bartos' album, *Communication*, was released at almost the same time as *Tour De France Soundtracks*. 'I Am The Message', 'Fifteen Minutes Of Fame' and 'Life' were among the strongest songs Bartos had written. 'I like both *Tour De France*

Soundtracks and *Communication,*' says designer and Kraftwerk fan Malcolm Garrett. 'But if you compare *Communication* side by side with the last Kraftwerk album, well, which one has got the songs? All those clever lyrics, all those kind of snappy couplets, they are all on Karl Bartos' album; and there are none of them on *Tour De France*. There is no clever lyric writing on *Tour De France*. There are words and technical wordplay but no conventional lyrics. Karl Bartos is obviously a crucial component that they now don't have.'

Bartos' album was a moderate success, and it kept him in the public eye. *Tour De France Soundtracks* performed well, even if in a market of drastically declining album and singles sales as the download revolution began to hit established record companies hard. The title track, released as a single for the third time, made the UK Top 20. In Germany, the album would become the band's first number one. Ralf called the feat, 'Amazing. In the Tour de France, it's called the yellow jersey.' Krafwerk supported the album with a series of live performances, including one at the very-high profile MTV Awards that November. No lesser icon than pop princess Kylie Minogue (whose 2001 hit 'Can't Get You Out Of My Head' had an unmistakable whiff of Kraftwerk in both song and video) would introduce them.[*]

'Cycling is the man-machine,' concluded Ralf. 'It's about dynamics, always continuing straight ahead, forwards, no stopping. He who stops falls over. It's always forwards...'

8.5 Electro Gods On The Road

When the new-look Kraftwerk took to the road they had abandoned the synths and now stood stock still, evenly spaced in a line, behind four laptop computers. 'It's much faster and more mobile,' Ralf told Jim DeRogatis. 'It functions very well, and we can do more updates during sound-check... It is more fun, because all these ideas that come to mind in the afternoon can be turned into reality.' In 2005, the band released their first live album, *Minimum-Maximum*, together with a DVD of concert performances. Both were culled from a variety of concerts, and although the authenticity of having

---

[*] Co-writer of the song Cathy Dennis revealed in an interview with PRS magazine that 'I had an idea which was kind of Kraftwerk-y' when she was working on ideas for the song.

a 'best of' of live performances masquerading as one show might be said to have been compromised (performances in Warsaw, Moscow, Berlin, London, Budapest, Tallinn, Riga, Tokyo, and San Francisco formed the composted aural whole),* what cannot be levelled as a piece of criticism is that the music itself isn't played. It just isn't played with instruments.

The new Kraftwerk live tour was contained on 10 Sony laptops. Six were used for the visuals; four, running Cubase, for the actual music. The result was strange, and, at times, strangely comical. The four *Musik-Arbeiter* would walk on stage, and stand almost motionless for the entire show. At times, when the music just became too powerful, too downright danceable, it was possible to discern, at first, a twitch, and then a very polite knee bend, followed by a toe-tap to the beat of the music by one of the members, but such terpsichorean tendencies, once noticed, were quickly restrained, and a defiant mien of inscrutability re-established. The audiences, in the main, were hit by a sonic uppercut right in the soma. The music was so pure, and so loud, that it seemed to resonate throughout the whole body, the huge, thudding low frequencies echoing round the rib cage, the higher notes shrilly beautiful without distortion. And behind the Post-Human Fabricated Four, perfectly sequenced graphics and images appeared on large screens as accompaniment to each song. For Joe Black the 2004 concert at the Royal Festival Hall in London was 'the best gig that I have ever seen in my life. It was just the perfect combination of audio-visual entertainment. It was really visceral. They had the smallest, most powerful PA I think that I have ever come across. For the first 15 to 20 minutes your solar plexus was taking an absolute pounding.' Joe Black brings out another point that many of Kraftwerk's male followers have found (and it is axiomatic that the core following is male): wives, partners, daughters have found, often to their surprise, that they are completely won over. 'I took my wife, and she said she felt really guilty about coming, because "There are people who would kill to come and see this."' She had 'only ever listened to half an hour of

---

* In an interview for *Mojo* Magazine, Ralf Hütter said that the best live show was recorded too late for inclusion. 'We have great recordings from Santiago, Chile, but couldn't incorporate them into *Minimum-Maximum* because we'd already mixed the album,' says Ralf. 'The Chileans are the only audience in the world who clap in time, in perfect synchronisation.'

Kraftwerk.' In the event, 'She sat through the whole gig with a huge smile on her face.'

'They still amaze me and my wife', says Kristoff Tilkin. 'If Kraftwerk come she always accompanies me. She started to listen extensively to Kraftwerk. And I sort of joined in; and she turned out to be a bigger Kraftwerk fan than I am. I have a son who is becoming a five year-old. He is the biggest Kraftwerk fan in the world. He knows the names of all the members, he can sing to any melody.' Yet, for some long-time Kraftwerk-watchers, the latest edition of Kraftwerk, standing as they did virtually immobile behind four lecterns, lacked entertainment value. 'It was like watching four old guys checking their email,' said Martyn Ware of Heaven 17.

Like many of their contemporaries in all shades of pop and rock, by the late nineties, Kraftwerk had become a touring band. The irony of this may have sat uneasily with Wolfgang and Karl who had spent year on end hoping that Kraftwerk would perform regularly and thus provide them with a secure income. However, the industry had changed. Playing live was where the money was, and the making and selling of records had become increasingly marginal. While Ralf would vehemently deny such a claim, Kraftwerk, with their legacy and back catalogue, not to mention the paucity of opportunities to see them in the past, were just about the most important 'heritage act' on the circuit. Ex-Kraftwerk member Eberhard Kranemann has offered his estimate of the fee for a Kraftwerk performance in the 21st century: 'When they make a performance, I think it is not possible to get the band for less than 100,000 Euros.' How does he know this? 'I spoke to some people; and I know the business. They have a lot of work to do; and there is a lot of technology involved. So this is very expensive to do it. Ralf and Florian, in recent years, they get maybe 10,000 Euros each, and I get 500, because they went the way of music for the greater mass of people – mass music.'

With trademark attention to sonic detail, to play effectively the group has constructed a fully digitalised scaled-down version of their own Kling Klang Studio, which is compact and mobile enough to be transported around the world for live concert appearances. The old analogue equipment was 'retired', although it is still maintained in working order. Rather than make new music, much of the then recent activity at Kling Klang was centred on preserving and refining existing sounds. 'I remember in Tokyo we were playing in this huge complex and there was no heat. It was like three degrees Celsius (37.4 degrees Fahrenheit), but everything worked really well,' claimed Hütter. 'And then we played in Melbourne, Australia, and it was close to 50 degrees Celsius (122 degrees Fahrenheit), and everything was still functioning very well.' Of course, a central part of the show were the robots, which would provide the non-human element of the show during the first encore, as well as the odd promotional appearance. 'They do a slow motorist dance, which some people call Tai Chi,' says Ralf. 'They have our faces.'

Every interview obligation would be taken on by Ralf. Now in his late-fifties, he still cut a relatively youthful figure. 'We know that time is sickening in its crimes, but the phrase "tanned and fit" would definitely apply,' says *Mojo*'s Ian Harrison of Ralf. 'When I interviewed him he had on a black shirt and trousers, and he looked in good nick. He spoke very good English. He was very courteous and he seemed like a person who was, what shall I say? He wasn't an unfriendly person, or dour or severe. He was amusing, you know. It was great because, as you know, you meet people in this game and sometimes it is unfortunate because you have these things that build up beforehand. I must admit that coming out of there I didn't find that he spoiled any of those things. He was cool; there was nothing that he couldn't talk about, then. I definitely got the impression that he was looking forward in this, that there were things he was still planning to do.'

However, other journalists formed a rather different view of Ralf, one of a man who spoke in carefully prepared sentences designed to give nothing of substance away. 'I had a chance to interview him over the phone,' says Kristoff Tilkin who interviewed Ralf for *Humo* magazine. 'He was very nice, but it was like a dicta-phone – he didn't really listen to my questions, I thought I had some interesting questions, but he didn't really listen. He started talking and I thought "Oh, my god, I have been reading this story in interviews for the last 15 years." He just says what he wants to say and he doesn't really listen to other people. He is very nice, he is very charming, but I think in a sort of a detached way. We didn't have a connection or something there. It was just another journalist to talk to, as he just keeps repeating "Yeah, you know all this, you know all this." I thought yes, you are absolutely right, I do know all this: and I didn't get anything else.'

At times, Kraftwerk would find themselves as tour support, second on the bill, for example, to Radiohead, and, at one festival, much to the incredulity of the artist himself, Moby: 'Four years ago I played this amazing festival in Serbia called the Exit Festival, and the opening acts that I had, and this is so strange, and so wrong, were three of my biggest influences: Patti Smith, Grandmaster Flash and Kraftwerk. It just seemed so wrong. If you had come to me aged 15, I would have been happy to have gone into Kraftwerk's dressing room, three hours after they had left, and stood there and looked around... Or if someone had asked me to go to the grocery store to buy Kraftwerk some coffee, that would have been enough for me. But to actually have been on the same bill as them and, oddly, to have them go on before me, felt so surreal and wrong. I mean, it was amazing standing at the side of the stage and watch them perform, but I really felt I should have been much more their humble servant and not some presumptuous electronic musician who had deigned to share the stage with them.'

A Kraftwerk concert was now an important event. Anyone with even the vaguest interest in electronic music knew that seeing the group live was just as important an event to them as still being able to see Bob Marley & the Wailers would be to a reggae fan, seeing the Beatles to a pop fan or being able to buy tickets for a Muddy Waters show for a blues fan. There was something hallowed about the sight of the band in concert. Jim DeRogatis of the *Chicago Sun Times,* in an interview with Ralf, asked him: 'For an entire generation of young electronic-oriented musicians, Kraftwerk is more influential than the Beatles. Is that legacy ever a burden?' 'No, not really, because it is giving us all the energy and the encouragement to keep going. Because we started in the late sixties, but we are still looking ahead. When we see the audience, and it ranges from the young computer kids to the university electronics or physics professor, we are very, very pleased.'

Although some critics disputed it, each Kraftwerk gig was different, if sometimes imperceptibly. Songs could be extended live, and mistakes did occur. 'So far the computers have worked very well,' Ralf said in 2003. 'Little failures here and there, but overall they have been very friendly with us and we have been friendly with the computers, so things are working very well.'

On one occasion, there would be an all-too human disturbance to a show. Kraftwerk were forced to cancel their concert in Melbourne for the Global Gathering Festival on November 22, 2008 when Fritz Hilpert collapsed backstage just 20 minutes before showtime. A visibly upset Ralf, already in his stage gear, made an announcement from the stage to the disappointed audience. But it was a sign that Kraftwerk weren't simply glorified mime artists or robots. It is believed that Hilpert had suffered heart failure but after a short hospitalisation was able to continue the tour the next day.

Kraftwerk played concerts around the world, not just in the major European cities, but also across North and South America, and in the East. 'We've been performing in different cultural contexts,' affirmed Ralf. 'We played a Tribal Gathering in England that was in the countryside in tents. In Italy, we will play outside in the old city centre. We played on the Lido in Venice. In Moscow, at Sports Palais. So it's like a little spaceship landed somewhere and we present our performance.'

One of the major reasons for their success across so many different territories was the fact that their music was so readily adaptable and understandable. With short texts, Kraftwerk could tailor a show to a given language group, switching from English to German wherever necessary. In Japan, a song such as 'Pocket Calculator' became 'Dentaku' with a text in Japanese. 'Numbers' could, again, be easily tweaked depending on location. Like mime artists for whom language barriers are never a problem to their global aspirations, Kraftwerk had created a unity of sounds and images, one which was not bound to any one culture, or generation. A robot, a motorway, a sequence of numbers, a computer screen, a high-speed train, the yellow radioactive warning sign were all well-known symbols in developed countries. Kraftwerk could be interpreted, across cultures, through a semiotic Esperanto.

8.6 Auf Wiedersehen, Herr Klang!

Footage of Florian's last performance with Kraftwerk, posted subsequently on YouTube given its significance to the faithful, was on 11th of the 11th in 2006 in Zaragoza. November 11 marks not just the Armistice but, in Germany, the start of carnival time, in Southern Germany of *Fasching*, an extended period of (some might say) forced jollity, with parties and balls, fancy dress, and conspicuous consumption, lasting until Lent, but only, of course, on pre-designated days, and in officially authorised locations. But there would be no jolliness in the demeanour of Mr Klang that night on stage in Spain. A brilliantly clattering rendition of 'Musique Non-Stop' closed the set with each band member soloing before taking his leave, stage left. When it came to his turn, Florian did not so much as walk as run off the stage.

Florian had been absent from the band's concerts in Ireland in 2008, and in an interview with the *New Zealand Herald* on September 27, 2008 ahead of the band's support gigs with Radiohead, Ralf stated: 'Yes, he never likes touring so in the last years he is working on other projects, technical things. So we are travelling with our live set-up as on the last American tour and now Europe. We are me, Mr Henning Schmitz, Mr Fritz Hilpert and Mr Stefan Pfaffe who is programming visuals with us.' Ralf was on vocals and keyboards, Henning controlled bass lines and sound equalisation, and Fritz controlled rhythms and percussive sounds.

It had been evident for many years that Florian found touring arduous. He was, after all, an inventor, content to work in the lab at Kling Klang on advanced techniques to mould and modulate the Kraftwerk sound, particularly in terms of vocal expression. But there seemed something inherently wrong when Kraftwerk took to the stage without him. His replacement was the then 29-year-old Kling Klang employee, Stefan Pfaffe, a tall and suitably inscrutable man who was decades younger than the others, and described by one journalist as a bit of a 'hottie'.

Competent though he may have been, his recruitment did seem to confirm the idea in the minds of many of their fans that Kraftwerk was simply Ralf's pet project. Ralf *was* Kraftwerk now. It had long been mooted that in terms of writing Florian's contribution had not been decisive for many years, so his departure didn't present Ralf with an insurmountable hurdle. Nevertheless, the absence of Florian's bald pate, his straight, superior nose, his mad-professor demeanour, his statuesque manner, his smile that always seemed about to break out any moment, removed Kraftwerk's most iconic figure. Show anyone a picture of Kraftwerk circa 1977 and ask them what country they came from and it would be Florian who would give the game away. Florian also brought to Kraftwerk a good deal of its humour, a touch of the offbeat and absurdist, that wide smile uniquely charming yet at the same time mildly sinister. In a band that had always presented itself as the embodiment of mechanical efficiency, Florian reminded fans that Kraftwerk were human after all.

Kraftwerk now had only one original member. Did it matter? Did anyone care that their live repertoire was now performed to a greater or lesser degree by people who were now no longer in Kraftwerk? The 2000s was a decade in which many groups from yore reformed without their iconic lead men. We had Slade without Noddy; we had the Undertones without Fergal; we even had Queen without Freddie. We also had the spectacle of the *Ersatz*, the tribute band; the popularity, for example, of the Australian Pink Floyd, a high production-recreation by skilled stand-ins, selling out large arenas across Europe; and Bjorn Again, Abba clones who implemented a franchise policy with different Bjorn Agains operating in different territories around the world. Nevertheless, the balance was always a tricky one to maintain. Where came the tipping point when the currency of an act was so devalued that the audience would decide it was too inauthentic to be viable? Could the Stones play without Keef? Could there be a U2 without the Edge? Had Kraftwerk now become a tribute act to itself? Or, simply, a solo act: *Ralfwerk*? Or was the final reality an inevitability? Kraftwerk had predicted a future whereby anyone – a robot, a projection, a stand-in, a tribute – could perform the same function as the originals for an uninterested, lazy but wealthy community of music fans. What was easier, a night with a tribute Pink Floyd, or the hard slog of actually listening to new music from a new era?

Perhaps this was too harsh on Kraftwerk. Ralf was always the acknowledged leader. Fritz and Henning had been onstage presences in the band for almost 20 years now, and maybe it was time to see them as bona fide members, rather than Wolfgang and Karl stand-ins, Kling Klang actors. However, for many fans, Kraftwerk without Florian was a crucial blow. 'He was the one who even could be Kraftwerk in the short period when Ralf was not around, you know, this period when he was working with Michael Rother,' says Ralf Dörper. 'For me, it was always Ralf and Florian. But for me it was Florian who was always the *"Robotnik."* I think he's great!'

Asked why he thought Florian had left, Wolfgang Flür's reply was terse, but probably accurate: 'Too old, not necessary any more, enough money, especially no more flying: he was tired of all that. I think he should have done it earlier, much earlier.'

According to Eberhard Kranemann, the split was not as amicable as one might have expected. 'I would like to play with Florian again, because I have heard Florian and Ralf now, they ... there are big problems between the two of them. They don't like each other any more: and they have problems with everything. Yesterday I got a telephone call from a friend and he told me that there are big problems between Florian and Ralf. Ralf is running the band alone without Florian, and Florian now wants to make his own music without Ralf, but Ralf doesn't allow him to do it. They work with lawyers. One lawyer says this, the other says this, and Kraftwerk have an agreement with EMI Elektrola to make one more record, and when this record is done, Florian is free, he can leave the group and he can make his own music, but not before. I would like to make music again with Florian Schneider, because we began the whole thing in 1967 and now we are some years older, I would like to go back to the beginning of the whole thing. Florian has some agreements with record companies with Ralf, so it is forbidden for him to make his own music. He is a slave of the music industry. As a musician working in the big-business circus you cannot do what you want to do. I wrote the song, "Say No!" about this situation: the fully developed ability to say NO is also the only valid background for YES, and only through both does real freedom take form. When Florian is freed from music business slavery, I would like to join him again. He is a good guy and a very good musician and it was always fun to make music with him.'

The statement above, of course, was one man's reading of the situation in an interview given in 2009. However, the probability of Florian being legally barred from releasing music as a solo artist is far from fanciful. It has also been suggested that as part of the financial deal with Ralf which saw Florian leave the band, he had to give up any legal rights he may have had to the Kraftwerk trademark. In fact, it would be odd if some sort of legal pact had not been made between Ralf and Florian, given that every record from *Autobahn* onwards has been denoted 'Kling Klang Produkt: Ralf Hütter/Florian Schneider'. 'I would imagine that Ralf and Florian have had a very big and long fight and discussion about the future of Kraftwerk,' says Wolfgang. 'I think at least it was Florian who was the one who put away his weapons and said, "OK, OK, I'll leave it, then. Do what you want. You can have the name." Maybe he had to pay a lot of money for it; I am sure Ralf had to take a lot of money from his bank and give it to Florian. Florian has nothing more to do with Kraftwerk. Maybe no rights, but maybe on the copyrights on the songs. I don't know the deal they have, but there was a deal. Florian wanted to be separated from everything.'

It was now obvious that, for Ralf, Kraftwerk was to be his life's work. Now well into his sixties, he showed absolutely no inclination of giving up. In fact, in the music business, it is virtually unknown for successful musicians to retire in the sense that they cease to perform *at all*. Almost everyone shores up their pension pot by clinging on to the festival tour, the pub circuit, or even cabaret. Some pretend they are out there for 'artistic' reasons; others point to the euphoria that grips their audiences, especially when they play their biggest hits. Paul McCartney performs shows that are heavily reliant on classic Beatles songs, every one interpreted as close as possible to the originals, with only a smattering of Wings and solo material. Keith Richards has pointed out that old blues pioneers keep going until they drop, so why shouldn't he? Approaching his three score years and ten, Roger Waters has toured with a solo interpretation of the Pink Floyd classic *The Wall*. On stage, Neil Young sounds as angry and aggressive at 70 as he did at 50, as do Pete Townshend and Roger Daltrey fronting a line-up of the Who that lacks both Keith Moon and John Entwistle. Ian Anderson solo, and Jethro Tull at Christmas, do big business. Even 'Laughing Len' Cohen could be found on stage, and valorised, particularly since his overlooked eighties track, 'Hallelujah', was now much-covered and reinstated a classic. David Bowie's media hibernation after his heart problems in 2004, together with Phil Collins' announcement of his intention to retire from making music at the age of 60, are, in fact, exceptions to the rule. In the second decade of the 21st century, there are many rock stars still writing, recording and performing over 70. Ian Hunter, Bob Dylan, Yoko Ono, Aretha Franklin, Seasick Steve, David Crosby, Bill Wyman, Ringo Starr, Paul Simon and Lou Reed spring immediately to mind, and there are many others, some deserving, most not. The old guard have become heritage acts, the importance of being young and beautiful now an irrelevance for all but those whose very existence was made meaningful by their ability to look preternaturally young. Ralf and Kraftwerk were in a different position entirely. He did not sing at a mic stand with an acoustic guitar as his only prop. He did not take to the stage supported by a pyroclastic flow of noise from a well-drilled rock band. No. He would soon be the first electronic pop pioneer to turn 70. Would he look ridiculous in his seventies producing beats rather than riffing an old blues tune?

Perhaps the answer to Ralf's unswerving desire to keep making music can be found 30 years ago, in an interview he gave to Chris Bohn at *NME*. Asked about computerising the Kling Klang Studio, he revealed quite clearly a psychological trait which was ingrained in him: 'Because we are German and there is a fatalistic German quality of going all the way. There is never a question of maybe using a little computer here and plugging it into the synthesizer there and keeping the rest of the group as it was before. We close the door for three years and don't open it. We try to do it all the way, imposing the process as a discipline on ourselves, really taking it all the way and then going out of the room to see where that takes us. I think that is very Germanic.' *Going all the way* ... To retire Kraftwerk was unthinkable. As one of Kraftwerk's current disciples, Hot Chip, would sing it: 'Over and over and over and over and over/ Like a monkey with a miniature cymbal/The joy of repetition really is in you.'

Kraftwerk, in fact, was becoming far more than some sort of manifest destiny for Ralf. Fiction and fact were eliding the gap between art and real life, becoming blurred as they merged together. 'In the German language, names are often occupations, like Müller [Miller] and Bauer [Farmer]. I don't feel like Mr Hütter any more but rather like Mr Kraftwerk. I feel like a robot.'

Official news of Florian's departure came in January 2009. One journalist drolly speculated that only in a group such as Kraftwerk could artistic differences split up the partnership... after 40 years. In typically Kraftwerkian style, no explanation was given for his departure. Another *Arbeiter* had simply left; a drone that could easily be replaced was the impression that might have been intended. 'Some fans, undoubtedly, will think it a shame that Schneider won't be sharing a stage with Hütter for any 40th anniversary concerts (they formed in 1970),' wrote reporter Andrew Eaton in *The Scotsman*. 'Looked at another way, his low-key, no fuss departure, on the eve of a major tour (including dates with long-time fans Radiohead) is very Kraftwerk. Their best creative years – from 1974's *Autobahn* to 1981's *Computer World* – may be long behind them, but the band remains inspiringly out-of-place in our celebrity-obsessed culture. Like Kate Bush, they are labelled eccentric partly because they are uninterested in participating in the media whirl. They simply have no desire to be famous.'

Since Florian's departure, Ralf has revealed very little, but there does appear to have been a degree of both sympathy and surprise on his part: 'What can I say? We have worked together for so many years but he has other projects. I'm a free artist so I can continue,' adding, 'We don't understand, but it's his private decision. He's done a couple of other projects, lecturing at university, things like that. Sometimes in life you take a different direction.' Ralf also revealed: 'He worked for many, many years on other projects: speech synthesis, and things like that. He was not really involved in Kraftwerk for many, many years.'

Before the depature, it was a very different matter. Asked about the importance of Florian a few years earlier, Ralf told the *Chicago Sun Times*: 'It's like an electronic marriage (laughs) – Mr Kling and Mr Klang. It's stereo, so it gives the music the overall dimension; Yin Yang, Kling Klang.' 'So you can't imagine making a Kraftwerk record without Florian?' quizzed the journalist: 'No, no. This is not possible. That's what Kraftwerk is all about. It's stereo.'

Florian's first public appearance after the announcement of his departure came at the MusikMesse in Frankfurt in 2009. Wearing a cap, looking relaxed and chewing gum, he was on good laconic form, firstly in a short interview, secondly, and with quite brilliant comic timing, popping his head into the view of the camera in an interview with Sebastian Niessen, the Munich-based instrument designer and a long-term associate of the band. Florian looked like a relieved man.

8.7 Kraftwerk Now

In 2009, with Florian now out of the group, Hütter and Co. abandoned the original Kling Klang Studio and moved out to the 'new' Kling Klang complex in Lise-Meitner-Strasse in Meerbusch-Osterath, roughly 10 kilometres west of Düsseldorf. With office space to co-ordinate the sale of Kling Klang product (CDs, T-shirts, cycling wear, luggage, mouse-pads, skateboards and the like), and a recording and rehearsal space, the new location might radiate the hi-tech aura that Kraftwerk had always displayed; but, as yet, it has failed to become a shrine for the faithful.

The same year saw the long-delayed reissue of the Kraftwerk back catalogue, or, more accurately, all eight studio albums from *Autobahn* to *Tour De France Soundtracks*. They were made available singly or in a box set, *The Catalogue* [*Der Katalog*], promoted by a short promotional video *1-2-3-4-5-6-7-8*, a vocodorised voice intoning each number in sequence revealing the original and the new cover artwork. Indeed, for most of the covers, the artwork had been tweaked and simplified, and the box set contained some pleasing 12″-sized booklets of period artwork for each album release, but there was nothing new except the renaming of *Electric Café* as *Techno Pop*, and the inclusion, on that album, of the instrumental 'Housephone'. There were even quibbles about the sound quality from some fans. *The Catalogue* was extensively reviewed in the media. Mostly, these were very favourable, but despite its elegance it failed to deliver what fans really wanted – new material, comment from Ralf, something out of the ordinary to make it an essential purchase.

Kraftwerk continued touring and improving their live presentation. The latest redefinition came with 3-D, and was given its British premiere in the second half of one of the band's most thrilling performances, at the Manchester Velodrome in July 2010. To promote the concert, Kraftwerk, or rather Ralf, or actually a robotic Ralf, or 'Ralfbot', gave an 'interview' to journalist Miranda Sawyer, who wore a red shirt and black tie in homage to one of her teen heroes. She mused on why there were so few female Kraftwerk fans (not something evidenced by the gender mix seen at most concerts), before trying to tease answers out of an interviewee who was rather more mechanical than most.

In 2003, Ralf had extolled the virtues of his robotic counterpart, stating, 'Where I am doing an interview, the robots can do a photo session, do some filming, so it's an industrial art process.' In a light-hearted exchange with the *San Francisco Chronicle*, Ralf was asked: 'Does it bother you that the robots still get more love than the band?' 'No. They've been travelling with us for quite a while. When we started this tour in September 2002 in Paris, the robots were in the Musee de la Musique, so they couldn't be with us. And then when we travelled into Australia and Japan they were not with us. They were in the museum for one year doing the exhibition. So now they're back with us... They want to be on the road with us.' 'Who ends up with the most chicks after the show, you or your android?' Ralf Hütter: 'Oh, that's a secret.'

'It was incredibly exciting,' Ian Harrison says of the Manchester Velodrome performance, 'very warm... and hot. When they played 'Tour De France', the British Olympic team rode out on bikes, which was a fantastic, hilarious, brilliant moment. You just wanted to laugh out loud.' It was, indeed, an utterly surreal moment. When the cyclists departed, Ralf added to the air of comic disbelief by adding: 'Next time, we bring our bikes.'

Andy McCluskey was also at the show, and was suitably bedazzled: 'It is now the most unbelievable multimedia extravaganza. They have got the music, they have got the robots, and they have got the reflective suits. They have got the gigantic screen. The whole back of the stage, 50 foot by 20 foot, was the screen. The whole second half of the show was in 3-D; and we wore our 3-D glasses. They keep taking the show to another level of multimedia. If you look at the designs, if you look at the way that they presented themselves, the artwork, everything about them, if the Futurists had computers they would have made music like Kraftwerk. I also found myself dancing around, although it is difficult to do a lot of dancing. I started to play 'air synth' during "Radio-Activity", and I stopped that immediately. My hand was up in the air and I thought "Don't put your hand up there and tap out the notes, you idiot!"'

For Andy, however, it was more than just a phenomenally innovative show; it was a statement of his own identity in sound and vision, and how Kraftwerk had shaped it. 'I spoke to Peter Saville after the show, I called him and said, "Peter, you weren't by any chance at the gig tonight, were you?" and he said "Yeah, yeah, yeah". He had the same experience because both of us were transported back to our youth, to a time when we were inventing ourselves. And what we got from and what we learnt from Kraftwerk were some of the most important building blocks in the construction of our vision of ourselves. So it was very, very nostalgic and very emotional for us.'

'It was appropriate that they opened with "The Man

Machine"', continues Peter Saville. 'It was quite an astonishing moment, for me. It was a lot of dots that you could draw a line through: and the line was an infinity loop. It was quite astonishing. A tear came to my eye, from the beginning.'

Saville saw a deep symbolism in the event. 'There was a moment of conclusion – of people, time and place, which was the moment when the Olympic cycling team came out. That was a convergent moment of "reciprocal evolution". The idea to have Kraftwerk in the Velodrome was Alex Poots'. The Velodrome is symbolic of the "new Manchester".

'So the building in which this happened would not have even been there had it had not been for something that Kraftwerk themselves were the inspiration of. That Velodrome is often cited as a tipping point in the evolution of the GB cycling team. So without the Velodrome, loosely speaking, there would be no Olympic gold winning team. So when you finally saw that team in that building, with Kraftwerk, it was a full circle moment. The International Festival itself owes something to Kraftwerk. The Festival's invitation to Kraftwerk could never have happened without Factory. Further, I think Manchester's role in the Industrial Revolution is quite well understood in Germany; and Manchester is known as the world's first industrial city. I think that was not lost on Ralf. I think that opening with the "The Man Machine" in the first industrial city was an appropriate moment.'

In October 2011 in Munich, and April 2012 in New York, Kraftwerk pulled off an audacious coup; live concerts in relatively small halls combined with a separate fee-paying art installation. The Munich concerts were staged at the Alter-Kongresshalle, the 3-D video at the Lenbachhaus. By now, the whole of the live show was in 3-D; it must have amused Ralf to see the whole audience wearing silly glasses. The mix of the audience was surprisingly heterogeneous, men and women from 17 to 70, and a few dressed in the trademark black and red of *The Man-Machine* days. The visuals were eye-popping. Robot arms seemed to reach out beyond you, numbers jumped out to chase you: we joined a spacelab in a weightless orbit and experienced the sensation of driving in a car along the autobahn with Ralf. During one YouTube clip of 'Numbers', one clearly over-excited male fan can be heard shouting, 'Oh my God! ... Oh yes! ... Wow! ... Wu-Woo!'

The electronic pulse of 'Musique Non Stop' was inevitably the band's closing number, with each member departing stage left in turn after 'soloing', again a knowing dig at rock authenticity. That the individual in sole charge of the visuals can solo is a real triumph of the simulated over the real. Ralf, the last to leave, usually checked his watch in a droll nod towards German punctuality. It's also a reminder that Kraftwerk are *Arbeiter* (workers) – they've done their shift (the gig), they've done the overtime (the encore), and now it's time to clock off.

If Munich was a success, Kraftwerk's residency at New York's Museum Of Modern Art (or MoMA as it is also known) garnered probably the most publicity the band had ever had in its entire career. It was their first appearance in the city since 2005, but, more than that, the plan was that all eight albums from *Autobahn* to *Tour De France Soundtracks* would be played on consecutive nights. In view of the ambitious nature of the concerts and the group's now legendary status, regardless of their line-up, it was perhaps inevitable that ticketing for the event became something of an omnishambles. Firstly, each applicant was restricted to just two tickets. This was, in theory, an attempt to please all potential punters but in actuality it alienated committed fans, a situation that was hilariously sent up in a 'Hitler reacts to Kraftwerk MoMA ticket limit' spoof on YouTube, which used a scene from the 2004 German film *Der Untergang* (*Downfall*), a well-established internet 'meme', and cast Hitler as an avid Kraftwerk fan enraged at finding out he would be unable to attend all eight shows: 'Perhaps I will see *Techno Pop* and *The Mix*? *Techno Pop*, AKA *Electric Café* is slightly underrated, which is to say that it's not as completely awful as most people say it is [long pause]. It just sounds like they were paging through the pre-sets on the DX 7.'*

Secondly, hardly any of the fans actually got tickets. What fans didn't know was that the capacity for each concert would be, reportedly, around 450 (and what percentage of these tickets was made available to the general public is unknown). The company responsible for the sale at least had the good grace to issue an explanation and an apology, pointing out that their normal ticketing arrangements were inadequate for the huge demand. 'While we're

---

* http://www.youtube.com/watch?v=b4yohA0ZVt4.

not able to disclose the number of tickets that were available for these performances, what I will say is that of the tens and tens of thousands of die-hard Kraftwerk fans from around the world that logged on at exactly noon EST yesterday to get these tickets, the venue capacity restrictions would only ever allow approximately 1.20% of them to actually be reserved,' stated the CEO of the company handling the sale. 'As you might imagine, this is an extremely large technical hurdle, particularly because of the tiny fraction of supply versus the demand.... I recognise that so many of you spent hours in front of your computer watching a spinning wheel – or watching the page go blank.' Reportedly one ticket tout, or 'scalper' as they are known in the USA, was offering a single ticket for $41,000.

Whilst most coverage of Kraftwerk in the British press in recent times has tended to genuflect, in America it was different, with a little light teasing cutting through many moments of adoration. Mike Rubin of *Rolling Stone* reviewed all eight concerts in what he dubbed 'Kraftweek'. Of the opening night, he wrote, 'Up in the second floor's atrium, a scrim was raised at the appointed hour to reveal the quartet – led by 65-year-old co-founder Ralf Hütter, providing all the vocoderfied vocals – squeezed like bratwurst into matching Tron-style spandex body-suits. They launched the night with their de facto theme song, "The Robots" (basically a cybernetic version of "hey, hey we're the Monkees").'

Rubin's reviews depicted an uneven week for Kraftwerk – many memorable moments but some disappointments too, among them the 1991 *The Mix* version of 'Radioactivity' played anachronistically on the night reserved for the *Radio-Activity* album itself; one was strident and technoid, the original, fragile and half-heard, and very different. Another complaint was the shortening of some of the classic pieces. However, most of the critics left amused and awed. 'Watching Kraftwerk's mesmerising presentation on Saturday night – the four men performed, unsmiling, in front of a giant projection of 3-D animations – I had two, intertwined realisations,' opined Michael Hogan of the *Huffington Post*. 'The first is that Kraftwerk was indeed right (as were, to be fair, plenty of other people): under the influence of technology, the human race is morphing into something new and strange. We're part of the way through now, but my guess is that the journey has just begun. The second is that I'm not scared by this. In fact, I find it exciting.'

'We didn't fall asleep,' Ralf told the *New York Times*, promising the next Kraftwerk record 'soon'. 'The 168-hour week is still going on since the beginning, since 1970.'

Seeing Ralf on stage, and the continuation of Kraftwerk, is not something that excites Wolfgang Flür: 'We were Kraftwerk. We lived Kraftwerk. There was nothing else besides that. It was our main theme. So that's why I know so much, much more maybe than today's musicians or robots who are hired there, because there is nothing new to invent today. Everything stopped when Karl and I left; and the bicycle stopped everything anyway. So there was nothing more to invent, to make anew and talk about. Maybe you could make it bigger, make it higher, make it "more", make the screens bigger, and the sound more digital. That's easy to do, you know; there is no invention in that. All you do is get some engineers and blow it up as they are doing on stage today.'

Although Wolfgang Flür sees the Kraftwerk project as long past its sell-by date, he looks back on his involvement in the group, his role as the 'Kraftwerk-Drummer', with mixed feelings. He is certainly proud to have been part of this remarkable endeavour, yet there is sadness and regret too, perhaps even bitterness and resentment. Listening to Wolfgang is like listening to an open wound that is able to speak: 'Ralf should do the same as Florian and replace himself by a hired robot. Then the whole thing would become intellectual! He would end up with his (wrong) idea that everyone is replaceable. It was his idea to put the robots on tour, and we can stay at home. But, now, he *cannot* stop it. I think it's a sad ending for Kraftwerk... How he, alone from the whole original thing, is left over. Kraftwerk is dead. He is open for anything which helps him to stay longer on stage, always again, and again, and again, to play "Autobahn" – at his age! He is 65 now.'

Wolfgang pauses to consider his words before continuing. 'I find that sad. I'm starting to think, "What happened after his accident? Is he ill?" And I think it's no longer healthy. If you see him in close-up pictures on tour, maybe in Wolfsburg, last year, when he gave some interviews. I was really horrified how he looked and how he spoke. His face – phew! I thought, "I wouldn't like to be close to him, to be near him." A bad feeling comes over me, when I see him today. There is no more life in his face. It's only work, slaving away, slaving. I think his thinking is that Kraftwerk is his life and his

'*Lebensprojekt*'[lifelong mission]. It all seems so dogged. He doesn't notice that he is himself already in the position of undermining his own project. Everyone wants to be [with] him, "Mr Hütter, Mr Hütter, Mr Hütter"... But it's only because of money, you know.'

Wolfgang now lives with his partner in a stylish though comparatively modest flat in Düsseldorf. He is charming, and retains a lovely sense of humour, but there's also, fleetingly, a sadness in his eyes. Images of the past sometimes intrude – a photograph here, a gold record there. He continues to write music, some of it potentially highly commercial, and bemoans the fact that the current state of the music business makes it so difficult for him to get it released. Wolfgang has also developed a second career as a novelist. His book *Neben Mir: Rheinland Grotesken* was written with his equally charming partner, Zuhal Korkmaz. He is also in demand on the live circuit. His new project, an extension of the idea of Kraftwerk as 'Robotniks', is the *Musik Soldat* (Music Soldier) in which Wolfgang parades up and down in full World War I regalia!

Karl Bartos lives with his wife of over 35 years, Bettina, a journalist, in Hamburg and, in 2013, will release a new album, *Off The Record*, which he will support with a live audio-visual show. Karl has returned to music full time after a spell working in academia. In 2004 he co-founded the Masters programme 'Sound Studies – Acoustic Communication' at the Berlin University of the Arts, where until 2009 he was a visiting professor teaching Auditory Media Design. 'The convergence of image and sound is the centre of my work,' he says.

We will have to wait for the publication of his autobiography for his true feelings about the years he spent in Kraftwerk, a time he admits now to find problematic discussing. That said, Bartos still performs Kraftwerk classics live, although understandably only those songs he either composed himself or had a hand in composing. Looking back on the group's career, Bartos charitably rates their 1974 breakthrough album as their finest. 'In my view the most important Kraftwerk album is *Autobahn*. The legendary Conny Plank was involved. I joined in 1975 and was initially booked for the upcoming live stuff in the USA. I had no idea at the time that I would be part of the Mensch Maschine for the next 15 years.'

Florian Schneider currently lives in Meerbusch-Büderich near Düsseldorf, and has a daughter named Lisa. Ralf Dörper: 'The way he is, even if, by chance, you could meet him, by walking near Kling Klang, because sometimes you meet him in a bar there, or in a coffee shop, even then he might not be prepared to talk to anyone! In a way he is even more erratic than the others in the way he relates to people. But I think he's great. For me he was, in a way, Kraftwerk.' Florian's mother, Eva-Maria, and his father, Paul, are recently deceased. His sister, Claudia, described as a 'character', lives in Monte Carlo.

There were other members of Kraftwerk too, despite the indelibility in the public perception of Krafwerk being Ralf, Florian, Wolfgang and Karl. The man who first began making music with Florian, Eberhard Kranemann, has had a long career working outside the mainstream. He formed the band Fritz Mueller and toured with a mixed-media show combining arts, theatre, literature, film and music. On reissue, the 1977 album *Fritz Mueller Rock* was described by *Mojo* as 'enjoyably maddening', and by *Record Collector* as 'an anarchistic, unsettling mix of Zappa-esque piss-taking and trashy straight-ahead rock'n'roll crank'. Asked if he sometimes wished he was still in the band when Ralf and Florian became successful, he laughs and is typically honest: 'Sometimes, yes!' Today, Eberhard continues to be as active as ever, mixing art and music in galleries and museums. In April 2012 he wrote: 'In autumn of this year there will be a Joseph Beuys exposition in New York City with three Kranemann contributions. In 1968 I had a performance with Joseph Beuys in Cream Cheese Düsseldorf, *Beuys = Handaktion* and I made acoustic terror with my band PISSOFF. I recorded the whole thing – it will run at the exposition. I made a poster that is shown and I have been asked to write something about it for the exposition.'

Sadly, two of the band's ex-members have now passed away.* Drummer Charly Weiss died in 2009, aged 69, and Klaus Dinger, who would later find fame as 50% of Neu!, died the year before, aged 62. 'He was proud of having taken more than 1,000 LSD trips,' says Michael Rother of his former musical partner, Dinger who actually posted this information on his own website in the nineties. 'He

---

* Indeed, there may have been more; my apology if this is so. According to Wikipedia, there are 15 ex-members of the band, ranging from those such as Wolfgang and Karl who played with the band for well over a decade to those who may have only played a few sessions in various early configurations.

thought that taking all these drugs cleared his mind and gave him a clearer view on what was really happening in the world, and that just led to him being separated from nearly everybody. And in the late eighties he started to drift away from many people around him, friends, and people who tried to take care of his projects, help him, and help Neu!.... In the end he was very lonely. Yes, and of course he also did crazy things with record companies, ruining some offices and, yes, demanding crazy sums. So people were starting to make fun of him in the business. It's a very, very sad story.'

Klaus Dinger's final years were dogged by impoverishment and deprivation, according to Eberhard Kranemann: 'What I heard from his girlfriend – she was with him for 30 years – she wanted to speak to me alone. We met in Düsseldorf to speak about all this. She said in the end he had so many enemies, because he had borrowed a lot of money and the musicians have got no money and all this. In the final stages – he did not go to a doctor, because he had no money. He did not even have medical insurance cover. Everyone in Germany has a *'Krankenversicherung'* [medical insurance, sickness cover] – but not Klaus! I don't understand it. Maybe, if he had gone to a doctor, it would have been OK. So he died because he had no money and no insurance.'

Michael Rother has been out of touch with the Kraftwerk founders for over 35 years: 'I haven't seen, or talked to them, since 1975, I guess. That was the last time they contacted me and asked me to join them again for the *Autobahn* tour, but at the time I was busy and very happy with Harmonia and preparing the release of *Neu! 75*. I wasn't interested at the time, so I have friends from Düsseldorf who know them, more or less closely. And that's about all I have as information from the past 30-something years.'

Michael remains a close friend of Karl Bartos, however, and, of course, remains active and hugely admired as a pioneering musician. In 2010 he helped co-ordinate the *Neu! Vinyl Box*, a career-spanning retrospective and performed as part of Hallogallo 2010 with drummer Steve Shelley (Sonic Youth) and bassist Aaron Mullan (Tall Firs). Of their performance at the Barbican Theatre in London in October of that year, Andy Gill wrote: 'The sound is like an overloaded bomber lumbering down a runway, straining for take-off, which comes just before the runway runs out as Rother sends the first of his characteristic, wiry guitar lines swirling off into the skies.

A wave of euphoria sweeps around the hall as the infectious trance-rock groove of "Hallogallo" does its stuff.'

By leaving Kraftwerk in 1971, Dinger and Rother gave us two very different groups. Although not as immediately visible, or as iconic as Kraftwerk in the mainstream, there is no doubting that Neu! have had an impact on popular music of the last 40 years. The interesting stuff, that is. Kraftwerk, by comparison, have invaded the very heart of popular music. Almost all of today's music that is produced electronically, with beats and repetitive sequencing, but which at the same time conveys respect for the romance of the machine, can be traced back to Kraftwerk.

'They don't sound like anyone else and never have. They abandoned every rock cliché and worked with what was left,' says John Foxx. 'They were aware of their limitations at the start and negotiated them into a solid style with great skill and tenacity. They spent a great deal of time perfecting their instruments and the sounds they produced. Each sound is an astounding sculptural event, and is always perfectly placed in its architectural space. You feel you can walk around those sounds in three dimensions. The result is pure sonic delight. Synaesthetics. The visual image is an equally potent work of art. It altered the fabric of space-time for generations of musicians, and quietly made the rest of popular music look like Spinal Tap.' 'Kraftwerk are like craftsmen,' David Bowie told Rolling Stone in 1987. 'They've decided they're gonna make this particular wooden chair that they designed, and each one will be very beautifully made, but it will be the same chair.'

Bowie's comment conveys the suggestion that Kraftwerk's music might be seen as elitist, and, in some respects, this has been the case. To understand the layers of irony in the music, and economy and beauty in almost everything they do, means that Kraftwerk can never be music for the 'casual' listener. Since so much music today is consumed almost passively, listened to uncritically, and enjoyed because of its inoffensiveness, Kraftwerk are an anachronism in that they have retained their immense reputation while bucking this trend. Their music can never be background music; it is, rather, music which asserts itself sonically – and very forcibly too. And if it isn't there, then the best replacement is nothing at all; better to have no music than music which brutalises sound. Better listening to the sound of industry, a car door slamming, the gentle mechanics of a well-tuned bike. 'It is beautiful to be lonely... silence is important...'

'When someone asks me about my top 10 records I always include silence,' Ralf opined in 1992. 'Turn off the record player and that is one of the most important sounds. And I hate all this zombie-like tranquilliser music, conditioning people in stores and in lifts and in all kind of places, it's just pollution. We always call it pollution music, and it has to go, because we want to hear the real sounds – I want to hear the sound of the escalator, I want to hear the sound of the plane, the sound of the train. Good-sounding trains, for themselves, they are musical instruments. That muzak, that uninteresting music from uninteresting people, we have to stop it. Whenever we can, in America, we have these little wire clippers, so we can clip the cables wherever we see them... We want to make people aware of reality, by bringing out in our compositions the sounds of cars and trains, and ideas of the beauty of the sounds themselves.'

Kraftwerk's career has been one dictated by a love of sound recording, and the switchover from their early work (up to and including most of *Computer World*) played analogue, to the much more polished digital soudscapes starting in the mid-eighties, is a history of how electronic music has embraced new technologies. But wasn't there something enchanting and liberating working in the old way? 'Limitations are actually the walls of your building,' says John Foxx. 'It all became even cleaner around the time of *Computer World*. Before that they used a few acoustic instruments, such as a Hohner Clavinet and even the odd wind instrument. I did like the early sounds on *Radio-Activity* – really primitive drum machines and beautifully imperfect synths and vocoders. Now we can have everything perfected, we're beginning to realise that it's actually the glitches and grit, the wonk and fut, that delight. In other words, what were considered imperfections can now be seen as qualities. You recognise the true signature. Conny Plank made great recordings of all that. You really feel as though you have access to a moment in time, whereas the later recordings exist in a more textureless space – all signatures carefully erased. They seem to have reached a sonic peak for recorded synth around Conny's time, then later reached peak efficiency through co-opting sound systems in *The Mix*. And of course, both of these have their respective qualities. Perhaps

Kraftwerk represent some trajectory of sonic history – from analogue glitch to digital perfection. They haven't yet accommodated the new aesthetic of joy in glitch.'

The reluctance, indeed, refusal to work with other musicians, has, one might reasonably assume, accounted for the slow pace of progress at the new Kling Klang. Again, there would be no shortage of willing pairs of hands and ears. 'It would be good to do something with them,' said John Foxx in 2010. 'I do think they need someone to do a Rick Rubin – strip away a few accretions. The only problem may be that the original line-up has dispersed – there is something real in that notion of chemistry. Easy to lose, even with the very best of intentions.'

Ralf and the band he fronts still retain their mythic corona. With a certain perversity befitting the contrary nature of the band, Kraftwerk's' official website, www.kraftwerk.com, is a relatively low-tech affair. There is a minimum of written content, no band history, no contact details, and no news section, in keeping with an operation dedicated to maintaining its mystique. 'Never explain' – the credo for any cult artist – is strictly adhered to. A message board or fan forum would be unthinkable, as to invite discussion would lead to demystification and criticism. The website is geared solely to publicising events and concerts, and selling their back catalogue and merchandise. One wonders how Ralf himself copes when shopping online in general when he is faced with the anti-fraud command, 'Please verify that you are not a robot.'

Tellingly, Ralf has revealed himself as an Internet sceptic. One suspects he thinks the World Wide Web has made things too easy for people, certainly too easy to 'pollute' the world with the meaningless and the inconsequential. 'I am not a fan of the Internet, I think it's overrated. Intelligent information is still intelligent information and an overflow of nonsense does not really help. In Germany it's called *Datenmüll*: data rubbish.'

Ralf is equally sceptical of social networking. The surveillance society the band described 30 years ago on *Computer World* has tightened its grip. Talking to journalist John Harris in 2009 he said: 'Everybody is becoming like... a Stasi agent, constantly observing himself or his friends.' As of 2009, Ralf did not own an mp3 player or iPod, claiming, 'I compose music – I don't listen to much.'

Way back in 1983, Ralf Hütter told the press: 'You, the journalists, you will be amazed. One day the robots will be the ones who will answer your questions.' The world according to Hütter hasn't quite materialised. We do not have cyborgs roaming society who can converse with a human intelligence. But in another, more quotidian way, Hütter has been proven completely correct. We can now book an airline flight, a table at a restaurant or buy almost anything we want without ever having to speak to a human being. When we want to book cinema tickets, renew a subscription or speak to anyone in a large organisation, we are almost always greeted not by a human voice, but by automation. Indeed, the impression is often given that whatever organisation we are calling is unwilling to present itself in human form, or at least its staff are no longer willing to talk to their customers. Today, we are used to speaking to 'robots', even if we forget that is what, in effect, we are doing. How the global society will develop in the next 20, 30 or 50 years is impossible to tell, but further incursions from the man-made seem inevitable.

With due respect to the three members other than Ralf who now play and record with Kraftwerk, two of whom have performed with the band for two decades, it is the classic formation of RFWK which, for most people, *is* Kraftwerk. If Ralf came on the phone today and asked to work with you again in Kraftwerk, what would you say? Karl Bartos: 'He would never call me. I think that, if he ever started to get emotional about the old days, the most he would do – being the easy-going type that he is – would be to instruct his lawyer or publisher to send me a formal e-mail. Come to think of it, since he never takes risks and since he owns the Kraftwerk trademark, he would probably just wait until his emotions had died down again. Seriously, though: as long as the public are prepared to believe that he and his collaborators/colleagues represent Kraftwerk, it will continue to work for him. However, I heard that, a while ago now, he wanted the band to be support for Depeche Mode, but Depeche Mode weren't interested, because it wasn't the real (original?) Kraftwerk. Be that as it may, there's a time for everything in life. As far as I'm concerned, all I want is to be independent and to be able to work how and when I want.'

Perhaps it makes just as much sense for the band not to appear at all on stage. This would be the logical conclusion to the Kraftwerk story as the group morphs into a pure stage presentation, a musical and visual experience, with no actual musicians playing in real time. Like Sun Ra and his Arkestra, could Kraftwerk continue for centuries to come? Are they more an idea, a concept, an invention, than an actual band – the band that has sought to remove itself, to merge with its technological signifiers, so that man and machine are one woven entity? Will Kraftwerk become a thought, an intelligence, rather than a living three-score-and-ten human entity?

8.8 Kraftwerk Forever

Imagine sitting in front of a TV and aimlessly channel-hopping the dozens of music channels on offer. Some offer a choice of new music, some cater for niche tastes, and many for nostalgia, be it for the nineties, for dance music, for the eighties, or further back still, to whenever it was when it seemed that guitars and drums were all that mattered. The aimless drift from one genre and one era to the next, with little or no regard for the historical context, or the origin of music, is nowadays the music experience for the majority. With music so readily available, and with so much of it, we simply repeat, shuffle and enjoy.

So much of this modern music which exists in this de-contextualised continuum of sound will show the secret hand of Kraftwerk.* It is present in the marching robot spacemen in Daft Punk's video of 'Around The World' in 1997; the synth beat of Röyksopp featuring Robyn and their love song, 'The Girl And The Robot' from 2009; the joys of staying in the same place that is Little Boots' 2008 dance classic 'Stuck On Repeat'; and the jumpy beats and vocodorised vocals of the Chemical Brothers' 1999 single, 'Music: Response'. Some groups borrow themes, some borrow melodies directly. Coldplay's Chris Martin wrote a letter to Ralf Hütter in his best schoolboy-level German to ask, very politely, permission to use the melody of 'Computer Love' in a song called 'Talk' from their *X & Y* album. Ralf said yes, one of the few times he has been minded so to do.

The Coldplay appropriation is significant. It shows that Kraftwerk's reach extends well beyond the genres of dance and

---

* One would need a book three times the length of this to explore fully the myriad ways in which Kraftwerk have influenced the work of others.

techno. Echoes of Kraftwerk (as well as Can, Harmonia, Cluster and Neu!) can be found in the music of many rock acts. Why? Because it's music which has not yet exhausted its potential. It still sounds odd and, more importantly, open-ended. The pulse of the 'Motorik' beat, the purity of a Kraftwerk melody carries with it still a measure of credibility and a cachet that signifies adventure and modernism. It is music which doesn't sound complete (unlike so much rock, blues, folk and country music, which sounds like the end, not the beginning, of a story), and so is easy to plug into, build upon and take in exciting new directions. Primal Scream did it with 'Autobahn 66' on their 2002 album, *Evil Heat*. Franz Ferdinand's 'Auf Achse' from their debut album of 2004 has the 'Motorik' spirit too. The melodies and oddly-formed rhythms found on Radiohead's *OK Computer*, *Kid A*, and *Amnesiac* are also in this tradition of risk-taking.

In the first few months of 2012, the radio continues to sound like Kraftwerk. Grimes' single 'Genesis' resurrects the sound of Conny Plank in an opening which sounds like an out-take from *Autobahn*. Even Cornershop, famous for their UK number one hit 'Brimful Of Asha (Norman Cook Remix),' would promote their 2012 album, *Urban Turban*, with the following PR gush: 'It's a summer breeze with an autobahn of electronic sound', their lead-off single, 'Non-Stop Radio', sung in French by songstress Celeste, could not have been made without Kraftwerk's 1986 single of almost the same name, or in fact, without Kraftwerk's 2003 'Aero Dynamik'. Both singles were referential, but supremely good. How many listening to them, however, would even know where the original inspiration lay?

Some outfits wear their admiration on their sleeves proudly. Take Client, described by *The Guardian* back in 2003 like this: 'Imagine Kraftwerk, but female, a bit kinky, from Halifax'. If this wasn't, in itself, a turn-on, their music was quite good too. With tracks such as 'Köln', 'Leipzig', and 'Drive', and their latest album release entitled *Command*, they were certainly under the influence. In concert and in photo shoots they would wear matching outfits such as airline hostesses' uniforms or fetish gear. Their very make-up was also indisputably Kraftwerkian: consisting of 'Client A', 'Client B', and 'Client C', the line-up changed with almost every release, with Kate Holmes their only ever-present member, and so their Ralf Hütter. Or take the duo Komputer. Originally signed to Mute Records under the equally Kraftwerk-influenced moniker I

Start Counting, they have produced music which neither pastiches nor parodies Kraftwerk, but in some strange way wants to be it. This is music which seems to use almost identical instruments, effects, chord progressions and vocal techniques to those used by Kraftwerk. Take their song 'Bill Gates', which consists of the name of the Microsoft supremo repeated and multiplied using vocodor in a melody which sounds like a 'Man Machine' for the new century, or their song 'We Are Komputer', a clone of 'The Robots': 'pressing keys and having fun/So many things to be done' before the six-word chorus, 'Work is pleasure/Pleasure is work'. It takes a good deal of wit and skill to make music which is so identikit, yet such good fun.

Tributes to the band have come in all different manners.* One of the best was in the form of a send-up by the British comedian and musician Bill Bailey on his *Part Troll* tour. His German-language version of 'The Hokey Cokey', performed unsmilingly in Kraftwerk costume against a video screen of black and white footage of old-age pensioners performing the dance gets to the core of Kraftwerk's appeal; taking something trivial or everyday and performing it with complete earnestness, its lyrics taking the parody to a truly absurd level: 'Man streckt den linken Arm ein, den linken Arm aus/Ein, aus, ein, aus, Man schüttelt alles rum'. Kraftwerk's music has always appealed to children too, not only in the simplicity and purity of its melodies but in its themes as well. With songs about robots, trains, cars, bikes and computers, not to mention spacelabs, counting, and going 'Boing!', the Kraftwerk repertoire is fascinating for the under-fives.

Kraftwerk's music, in its simplicity, its purity, deconstructed the tired currency of rock and pop. A report on MTV claimed that 92% of all Top 10 songs on the American *Billboard* chart in 2009 contained what they called 'reproductive messages'. Pop and rock has traditionally been obsessed by love, romance, courtship, and sex. Not so with Kraftwerk. 'Even at its most full-on, there is a delicacy, even a naivety to Kraftwerk's music. Not for them the traditional pop/rock preoccupations of sex and drugs and crypto-adolescent angst,' writes Kiran Sande. 'Throughout their career they've elected to sing of more innocent, frankly nerdier pleasures: train travel,

---

* See the 'Appendix' for more information on tributes to Kraftwerk, along with more information on Kraftwerk samples in use.

cycling, tuning the shortwave radio – that sort of thing. Even in the band's embryonic stages their music displayed a de-sexualised, non-carnal quality which would become more deeply entrenched and encoded as their interest in computers grew. Looking back on their early recordings, it's almost as if they willed the digital age into being, with all its attendant disembodiment and facelessness.'

Kraftwerk, now down to just one original member, has become less a band and more of an idea. It must be said that the conceptualist, the genius behind so much of Kraftwerk, the person of Ralf Hütter, has been the one single individual who has kept the Kraftwerk story moving forward. As a result, understandably, there are now jealousies and issues. No group lasts 45 years without this being so.

'A quintessential point struck me in Manchester, when there were four shadowy figures behind a screen at the beginning of the Festival performance. I thought "Who are these people?" Because I knew that Ralf was the only original one, but then I thought – did it really matter? Cannot somebody always be Kraftwerk? IBM has not closed with the passing of its founders. Apple will not close when Steve Jobs goes. Microsoft will not go when Bill Gates retires and then dies. Why can somebody not always be Kraftwerk? They have their own canon of music, can't somebody always be Kraftwerk? Well, I quite like that idea.'

In 2003 Ralf was asked whether Kraftwerk had become immortal. His answer was clear, and, perhaps, just a little chilling. 'In a way, yes. In German there is a saying: *Ewig währt am längsten* – forever lasts longest.'

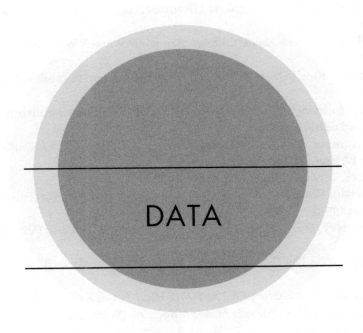

DATA

SOURCES

BOOKS

Albiez, Sean & David Pattie eds. *Kraftwerk: Music Non-Stop*
(Continuum, 2011)
Barker, Hugh & Yuval Taylor. *Faking It: The Quest For Authenticity
In Popular Music* (Faber & Faber, 2007)
Barr, Tim. *Kraftwerk: From Düsseldorf To The Future (With Love)*
(Ebury Press, 1998)
Beckett, Francis. *What Did The Baby Boomers Ever Do For Us?*
(Biteback Publishing, 2010)

Bussy, Pascal. *Kraftwerk: Man, Machine And Music* (S.A.F. third edition, 2005)

Bangs, Lester. *Psychotic Reactions & Carburetor Dung: Literature As Rock'n'Roll, Rock'n'Roll As Literature*, Greil Marcus, ed., (Mandarin, 1991)

Dellinger, Jade & David Giffels. *'Are We Not Men? We Are Devo!'* (S.A.F. 2003)

Fletcher, Keith. *Dear Boy: The Life Of Keith Moon* (Omnibus Press, 1998)

Flür, Wolfgang. *Kraftwerk: I Was A Robot* (Sanctuary Publishing, second edition, 2003)

Frith, Simon, and Andrew Goodwin, eds. *On Record: Rock, Pop And The Written Word* (Routledge, 1990).

James, Oliver. *Affluenza* (Vermilion, 2007)

Kureishi, Hanif & Jon Savage eds. *The Faber Book Of Pop* (Faber & Faber, 1995)

Kurlansky, Mark. *1968: The Year That Rocked The World* (Vintage, 2005)

Leroy, Dan. *The Greatest Music Never Sold* (Backbeat Books, 2007)

Long, Pat. *The History Of The NME: High Times And Low Lives At The World's Most Famous Music Magazine* (Portico, 2012)

Longhurst, Brian. *Popular Music & Society* (Polity Press, second edition, 2007)

Morley, Paul. *Words And Music: A History of Pop In The Shape Of A City* (Bloomsbury, 2003)

Moy, Ron. *An Analysis Of The Position And Status Of Sound Ratio In Contemporary Society* (Edwin Mellen Press, 2000)

Palm, Carl Magnus. *Bright Lights Dark Shadows: The Real Story Of Abba* (Omnibus Press, third edition, 2008)

Prendergast, Mark. *The Ambient Century: From Mahler To Moby – The Evolution Of Sound In The Electronic Age* (Bloomsbury, 2003)

Reynolds, Simon. *Blissed Out: The Raptures Of Rock* (Serpent's Tail, 1990)

Reynolds, Simon. *Energy Flash* (Picador, 1998)

Reynolds, Simon. *Rip It Up And Start Again: Postpunk 1978-1984* (Faber & Faber, 2005)

Reynolds, Simon. *Retromania: Pop Culture's Addiction To Its Own Past* (Faber & Faber, 2011)

Reynolds, Simon, and Press, Joy. *The Sex Revolts: Gender, Rebellion And Rock'n'Roll,* (Serpent's Tail, 1995)

Shuker, Roy. *Understanding Popular Music Culture* (third edition, Routledge, 2008)

Shuker, Roy. *Popular Music Culture: The Key Concepts* (third edition, Routledge, 2012)

Winder, Simon. *Germania: A Personal History Of Germans Ancient And Modern* (Picador, 2010)

ARTICLES

I have consulted over 200 articles from the following publications and websites:

Afisha Magazine, The Arts Desk, BBC.co.uk, Chicago Sun Times, Clash Music, Creem, The Daily Note, The Daily Telegraph, De Morgen, DJ History.com, Dummy Magazine, Humo, Electronic Musician, Electronics And Music Maker Magazine, Fact, Fast Forward Magazine, Frieze, The Guardian, MTV.com, The Independent, Icon, Interview, Keyboard Magazine, LA Weekly, Mojo, NME, New Zealand Herald, Now Toronto, Pitchfork, Q, The Quietus, Record Mirror, Rock And Folk Magazine, Rolling Stone, San Francisco Chronicle, The Scotsman, Sounds, Sonntagszeitung, Der Spiegel, Stern, Synapse Magazine, TC Electronics, Techno Pop, The Telegraph, The Times, Triad, Uncut, Waxpaper, Wired.

ONLINE

The *Techno Pop* website (*http://www.technopop-archive.com*) has an excellent online collection of articles, including many non-English articles which have been translated. Kraftwerk's influence on the DNA of modern music has been decisive and unique. The Kraftwerk Influence (*http://www.cuug.ab.ca/~lapierrs/creative/kraftwerk*) contains sections on covers (from artists as diverse as the Divine Comedy, Rammstein, OMD, U2 and Siouxsie & the Banshees), tributes, samples and a final section, references, which lists mentions in the media, and from other musical artists. Another fan site, I Believe The Truth Is Out There (*http://www.cheebadesign.com/perfect/kraftwerk/index.html*) has an excellent section on Kraftwerk samples, covers and tributes (listing artists such as Fat Boy Slim, Coldplay, Depeche Mode, Prodigy, Beck, Devo, Destiny's Child and Madonna.

The Quietus (*http://thequietus.com*), a relatively new online music magazine, has given extensive and thought-provoking coverage to Kraftwerk, Neu! and electronic music in general. The best website devoted specifically to synth music both old and new is *Electronically Yours* found at *http://www.league-online.com*, whilst This Is Not Retro (*http://www.thisisnotretro.com*) runs news, interviews and reviews of a wide variety of artists whose careers took in the coolest decade in music, the eighties. Finally, my thanks to Barney Hoskyns and everyone at Rock's Backpages (*http://www.rocksbackpages.com*), a velvet goldmine of information.

Other helpful websites for the budding Kraftwerk scholar are:

Afrika Bambaataa (Official Site) (*http://www.zulunation.com/afrika.html*)
Aktivität online (Fan Site) (*http://www.aktivitaet-fanzine.com/index.html*)
Antenna (Fan Site) (*http://kraftwerk.hu/antenna*)
Boing (Fan Site) (*http://www.kraftwerk.kx.cz/en/news*)
DJhistory.com (*http://www.djhistory.com*)
Eberhard Kranemann (Official Site) (*http://www.e-kranemann.de/index.htm*)

Emil Schult (Official Site) (*http://www.emilschult.eu*)
Giorgio Moroder (Official Site) (*http://www.giorgiomoroder.com*)
Karl Bartos Official Site (*http://www.karlbartos.com*)
Keep Werking (Fan Site) (*http://www.keepwerking. co.uk/index. php*)
Kraftwerk Information (Fan Site) (*http://www.elektrodaten.com*)
Kraftwerk (Official Site) (*http://www.kraftwerk.com*)
Michael Rother (Official Site) (*http://www.michaelrother.de/en*)
Rebecca Allen (Official Site) (*http://rebeccaallen.com*)
The Blitz Club (*http://www.theblitzclub.com*)
Twingo Kraftwerk (Fan Site) (*http://twingokraftwerk.com/index. html*)

DVD

For an excellent and detailed analysis of Kraftwerk and modern German electronic music, the DVD *Kraftwerk And The Electronic Revolution* (Chrome Dreams, 2008), produced by Rob Johnstone, is essential. Not only does it contain excellent archive footage of Kraftwerk and their contemporaries, but it also contains invaluable input from writers, academics and musicians. The 2009 BBC documentary *Synth Britannia*, directed by Benjamin Whalley, is a broader overview of the electronic music scene of the seventies and eighties. And of course many classic Kraftwerk moments such as their 1975 appearance on *Tomorrow's World* can be found on YouTube.

Kraftwerk have yet to release a career-spanning retrospective DVD in the same manner that no Greatest Hits package exists. However, their tour DVD *Minimum-Maximum* (EMI, 2005) gives a flavour of the astonishing visual spectacular of Kraftwerk in concert.

SELECTED DISCOGRAPHY

ALBUMS

Kraftwerk's biggest-selling album remains their 1974 breakthrough, *Autobahn*, followed by their 1978 album, *The Man-Machine*, which was awarded a gold disc in the UK in February 1982. Top 75 chart positions are for the UK, Germany, France and USA only.

Kraftwerk
November 1970
Philips/Vertigo – 30 (Germany)

Kraftwerk 2
January 1972
Philips/Vertigo – 36 (Germany)

Ralf And Florian (Ralf und Florian)
October 1973
Philips/Vertigo

Autobahn
November 1974
Philips/Vertigo – 7 (Germany), 4 (UK), 5 (USA)

Radio-Activity (Radio-Aktivität)
October 1975
Kling Klang/EMI-Electrola/Capitol – 22 (Germany), 1 (France)

Trans-Europe Express (Trans-Europa Express)
May 1977
Kling Klang/EMI-Electrola/Capitol – 32 (Germany), 49 (UK), 2 (France)

The Man-Machine (Die Mensch-Maschine)
May 1978
Kling Klang/EMI-Electrola/Capitol – 12 Germany, 9 (UK), 14 (France)

286

Computer World (Computerwelt)
May 1981
Kling Klang/EMI-Electrola/Warner Bros – 7 (Germany), 15 (UK),
72 (USA)

Electric Café
December 1986
Kling Klang/EMI/Warner Bros – 23 (Germany), 58 (UK)

The Mix
June 1991
Kling Klang/EMI/Elektra – 6 (Germany), 15 (UK)

Tour De France Soundtracks
August 2003
Kling Klang/EMI/Astralwerks – 1 (Germany), 21 (UK)

Minimum-Maximum
June 2005
Kling Klang/EMI/Astralwerks – 26 (Germany)

The Catalogue (Der Katalog)
October 2009
Kling Klang/EMI/Mute/Astralwerks – 34 (Germany)

SINGLES

Note: only singles which have reached the Top 40 in one or more
territory have been included. Chart positions are for the UK,
Germany, France, and USA only.

The single 'Computer Love' was originally released as the
second single off the *Computer World* album and reached number
36 in the UK charts. In December 1981, the single was re-promoted
using the 'B' side, 'The Model', from their previous album, *The Man-
Machine* as the 'A' side and the single reached number one in the UK
in February 1982, the first single by a German act to top the UK charts.
'Tour De France' has entered the UK Top 75 no less than four times
in various remixes and re-recordings making it, by chart longevity,
Kraftwerk's most successful single with a total of 24 weeks in the
singles charts. 'The Model'/'Computer Love' spent 21 weeks in the
UK charts.

In Britain, Kraftwerk's biggest-selling single is 'The Model/
Computer Love' with total sales of around 550,000. 'Radio-Activity'
sold around 500,000 copies in France. However, the single to chart
in most countries worldwide is 'Autobahn.'

'Autobahn'
May 1975
Philips/Vertigo – 9 (Germany), 11 (UK), 25 (USA)

'Radio-Activity'
May 1976 – 1 (France)

'The Robots'
June 1978
Kling Klang/EMI-Electrola/Capitol – 18 (Germany)

'Pocket Calculator'
May 1981
Kling Klang/EMI-Electrola/Warner Bros – 39 (UK)

'Computer Love'
July 1981
Kling Klang/EMI-Electrola/Warner Bros – 36 (UK)

'The Model'/'Computer Love'
Dec 1981
Kling Klang/EMI-Electrola/Warner Bros – 7 (Germany), 1 (UK).

'Showroom Dummies'
Feb 1982
Kling Klang/EMI-Electrola/Capitol – 25 (UK)

'Tour De France'
July 1983
Kling Klang/EMI/Warner Bros – 22 (UK)

'Tour De France' (remix)
August 1984
Kling Klang/EMI/Warner Bros – 24 (UK)

'Musique Non Stop'
October 1986
Kling Klang/EMI/Warner Bros – 13 (Germany)

'The Robots' (1991 remix)
May 1991
Kling Klang/EMI – 20 (UK)

'Expo 2000'
December 1999
Kling Klang/EMI/Astralwerks – 35 (Germany), 27 (UK)

'Tour De France 2003'
July 2003
Kling Klang/EMI/Astralwerks – 20 (UK)

'Aerodynamik'
March 2004
Kling Klang/EMI/Astralwerks – 33 (UK)

CLASSIC KRAFTWERK in 20 BITS

Kraftwerk are a rare breed indeed; in a career stretching over 40 years they are an outfit who have never made a truly poor record. The first two Kraftwerk albums are enjoyable slabs of early-seventies Cosmic Music though only hint at the greatness to come. From 1973 onwards, Kraftwerk developed a distinctive and utterly seductive electronic style, reaching its zenith on three essential recordings, *Trans-Europe Express*, *The Man-Machine*, and *Computer World*, the latter arguably their defining statement. With no official greatest hits compilation on the market, the following is my guide to the 20 essential Kraftwerk tracks.

1	'Computer Love'	Find it	*Computer World* (1981)
2	'Autobahn' (single edit)	Find it	single (1975)
3	'Europe Endless'	Find it	*Trans-Europe Express* (1977)
4	'Numbers'	Find it	*Computer World* (1981)
5	'Trans-Europe Express'	Find it	*Trans-Europe Express* (1977)
6	'Radio-Activity'	Find it	*Radio-Activity* (1975)
7	'Computer World'	Find it	*Computer World* (1981)
8	'Kometenmelodie 2'	Find it	*Autobahn* (1974)
9	'The Hall Of Mirrors'	Find it	*Trans-Europe Express* (1977)
10	'The Model'	Find It	*The Man-Machine* (1978)
11	'Tour De France'	Find it	single (1983)
12	'Neon Lights'	Find it	*The Man-Machine* (1978)
13	'Music Non-Stop'	Find it	*Minimum-Maximum* (2005)
14	'La Forme'	Find it	*Tour De France Soundtracks* (2003)
15	'Radioactivity' (1991)	Find It	*The Mix* (1991)
16	'Pocket Calculator'	Find it	*Computer World* (1981)
17	'Spacelab'	Find it	*The Man-Machine* (1978)
18	'Kristallo'	Find it	*Ralf And Florian* (1973)
19	'Airwaves'	Find it	*Radio-Activity* (1975)
20	'The Telephone Call'	Find it	*Electric Café/Techno Pop* (1986)

Agree? Disagree?
Let me know your thoughts at *info@david-buckley.com*

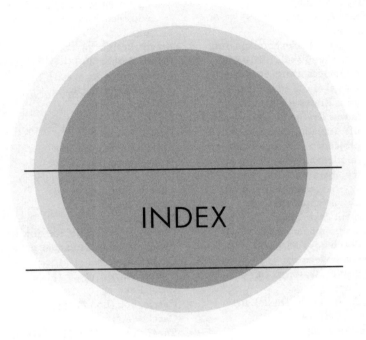

INDEX

292

8/12(184210)